SLIPPERY JIM or
PATRIOTIC STATESMAN?

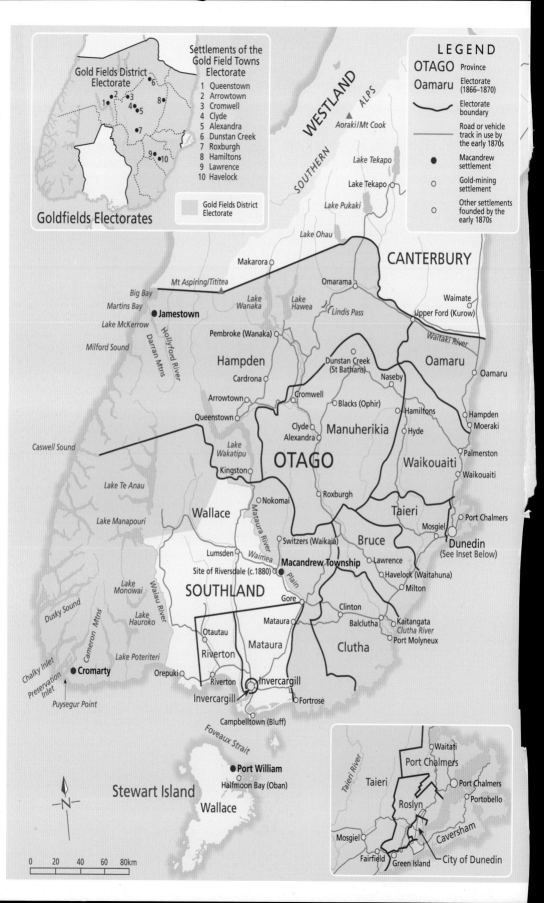

Goldfields Electorates

Settlements of the Gold Field Towns Electorate

1 Queenstown
2 Arrowtown
3 Cromwell
4 Clyde
5 Alexandra
6 Dunstan Creek
7 Roxburgh
8 Hamiltons
9 Lawrence
10 Havelock

Gold Fields District Electorate

Gold Fields District Electorate

LEGEND

OTATGO Province

Oamaru Electorate (1866–1870)

Electorate boundary

Road or vehicle track in use by the early 1870s

● Macandrew settlement

○ Gold-mining settlement

○ Other settlements founded by the early 1870s

WESTLAND

SOUTHERN ALPS

▲ Aoraki/Mt Cook

Lake Tekapo

Lake Tekapo

Lake Pukaki

Lake Ohau

CANTERBURY

Makarora

Omarama

Waimate

Upper Ford (Kurow)

Big Bay

Mt Aspiring/Tititea ▲

Martins Bay

Lake Wanaka

Lake Hawea

Lindis Pass

Waitaki River

Lake McKerrow

● Jamestown

Pembroke (Wanaka)

Milford Sound

Hollyford River

Darran Mtns

Hampden

Dunstan Creek (St Bathans)

Naseby

Oamaru

Oamaru

Cardrona

Hampden

Arrowtown

Cromwell

Blacks (Ophir)

Hamiltons

Moeraki

Queenstown

Clyde

Manuherikia

Hyde

Caswell Sound

Alexandra

Palmerston

Lake Wakatipu

OTAGO

Waikouaiti

Kingston

Waikouaiti

Lake Te Anau

Nokomai

Roxburgh

Taieri

Port Chalmers

Lake Manapouri

Wallace

Mataura River

Mosgiel

Switzers (Waikaia)

Bruce

Dunedin (See Inset Below)

Lumsden

Waimea

Lawrence

Macandrew Township

Site of Riversdale (c.1880)

Plain

Havelock (Waitahuna)

Lake Monowai

SOUTHLAND

Milton

Dusky Sound

Gore

Cameron Mtns

Lake Haurroko

Clinton

Waiau River

Mataura

Balclutha

Kaitangata

Clutha River

Otautau

Mataura

Clutha

Port Molyneux

Lake Poteriteri

Riverton

Chalky Inlet

Orepuki

● Cromarty

Preservation Inlet

Riverton

Invercargill

Puysegur Point

Invercargill

Fortrose

Campbelltown (Bluff)

Foveaux Strait

● Port William

Halfmoon Bay (Oban)

Stewart Island

Wallace

Waitati

Taieri River

Port Chalmers

Port Chalmers

Taieri

Port Chalmers

Roslyn

Portobello

Mosgiel

Caversham

Fairfield

Green Island

City of Dunedin

N

0 20 40 60 80km

SLIPPERY JIM or PATRIOTIC STATESMAN?

James Macandrew of Otago

R.J. Bunce

OTAGO

To Elizabeth, and to John Haynes who showed the way.

Published by Otago University Press
Level 1, 398 Cumberland Street
Dunedin, New Zealand
university.press@otago.ac.nz
www.otago.ac.nz/press

First published 2018
Copyright © R. J. Bunce
The moral rights of the author have been asserted.

ISBN 978-1-98-853135-9

Front cover: This portrait of Macandrew by Kate Sperry hangs in the
stairwell of the University of Otago's Clocktower Building. Photography
Allan Ramsay.
Back cover: The only extant bust of James Macandrew stands outside Toitū
Otago Settlers Museum in Dunedin. Author photograph.

Editor: Imogen Coxhead
Design/layout: Lucy Richardson
Indexer: Carol Dawber
Printed in Christchurch by Caxton.

Contents

Acknowledgements

James Macandrew spent much of his life in the public spotlight, so a large collection of newspaper reportage on his activities is available. Any collection of personal papers, so vital to biography to explain his private life and to understand what motivated him, is absent, which may explain why he has been overlooked. Public records and the private views of his contemporaries provide most of the material for this biography, which focuses particularly on his public service and his political career.

Macandrew's descendants have been enthusiastically helpful with discussion and the loan of family records. I particularly wish to thank Ruth Anderson, Marsha and Hunter Donaldson, Jane Harcourt, Anne Hubbard, Neal Macandrew and Sheryl Macandrew Morton. Denis Le Cren, in his family history of the Rich and Macandrew families, has provided a valuable summary of Macandrew's life. Kate Wilson, a great-granddaughter of Macandrew, kindly made available her collection of Macandrew family papers, which includes five letters written by James Macandrew – one to his wife, three to his daughter Mabel and one to his son Hunter.

Charles Waddy, a descendant of Thomas Reynolds Jnr, lent me his detailed but unpublished history of the Reynolds family and generously made time to review my manuscript.

I was encouraged to write this biography by Professors David McKenzie and Tom Brooking of the University of Otago. Supervision of the doctoral thesis at Victoria University of Wellington, from which this book emerged, was provided by Associate Professor Jim McAloon and Professor James Belich.

My thanks go to Dr André Brett of the University of Wollongong, who gave me invaluable guidance and encouragement during the writing of the manuscript, and to Dr Michael Stevens of the University of Otago, who set me right on Ngāi Tahu history.

Professional assistance was provided in Dunedin by Alison Breeze of Dunedin City Archives, Jill Haley of Toitū Otago Settlers Museum, Alison Clarke of the Hocken Collections, Gregor Macaulay of the University of Otago and Jane Smallfield of Otago Girls' High School. In Wellington, assistance came from Katie de Roo of Archives New Zealand, David Colquhoun of the Alexander Turnbull Library and Lindsay Milne at the Parliamentary Library. Derek Oliver of the National Library of Scotland in Edinburgh located a number of Macandrew's letters and a previously unsighted business card.

I am grateful to Lydia Wevers, who provided technical support and good company while I wrote this book, and the Stout Research Centre for New Zealand Studies at Victoria University of Wellington, which provided a distraction-free environment.

Publisher Rachel Scott of Otago University Press has made this book a reality, and editor Imogen Coxhead showed me how to improve the original manuscript immeasurably: thank you both.

Finally, I wish to thank my wife Elizabeth for her encouragement and support during the writing of this biography, and my children, Jeremy, Oliver and Melanie and their partners Angela, Greer and Genevieve: you keep my feet on the ground.

Introduction

On a mild summer's day in January 1851, 31-year-old Scotsman James Macandrew disembarked from a barge onto Dunedin's mānuka jetty at the head of Otago Harbour in search of lodgings for his family members, who awaited him aboard the schooner *Titan* at Port Chalmers.[1] The jetty stood between the muddy strip at the mouth of Toitū Stream, where the first Scottish settlers had landed in 1848, and a ribbon of strand where local Māori beached their waka. The houses, hotels and businesses of the three-year-old settlement, home to some 1400 people, straggled along the shoreline over waterlogged land striped with ridges and gullies and enclosed by a circle of hills crowned with 'an irregular crescent of reserve', the distinctive Town Belt.[2] A Presbyterian manse occupied the land to the left of the wharf; to the right a church and a schoolhouse stood at the bottom of a steep hill, beyond which lay the flat northern reaches of the town.

A short walk up Jetty Street led Macandrew to Princes Street, the settlement's main thoroughfare. This ran south to a tidal inlet, later reclaimed as the Market Reserve, and to the north spanned Toitū Stream, scaled Bell Hill and crossed Moray Place and its central reserve (later known as the Octagon). Here it was renamed George Street and continued through swampy ground to a river known as the Water of Leith.[3] Several stores, a smithy and a number of hotels were clustered on Princes Street beneath Bell Hill and cottages dotted the slopes above; few buildings had been erected to the north of the hill.[4] The streets were muddy, the bogs were foul with sewage and the streams were tainted.[5]

This unprepossessing village would be the base for Macandrew's spectacular business and political careers, and he would be involved in many aspects of its meteoric growth. By the time of his death in a carriage accident in 1887, Dunedin would have 45,514 European residents and would be the second city of New Zealand, its streets paved by the gold extracted from the hinterland.[6] It would boast substantial civic buildings, stone churches, the country's first university, factories, steam trams, a cable car to the spreading hill suburbs and a ferry service to the harbour-side settlements.

James Macandrew landed on this jetty in 1851. This is reputed to be the earliest known photograph of Dunedin, taken in 1852 from Bell Hill, looking south along Princes Street. Macandrew's Manse Street store, with its long roof and three dormer windows, is visible to the right of Princes Street, nearer to the hill.

Muir & Moodie reprint, Album 359 P1990-015-36-001, Hocken Collections, Uare Taoka o Hākena, University of Otago

James Macandrew (1819–1887) had arrived in the land of his dreams.[7] He was welcomed as a successful and wealthy Scottish entrepreneur, his reputation enhanced by business experience acquired in London and by the fact that he had arrived on his own ship. His life over the next four decades is a remarkable tale of unwavering faith in his own judgement, challenges to the established order, risk-taking, undreamed of financial success and utter failure, and a determination to shape the new colony in his own image. He was the very model of the 'merchant adventurer, [the] commercial entrepreneur' – the sort of man who helped to build the British Empire.[8]

Few people today know of James Macandrew, yet for 36 years from 1851 there was scarcely a day when he did not feature, for reasons both admirable and notorious, in one of New Zealand's many newspapers. His political career spanned three unique periods of New Zealand's history: he was directly involved with the establishment of self-government, the abolition of provincial government and George Grey's 1877–79 ministry. New Zealand's parliament

Dunedin developed rapidly during the 1860s gold rush. This 1867 photo looks down Jetty Street from Princes Street to the wharf where, 16 years later, Macandrew first landed in Dunedin.
J.W. Allen photograph. Album 10, p. 20, P1910-046-020, Hocken Collections, Uare Taoka o Hākena, University of Otago

attracted talented men during Queen Victoria's reign, and service at both provincial and colonial levels of government was obligatory for a small clique of the colony's earliest European settlers.[9] According to historian Edmund Bohan, 'Those men who sat in parliament between 1854 and the 1870s included some of the best educated, most accomplished, widely travelled, colourful and interesting personalities who have ever involved themselves in this country's public life.'[10] In the bear pit that was the General Assembly, powerful personalities dominated and opportunities abounded for intrigue and powerbroking.

Macandrew thrived in this environment. He was intimately associated with some of New Zealand's most original thinkers and unconventional politicians, including the Wakefield family in the 1840s and 1850s, Julius Vogel in the 1860s and George Grey in the 1870s. He was a member of Otago Provincial Council for 10 years and superintendent of Otago Province for a decade. He served concurrently in the House of Representatives for 29 years, both as a backbencher and as a minister in Grey's Cabinet; he was leader of his parliamentary faction, and in 1879 the premiership eluded him by just four votes. At the time of his death he was father of the House. Macandrew served in most of the positions available on Otago Provincial Council as well as sitting in the first nine New Zealand parliaments. In all, he was a constant advocate for the interests of Otago.[11]

From the day he landed in Dunedin, Macandrew began to shape events. He was a passionate campaigner for the development of infrastructure to stimulate rapid, predominantly English-speaking settlement. He sought to provide satisfactory physical, intellectual and emotional conditions for all settlers, and was a driving force behind the establishment of the School of Art, the Normal School for teacher training, the Caversham Industrial School, high schools and the University of Otago. He initiated a steamer service between New Zealand and Australia in 1858 and, despite its failure, maintained his crusade for international shipping services. He was one of the prime movers in the construction of the Oamaru breakwater, the Dunedin to Port Chalmers and the Clutha railways and many other public works, and was responsible for the building of the Otago graving dock at Port Chalmers.[12] As minister of public works in Grey's ministry from 1878 to 1879, his monument is the public works statement of 1878 with its commitment to a national railway system as well as numerous bridges, roads and wharves.

Macandrew's guiding beliefs were simple. He identified closely with the precepts of the Free Church of Scotland and the aims of the Otago settlement: his drivers were 'education and religion, agriculture and commerce'.[13] These beliefs evolved into his political creed, encapsulated at his death in four words: 'roads, population, bridges, capital'.[14] When he arrived in Dunedin, a community founded on self-sufficiency, his economic philosophy was typically Victorian laissez-faire, but he soon realised that a larger population would stimulate faster growth in this undeveloped country. In the absence of private investors with capital to build the province's infrastructure, Macandrew modified his views on self-reliance and advocated instead for the use of state resources to build roads, railways, harbours and more. As New Zealand's economy faltered in the 1870s he recognised the need for state assistance for individuals, and became a proponent of deferred payment for land and state loans to settlers. In parliament he sought access to land for all settlers and liberal social legislation, the latter enacted a decade later by the Seddon government; and it was Macandew who suggested unemployed colonists be given free land to enable them to be self-supporting.

Macandrew's role in New Zealand politics has been neither widely nor impartially discussed, and few historians have acknowledged his contribution to social conditions in the colony. Instead, Macandrew is largely remembered for his audacious behaviour, and is most commonly recalled as the politician who was imprisoned in Dunedin for personal debt during his first, brief term as superintendent of Otago. Using the authority of that position he declared his private residence a prison and continued to conduct the province's business from home, until dismissed by Governor Thomas Gore Browne and returned to the public gaol. Even there his chutzpah was unbounded: in the ensuing election to choose his successor he mounted a campaign from prison and came a respectable second.

The major historians of Otago – A.H. McLintock, William Morrell and Erik Olssen – provide an outline of Macandrew's life and trenchant criticism. McLintock comments, 'when the fire of Macandrew's eloquence had died and the embers were raked, little of any value remained'. Morrell considers Macandrew an ultra-provincialist and the employer of 'irregular proceedings'; his description of Macandrew as 'energetic and self-confident' is disparaging. Olssen calls him 'a gambler and speculator … Impulsive, at times reckless.'[15] Macandrew's contemporary, Thomas Bracken, called him 'a leader staunch and true', but others have described him as a man 'whose cool audacity was matched only by his political opportunism'; one who demonstrated 'the most marked exhibitions of imprudence': a 'Slippery Jim'.[16]

Ironically, given his concern with public expenditure, a considerable amount of the colony's time and resources were spent on preventing any repetition of his behaviour. By 1867, when he began his second term as superintendent, he had precipitated three Otago Provincial Council select committees, two enquiries by the country's auditor-general, an entry in the *Appendices to the Journals of the House of Representatives* (*AJHR*) and six Acts of parliament. As a minister he precipitated a further two select committees, and in 1880 two royal commissions investigated his ministerial performance.

His business practices provoked a similar degree of censure. The first years of European settlement in New Zealand saw explosive settlement and unrestrained expansion as a stream of colonists was matched with apparently unlimited land, and internal and external markets were ripe for development. Macandrew was one of a small group of settlers shrewd enough to grasp the opportunities to exploit the seemingly endless resources in this untapped country.[17] A sharp-witted businessman could skim a commission from almost every human transaction in his locality, and indeed, in his first decade in Otago Macandrew accumulated assets that today would make him a multi-millionaire.

The *Southland Times*, critical of Macandrew for much of his career, at his death in 1887 noted:

> There are some politicians who are always in office and others who are always in power –which is quite a different thing. Mr Macandrew belonged essentially to the latter class. He was in office for many years, but he was in power from the time he landed in Otago …[18]

That Macandrew appealed to the Otago voters and was an outstandingly successful politician is indisputable. Of the 19 positions he ran for in his lifetime, he won three elections to Otago Provincial Council, four of the five elections he contested for superintendent, and lost only one of his 11 Assembly races. In Otago his followers alternately abused and praised him, but when the provinces ended, his career was depicted in largely respectful terms:

> The time has not yet come to write the history of this remarkable man, but the materials for a most striking biography are most abundant, and the variety of light and shade scattered through an eventful life in Scotland, England, and New Zealand will be read with interest some day … While there is much in it to warn, there is much to imitate.[19]

The first tier of colonial nineteenth-century politicians is well represented in New Zealand biography. Ten of the 17 premiers – FitzGerald, Stafford, Weld, Vogel, Atkinson, Grey, Hall, Stout, Ballance and Seddon – have their biographers, but less interest has been shown in the contributions made by provincial leaders. Of the 44 superintendents, only FitzGerald, Stafford, Grey, Campbell, McLean, Rolleston and Cargill have had their lives publicly examined. This biography provides a view of New Zealand from the second tier, the provincial periphery, and places Macandrew as a skilful businessman and politician, able to advance the interests of his constituents while serving the demands of the country during a period of rapid change.

Macandrew polarised onlookers, engendered both intense loyalty and enmity in his fellow citizens, and played an important role in the making of Dunedin, Otago and New Zealand. He was active in most of New Zealand's political institutions during almost four decades of public life and mixed with the country's movers and shakers. His many-faceted life in Dunedin – his involvement in a range of commercial activities, his imprisonment as a defaulting debtor and his lengthy public service – as well as his extended parliamentary service, his brief ministerial career and his presence at many important events in New Zealand's history, make him a subject worthy of his own biography.

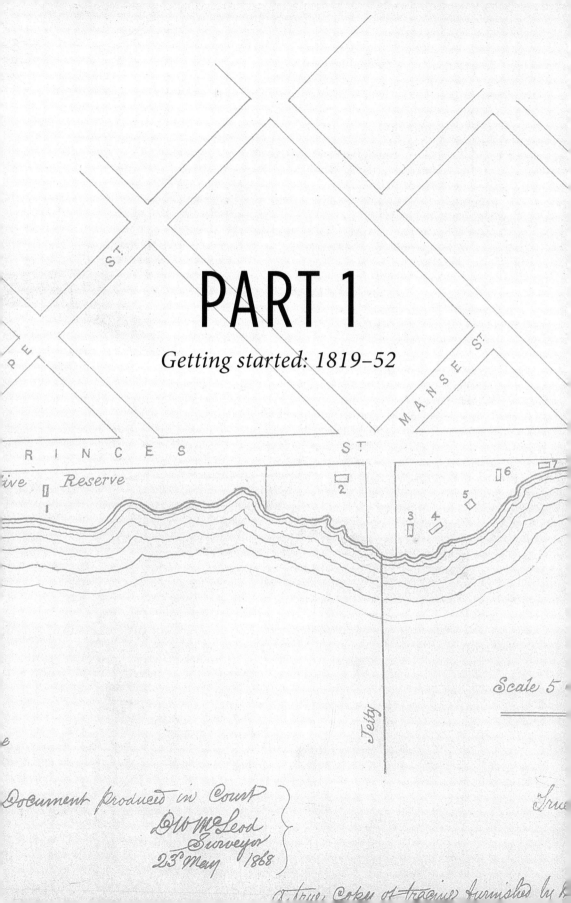

PART 1

Getting started: 1819–52

Chapter 1

James Macandrew was born into the social and economic upheaval left in the wake of the Napoleonic Wars, in a world shaped by the Scottish Enlightenment. During the 18th and early 19th centuries the humanist tenets of the European Enlightenment were adopted by Scottish thinkers, who rejected any authority not justified by reason. Scottish intellectual activity was noteworthy for its emphasis on empiricism and a determination to improve the life of the individual as well as improving society. According to historian Erik Olssen, the 'main themes of the [Scottish] Enlightenment were fairly constant – liberalism, rationalism, naturalism, empiricism, and materialism … the central principles of social engineering'.[1] In 1750 these, combined with a Presbyterian emphasis on individual salvation based on the teachings of the Bible, produced a Scottish male literacy rate of almost 75 per cent, compared with 53 per cent in England.[2] The Scottish parliament's 1696 Act for Settling of Schools had resulted in a school in every parish and a rapid increase in libraries, where works such as the American Declaration of Independence, Adam Smith's *The Wealth of Nations*, Edward Gibbon's *Decline and Fall of the Roman Empire* and Jeremy Bentham's *A Fragment on Government*, all published in 1776, were available.

As an avid reader, Macandrew was likely influenced by these books and the discussions they stimulated. From them he would have absorbed many of the values that shaped his life, such as his creed that an individual was responsible for his relationship with God and his own success in life. He also believed society could be – and must be – improved wherever possible, to allow all people the opportunity to advance themselves.

Macandrew lived in and about Aberdeen, a city adjoining the Highlands and influenced by Highlands traditions. He was a young man there during the period of fierce religious debate that led to the Disruption of the Church of Scotland in 1843, when more than four hundred evangelical ministers demanded an end to state intervention in spiritual matters. Opposed to patronage in the appointment of ministers, they broke ranks to establish the Free Church of Scotland, taking at least a third of the existing congregations with them.

The young Macandrew was shaped by working-class Scottish and middle-class English societies and knew about insecurity: the English middle class was 'an immensely privileged group in a society of great inequality', whose income and lifestyle were based on a cycle of property acquisition and accumulation, over-shadowed with the ever-present threats of illness, economic ruin and death.[3] After the decades of the Napoleonic Wars, a period of fluctuating trade and social upheaval meant that provincial middle-class families faced 'unrelenting physical and economic insecurity intensified by the rigidity of their self-imposed morality'.[4] Concern for their reputations added to their insecurity and, for most, the only effective agency for spreading risk was their family network.

Details of Macandrew's life as a child in Scotland and a young man in England are sparse, and particulars reported in some previous accounts of his life may be incorrect.[5] The family originated in the Black Isle, northeast of Inverness, where his family is commemorated on a gravestone in the grounds of Fortrose Cathedral.[6] James' father Colin (1794–1852) spelled his name 'McAndrew' and is variously identified as a shoemaker and a leather merchant. His mother Barbara Johnston (1797–1873) was born to a Quaker family.[7] Their son's baptism on 18 May 1819 is noted in the baptismal records of the Old Machar Parish Church – the Cathedral of St Machar's in Old Aberdeen – although an entry in the Macandrew family Bible in James' handwriting gives his birth date as 17 May 1820.[8] The error is repeated in the UK census of 1841 where his age is listed as 21, and is perpetuated on his wedding certificate in 1848 where his age is entered as 28.[9] Such details may have been genuine mistakes – or they may indicate Macandrew's casual attitude to accuracy, which in later financial dealings would lead him into serious strife.

The family moved to the village of Rosemarkie after James' birth, and there his siblings were born: Daniel in 1821, Jane in 1823 and Lewis in 1825.[10] James' commitment to his extended family was strong: his brother Daniel accompanied him to Dunedin in 1850 along with James' parents-in-law, his brother-in-law and the three children of another brother-in-law.[11] Daniel remained in Dunedin for three years before returning to Aberdeen, and he and James co-operated in a number of business ventures.[12] Their sister Jane would marry Alex Gillespie, who became a London merchant. Lewis died before reaching his first birth-day.[13] After Colin McAndrew's death in 1825 the family shifted to Drumoak on Deeside, 19 kilometres inland from Aberdeen, where James attended a parish school until he was at least 13 years old – advanced schooling for that period.[14] Although one source states that he attended Ayr Academy, this is unlikely given that Ayr is a considerable distance from Aberdeen.[15] James' personal skills were improved at his church; it was later noted that 'he was greatly indebted for his political education to Young Men's Debating Clubs in connection with Trinity Church, Aberdeen, under the Rev. David Simpson, and London Wall Presbyterian Church, under Dr Tweedie'.[16]

In 1836 James was apprenticed to Aberdeen paper merchants Pirie and Co. That year a letter from his Edinburgh-based cousin, also named James, outlined the preoccupations of their poor but genteel class: 'I am happy to learn you are in a good situation. Yours is a delightful business for making a fortune fast, altho' in some instances by speculation too largely you may founder & go at once from affluence to poverty.' He added – with prescience, given James' later career – 'I find the accountant profession a very good one … I advise you however to endeavour to keep out of our clutches in the Bankrupt way I mean.'[17]

James' uncle John Macandrew contributed to his nephew's upbringing, both financially and emotionally, providing him with the support he might have received from Colin had he lived longer. In 1838 as James was about to transfer to London, his uncle wrote with advice. His words evoke the values typical of those with little capital who had to make their own way in the world:

> I am glad to observe that you are sensible that in the great City of London, you will be exposed to new temptations, and that you need the protection of the Father of the fatherless … My dear James, if you are spared, & preserved in the paths of virtue (which may God grant of his great goodness) I think you are in a fair way of gradually (and that is the only safe way) working up into perhaps a situation of importance & emolument, and becoming yourself through time a British merchant of some eminence … Do all in your power, in a lawful way, to promote the interest of your employers, at their back, equally as when their eyes are on you – and depend upon it that in the long run, you, as well as they in the meantime, will reap the reward …[18]

John Macandrew reminded 18-year-old James to avoid the temptations of London and to be virtuous, law abiding, to love his family and be respectful of his employers. Hard work would eventually bring rewards.

Raised in a religious family, Macandrew had a strong Christian faith: in the few extant letters written to his children he invariably invoked God's protection, and his everyday language was laced with Old Testament references. When he died, one obituarist observed: 'All Mr Macandrew's speeches abound in Biblical quotations, thus proving that he was a constant student of the good old book. With the exception of a stray quotation from his national poet, Burns, nearly all the others are from the Bible.'[19]

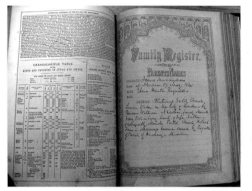

London was Macandrew's home from 1838 until 1850, and there he honed his business skills, enjoyed a middle-class lifestyle, married and began a family. While the country endured the Hungry Forties, London was undergoing a transformation. Large numbers of refugees from the Irish Famine and members of the Scottish diaspora had streamed into the capital. Slums were being replaced by brick terrace housing, and centrepieces such as Trafalgar Square and the Houses of Parliament were under development. The city was a far from savoury place, however: cholera epidemics killed at least 14,000 in 1849 and 10,000 in 1854, before effective sanitation and better housing finally eradicated the disease late in the century.[20]

The rapidly growing population led to ample business opportunities for Macandrew, and his stay with Pirie and Co. was brief. James Adam, one of his Dunedin business contemporaries, later recorded Macandrew's own description of his career:

> He entered the office of a large establishment, whose ramifications extended
> to the limits of commerce, and from the desk of a junior clerk he rapidly rose
> to the highest post in the concern – that of chief correspondent. This latter
> he also gave up and started as a merchant on his own account.[21]

The 'large establishment' was owned by the paper merchant Robert Ragg, who introduced Macandrew to the congregation of Scotch Church at London Wall, where he met Robert Garden. Born in 1818 in Montreal, by 1842 Garden was in business in London on his own account: he acted as an agent for Messrs Oliver & Boyd, booksellers of Edinburgh, pursuing debtors, selling advertising and distributing their books in London.[22] Macandrew joined Garden in 1845, and their business activities included locating lost consignments, dealing with the excise and soliciting advertising for Oliver & Boyd.[23] By 1847 the pair, now

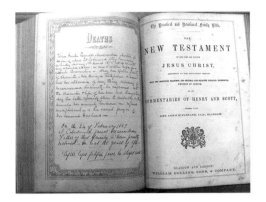

The Macandrew Family Bible, which is held by Toitū Otago Settlers Museum, Dunedin. Author photographs

iron merchants, occupied premises at 27 Queen Street, Cheapside, and by 1851 were operating from two offices, in Queen Street and Dowgate-hill. Garden & Macandrew's enterprises covered a wide range of activities, and their agency for yellow metals (bronze castings) indicates that they were dealing in the expensive end of the market, no doubt with a higher rate of profit. Railway companies were important customers for the pair, and as the business expanded Macandrew also broadened his knowledge of the mining and maritime worlds.

Ill-health and business failure haunted the self-employed, and if middle-class men like Macandrew aspired to a certain lifestyle, then using family connections in the pursuit of business was necessary. A letter from his cousin Donald Macandrew, an Edinburgh commission agent, discussed the sort of employment considered appropriate for men of their class: sales and commission work.[24] Donald could not help James to establish an agency for 'scotch pig iron' but added, 'I am … happy that you have abandoned the offered post abroad, and I hope that you will give up the idea entirely now and plod away at home.' While the more ambitious James appears to have considered and rejected migration, it is unclear where and what the 'offered post abroad' had been. When he did migrate three years later, likely spurred by the economic depression and the cholera epidemics of the late 1840s, it was on his own terms, on his own ship.

James Macandrew was active, committed to self-improvement and had an early interest in politics. He was 'a frequent visitor to the strangers' gallery [of the House of Commons]'.[25] As well as familiarising himself with the parliamentary system, he spent time in London with officials at the colonial office, who managed the affairs of the empire.

The Scotch Church at London Wall was a meeting place for evangelical Presbyterian expatriates, and Macandrew joined the congregation in 1838.[26] After the Disruption in 1843 and the establishment of the breakaway Free Church of Scotland, it became an active centre for émigré Free Church adherents and eventually cut its formal ties with other Scottish denominations.[27] Here Macandrew would have met promoters of the Otago settlement in New Zealand, and it was here also that he first met the Reynolds family when they joined the church in 1841: Thomas and Marion, their son William, born in Kent in 1822, and their daughter Eliza, born in Oporto in 1827.[28]

Thomas Reynolds was born in 1783 and had served in the Royal Navy before becoming the proprietor of cork plantations in Spain and Portugal.[29] The family departed Portugal for Edinburgh on the outbreak of revolution in 1828 and returned to Lisbon in 1834. That the business was prosperous is confirmed in William's obituary, which states that he returned to London in 1842 to run the family firm where 'as much as £180,000 a year passed through his hands'.[30] Macandrew was clearly acceptable to the Reynolds family, and he and Eliza were married on 17 October 1848. They resided in respectable Hackney where their first son, Colin, was born on 7 August 1849.[31] Macandrew's close bond with the wealthy and socially well-established Reynolds family no doubt boosted his confidence, further shaped his values and bolstered his finances.

It is not clear who initially conceived the plan to migrate to New Zealand, but the Reynolds clan shared his world view and saw prosperous opportunities in another country. In September 1850 Macandrew, Eliza and most of the family departed in the iron-hulled schooner *Titan* for a new life in New Zealand.

Migration 'sustained without interruption not only over decades and generations but across centuries' has been a consistent feature of Scottish life.[32] After the Clearances the Scots viewed emigration positively, both because it encouraged the pursuit of opportunities not available at home, and because it acted as a safety valve by reducing the population and pressure on the Scottish economy. Macandrew's moves – first to London and then to New Zealand – followed a common pattern. Between 1825 and 1914, 1.84 million Scots sailed to non-European destinations, a huge outpouring from a small country whose total population in 1911 was less than five million. Twenty-five per cent of these were bound for Australasia, with New Zealand a popular destination.[33] In 1871 Scots made up 10 per cent of the UK population; in New Zealand they made up 27.3 per cent of the UK-born population.[34] Historian James Belich records that over 80 per cent of those in New Zealand were Lowlanders and were seen as 'archetypically egalitarian, competent, undemonstrative and somewhat dour', the prototype of the emerging New Zealander.[35] UK historian Tanja Bueltmann

Macandrew came prepared: a business card distributed with his circular letter in August 1850. MSS, Acc 5000/Vol. 207, National Library of Scotland

suggests that because 'the Scots were early arrivers and eventually represented up to one-quarter of the settler population, they were … de facto disproportionately responsible for New Zealand's foundational culture'.[36]

The Scottish Enlightenment's emphasis on literacy and equality meant that the Scots had a strong influence in their new countries. Many were well educated and had prior business experience and capital reserves, so it is not surprising that they did well in their adopted lands. Macandrew stood out: as a Highlander, resolute, well read and with healthy capital to his name, he would initially enjoy membership of the New Zealand elite.

Chapter 2

Confident that they would receive a charter to settle English folk in New Zealand, the New Zealand Company despatched the sailing vessel *Tory* from Plymouth bound for New Zealand on 12 May 1839. On board was a team of surveyors who would purchase land and prepare it for settler groups. They were followed soon after by nine migrant ships whose passengers established the settlements of Wellington, Nelson, Whanganui and New Plymouth.[1]

The New Zealand Company was founded on a proposal for the 'systematic' settlement of New Zealand advanced by Edward Gibbon Wakefield, an imaginative Englishman who achieved fame as an educationalist and a writer of colonising policy. Wakefield wanted to avoid haphazard colonisation based on free land grants; instead he proposed selling land at a 'sufficient price' to support the subsidised migration of labourers, who would work towards the purchase of their own farms. Wakefield had damaged both his reputation and his diplomatic career by abducting a young woman, a crime for which he had served time in prison, but despite his reputation, with this proposal he managed to attract a coterie of establishment backers. Following the 1840 signing of the Treaty of Waitangi, New Zealand's founding document and a statement of partnership between Māori and the British Crown, the British government granted the company a charter for land sales and sole rights to sponsor any settlements in New Zealand.[2]

In July 1842 Scotsman George Rennie approached the directors of the New Zealand Company with a scheme to 'save the institutions of England from being swept away in an uncontrollable rebellion of the stomach' by assisting 'the unemployed and destitute masses' to migrate. Somewhat undiplomatically, he claimed that earlier settlements in New Zealand had been poorly planned; he proposed that an advance party establish the necessary infrastructure for a new settlement before a main body of settlers departed Britain.[3] The directors of the New Zealand Company, whose plans for further migration were meeting resistance from an unsympathetic Tory government and the Colonial Office as a result of confusion over land titles and perceived Māori hostility to European settlers, rebuffed Rennie's approach.

In May 1843 Rennie, now associated with 59-year-old Captain William Cargill, returned to the company with a revised proposal for a Scottish class settlement.[4] In it he claimed that:

> the great bulk of the colonists, as well capitalist as laborers, who have
> emigrated in connection with the New Zealand Company have proceeded
> from England … Scotland has taken but small part in an enterprise for
> which her people are eminently qualified by their self-reliance, industry,
> perseverance, and prudence. We are desirous, therefore, that the proposed
> Colony should be made particularly eligible for Scottish immigrants of all
> the various classes which constitute society … we propose that the plan
> of the Colony shall comprise a provision for religious and educational
> purposes, in connection with the Presbyterian Church of Scotland; and that
> the whole of the emigration fund arising from the sale of the Company's
> lands in the settlement, shall be employed in promoting the emigration of
> persons of the labouring class of Scotland only.

The company this time approved their proposal, and Rennie and Cargill arranged for Rev Dr Candlish and Robert Cargill (William Cargill's brother) to present the proposal to the acting committee of the Colonial Scheme of the Free Church of Scotland in June 1843. This body warmly endorsed it and promised to find a minister and a schoolmaster for the expedition. The committee apparently thought the proposal referred to the Free Church rather than the continuing Church of Scotland; just which branch of the Presbyterian Church of Scotland Rennie meant has been debated ever since.[5]

In October 1843, at the second meeting of the Free Church of Scotland Assembly, it was announced that 47-year-old Rev Thomas Burns would be the first minister of the proposed colony.[6] Burns had held the prestigious Church of Scotland 'living' at Monckton in Ayrshire for the previous 13 years, but had left the Established Church at the Disruption of 1843 and was now without a parish. He was considered a pious and highly principled man, capable of undertaking the difficult task of colonising a new country. However, his determination that the new colony would be a strictly Free Church settlement led to a close relationship with William Cargill and a complete split with Rennie.[7]

The Free Church was prepared to give its blessing as it had in June, but refused to adopt the scheme as an official church undertaking. One reason for this lack of support was given by the Rev Dr Candlish, who did not 'like our Church courts to be saying much about emigration in any shape just now: it looks so like playing into the hands of Lairds and factors, taking up their cuckoo song, and seeking to do what they so cruelly want to do; viz. drive away the people to make their lands a desert.[8] Crop failures, famine, cholera outbreaks and the Clearances were taking their toll on the Scottish population; another emigration scheme, although well-meaning, could have negative implications for the country.

In 1845 supportive citizens and potential settlers formed an independent Lay Association of Scotland in Glasgow for promoting settlement of 'the colony of Otago', because it was felt that 'the Free Church supporters of the Otago scheme would more readily place their confidence in a purely Scottish concern mainly because the New Zealand Company, by reason of its protracted negotiations with the Government, was fast losing the confidence of investors'.[9] Burns also wanted to disassociate the scheme from the New Zealand Company because he considered that '[Edward] Gibbon Wakefield's name in Scotland would bring no favour, no confidence with it'.[10] However, as the New Zealand Company was the only body with a charter from the British government to organise migration to New Zealand, the Otago Lay Association remained under the company's aegis and never actually acquired its own charter.

Land for Rennie's original New Edinburgh settlement was selected in 1844 by Frederick Tuckett, principal surveyor of the New Zealand Company's Nelson settlement. Tuckett had been commissioned by the company's Wellington-based principal agent, Edward Gibbon's brother Colonel William Wakefield, to select a site in the Middle (South) Island for a proposed Scottish settlement. After exploring and rejecting possible sites in what would become Canterbury, North Otago and Southland, Tuckett, on behalf of the company, signed a memorandum on 31 July 1844 with 25 Otago Ngāi Tahu rangatira, including Hoani Tūhawaiki, Te Matenga Taiaroa and Kōrako Karetai, for a 'block of country from Otago Harbour to the Molyneux, with the exception of certain areas to be set aside as native reserves, for the sum of two thousand four hundred pounds'.[11] This was to be the Otago Block of 400,000 acres (160,000ha). After much discussion, in September 1845 the Otago Lay Association, now headed by Captain William Cargill (who had accepted the appointment as the New Zealand Company's resident agent in Otago with a salary of £500 per year) and the Rev Thomas Burns, finalised arrangements with the New Zealand Company and agreed to establish the Otago settlement on a smaller block of 144,600 acres (57,274ha).

The Otago Block was to be divided into 2400 properties of 60¼ acres (25ha), each consisting of three packages: a town allotment (one-quarter acre/0.1ha), a suburban allotment (10 acres/4ha) and a rural allotment (50 acres/20ha). Of these, 2000 properties were to be sold to settlers, 100 were to be bought by the local municipal government, 100 were to be bought by the trustees of the Fund for Religious and Educational Uses, and 200 were to be bought by the New Zealand Company. At £2 per acre, sales would generate £289,200, of which three-eighths would be spent on emigration and the supply of labour by way of subsidised passages; two-eighths on civil uses to provide infrastructure for the settlement; one-eighth for religious and educational uses; and two-eighths would be paid to the New Zealand Company as a return on its investment.[12]

First steps to migrations

Macandrew's interest in migration and his Free Church membership led him to join the London committee of the Otago Lay Association in 1845; his brother-in-law William Reynolds also formed a connection with the association. As a man who keenly sought to influence events, Macandrew threw himself into the organisation of the Otago expedition and came to wield a certain amount of power. On the committee he mixed with the enthusiasts and advocates, the politicians and civil servants who were determining the fate of New Zealand. The London committee met in New Zealand House, the New Zealand Company's offices in London's Broad Street, and there Macandrew would have met Edward Gibbon Wakefield and his clansmen and been exposed to Wakefield's colonising theories, while committee work introduced him to the modus operandi of both the Whig and Tory secretaries of state for war and the colonies.

The years 1845–47 were discouraging ones in which little action took place, but in June 1846 Lord John Russell's pro-emigration, pro-colonising Whig party was elected to power and, with the backing of Colonial Secretary Earl Grey, the New Zealand Government Act was passed in December (see chapter 3). This spurred the issue of a revised version of the Otago Terms of Purchase by the New Zealand Company in June 1847.[13] The dormant Otago Lay Association now began advertising for and recruiting settlers,[14] and by the end of 1847 the first Otago-bound ships had set sail: the *John Wickliffe* departed on 24 November with 97 emigrants headed by William Cargill, and the *Philip Laing* left three days later with Burns in charge of a further 247 settlers.[15] These were followed by three more vessels in 1848, eight in 1849 and five in 1850.

The members of the Otago Lay Association were not noticeably enthused by the departure of these ships; support for the settlement had been limited and explanations were sought.[16] A report of the Edinburgh committee to the special general meeting of the association noted that as far as publicity was concerned, 'a considerable portion of this distribution has not yet had time to fructify';

regarding land sales, 'the undertaking has had to contend against the pernicious effects of detraction' and 'the infrequency of intelligence has operated unfavourably'; of all obstacles, 'what Dr Chalmers used to call "the unimpressibility of the masses" is the greatest'.[17] It may simply be that the £120.10/- required for a property package in Otago was the major deterrent in Scotland where, in 1867, 90 per cent of the population had an annual income of less than £50.[18]

Poor land sales in Otago meant development costs were not being met and the New Zealand Company had to cover the association's costs. By May 1850 the association owed £30,000, and the New Zealand Company refused any further advances.[19] As a member of the London committee and a confidant of John McGlashan, the association's Edinburgh-based secretary, Macandrew would have known of the looming financial crisis, but still chose to commit his future to Otago. In June 1850 he applied for land there, just a few weeks before the financial collapse of the New Zealand Company. Perhaps he hoped that the Otago Lay Association, released from the control of the New Zealand Company, would be free to deal directly with the British government – which might bring self-government for the settlement one step closer.

Despite the gloomy outlook, Macandrew played an increasingly active part in the foundation of Otago. His attitude to money and eye for a bargain are revealed in his letter of 14 June 1850 to McGlashan:

> I enclose a cheque for £120.10/ being the purchase money for one property in Otago … I intend to apply for two other properties but as the parties for whom I am to purchase them do not sail until September, I do not wish to have the money lying idle until then, and I would not have paid for one now, but for the sake of obtaining a passage for a man and his wife whom I intend to send out by the July vessel … I observe from the papers sent up lately for the consideration of the London Committee that the New Zealand Company seem to underrate the exertion of the Association in making sales, and therefor it is that I intend to trouble you with my payment, so that you may at least have the credit of them.[20]

This was powerful leverage: Macandrew made the minimum outlay for the maximum return – in this case, a sponsored passage for others, credit for unpaid-for sections and a percentage for the association, as well as an early choice of desirable land. His self-assurance and Scottish origins are apparent as he took it upon himself to criticise McGlashan's work:

> I feel perfectly assured of this that had proper steps been taken to make the London Committee something more than a mere name, if it had got a

habitation and an active paid Secretary, the Settlement of Otago might have been ere now nearly all bought up [as] there is an immence field here ... I am inclined to think that the Association and its functions are made very light of and that to use a scotch phrase they [the New Zealand Company] are now calling out stinkin fish.[21]

He added, 'I am convinced that if the Association were to act with spirit they might be in the same position as the Canterbury Association, and have the formation of the colony entirely in their own hands. [A]s it is now the influence of the Otago Association, upon the character of the Colony (excepting in as far as the emigrants are concerned) is a perfect farce.' While happy to give unsolicited advice for improving the association's situation, he was cautious, however: 'As regards your suggestion of having the head office of the Association here [in London] – it would require a great deal of consideration – I am not sure that such a step would be advisable although I think the vessels should be dispatched from here as there will be little chance of their procuring *cargo* in Scotland.'[22]

Macandrew's inclination to take control of events, his drive to shape the Otago settlement and his tendency to endow plans with grand and fanciful outcomes is evident through the events of this time. He concluded this letter with talk of a superior ship, his plan to establish a branch of his London 'house' in New Zealand, and reference to a bank he proposed to found in Otago: 'I mention it to you in confidence – if however you should find the knowledge of the fact, likely to be useful in operating upon parties about to proceed to the Settlement, you are at liberty to make use of the information.'

At the time, Macandrew was not committed to permanent emigration. He further noted: '[O]ur house here has lately been extending its business and operations in our Southern colonies, and that with the view of further extension and consolidation, it is probable that I shall go out for some years myself, making Otago my headquarters.'[23]

The quest for charter

The Otago settlement was experiencing teething pains: the surveying and allocation of sections was slow, and a small group of settlers was creating discord. In a progress report to William Cargill, now the leader of the Otago Lay Association settlers in Dunedin and the New Zealand Company agent for Otago, McGlashan summarised the problems the association was facing on both sides of the globe:

Our progress in Landsales continues to be depressingly slow; but what else could be expected, in the whole circumstances – the New Zealand Company denounced by Mr Wakefield – its members clamouring for its dissolution – its terms of existence approaching, when die it must unless it receive an addition to its days – the hostility of the Otago News, which is doing more harm than I could have supposed from Settlers injudiciously supporting it, and sending home, I would almost say maliciously sending home, copies of it – complaints from the Settlers of want of energy and, apparently, means, among many of the Land owners – complaints of the roads, which are represented to be wet weather canals of liquid mud …[24]

McGlashan's thankless role as a home agent required a degree of optimism and tact. He remembered to include good news for Cargill in Dunedin: 'But yet we are not without some progress. Besides the New Zealand Company's own ships, there are no less than three private adventure ships about to proceed … The one direct is a ship of Messrs. Garden and MacAndrew; which is to carry out only First Class passengers, who are Capitalists and are to make Otago their home.' Four days later, in a burst of exaggeration, McGlashan advised Thomas Harington, secretary of the New Zealand Company, of 'a Bank about to be formed in Dunedin by a party of capitalists principally Free Churchmen – and such an amount of Capital the Association has been assured by one of the projectors, is to be employed in the business as will place the bank on a solid foundation'.[25] In his next dispatch to Otago, McGlashan buoyed expectations even further: 'A number of Capitalists are about to settle in Otago. Amongst them is Mr Jas Macandrew who with others propose to establish a Bank with a capital amply sufficient. Their party leaves in a ship of their own in August next. They are staunchly Free Church.'[26]

On 28 June 1850 Macandrew put the case to McGlashan for a paid secretary for the London committee of the association, and proposed that the minister of his London Wall church, the Rev William Nicolson, accompany him to Otago. He wrote, 'the grand point which I am anxious to secure is a standing thero [sic], either ministerially, or as the founder of a superior educational institute which might ultimately emerge into a Free Church College'.[27] This was the first reference to a university in Otago, and possibly another of Macandrew's flights of fancy. No secretary was appointed, however, and although Nicolson did accompany the Macandrew family to New Zealand, it was neither as an academic nor to minister in Otago: he eventually settled in Tasmania.

The demise of the New Zealand Company on 5 July 1850 meant the Otago Lay Association lost its authority to buy land and send settlers.[28] Macandrew saw opportunity in adversity, however, and wrote to McGlashan: 'Now is the time for the Association to step in and occupy the same position as the Canterbury people … I would strongly impress upon you the necessity of making the attempt at least to get the whole affair into our hands.' Nor did the Otago settlement have to be purely Scottish: 'No doubt Scotland is the place to look to for the kind of labour which we want, but London is the grand source from whence Capital and Capitalists may be most readily drawn.'[29] Macandrew no doubt encouraged his brother-in-law William Reynolds, who also wrote to McGlashan reiterating that 'if proper means were adopted' the association 'would … secure the sympathies and support of English people, (and Dissenters from the Church of England especially)'.[30] Together the brothers-in-law were a prevailing force, promoting recruitment from all classes of society for the projected settlement. Their suggestion of wider recruitment was accepted, although the presence in Otago of a band of Englishmen was to have an unhappy outcome and would eventually lead to opposition to Free Church control of the settlement.

Macandrew encouraged McGlashan to step up pressure on the government for a charter.[31] Reynolds reported on 15 July 1850 that Macandrew had requested Otago's long-time backer, the Rev William Chalmers, to ask his parishioners, Fox Maule MP and the Marquis of Breadalbane, to act as go-betweens and arrange a meeting with higher Colonial Office officials.[32] Macandrew reported a useful lobbying visit on 17 July and issued further instructions to McGlashan: 'I need not enlarge upon the subject further than to express the hope that you will lose no time in drawing up the draft of a Charter. From the disposition of the Colonial Office I have every reason to think that the Association may fix its own terms – and the Authorities there seem to be quite alive to the necessity of dispatch.'[33]

EMIGRATION to OTAGO, NEW
ZEALAND.—The OTAGO ASSOCIATION announce that new arrangements having become necessary in consequence of the Dissolution of the New Nealand Company, relations have been establishment with Government, under whose immediate auspices the Association's Colonising operations are now conducted; and that the Association are presently organising a party which will proceed to the Settlement under highly advantageous circumstances.

PRICE OF LAND.

1-4th of an Acre of Town Land	..	..	..	.. £12	10 0
10 Acres of Suburban Land	..	..	..	.. 30	0 0
25 Acres of Rural Land	..	..	..	.. 50	0 0
60½ Acres, forming an Entire Property, and consisting of three allotments, viz. ¼ of an Acre of Town Land, 10 Acres of Suburban, and 50 Acres of Rural Land			120	10	0

The Ownership of certain Quantities of Land gives a Privilege of Extensive Pasturage to the Proprietor or his Tenant.

7s. 6d. in £1, or 37½ per cent., allowed towards the cost of the passage of the purchaser, his family and servants.

First-Class Passenger Ships will be despatched to Otago monthly, and care will be taken to appoint experienced Surgeons, and provide Medicines, Medical Comforts, and an ample Dietary for each Class of Passengers.

. The OTAGO JOURNAL.—Five Numbers Published—Price 2d., or by post 4d. each.

For further particulars apply in London to James Watson, Esq., 21, Berners-street; or to Messrs. Garden and Macandrew, 34, Dowgate-hill; or at the Offices of the Otago Association, 1, Royal Bank-place, Glasgow, and 27, Hanover-street, Edinburgh.

J. M'GLASHAN, Secretary.

The Otago Association's advertisement in the *Illustrated London News*, 28 September 1850, announcing the revised arrangements for settlement in Otago following the demise of the New Zealand Company. Garden & Macandrew is one of the addressees.

McGlashan followed Macandrew's directions with a letter to Colonial Secretary Earl Grey in which he applied subtle pressure by informing Grey, among other things, that 'several capitalists' were about to depart for Otago to establish a bank; the 'capital intended to be employed will not be less than from sixty to seventy thousand pounds'.[34] Other parties, he said, also wanted to buy land; if they could not go soon they would not go at all. McGlashan also asked for £400 a year to run an office in London, and softened the original exclusive Terms of Purchase: 'The Association do not exclude from the benefits of the Scheme Episcopalians and others, who are satisfied with the Institutions in Otago, and who are themselves of good character – all that they ask is proof of character and friendliness to the institutions.' He reported that a number of families from other denominations had signed up to emigrate.

It was beginning to seem that the association might become a legal body with its own charter, which would give it an independent commercial footing.[35] On 4 September 1850 Macandrew, McGlashan and other members of the association met with Colonial Under-secretary Herman Merivale to discuss ways for the association to continue its operations.[36] However, no progress was made,[37] and Grey now baulked at their requests and placed the association under the temporary aegis of the Colonial Land and Emigration Commission, a branch of the Colonial Office – definitely not an outcome desired by the association members.[38] In early 1851 Grey ruled that the revised Terms of Purchase signed in June 1849 would remain in force and no charter would be granted to the association. The proportion of land-sale monies that had previously gone to the New Zealand Company from the Otago Lay Association would now go to the Crown because it had taken over the company's liabilities; the association would be granted a five per cent commission on land sales for its own use. If the association was determined to have a charter, the Crown would take no responsibility for the association's liabilities.

At this the clamour for a charter ceased. Macandrew, however, emerged smelling of roses, something that would happen many times in his lifetime. Forty years after the event one obituarist wrote that in the 'tedious and difficult negotiations with the New Zealand Company and the Colonial Office, it is said, and is easily credible, that Mr Macandrew's great industry and tact, and doubtless his irrepressible hopefulness had much to do with the success of the scheme'.[39] Given the outcome, it is unclear that Macandrew or anyone on the deputation had achieved anything, but the story improved over time, probably through his own telling.

The Anglo settler revolution

New Zealand historian James Belich has defined a unique Anglo 'settler evolution' in the nineteenth century, when population pressures in Britain made emigration acceptable to people of all classes. He identifies four phases of settlement in the new territories.[40] The first, 'incremental settlement', describes the arrival of the new race, who survived by subsistence farming in the new land. This was followed by 'explosive settlement', often marked by unrepeatable events such as gold strikes, the unrestrained export of animal products or the exploitation and exhaustion of virgin land. The explosive phase was usually accompanied by dramatic swings of boom and bust: 'boosters'– men who committed themselves to a new land then encouraged maximum investment by others in order to raise the value of their own property – talked up their particular region to encourage new settlers, who then flooded in.[41] Investors in Britain, beguiled by dreams of the riches to be extracted from the young settlement, poured their money into often impossible projects. Growth fed on growth, usually based on unsustainable financial schemes that inevitably led to economic collapse.

Belich's third phase of settlement, 'recolonisation' – the inflow of further settlers – usually followed as each 'bust' was rescued by successive waves of immigration and investment. The fourth phase was independence from the homeland; however, for most colonies, who were channelling produce to their sole market, Britain, complete self-government was postponed.

Macandrew arrived in New Zealand at a time of expanding settlement and lived through three of Belich's phases: incremental, explosive and recolonising settlement. An early booster, Macandrew saw the endless opportunities offered in New Zealand: he amassed and lost great wealth but was able to rebound from each failure. His enduring view of New Zealand as 'the Great Britain of the south' inspired his commercial enterprises and encouraged his development of shipping and overseas markets, which made significant contributions to the colony's progress through the explosive and recolonising phases.

His unquenchable optimism, at this time based on speculation, was apparent in a letter distributed under the name of Garden & Macandrew in July 1850 (see Appendix 1).[42] This may be one of the most sanguine views of the future of New Zealand ever penned, exceeding even E.G. Wakefield's paeans, and in it Macandrew demonstrated his ability to paint with a very broad brush. The letter announced that Garden & Macandrew had established a trading branch in New Zealand, and claimed New Zealand's future was assured: 'There can be no doubt that from its locality, climate & capability, it is fitted and destined to

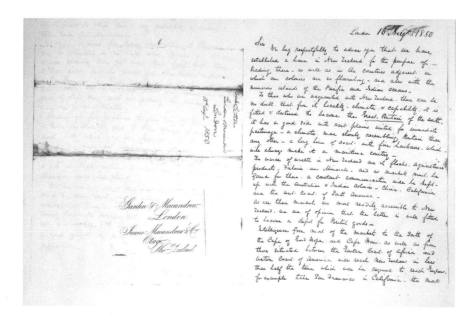

become the Great Britain of the south.' Macandrew praised the country's grasslands and excellent harbours, and suggested that New Zealand's wealth would come from 'its flocks, agricultural products, Fisheries and Minerals'. A depot there for British goods would be able to serve 'most of the markets to the South of the Cape of Good Hope and Cape Horn', as well as those situated 'between the Eastern Coast of Africa and Western Coast of America' – a wide area indeed. 'The voyage at present from Sydney & New Zealand to Panama may be estimated at six weeks. When steamers are established it will probably take not more than half that time.' This, the writer promised, would eventually enable goods to be ordered from New Zealand and delivered to San Francisco in three months – half the delivery time from Britain. The letter ended with a promise: 'We are sending out a very fast vessel, our purpose having one or two more such, to be entirely engaged in the intercolonial trade', and solicited support 'by way of sample'.

From 1838 the purpose-built side-wheel paddle steamers *Sirius* and *Great Western* had provided regular trans-Atlantic crossings, and Macandrew would have seen steamers departing from London for increasingly longer voyages around the world.[43] He would also have been aware that the New Zealand Company had issued tender documents in 1849 for steamship services around the New Zealand coast and to Australia.[44] The circular demonstrated his enthusiasm for new technologies and his ability to identify trends and opportunities

Macandrew's circular letter, 15 August 1850, encouraging investment in 'the Great Britain of the south'. MSS, Acc 5000/Vol. 207, National Library of Scotland

ahead of others – and to promote them ardently. These skills would repay him handsomely.

Macandrew's ability to think in sweeping terms is apparent in his portrayal of half the world, from Africa to America, as a market that could be serviced from New Zealand. He also appears to have been well informed about conditions on the other side of the world: his knowledge of New Zealand's temperate climate enabled him to make optimistic predictions about agricultural productivity, and he was aware of the booming economy in Australia and the expanding settlement in Victoria. For migrants who expected to take three months or more to reach New Zealand, Victoria would have appeared a promising and not-too-distant market for New Zealand produce.[45]

When the extended Reynolds family agreed to migrate to Otago, Macandrew shrewdly realised it would be economical to charter his own vessel to convey his large group of relatives along with paying passengers and a cargo of trade goods. The *Titan*, just 86ft (26.3m) long, 21ft (6.5m) wide and weighing 161 tons, was bought on credit from shipbuilders Robinson and Russell of Millwall, and registered by Garden & Macandrew on 3 August 1850. The ship was then chartered to Macandrew & Co., a new company formed by Macandrew and Reynolds.[46] Robert Garden retained a power of attorney to enable him to continue to manage Garden & Macandrew and to reclaim his share of the investment through sale of the ship when it reached New Zealand.[47]

Getting there

On 12 June 1850 Macandrew advertised in the *Aberdeen Journal* for passengers on a ship that would proceed to New Zealand; further details, including the ship's name, size, departure date and the captain's name, were specified in an advertisement in *The Times* on 25 July 1850.[48] A second advertisement in the *Aberdeen Journal* on 31 July 1850 listed the departure date as '26th August next' and the projected duration of the voyage: 90 days.[49]

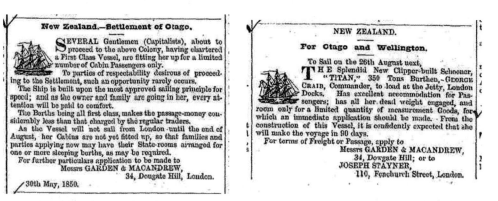

Garden & Macandrew's advertisement in the *Aberdeen Journal* of 12 June 1850 offering passage to Otago in their 'First Class vessel'. A similar advertisement on 31 July 1850 named the *Titan* and a departure date of 26 August 1850. The projected 90-day voyage took 132 days.

Macandrew would have been aware of the contents of McGlashan's letter to Cargill of 14 June 1850 and the problems brewing in Otago: the underperformance of the New Zealand Company, the lack of investment in infrastructure, the rift between those who were Free Church adherents and those who were not (dubbed the 'Little Enemy' by Scottish settlers – an indication of the intensity of feelings).[50] He knew that Henry Graham, editor of the *Otago News*, the region's only paper, was antagonistic towards the leadership of the settlement, and he would have seen the impact of Graham's critical copy in Britain, where it had effectively undermined the marketing of the new settlement. According to McGlashan, Macandrew was well equipped to meet these challenges, and sailed carrying 'a large amount in specie for the establishment of a Bank and Type &c for a newspaper', although efforts to recruit an editor to travel with him had apparently been unsuccessful.[51]

The *Titan* sailed on 7 September 1850 and arrived in Port Chalmers on 17 January 1851 after a stopover in Cape Town en route.[52] Nothing untoward was reported during the voyage, although Cargill observed to McGlashan: 'Your letter by the "Titan" did not reach till the 16th inst. having been 132 days on the way. No fault it is stated in the sailing qualities of the vessel, but still the longest voyage that had been made.' It was a far cry from the optimistic estimate of 90 days.[53]

The advertisements for the *Titan* clearly did not attract any extra passengers, as Macandrew's family, staff and friends appear to have been the only passengers. Thomas Hocken recorded the 19 passengers and an unknown number of crewmen, commanded by George Craig, who were welcomed in Dunedin as a 'galaxy of Free Church talent'.[54] The passengers included James (31) and Eliza (24) Macandrew and their son Colin (1); James' brother Daniel(27, architect); Thomas (67) and Marion (65) Reynolds and their son William (26, merchant); Thomas (13), Maria (11) and Robert (10) Reynolds, the children of Thomas Reynolds Jnr who had remained in Portugal; Rev William Nicolson(55), Macandrew's minister from the Scotch Church, London Wall, and his son Ralph (23, pharmacist); Job Wain (14, employed to mind baby Colin); Beatrice Fowler (25, servant); James Saunders (24, bank clerk); George Shaw (artist and engraver); J. Smith (carpenter); and James Scott (22, carpenter), 'a native of Aberdeen, and was born and spent his early years in the same street as the Macandrew family'.[55] Passenger W. Blyth had died en route and had been buried at sea.

James Macandrew had arrived in his Great Britain of the south. His connection with the Otago Lay Association demonstrated that he was an effective committeeman and administrator, and he had helped to animate the torpid organisation. He had the organisational capacity to move his extended family and worldly goods to the Antipodes, as well as broad experience and a comprehensive knowledge of practical, technical and political matters, including theories of government. He was an energetic man whose Presbyterian values did not hamper his hard-nosed commercial endeavours. Self-assured and socially adept, he was equally at ease with the educated Englishmen who were filling government positions as with his artisan and labouring fellow immigrants.

Macandrew would astonish New Zealand audiences with his grand visions, and historian Tom Brooking's description of him – as one of the three great optimists of the nineteenth-century Pākehā world alongside Edward Gibbon Wakefield and Julius Vogel – is warranted.[56] The next decade would see him become first wealthy beyond his dreams, then destitute, subjected to the indignities of poverty and rejected by many.

Chapter 3

When James Macandrew reached Dunedin in 1851 the settlement was three years old and had a population of 1455, more than four times the number of original settlers who had arrived in 1847. This was rapid growth for a distant and isolated outpost.[1] Scots, chiefly Lowlanders, were still in the majority, but the intended Free Church ethos had been diluted.[2]

In John McGlashan's opinion, the community at Otago was ideal:

> The Settlement … is peculiarly a Scotch one – it is composed of no single class or sect but forms an epitome of Home Society in the lower, and through different grades to the apex of the Middle Classes. The greatest care having been taken in the selection of the laboring class, it is of the elite of the Scottish Peasantry; and altogether, according to the testimony of disinterested and impartial witnesses its Community is highly moral intelligent and enterprising.[3]

The community lacked harmony, however. While the settlers may have been principled and resourceful, from the start they were remarkably disputatious. People bickered over minor decisions and argued over administrative, financial, educational and infrastructural matters.[4] Outside observers perceived Otago as a province riven by querulous factions, and one Auckland newspaper was sharply critical: 'We regret to observe nothing is more prominent than the spirit of strife, disputation, and political partisanship which seems to have acquired an ascendancy amongst the "Pilgrim Fathers".'[5] The account continued:

> As respects the GOVERNOR-IN-CHIEF, in addition to any previous quarrels they had, or supposed they had, with his administration, there has lately been a new infusion of bitterness, extracted from his strictures on the 'class' character of the Canterbury Association, which the Otago Associationists regard as bearing with almost equal force on their scheme, and on account of which they are fully inclined to make it a common cause – Presbyterianism and Prelacy for the time uniting in opposition to the Government. An 'Otago Settlers' Association' has been for some months in operation and its proceedings have been marked from time to time by no trifling contentions.

'The Coming Man', James Macandrew, with his carpet bag. This 1852 James Brown cartoon has been labelled 'New Zealand's first political cartoon/caricature' (Ian F. Grant, *The Unauthorized Version: A cartoon history of New Zealand*, Auckland: Cassell, 1980, 9).

Acc 7734, Hocken Collections, Uare Taoka o Hākena, University of Otago

Macandrew flourished in the emerging community, where he was considered a welcome addition to the Free Church congregation and 'accorded a place in society which doubtless coincided with his ambitions'.[6] Within six weeks of arrival he was appointed to three committees: one charged with building a road from Dunedin to Port Chalmers, another with constructing jetties at both ports, and a third to consider changing the pasturage regulations.[7] At a meeting of the Otago Horticultural Society, where it was resolved to form a corresponding branch of the Highland and Agricultural Society of Scotland, to be called the Otago Agricultural Association, he was appointed to the management council.[8]

In the first few years he seemed to be patron, appointee or committee member of almost every official, quasi-official or community body in Otago. Thirty years later he would recall that he had, 'in the course of a busy and eventful life … run everything, from a province to a newspaper'.[9] One local cartoonist in 1852 depicted him marching forth carrying a carpet bag, with the caption 'Macandrew, the Coming Man!'[10] Young, fit and healthy, he was rarely idle. He attended most public and congregational meetings and festive occasions, frequently taking the chair or in some way overseeing events. His roles were many: landowner, churchman, family man, community stalwart and businessman, and over time he came to occupy virtually all the elective positions available in local, provincial and colonial politics.

There was no doubt in Macandrew's mind about the place of business in the world. He once proclaimed, 'Let them set up the genius of Commerce, with all its soul-expanding and elevating tendencies. Next to Christianity, it was the most powerful instrument in promoting the happiness of the human race.'[11] He had ideas for achieving that happiness: 'Otago settlers should take a leaf out of the American book … they should borrow as much money as they possibly could invest in the productive development of the resources of the Province.'

Setting up business

On his arrival, Macandrew already owned a package of 60¼ acres (25ha) for which he had paid £120.10/-, an investment that inflated rapidly as values soared in the new settlement.[12] He immediately leased two sections from the local municipality on the south side of Manse Street and arranged to have a store built there.[13]

He set sail for Lyttelton and Wellington on the *Titan* on 25 January 1851 to acquire further supplies and to investigate trading opportunities and markets in Wellington and Canterbury. On his return on 26 February he rented further accommodation for his merchandise, stocked his store with the *Titan's* cargo, and advertised for business on 22 March 1851.[14] James Macandrew & Co.'s first store, stocked with British and some locally purchased goods, was opened on 17 May 1851.[15] The firm would operate the Dunedin outlet, and others at Port Molyneux and Invercargill, until Macandrew and William Reynolds dissolved their partnership in 1858. The renamed Macandrew & Co. was then sold to James Paterson & Co. in September 1859.[16]

The *Titan* was in the news again when Reynolds sailed for Hobart on 20 March 1851 with some of the original cargo from London and items from New Zealand.[17] He returned on 26 May with a varied cargo, loaded more goods and sailed on 3 June for the insatiable markets of the Californian goldfields.[18] With the extraordinary luck that accompanied so many of Macandrew and Reynolds' enterprises, Reynolds arrived in San Francisco soon after the fires of May and June 1851 had destroyed much of that city. An absence of storage space meant he could sell high: it was reported that 'the Otago lime, of which [the *Titan*] took a considerable quantity as ballast, has realised about 14s. a bushel'.[19] He also purchased goods 'at exceptionally low prices, in some instances at prices equal to 90 per cent below the cost at the port of shipment'.[20] Almost a year later Reynolds returned to Sydney with paying passengers, sold most of his cargo, loaded cattle and sheep and returned to Otago where, 'after the payment of all expenses, including the charter of the ship, this venture returned him a profit of £8000 or £9000'.[21] Such a large sum would have maintained the two men and their relatives in comfort for some time.

PURSUANT to an Order of the High Court of Chancery made in a cause THOMAS BOYD v. RICHARD ALEXANDER ROBINSON, the CREDITORS of ROBERT GARDEN and JAMES MACANDREW, formerly of Dowgate-hill, in the City of London, and of the Colony of New Zealand, merchants, and co-partners, trading under the firm or style of "Garden and Macandrew" at the date of a certain indenture of assignment, executed by the said firm, for the benefit of their creditors, on the 19th day of June, 1851, and who executed or assented to the said indenture, are by their solicitors, on or before the 2nd day of November, 1860, to come in and prove their debts at the Chambers of the Master of the Rolls, in the Rolls-yard, Chancery-lane, Middlesex; or, in default thereof, they will be peremptorily excluded from the benefit of the said Order. WEDNESDAY, the 7th day of November, 1860, at 3 o'clock in the afternoon, at the said Chambers, is appointed for hearing and adjudicating upon the claims.

Dated this 8th day of August, 1860.

GEO. WHITING, Chief Clerk.
HENRY HARRIS, 84A, Moorgate-street, London, Plaintiff's Solicitor.

A notice in the London *Daily News* of 14 August 1860, alerting the creditors of foreclosure on Garden & Macandrew 10 years after Macandrew left London.

MESSRS. MACANDREW, CRANE, and
Co., of LONDON, beg to state that they
are prepared to transact every kind of business
between the Settlement of Otago and the
Mother-Country.

From their extensive connexions, experience,
and knowledge of the Markets at Home, they
are enabled to send out Goods upon the most
advantageous terms. All orders transmitted
through their House in the Colony (MESSRS.
JAMES MACANDREW, & Co.) will meet with
due attention.

MESSRS. MACANDREW, CRANE, & Co., beg
further to state, for the information of such
parties as may be receiving Money from Home,
that they are ready to grant Letters of Credit,
or Bills of Exchange, AT PAR, upon their
House in the Colony, payable in gold; thereby
obviating the expense which has hitherto been
incurred in its transmission, either through the
banks or by ships.

An advertisement in the *Otago Witness*, 8 March 1851, for the mysterious Macandrew, Crane & Co.

New Zealand required food, liquor, animals, ships and labour, and Macandrew supplied these in growing quantities. Alcohol, a major concern for the community's moral custodians, was an important part of his custom.[22] A. H. McLintock notes that although the duty on British and foreign spirits was as low as five shillings per gallon, customs returns for the year 1848–49 were 'little short of one thousand pounds, an appalling figure when one considers the size of the population'.[23]

Thomas White joined James Macandrew & Co. as a partner in 1851 and was dispatched to London to restock the store: he returned in 1853 with a large and varied assortment of goods from Scotch ploughs to tobacco pipes, and joined George Hepburn in running the business.[24]

Macandrew's commercial proposals, however, were often undermined by his propensity for risk-taking and his casual use of other people's money. In March 1851 a new company, Macandrew, Crane, & Co., advertised in the *Otago Witness* its willingness to transact 'every kind of business'.

Six months later, a year after Macandrew's departure from Britain, a public notice appeared in London's *Daily News* under the heading 'Macandrew, Crane and Co and Garden and Macandrew': 'The Creditors of Robert Garden and James Macandrew, being two of a firm of three persons styled Macandrew, Crane, and Co. … who have not signed the Deed of Trust for the benefit of the Creditors of Robert Garden and James Macandrew are requested to sign the same.'[25] A similar notice appeared in the *Glasgow Herald* a week later.[26] Garden had exercised his power of attorney and begun the process of winding up their firm. He sold the *Titan* on 11 April 1851, although the charter to Macandrew & Co. was continued.[27] However, it was another nine years before Garden &

Macandrew was foreclosed. Another public notice appeared in both the *Daily News* and *The Times* in August 1860:

> The CREDITORS of ROBERT GARDEN and JAMES MACANDREW, formerly of Dowgate-hill, in the City of London, and of the Colony of New Zealand, merchants and co-partners, trading under the firm or style of Garden and Macandrew at the date of a certain indenture of assignment executed by the said firm for the benefit of their creditors on the 19th day of June 1851, and who executed or assented to the said indenture, are, by their solicitors on or before the 2d day of November, 1860, to come in and prove their debts at the Chambers of the Master of the Rolls, in the Rolls-yard, Chancery-lane, Middlesex…[28]

Not much record remains of the mysterious New Zealand firm Macandrew, Crane, & Co., but the firm caused concern, and a study of some of its activities reveals something of Victorian financial processes. Cargill made use of this firm's services to send money to Britain but the response, after the usual six months' turnaround, was disturbing.[29] The London-based Macandrew, Crane & Co. declined to honour Macandrew & Co.'s draft for £25.[30] This happened again in January 1852, for larger amounts, but in a letter to Cargill, McGlashan defended Macandrew: '[T]he energy of the Messrs Macandrew and their enterprise were laudable, and deepen the regret at what has so unexpectedly occurred.'[31] When McGlashan wrote to Thomas Harington at the New Zealand Company in July he identified Crane as 'Patrick Moir Crane, 18 Canonbury Villas, Islington, London' and noted: 'I understand Mr. Crane has admitted to parties that he is a partner with Mr. Macandrew.'[32] McGlashan received a stinging reply and the news that the matter of non-payment had gone higher, to the secretary of state no less. Harington replied that the directors

> have been somewhat at a loss to understand what can have been your motive, either in taking a private Bill [of exchange] … as a channel of transmission and payment to the Commissioners of Colonial Lands and Emigration … upon further enquiry, a statement is made to the effect that the Firm of 'Messrs Macandrew Crane & Co.' was only a contemplated Firm, which had no actual existence. Under the circumstances, the Bill in question has been forwarded to the Secretary of State for the Colonies, specially endorsed over to the Colonial Land and Emigration Commissioners, and will in all probability be returned to the Colony burdened with Protest Charges … I am instructed to request that you will on no account consider yourself as authorized to enter into any similar transaction, or indeed, into any transaction, whatever, on behalf of the company.[33]

McGlashan had to tell Cargill that the account remained unpaid. Macandrew's debts were discharged 18 months later in a way that demonstrated the difficulty of doing business half a world away: with no banks to transmit funds, an account was considered settled only when cash was presented or a bill of exchange received from a debtor.[34] With these payments, the matter was wound up without damage to Macandrew's reputation in Otago where, despite his tardy payment having been reported to the Colonial Office, Cargill had already endorsed him as a political candidate, saying, 'Macandrew will … be the mainspring of our representative element and you may fully rely upon him.'[35]

McLintock claims that Macandrew, Crane & Co. 'existed solely as a figment of Macandrew's imagination … [and] was known to one man and one man alone, and he for obvious reasons, was not prepared to enlighten a credulous community of the nebulous character of his financial entanglements.'[36]

Light was shone on Macandrew's financial problems in July 1861 in the Dunedin Supreme Court when Macandrew described his cashflow problems during his application for discharge from debtors' prison: 'I lost altogether £8300 on account of a partnership in London, for the debts of which I have been held liable through the dissolution of partnership not being gazetted.'[37] Garden had sold the *Titan* in 1851 but had not repaid the shipbuilders. He had not paid the firm's debts to publishers in Edinburgh, nor had he wound up Garden & Macandrew. He was now employed as a clerk for a life assurance company and presumably unable to repay the debts. As a result the creditors went after Macandrew, a public figure who appeared to be in a better financial position. The settlement date was 2 November 1860 in London.[38] Macandrew must surely have been aware of the debts hanging over his head all those years, and showed scant sympathy for his creditors in Britain. It was but one example of his tendency to blame others for his misfortunes – a characteristic that would emerge when his questionable business practices were exposed.

Becoming a leading citizen

The *Otago Witness* announced in March 1851: 'Appointment by His Excellency The Governor-in-Chief: James Macandrew, Esq., Otago, to be a Magistrate of the Province of New Munster.'[33] It is likely that Macandrew engineered his own appointment to the bench, as he had earlier arranged to meet officials, including Governor George Grey, and had collected the appropriate Book of Ordinances during a business visit to the north.[34]

The Dunedin magistrate's bench was dominated by educated and financially independent Englishmen, so the appointment of a Free Church compatriot, followed soon after in May by the appointment of William Reynolds, gave William Cargill some desirable allies. As magistrate, Macandrew once appeared as a complainant after laying a charge of assault against another Justice of the Peace, who had punched him at his store.[35] That an individual could be both victim and judge at the one court hearing appears not to have bothered too many citizens of this era.

The bench had a wide range of responsibilities, from the straightforward punishment of drunks to more complex cases, and was backed by an arsenal of sanctions. It also advised Governor Grey on constitutional matters. On 30 January 1852 it advised on the wisdom of proclaiming, in the district of Otago, one or several 'Hundreds' – areas of land set aside for division into small holdings for close settlement. Other matters were discussed such as roading, bridge-building and mail delivery, and recommendations included that the harbour pilot have a boat's crew for his work, and that the customhouse be moved from Port Chalmers to Dunedin. The bench also acted as a de facto town council, making recommendations for the expenditure of government funds allocated to Otago.[36]

Macandrew was a regular churchgoer, and his membership of the Free Church gave him further influence in the community.[37] He joined the First Church of Otago on arrival, and within a month had taken on administrative duties as a trustee for the Fund for Religious and Educational Uses, a role in which he made his foremost contribution to church life.[38] The fund received one-eighth of the purchase money for all land sold in the Otago Block; this was invested in an estate and the profits used to establish and maintain churches and schools.[39] The trustees were autonomous; although they initially reported annually to the Deacons' Court of First Church, and from 1854 to the Presbytery of Otago, they were beholden to no one. To many settlers, however, this fund characterised the Free Church's disproportionate control of land and funds, and Macandrew's connection with it made him a target for public criticism for many years. Settlers also criticised the practice of allocating the income from land sales to a fund for the benefit of just one denomination, especially as land prices were kept higher in Otago than in other settlements. Dissension grew until the provincial council was established in 1853, at which point, in McLintock's words, 'the period of paternalism in government, of theocratic control' finally ended.[40]

With his easy style of public speaking and his skill in managing crowds, Macandrew quickly became a regular chairman of formal dinners, which were a popular form of entertainment. His increasing status can be measured by the growing importance of the events he managed. In April 1853 he was the chairman of a dinner for 214 guests in honour of Captain Cargill, to mark the advent of self-government and the conclusion of Cargill's role as the settlers' leader; the printed speeches for this event occupied two and a half pages of the *Otago Witness*.[41] In June 1859 he was chair at a soirée for 500 people, at which a silver tea service was presented to Rev Thomas Burns.[42]

Macandrew was elected as chair of the management committee when the Dunedin Mechanics' Institute was launched in July 1851. As a venue for adult education, the objects of the institute were to provide:

> Lectures and Classes for Public Instruction, upon such subjects as Natural Philosophy, History, Astronomy, Geology, Chemistry, Political Economy, Architectural and Mechanical Drawing, Music, language, &c; and also to have regular Fortnightly Meetings of the Members for Mutual Improvement, by Essay-reading and conversational enquiry.[43]

Newspaper advertisements announced the intention 'to have a Reading Room, supplied with British and Colonial papers and periodicals, to be open daily. A Library and a Museum is also in contemplation … It has been resolved to erect a suitable Building immediately.'[44] The building fund stood at £130.5.0 (donated by 44 settlers), and the Mechanics' Institute was officially opened on 3 January 1853.[45] Built at the water's edge on land bordered by High, Rattray and Princes streets, the solid, square structure had a large space that could accommodate 100 people and two reading rooms that doubled as classrooms.[46] It was to be the meeting place of Dunedin's multifarious boards, councils and committees for many years, before becoming the office for the Oriental Bank and finally a butcher's shop.[47]

The slow journey to self-government

As one of the later-settled colonies in the British Empire, New Zealand benefitted from the election of the Whig government of Lord Russell in 1846, which held office until 1852. British governments' gradual acceptance of a limited form of self-government for some of the colonies saw New Zealand settlers granted a large degree of autonomy in 1852 to manage their own affairs.

The third Earl Grey, Henry George Grey, had been under-secretary of state for war and the colonies from 1830–34, then secretary at war from 1835–39, and was appointed secretary of state for war and the colonies when the Whigs returned to power in 1846. As a supporter of empire free trade, and sympathetic to the model of systematic colonisation advanced by Edward Gibbon Wakefield, he was disinclined to listen to the humanists and missionary societies who had championed the 1840 Treaty of Waitangi and the rights of indigenous people during five years of Conservative rule. The Treaty had 'turned over a new leaf in British colonial policy and offered the natives a guarantee that colonisation, inevitable though it might be, should not proceed without regard to their just claims'.[48] But despite the input of the missionaries, within six months of his taking office, Earl Grey's New Zealand Government Act was passed, shaped in part by the 1839 Durham Report. (This had recommended self-government for Canada's then two provinces, although they did not achieve this status when they were integrated as the Province of Canada in 1841.)[49]

The New Zealand Government Act marked a revolution in colonial governance, but proved unwieldy and singularly unrepresentative. It divided New Zealand into two provinces, with land that had been purchased from Māori further divided into municipalities.[50] Each province was to have its own governor, a Legislative Council of Crown appointees, and a Lower House elected by municipal representatives. These were given extensive powers of self-government, including taxation and legislation. The General Assembly of New Zealand, which would sit above these bodies, consisted of the governor-in-chief, a Legislative Council of Crown appointees, and a House of Representatives elected by the provincial Houses. It was to be responsible for nine areas of national importance: customs duties; the establishment of, jurisdiction and procedure of a Supreme Court; currency and coinage; weights and measures; the Post Office; bankruptcy and insolvency; beacons and lighthouses; and shipping dues.[51]

The franchise for electing the municipal representatives was so limited, however, that only the few hundred potential voters – those who were European, male, able to read and write English, of good character and not aliens, felons or paupers, and who had been property holders for at least six months – would elect the mayors, aldermen and councillors, who in turn would elect the provincial assemblymen. These in turn would elect the members of the House of Representatives, while members of the Legislative Councils at both levels would be appointed by the Crown – prompting critics to suggest that 'this so-called Representation Act was in reality a cast-iron frame of political bondage from which the people of New Zealand could not have escaped without the consent of the [New Zealand] Company, which would never have been given'.[52]

Governor George Grey, in command in New Zealand from 1845–53 and faced with implementing the Act, was sceptical of its utility:

New Zealand is divided into several settlements, separated by long intervals, having in some respects interests totally different from each other, and none of them exceeding the other so much in wealth and importance as to possess a preponderating influence and recognised superiority.[53]

Grey had strong reservations about the workability of such a complex governance structure and asked how it would be possible for a single governor and his executive council to legislate satisfactorily for the colony. He was successful in having the Act suspended in 1848 on the grounds that it would obstruct Māori, who were disenfranchised by the property and language requirements, and because there were too few capable men to fill the numerous positions. The proposed division of the colony into smaller sub-units of government was not carried out, but Grey was encouraged to proceed with some of the Act's provisions. The result was the creation of two provinces: New Ulster and New Munster. It was an experiment in power sharing that tested the legislative boundaries between local and national government.

Although made in the interests of the settlers, the governor's decision that this complicated, quasi-federal, quasi-feudal edifice for fewer than 13,000 Europeans was unworkable outraged many. His apparent refusal to accommodate settler demands for elected representatives was marked by protests throughout the country, even including the independent-minded settlers of Auckland.[54] This was followed by the formation of settlers' constitutional associations in Wellington, Nelson, Canterbury and Otago, which, although often concerned with parochial matters, became effective vehicles for pursuing wider political change. By 1850 Grey was faced with opposition throughout the entire country.[55]

Governor Grey had visited Otago in November 1850 prior to Macandrew's arrival, and there received a request from the settlers for a municipal charter 'with powers to legislate and rule, and also to administer Revenue within the boundaries of their District [which they preferred] because of its authorities being suited, in their view, to the limited population and Revenue of the District'.[56] Grey had pointed out that it would be impossible to delegate such power to a municipality; he suggested that what they wanted – incorporation as a separate province – could be achieved through a modification of the Provincial Legislative Councils Bill. The settlers accepted this, and also resolved that 'a Legislative Council, of which two-thirds to be elected by the people, and one-third by the Governor-in-Chief, is satisfactory in principle'. Grey agreed to this ratio and in 1851 modified legislation to elect some members of the Legislative Councils of New Ulster and New Munster. However, he insisted that the Legislative Council of New Zealand remain a nominee body. This resulted in a public meeting in Dunedin on 13 May 1851, called:

> for the purpose of requesting [Otago settler] Englishman William Henry Valpy, Esq., not to accept his nomination to be a Member of the Legislative Council of New Zealand; it being inconsistent with the feelings and principles of the Otago settlers ... to have anything to do with an exclusively Nominee Council, or that they should have the REMOTEST APPEARANCE of being represented, without their ACTUALLY being so.[57]

Valpy had migrated to Dunedin in 1849 after a profitable career in the East India Company and government service in India, and was probably the only wealthy capitalist in the settlement. He agreed with Grey's opinion that the colony was not ready for self-government.[58]

Stormy speeches opposing nomineeism were made, and Macandrew demonstrated his skill at appealing to both sides of a case:

> [Macandrew] disclaimed being actuated by any desire to embarrass the Government, or to oppose Mr. Valpy, towards whom he entertained the highest respect ... but he did entreat, that the meeting would not allow any feelings of respect, or any feelings of delicacy towards the Government, to deter them from asserting a great principle, and vindicating their rights as free men – men born in a free country – men who had left the land of their fathers in the full confidence, and with every assurance, that they were to live under and enjoy the privileges of the representative and responsible government, for which their forefathers had struggled.[59]

Whether Macandrew would have spoken as strongly against a co-religionist is a moot point, but Valpy, an Englishman and an Anglican, would not yield. In the event, his health declined and he died in September 1852 without occupying his seat on the Legislative Council.

Macandrew had arrived in Otago certain that the Otago Lay Association had secured its own charter with the British government and that self-government for Otago was on its way, only to discover that Earl Grey had reneged on his agreement and Governor Grey was insisting that the Legislative Council comprise Crown nominees only. Macandrew had no hesitation in engaging with the governor on legislative matters even as he was responsible for gathering the evidence the Otago Lay Association needed to convince Sir John Pakington, colonial secretary in the Earl of Derby's 10-month 1852 Conservative government, that the Otago settlers did indeed want a charter – though a large group of them patently did not.[60]

The Otago Settlers' Association was established at this time, primarily to monitor the use of money allocated by the 1847 Deed of Trust to the Emigration, the Civil and the Religious and Educational Funds, which were assigned a share of land-sale money to be used for the benefit of the settlers. The association was also keen to obtain a share of customs dues to develop local amenities, in particular roads.[61] An inaugural committee meeting was held on 31 May 1851 soon after the 'Valpy' meeting.[62] At the first general meeting on 11 June 1851, Macandrew was appointed treasurer.[63]

Macandrew's political career was launched with his activities in the Otago Settlers' Association, where his lifelong habit of driving the business of any forum soon became apparent. He was a regular attendee, and was present at the second meeting of the committee when the chairman, Dr Robert Williams, suggested that the subjects for the society's investigation include 'our present position as to Government'.[64] At a general meeting on 8 September 1851 Macandrew demonstrated his familiarity with the British parliamentary system, by moving 'that the Sub-Committee be re-appointed, with instructions to draw up a Petition to the Imperial Parliament embodying the general grievances of the settlement, and craving redress'.[65] Macandrew had an eye for a wider audience, and was no doubt aware that the views of the Otago settlers were reaching influential ears in Britain.

In this isolated settlement it was not unusual for people to hold apparently conflicting roles. As well as being treasurer for the Otago Settlers' Association, Macandrew was a trustee for the Fund for Religious and Educational Uses, whose money the settlers also wanted for road building. Opposing roles never seemed to bother him, however; it is likely he accepted the treasurer's position in order to keep a watching brief on events.[66] Perhaps he was politician enough to recognise that the settlers' association would become the prevailing body in the transition to self-government, and desired to be part of it. While indubitably a man of conviction who was following the dictates of his conscience in his political activities, Macandrew certainly used the Otago Settlers' Association to advance his views and, eventually, his political career.[67]

Expansion

Macandrew's capital and his gambler's approach gave him an edge over more cautious businessmen; he wasted no time in expanding his business affairs, and the range of his activities during the next eight years is breathtaking given the isolation and population of Otago. He quickly complemented his land holding by leasing a sizeable portfolio of sheep-grazing and farming properties, and was associated with a number of other properties as owner, lessee or mortgagee. He and Reynolds leased a block of 35,000 acres (14,164ha) to the east of the Taieri River in 1851 with the intention of running 5000 sheep;[68] a second block leased in their names was described as a run 'in the vicinity of their Allotments. Boundaries not stated', while a third run was bounded by the Clutha and Pomahaka rivers.[69]

Early pastoralists living in remote parts of the province usually engaged a merchant firm to act as their town agent to supply goods and negotiate with officialdom, and were another source of income for Macandrew and Reynolds. James Macandrew & Co. applied for three pastoral runs in the Clutha district on behalf of other settlers, presumably on commission, and also supplied building and farming materials.[70] The company advertised bricks for sale in February 1852 ('15,000 very superior Kiln-burn Bricks … at 33s. per thousand'), bought and sold sawn timber, roofing materials and 'grey sea-stone lime from Captain Blackie's Caversham sections', and developed its own supply of lime, as Cargill wrote in a letter to McGlashan:

> Mr Macandrew's object is to put down instanter at a cost of some £150 a
> regular lime-kiln not only to supply the neighbourhood, but to produce,
> as he calculates at a low enough figure to make it an article of export. – Mr
> Daniel Macandrew (who joined us with his brother) was the first to discover
> and point out the abundance of Lime Stone which is now being burned in
> a simple way and in several localities for their own use, so that monopoly is
> out of the question, but without a scientific kiln it could not be turned out
> cheap enough and largely enough for export. The quality is first rate, and a
> powerful mastic.[71]

By May a tramway and storage shed had been built and a regular supply of lime was available, but as with so many of Macandrew's enterprises, the lime operation was sold before long to underwrite the next project.[72] Tenders for a flour mill were called by J. Macandrew & Co. in 1853, and in 1857 and 1858 Macandrew leased a section – now 24 Filleul Street – to Robert Henry for use as a brickfield.[73] He established another brickworks in 1859 in Stafford Street near the town belt, and at its opening offered for sale 40,000 'hard-burnt bricks'.[74]

Reynolds became a Lloyd's agent in 1851, and in May 1854 was granted an auctioneer's licence, and James Macandrew & Co. became fire insurance agents for the Northern Assurance Company in August of that year.[75] The firm extended its activities to become land agents and then estate managers, and leased the Otago jetty, which had fallen into a state of disrepair.[76] This gave the firm's goods precedence for landing, while the collection of wharfage dues assisted with cash flow. Macandrew also owned property in the lee of Bell Hill (the present 30 Dowling Street) and the English barracks, which he had leased from the Crown in 1851 for use as a warehouse.[77]

With pastoralist clients requiring regular deliveries of supplies, transport was Macandrew's next venture. He commissioned the building of the 40-ton sailing barge *Bon Accord*, launched on 22 January 1852, followed by another, the *Star*, and set up services on the Taieri River to Lake Waihola and further south on the coast to the Clutha River.[78] In March 1852 he announced the departure of a third craft, the *Endeavour*, for the Clutha River.[79] Larger ships would expand his fleet in the coming years.

Macandrew's involvement in another business enterprise, while not profitable, provided him with a mouthpiece and widespread influence. Otago's first newspaper, the *Otago News*, had been launched on 13 December 1848 by Henry Graham under the optimistic banner, 'There's Pippins and Cheese to come.' Its success was fleeting.[80] Graham, an Englishman and an Anglican, was soon attacked for pointing out the limitations of the land around Dunedin for development and expansion, and the unsuitability of some settlers for a life of farming. Battle lines were drawn, and the paper became the mouthpiece of the 'Little Enemy' until Graham ceased publication in December 1850.

Two months later a group of 11 Free Church shareholders, including Macandrew and Reynolds, bought the press, and on 8 February 1851 they launched the *Otago Witness*. Initially it was edited by the shareholders, then by a subcommittee of the proprietors, until William Cutten was appointed as editor. Eighteen months later 'the printing press and types, together with the whole interests of the proprietors in the *Otago Witness* were presented to the editor gratuitously'.[81]

Macandrew was a skilful writer and publicist, and contributed regular editorials on subjects of significance to the settlement, but a quarrel in 1854 ended his association with the paper. Cutten, now one of William Cargill's sons-in-law, attacked Macandrew so vehemently via the *Otago Witness* that Macandrew was provoked to start a competing paper. The *Otago Colonist*, edited by William Lambert, was launched on 26 December 1856 and remained in Macandrew's hands until his financial collapse in 1860, at which point it too turned on Macandrew and 'poured forth its scorn … in language more extravagant than that employed by Cutten's paper, the *Witness*'.[82]

Before leaving Britain, Reynolds and Macandrew had committed themselves to the establishment of a bank in Otago; they brought with them 'a large batch of notes for 10/-, £1 and £5 value' that were never used.[83] Macandrew's plans for a

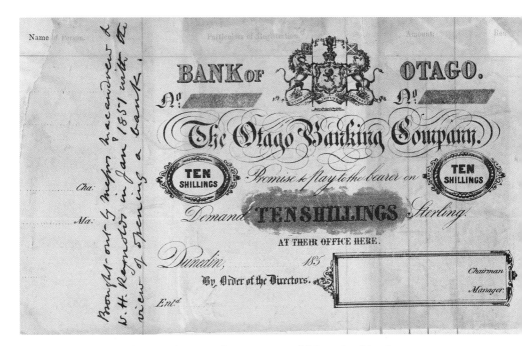

A 10 shilling note printed in 1850 for Macandrew's unsuccessful Otago Banking Company.
Misc-MS-1535-1/4, Hocken Collections, Uare Taoka o Hākena, University of Otago

'native' bank were published two months after he made landfall, when he claimed that a bank 'would be to industry and labor what fuel is to the steam engine – setting all its wheels and parts in motion'.[84] He lauded the success of Scottish banks that were owned by local shareholders and issued their own banknotes; at the same time, he lamented the restrictions on commerce caused by the absence of a bank in Otago, and criticised the New Zealand law that blocked the Scottish model by requiring a bank's shareholders to subscribe the bank's entire capital within four years.[85]

Despite the enthusiasm of its boosters and the support of the community, however, Macandrew's bank was stalled by Grey, according to James Barr, an Otago settler of this period, who 'did not decline to comply with the application for a charter, yet he allowed it to get into the circumlocution office, where, in the weary round of its many chambers, it was quietly but surely ... anodyned to death'.[86] Thomas Hocken suggests this was to prevent competition with 'the Government paper currency of the Bank of Issue and with the monopoly enjoyed by the Union Bank', while Barr claims the result emanated from the antipathy that existed between Grey and the Scottish settlers.[87]

In 1852 settlers petitioned James Macandrew & Co. to issue 'Promissory Notes for small amounts at short dates' to be 'at any time … taken as Cash in payment of goods or produce at your store'. Cannily, the firm was happy to do this until such time as the proposed Otago Banking Company should become established, and the promissory notes circulated for over three years until a bank was launched.[88] There was some resistance to them, as described by McGlashan: 'Parties in Dunedin who have taken them in payment, have been obliged to pass them off at a discount to meet their engagements … some merchants in the place refuse to take them without a discount.'[89] Naturally, only business-men profited from the use of the notes.[90] But there was one amusing outcome: Hocken reports that a competing merchant, John Jones (widely known as Johnny Jones), attempted to 'break the bank' by accumulating notes for several thousand pounds, which he then asked Macandrew & Co. to convert to cash.[91] This ploy had been anticipated, and his bluff was called by payment with 'bag after bag of sovereigns'. This marked the end of any opposition to their use, and Jones then issued his own notes.

Having an architect in the family was useful. In the spring of 1851, Macandrew's brother Daniel oversaw the construction of one house for the Reynolds family and another for the Macandrew family in Stafford Street, close to the Manse Street store and yards.[92] By this time Macandrew and Eliza had two children and would eventually have nine more. Apart from Colin, who had accompanied his parents on the *Titan*, all were born in Dunedin; two died at birth, in 1852 and 1855.[93] It is unlikely that Macandrew spent much time with the family in his early Dunedin years, given the demands of his business and community activities. That he was a God-fearing and loving father shines through in the few existing letters he wrote to his children, in which he dispatched firm guidance and showed an affectionate interest in their health.

Little information exists about Eliza, but no doubt the business of childrear-ing and running the home would have kept her fully occupied. She was positive about life in Dunedin, and a year after arriving described the settlement in a letter to her brother Thomas:

> It is a very healthy place. A doctor is never needed for anything but
> confinement. It is also a quiet place. You live as you like and dress as you
> like. There are no taxes and no house rent and the ground when well cleared
> certainly is very productive, so that with a little labour you may live as
> independent as a prince but I cannot deny that there are many luxuries at
> home in England at least that you cannot get here. There is no amusements,

Eliza Macandrew in her early forties. John Richard Morris, photographer, 1869, Kate Wilson Collection

no cabs, no operas, in fact it is just a sober church going Scotch village. It has one great advantage, the more children the better. You can turn them all to account and as for education that will soon be remedied.[94]

Macandrew was a regular donor to many worthy causes. His was an enviable position: as a merchant he was able to put his energy into meetings, planning and administration rather than the hard labour of taming the land, erecting shelter and growing food. He was often the first named for a good cause and the most generous, and his contributions, in cash and in kind, were spread widely and even-handedly among many projects and to both the Presbyterian and Anglican churches.[95] His patronage no doubt improved his chances of appointment to formal positions in the colony, and these were soon forthcoming.

PART 2

Building a reputation: 1853–60

Chapter 4

The New Zealand Constitution Act 1852 was simpler than its predecessor, the New Zealand Government Act 1846. It granted a wider franchise; increased the number of provinces to six; and provided a simpler governance structure of six provincial councils and a General Assembly, which consisted of the governor, an appointed Legislative Council and an elected House of Representatives. Clause 70 authorised the creation of municipalities,[1] and other clauses dealt with Native law and lands, the disposal of waste lands, and the wash-up of New Zealand Company debts.[2] Three were specific to the Canterbury, Nelson and Otago settlements, one defined New Zealand's geographical borders, and the final two comprised instructions for the proclamation of the Act when it reached New Zealand. The establishment of a workable government would be a long and painful process as the Act was interpreted and applied, roles were defined, and parliamentarians who could lead the country to peace and prosperity were chosen.

As a proprietor of the *Otago Witness*, Macandrew was the likely author of an editorial in August 1852 which took issue with Grey's notion that there was a shortage of settlers capable of serving in political roles – one of the justifications the governor had given for delaying the introduction of an elected Assembly.[3] Macandrew described the ideal colonial political representative:

> They should be men of education at least, if not men of some position and standing in society; – they ought to be vigorous and energetic, men of business habits and knowledge; and if they should possess a large personal and pecuniary interest in the property of the settlement, so much the better.[4]

The editorial was published after the New Zealand Constitution Act 1852 was enacted in London in June 1852, and can be viewed as the opening shot in Macandrew's election campaign. He further enhanced his reputation by helping to organise the celebrations when the Constitution Act arrived in Dunedin on 5 November 1852: 'Cartloads of old cases, shavings and tar barrels … were conveyed to the Church Hill to make a bonfire, the public in all directions contributing wood, old crates, and such rubbish as they could lay their hands on.'[5] Bells were rung, flags were flown, guns were fired and dancing broke out on the jetty.

The New Zealand Constitution Act 1852

Members of the House of Commons had accepted that the time for the colony's self-government had arrived. During debate on the New Zealand Government Bill they limited their discussion to the role of the provinces, the appointment of superintendents, the appointment of the Legislative Council, and the division of powers between provincial and central government. Colonial Secretary John Pakington believed that self-government would be satisfied if the settlements became 'strong municipalities', even though some settlers had lobbied for more autonomy and a federal structure.[6] Sir William Molesworth quoted from a Blue Book, a collection of statistics compiled by settlers in Wellington and Nelson:

> One centrally-situated Executive, with the aid of steam vessels to keep
> up a rapid and regular communication between the settlements, would
> be infinitely more direct and efficient in its action, and far less costly in
> its maintenance, than any number of provincial councils could hope to
> be; while, to meet the wants of each separate district, municipalities, with
> extensive powers of legislation on questions merely relating to such districts,
> would amply suffice for all their local wants.[7]

Molesworth was concerned that the isolated communities would become permanently divided if given too much independence, and continued:

> The various settlements of New Zealand had been founded upon distinct
> and exclusive principles; that 1500 Presbyterians had gone to one corner;
> that 3000 Episcopalians had emigrated to another spot; and that 4000
> 'what-do-ye-call-'ems' had settled in a third place, and 1400 bumpkins in
> a fourth, and the two remaining settlements, with a population of about
> 7000 each, were composed of publicans and sinners. It was said that the
> Presbyterians had carried to New Zealand their antipathy to a bishop; that
> the Episcopalians had taken a bishop along with them as an advertisement;
> that the 'what-do-ye-call-'ems' were voluntaries, the bumpkins were devoted
> to agriculture, and that the publicans and sinners stunk in the nostrils of
> the Pharisees of New Zealand. Therefore, it was said that each of these
> exclusive Lilliputian settlements should have its own little kingdom of
> Brentford, with its own peculiar and exclusive laws. He should be very sorry
> if the exclusive character of these settlements could be preserved, with their
> narrow animosities, religious feuds, and jealousies … Efforts should be made
> to unite the Colony together, to remove local ignorance and prejudice, and
> to counteract, in short, the narrowness of view and selfishness which never
> failed to arise in isolated communities.[8]

Although the establishment in New Zealand of local bodies with widespread powers to run their own affairs was inherent in both of the Constitution Acts, the eventual provincial councils exercised greater powers than those envisaged by the Colonial Office, and certainly more than British municipal councils possessed. This is not surprising given the geographical isolation and the strong parochialism of the settlements. The General Assembly, on the other hand, took many years to achieve its anticipated authority.[9]

Some historians have suggested that Grey allowed the provinces 'to acquire substantial and unpremeditated powers, which they were subsequently loath to give up', but historians Morrell and D.G. Herron disagree.[10] They note that Grey, who was a significant contributor to the 1852 Constitution Act, had proposed that provincial councils should meet first in order to elect the Upper House. When this proposal was dropped in favour of a Crown-appointed Legislative Council, and in the absence of instructions to the contrary, he retained this time-table. The writs for calling the Assembly took months to make their way back to Auckland, by which time Grey had departed for Britain on leave. He sailed without leaving explicit instructions for his replacement, Lieutenant Colonel Robert Henry Wynyard (previously lieutenant-governor of the province of New Ulster, then superintendent of Auckland Province and now administrator of the colony) to call the members of the Assembly together.[11]

Appointment to the Legislative Council was modelled on the Life Peers in the House of Lords, who were appointed for life by the Crown.[12] A Legislative Council of elected provincial representatives may have safeguarded provincial interests more closely and precluded abolition, but McLintock for one is adamant that the British lawmakers never intended to create a federal government.[13] According to McLintock, 'Sir John Pakington defended this undemocratic system on the ground that there existed in the British Empire no precedent for an elective legislative council.' There was an American precedent, but this was seemingly a step too democratic.[14]

According to Clause 53 of the Act, the responsibilities of the General Assembly were the same as those declared for the provincial councils: 'to make Laws for the Peace, Order, and good Government of New Zealand'. The Assembly trumped the provinces' powers, however: any provincial ordinance considered 'repugnant to or inconsistent with any Act passed by the General Assembly' could be rendered null and void. According to Morrell, 'The most important principles of the constitution – the generous measure of representative government, the extension and liberalisation of the provincial system, the surrender of control of lands, the power of amendment – were well calculated to appeal to the colonists of New Zealand.'[15]

The Act established the provinces of Auckland, New Plymouth, Wellington, Nelson, Canterbury and Otago, each with a council of no more than nine members, to be elected for a maximum four-year term, and a superintendent elected separately for the same period as his council. Electors had to be male, over 21, and to have possessed freehold land worth £50 for at least six months or leasehold worth £10 for not less than three years, or occupy a tenement worth £10 if in a town or £5 outside the urban area. This meant that in 1853 when the first election was held, 'for every hundred of the population there were twenty names on the electoral rolls. In the United Kingdom at this time the figure was four.'[16] For most settlers, the novel experience of access to political power as a result of land ownership is one possible explanation for the many pieces of land legislation passed in the provincial period.

The superintendent's role

In the original bill, superintendents were to be appointed by the governor, which would have given him a measure of control over events in the provinces. But Pakington, envisaging that superintendents would have the same responsibilities to their constituents as mayors, changed his mind; in the Act, the position became an elective one.[17]

The responsibilities of the superintendent were laid down in Clause 18:

> It shall be lawful for the Superintendent of each Province, with the Advice and Consent of the Provincial Council thereof, to make and ordain all such Laws and Ordinances (except and subject as herein-after mentioned) as may be required for the Peace, Order, and good Government of such Provinces, provided that the same be not repugnant to the Law of *England*.[18]

The superintendent was the province's chief executive officer, who assembled and prorogued the council; he initiated all money bills and could give his council drafts of ordinances to consider. He could suggest amendments to bills – something the governor could not do for the General Assembly since that was the responsibility of the Legislative Council – and he had the power to endorse ordinances (which then required the governor's confirming assent), or to send them directly to the governor for approval. A superintendent's fate was not solely in the hands of the electors, however: his election could be disallowed, or he could be removed by the governor if the council so requested.[19]

An elected provincial chief executive was a novelty; in other British colonies the (supposedly) comparable position was an appointment made by the Crown. Unfortunately, however, the Act did not explicitly define the position and rights of superintendents. The New Zealand parliament was to acknowledge that there was some difficulty in determining 'the order of precedence of the Superintendents, Judge, Sheriff, and Military', and the status and authority of these continued to be debated until 1874.[20] Morrell suggests the superintendent was, in effect, made 'a provincial Second Chamber', and the relationship between a superintendent and his provincial council was similar to that between the governor and the legislature until 1856. In reality, a superintendent's powers fell between those of the governor and the premier.[21] According to Morrell:

> The Superintendent of a New Zealand province, though of course he played all his parts on a restricted stage, was often able to combine three roles: he had the official dignity of a Canadian Lieutenant-governor, he performed administrative functions like a provincial administrator in South Africa, and he was a popular leader, taking part in that capacity not only in provincial but in general politics.[22]

Defining the role and powers of the superintendent certainly took time. Following a levee held on the Queen's birthday on 24 May 1855, Acting-Governor Wynyard reported:

> In Auckland it has been alledged [sic] that the Superintendent took precedence of every other person in the Province, and that unless he was so received, he would attend in his private, not his public capacity ... It is very advisable to ascertain distinctly the relative position of the Superintendents in New Zealand, not only to Officers of the General Government, but to each other.[23]

He asked Secretary of State for the Colonies Henry Labouchere for guidance. Two weeks later he asked for further direction, after he received a letter protesting against the customary channel of communication between superintendent and governor through the colonial secretary (the leader of the government, later called the premier), 'on the grounds that the Superintendents are placed in the position of Lieutenant-Governors and as such possess the right of addressing her Majesty's Representative direct.'[24] Wynyard felt strongly on this matter: to allow it would 'render the office of Colonial Secretary ... superfluous, lead to endless confusion ... correspondence would frequently be disjointed and the Registry would be incomplete, besides opening a door for personalities which in official correspondence must ever be most advisable to avoid.' He concluded: 'I have long seen a disposition to assume the authority and position of Lieutenant-Governors on the part of the elected Superintendents but till now never possessed any grounds to warrant a direct reference on this express point.'[25]

In his reply to both dispatches, Labouchere admitted that neither the Constitution Act nor Pakington's accompanying dispatch contained 'anything decisive on these questions'. He acknowledged there was 'no precedent applicable to officers of this class. But since reference is made to Her Majesty's government on these points, it becomes necessary that I should convey to you their instructions founded on the best consideration which they can give to the subject.'[26] This was policy created on the run, and he continued:

> With every disposition to recognise the high position occupied by these officers as elected by the people of each Province to fulfil functions of importance within it, Her Majesty's Government cannot admit that this can give a claim to the Superintendent of Auckland for precedency above high officers of the General Government and Legislature. Even admitting that there were an analogy between the position of the Provincial Superintendents under the New Zealand Constitution and that of the officers formerly so styled in different colonies, (which is hardly the case their duties being wholly different,) that analogy would fail here, because no local Superintendent under the old Colonial system, could have been at once 'in his Province' and at the 'seat of government'. The rank of Superintendent at Auckland cannot be placed higher than that of the 'Commissioners or Government agents of Provinces or Districts' in the table contained in the Colonial Regulations. But in other Provinces there being at present no Lieutenant-Governor, the Superintendent should have precedence of all other persons.[27]

He directed that precedence among superintendents should be based on time served and was definite that 'the Superintendents are certainly not invested with the power of Lieutenant-Governors, or any Executive powers by the Constitution'. On the matter of official correspondence he acknowledged that the superintendents did have legislative duties defined by the constitution: 'Her Majesty's Government think that the dignity and peculiar functions of the Superintendents entitle them to carry it on direct with the Governor, and not through the medium of the Colonial Secretary.'[28] All communication between the superintendents and the secretary of state for the colonies was to go through the governor. This confusing dispatch certainly did not satisfy anybody: it seemed that superintendents had the status of a lieutenant-governor, sometimes, but not the powers; and they had the right to correspond with the governor on certain matters but not on others.

The matter of precedence arose again the following year, once more at the Queen's birthday levee, and the new governor, Thomas Gore Browne, had to request further guidance from London. In a dispatch to Labouchere he noted: 'The Superintendents of Auckland and Nelson, speaking on behalf of all the Superintendents, informed me that they would not appear at the Levee unless their precedence was recognised as following immediately after the Members of the Executive Council, nor would they come as individual members of the Assembly.'[29] He added: 'At present the Superintendents are really in possession of greater powers than any Lieut. Governor ever possessed.' If this were the case, he felt 'their views are not unreasonable'.[30] Labouchere did not respond directly to this issue in his omnibus dispatch of December 1856, in which he acknowledged Browne's problems, but he noted that 'the proper remedy for them will be found in the exercise of those legislative powers which have been freely given to the colonists through the General Assembly, rather than in the interference of the Imperial Parliament'; he emphasised that 'the Provincial Legislatures are made by the Constitution absolutely subordinate to the General Assembly'.[31]

Provincial precedence was still an issue in 1873. Governor Sir James Fergusson had no sooner arrived in the country than he also was asked to rule on the 'precendency to be accorded to the Superintendents of the Provinces of New Zealand'; he wrote to Downing Street for advice.[32] With the seat of government now in Wellington, the governor occasionally took up residence in other centres where he might hold meetings of the Executive Council. Usually the superintendent had precedence over all other persons in his own province, but when the governor and government were present he was demoted. Fergusson wrote, 'as such Provincial capitals increase in importance, it is hardly probable that the position of Superintendents will diminish in consequence'. The Earl of Kimberley's reply was straight to the point: the rule of 1855 was to be followed:

> During the presence of the Governor in any province, the Superintendent
> of that province should not be placed above other high officers of the
> Government who may be there with the Governor, but in the absence of the
> Governor from the Province, the Superintendent should have precedence
> over all others in the Province, including any officer of the Government who
> may reside in the Province or happen to be there on a visit.[33]

It was amid such confusion and against a backdrop of conflicting provincial and colonial authority that Macandrew's political career was played out. It was a world that he was well able to manipulate to his advantage.

When the Constitution Act brought self-government in 1852, another task fell to the magistrates' bench – that of vetting the list of settlers to decide whether they were entitled to vote. In September 1852 in Dunedin, justices determined such issues as whether a squatter with more than six months' residency on a property qualified as a voter; whether properties were worth more than £10, the required value to gain a vote; whether one property could sustain more than one vote; and whether a voter had to live on a property in order to secure his vote.[34] Macandrew, a judge at the sitting, was caught up in this process when he and his store manager Thomas White claimed to be householders on the same property and, as such, both entitled to a vote. The court disallowed this. Macandrew then reverted from applicant to judge and continued hearing applicants.[35]

For Macandrew, membership of a number of other official bodies followed swiftly on the heels of responsible government in 1853. He was appointed to the Board of Commissioners for the Management of the Public Lands in Dunedin and the Jetty Committee in May 1854, elected to the Dunedin Town Board in August 1855 and the Town District Board of Road Trustees in May 1856, and appointed to the Waste Lands Board in September 1856.[36]

Otago Provincial Council

During the 1850s the provinces of the Middle Island developed their infra-structure in peace, untroubled by the friction occurring between Māori and settlers in the North Island. The scope of provincial council business was clearly delineated: to make and administer laws 'for the Peace, Order, and good Govern-ment of each Province'.[37] This included all matters that were one step above the municipal responsibilities of rates, roads, potholes and sewage. Perennial issues such as land sales, public works, immigration, law and order and education were dealt with thoroughly, even if the outcomes did not always satisfy all members.

It was almost a year before elections were called in Dunedin on 10 Septem-ber 1853, whereupon Macandrew ensured the Free Church retained leadership of the province by nominating Captain William Cargill as superintendent.[38] Cargill was a stubborn, clever politician with whom Macandrew was to cross swords frequently. He had served for 17 years in the 74th Highlanders and was disciplined, tenacious and rigid. He was 69 on his election, a relatively old man in a youthful community (in 1848 the average ages of the *John Wickliffe* passengers had been calculated as married men 36; married women 30; single men 22; single women 26).[39] Charlotte Godley described him in 1850:

HOUSE
OF
REPRESENTATIVES.

NAME.	ELECTORAL DISTRICTS.
Bacot, John T. W.	The Pensioner Settlements.
Bartley, Thomas H.	City of Auckland.
Cargill, John	Dunedin Country District.
Carleton, Hugh	Bay of Islands.
Clifford, Charles	City of Wellington.
Crompton, W. M.	Omata District.
Cutten, William Henry	Dunedin Country District.
Featherston, Isaac Earl	Whanganui and Rangitikai Districts.
FitzGerald, J. E.	Town of Lyttelton.
Forsaith, Thomas S.	Northern Division.
Gledhill, F. E.	Town of New Plymouth.
Gray, John	Southern Division.
Greenwood, Joseph	Pensioner Settlements.
Hart, Robert	City of Wellington.
Kelham, James	City of Wellington.
King, Thomas	Grey and Bell Districts.
Lee, Walter	Northern Division.
Ludlam, Alfred	Hutt District.
Macandrew, James	Town of Dunedin.
Mackay, James	Town of Nelson
Merriman, R. W.	Suburbs of Auckland.
Monro, David	Waimea District.
Monhouse, W. S.	Akaroa District.
O'Brien, Loughlin	City of Auckland.
O'Neill, James	City of Auckland.
Picard, A. S.	Motueka and Massacre Bay Districts.
Porter, W. F.	Suburbs of Auckland.
Revans, Samuel	Wairarapa and Hawke's Bay District.
Rhodes, W. B.	Wellington Country District.
Sewell, Henry	Town of Christchurch.
Taylor, J. C.	Southern Division.
Wakefield, E. G.	Hutt District.
Weld, F. A.	Wairau District.
Wortley, Honourable J. S.	Christchurch Country District.
Wakefield, E. J.	Christchurch Country District.
	Waimea District.
	Town of Nelson.

A list of the members of New Zealand's first parliament, 1853, immediately after the election in which James Macandrew was elected for the Town of Dunedin.

Eph-D-POLITICS-1853-01/22881356, Alexander Turnbull Library, Wellington.

a funny looking little old man with a very large head covered with thick upright hair, that has been red, which also forms a white frill under his chin. He is Presbyterian, and Free Kirk, and talks broad Scotch, and he is exactly like some of the old Covenanter fathers of families in Walter Scott's novels.[40]

Cargill had been appointed Commissioner of Lands for the Otago Block by Governor Grey when the New Zealand Company ceased operations, but could not resist local politicking – considered unseemly behaviour for a government official – and was sacked, a move that intensified his animosity towards Grey.

Macandrew was nominated for a seat on Otago Provincial Council by William Cutten, who would later become his persistent critic.[41] On 28 September he was elected to the provincial council as a member for Dunedin Country, one of six representing the electorate.[42] The following day he was appointed, unopposed, as the member for the Town of Dunedin in the House of Representatives; William Cutten and John Cargill were appointed to represent the Dunedin Country district.[43]

Eight of the nine elected Otago provincial councillors convened in the Mechanics' Institute hall on 30 December 1853 for the first meeting of this long-sought-after body, and in the restrained manner of Presbyterian Otago, there were no decorations or special ceremonies to mark the auspicious occasion.[44] In his opening speech Superintendent Cargill observed that the position of the council was uncertain, as 'objectors in other provinces have raised the question of illegality as to the disposal of public revenue'.[45] He recommended that the council 'take all that is given and use it for the public good, but at the same time under protest against every infraction or suspension of the Constitution in all its fullness'. His priorities, he said, were the immediate challenges facing Otago settlers who were struggling to eke out a living from the land: to obtain money for public works and immigration; to survey road lines to enable land sales to proceed; to build roads; and to continue with the administration of the Otago Block under the Terms of Purchase of 1849. Cargill promised to appoint a provincial treasurer immediately and a surveyor as soon as possible.

Macandrew was elected as Speaker, but resigned after only three weeks to join the three-man Executive Council, appointed to advise the superintendent and act as his Cabinet. By the end of the session, however, this body had dwindled to one member with 'Mr. Macandrew holding the unique office'.[46] Fifteen bills were presented during the session, 11 of them by Macandrew, on topics as diverse as the establishment of an Executive Council, Dunedin public lands, scab and catarrh, a government gazette, provincial revenue, ferries, dog nuisance, land purchase, and jetties and wharves.[47]

Members of the provincial council disagreed from the start, ostensibly over land prices but more fundamentally over the future of Otago. Different philosophies divided the settlers. Cargill's conservative supporters – Cutten, Macandrew and Reynolds – wanted to maintain the Terms of Purchase and preserve the Presbyterian and socially stratified character of Otago; the opposing camp – John Gillies, John Hyde Harris and Edward McGlashan – supported Governor Grey's General Land Regulations of 4 March 1853, which had reduced the price of land colony-wide from 20s to 10s and even 5s an acre.[48] Cheaper land meant reduced contributions from land sales for the immigration, education and public works funds, and this in turn reduced the Otago Lay Association's ability to select and subsidise the 'right' type of settler, thereby undermining the Free Church ethos of the settlement. Inevitably, other settlers wanted to abolish the Church's control.[49] Battle lines were drawn when Cutten and Reynolds moved 'that public lands should not be alienated, except at a price that should cover the expense of surveys, and make suitable provision for immigration'.[50] From this time on, Gillies, Harris and McGlashan – in favour of cheaper land and more liberal terms of immigration – voted in opposition to many of the council's proceedings, which led Cargill to challenge their definition of a councillor's role. He suggested that 'by passing these resolutions the Council have assumed a power which at most they possess in conjunction with the Superintendent. I am therefore to learn on what ground they consider themselves entitled to pass Resolutions not simply assenting to, or recommending a measure, but absolutely enjoining it, and requesting the Superintendent to intimate it to the government'.[51] It was many years before councillors became comfortable with Westminster government.

Macandrew, Cutten and John Cargill departed for Auckland on the government brig *Victory* on 28 March 1854 for the first sitting of the House of Representatives, scheduled for May, thereby missing the final seven sitting days of the council. Macandrew and Cutten's departure meant the loss of Captain Cargill's majority support; he prorogued the council on 25 April 1854 with a typically blunt speech in which he expressed his frustration with members who had brought the council to stalemate and challenged his authority.[52] Cargill claimed, somewhat excessively, that opposition to his policies was comparable to an attack on human society. Such behaviour was predictable, however, as the new body tested the limits of its powers.

The General Assembly

Early elections for the General Assembly were drawn-out events in which each constituency held its ballot on a separate day. Voting for the first election in

New Zealand's first parliament house, 'The Shedifice', Auckland, 1854. This building housed parliament from 1854 to 1865. 7-A11714, Sir George Grey Collection, Auckland Libraries.

1853 began in the Bay of Islands on 14 July and finished in Dunedin Country on 1 October. This prolonged polling system continued until 1881, when voting for general list and Māori seats was held on two separate days; not until 1951 did all New Zealanders go to the polling booths on the same day. Until 1890 plural voting was permitted, meaning that a man could both vote and be nominated as a candidate in each electorate in which he owned the requisite property. Thus the extended election period could work in a determined candidate's favour: later in his political career Macandrew was defeated in Clutha on 31 January 1871, but was nominated and won in Port Chalmers on 16 February 1871. The Electoral Act 1893 would eventually remove all elements of plural voting and grant the franchise to all persons over 21, making New Zealand the first self-governing country in the world to grant the vote to women.

In the half-century between 1856 and 1906 New Zealand's parliament was led by 15 premiers and their 27 ministries. The briefest lasted for seven days (Harry Atkinson, 1884), the longest for 14 years (Richard Seddon, 1893–1906), and only seven exceeded two years. Repeated incumbency was common: Atkinson was appointed five times, William Fox four, Edward Stafford three and Julius Vogel, Robert Stout and Frederick Whitaker each led twice.[53] Political parties as we now know them did not exist, manifestos were unheard of, party discipline was non-existent and instability was the norm. Parliamentary leaders commanded if they could attract sufficient members to support their particular stance, usually shaped by the state of the economy at the time, and members often switched allegiances. With no guarantee of payment, financial independence was a prerequisite. Members tended to be from New Zealand's middle class – professionals, merchants, substantial farmers and runholders – and turnover was rapid: over half the members of every parliament elected before 1876 were newcomers to the House.[54]

On the voyage to Auckland the *Victory* was blown back to Cook Strait from the west coast route and forced to go via the east coast. The resultant 70-day voyage would have allowed Macandrew to renew his London friendship with Edward Gibbon Wakefield, who boarded in Wellington.[55] Wakefield was to dominate proceedings in the forthcoming Assembly by virtue of his political experience in Canada and Britain, but was unable to bend it to his will despite his influence with Robert Wynyard. Henry Sewell, a prominent Canterbury settler who expected Wakefield to be a powerbroker in Auckland, described Macandrew as 'expectant of office under Wakefield'.[56] Meantime the animosity, fuelled by political and personal differences, smouldered between Macandrew and Cutten.[57] While in Auckland an impecunious Cutten complained to his wife that Macandrew had refused to lend him any money: 'Since my coolness with Macandrew I have been so short of cash having asked him for £3 which he has neglected to give me that I did not go to church on two Sundays for want of a clean shirt.'[58] On their return to Dunedin, Cutten would continue to assail Macandrew in the pages of the *Otago Witness* as well as on the floor of the provincial council.

The first parliament met in a two-storey wooden building dubbed 'the Shedifice', which sat above Mechanics Bay not far from Government House. The building was unfinished, facilities were non-existent and there was scant comfort for the politicians. The 37 elected members gathered on 24 May to swear the oath of affirmation and appoint a Speaker.[59] At the next meeting on 26 May Macandrew precipitated the first-ever division in the New Zealand parliament with his motion that 'the first act of the House of Representatives shall be a public acknowledgment of the divine being, and a public supplication for His favour on its future labours'.[60] In a letter to Eliza, Macandrew reported:

> there was a very long and animated discussion upon a motion put forward by me to the effect that the meeting should be opened by prayer. I had all sorts of entreating to withdraw the motion for a day – however I kept faith and pressed the matter to a division, the result of which you will see from the papers.[61]

Macandrew's motion was carried, and to this day New Zealand's parliament still opens with a prayer read by the Speaker.

Wynyard opened the first parliament on 27 May 1854. In his speech from the throne he acknowledged the 'experiment in Constitutional Democracy about to be attempted in New Zealand', and outlined what he considered to be the major issue facing the colony:

> In order that New Zealand islands may ultimately become one great country; that they may be united by a feeling of common patriotism, be subjected to one general authority, and governed by the same law, the power of the central Government will require to be strengthened and extended; while the legislative authority of the Provinces will need at the same time to be rather narrowed in range.[62]

Initial business involved appointing committees and sorting out procedures. Although many New Zealand parliamentary procedures were those of the House of Commons, there were no recognisable and cohesive parties; and although there was a major division between provincialists and centrists, voting blocs were fluid and unpredictable. The first parliament was rumbustious and conflicting attitudes to land sales and responsible government divided the members as procedures and positions were hammered out and allegiances formed.

Behaviour in the House deteriorated after the formal opening, and members appeared more concerned with the appointment of an Executive Council and its powers than with the governance structures of the country. In the first session, James FitzGerald, Henry Sewell and Frederick Weld were appointed by the governor as members without portfolio to the first Executive Council under the constitution.[63] The Executive was headed by FitzGerald and consisted of the governor, the civil secretary, three permanent officials and two members of the Legislative Council, who were appointed soon after. This structure was unacceptable to members: they demanded an Executive chosen by and responsible to parliament.[64] Wynyard refused to agree to this without confirmation from the Colonial Office, supposedly on the advice of Wakefield, whose reputation made him a dominant figure in the first meetings of the House when members were slow to find their feet. Wakefield instigated the defeat of FitzGerald's ministry on 2 August.[65]

On 17 August feelings regarding Wynyard's refusal boiled over and a melee occurred in the chamber. In an effort to form another ministry, Wynyard wished to prorogue the session for two weeks. Forewarned of his intention, however, FitzGerald immediately called for a division to suspend Standing Orders in order to allow a debate before the prorogation order was read. Wakefield's minority bloc, of which Macandrew was one, wanted the prorogation to proceed. In an attempt to preclude a quorum and thus prevent the division and cause the House to be suspended, they hastily left the Chamber. They were unsuccessful: the quorum survived, and some of Wakefield's followers returned to disrupt proceedings instead. Sewell attempted to manhandle James Mackay of Nelson from the room, after which Macandrew provocatively re-entered the Chamber to collect 'his walking stick and plaid' and, against Standing Orders, kept his hat on until ordered to remove it.[66] The next day the House agreed that Mackay was 'guilty of a gross and premeditated contempt of the House'; Macandrew was charged with contempt of the House but the motion was withdrawn.[67] The House then adjourned and the session ended. The members met for a second session on 31 August with the appointment of Forsaith's ministry and adjourned finally on 16 September.

In the life of this Assembly, Macandrew usually spoke early and succinctly in debates, and was swift to second motions, commit bills and move adjournments. He sat on nine of the 24 select committees that met during these two sessions.[68] To begin with he was in favour of responsible government, and in one typically blunt speech demanded that the ministry be appointed by the Assembly, not by the governor:

> if there were not men in that House qualified and, if need be, ready to make personal sacrifice in order to conduct the government – the people of New Zealand were not ready for free institutions, and the Constitution Act had been conferred too soon … [I] would take any number of members of that House in preference to an equal number of men who had not undergone the same ordeal of election.[69]

Macandrew would later reverse his position on responsible government, most likely to ensure that the governor and the House supported his stand on maintaining a high price for waste lands in Otago. He criticised members who opposed the acting governor, and declared that he was prepared to wait for Wynyard to receive the proper authority from Britain to establish responsible government.[70]

The issue of the sale of waste lands occupied much of that first parliament's time, and Macandrew insisted that any changes to the sales regulations be implemented with the proper authority. An adamant supporter of the provinces until their dissolution in 1877, he disclosed his provincial bias in the 1854 debate:

> While disapproving of what he could not but consider as an evasion of the
> Constitution Act, he at the same time felt that the waste lands would be best
> administered by the Provincial Legislature, and that the General Assembly
> ought at once to apply for power from the Imperial Parliament in order to
> enable it to hand over the waste lands, on such terms and conditions that it
> might then see fit.[71]

It is likely that Macandrew's association with Wakefield, who continued to
proffer advice to Wynyard, secured him the administrator's approbation and
a seat in the succeeding 'clean shirt ministry' of Thomas Forsaith. This was an
amalgam of officials and elected members appointed on 31 August that lost a
vote of confidence on 2 September, making it the shortest-lived government in
New Zealand history.[72] Frederick Weld, premier for 11 months in 1865, described
them as 'a most miserable set, not one of them with the feeling of a gentleman'.[73]

In the final weeks of the first parliament Macandrew revealed his conservative fiscal values. Believing it one of parliament's duties to regulate public
expenditure, he initially opposed payment to members of anything other than
their actual expenses; in his opinion, members of the Legislative Council should
be 'men of property: if not, they ought not to be there'. He spoke against granting
a pension to the widow of a civil servant, opposed a Supreme Court for Otago,
and even opposed increasing a subsidy to enable a coastal steamer to include
Otago in its itinerary. He was clear about the responsibilities of government,
however, and sought money to establish an industrial school in Otago to accommodate local Māori. With time, Macandrew became more sympathetic to people
of limited means.

In a letter to his brother-in-law Thomas Reynolds, who was contemplating
migrating from Spain to New Zealand, Macandrew enthused about life in the
colony, saying, 'your brother & myself, have got settled in comfort with plenty
and independence'.[74] He described lessons learnt in his first three years in
the colonial settlement: 'The great error committed by William and myself at
Otago has been that we did not devote all our attention to sheep & cattle and to
agriculture, had we done so at first, we would have been much more independent now'. The letter is crammed with hard-won information about items that
Thomas should bring with him: 'the best merino breed of sheep you can procure',
Arabian horses, Spanish mules, ponies and donkeys; '£500 worth of really good
wine Port & Sherry ... and £500 of the *cheapest* sherry or any other wine ... £1000
worth of wine well selected in such proportion as I have indicated would nett
at least £1000 profit'; and dry goods such as raisins, figs, currants, nuts, seed
wheat, barley and other cereals. Macandrew included political news too:

The House of Representatives has been engaged since it met in striving to obtain responsible government, in which I am happy to say that we have succeeded, the consequence is that … executive power will be in the hands of the men chosen by and possessing the confidence of the people, and you need not be surprised if some morning you find that the writer is a member of the Government.[75]

News that the British government had granted permission for a fully responsible ministry of elected members was not circulated in time, and as a result few parliamentarians bothered to travel to Auckland in 1855. Although parliament was an excellent place to form networks of acquaintances and garner useful business advice, attendance was expensive, time-consuming and, given the limited range of topics handled and the Assembly's limited authority, often considered unimportant by members.

Over the three decades following his 1853 election Macandrew would spend long periods of time away from Dunedin and his family. In the first 10 years he attended the Auckland parliament in 1854 and 1856 and absented himself in 1855, 1858 and 1860, claiming pressing business matters. Parliament did not meet in 1857 and 1859. Following his bankruptcy in 1861 he was absent for four years, but in 1865 returned to the House, now removed to Wellington, and attended all sittings there until 1887. In total, he served as a member of the House for 30 years and, by a quirk of parliamentary timing, belonged to all of the first nine parliaments. With his comprehensive knowledge of parliamentary procedure, acquired during long hours observing in the House of Commons, he became a clever and calculating parliamentarian and a notable powerbroker.

Provincial council issues

In Dunedin the superintendent's faction and the opposition bloc continued to debate the issues of public works, immigration and land sales. These cloaked the demarcation dispute over the powers of the superintendent, the role of the Executive Council and the future of Otago, issues that saw intermittent sittings of the second session of the council extend from October 1854 to September 1855. The dissident bloc of Gillies, Harris, McGlashan and Cutten – the latter having parted company from Macandrew at the General Assembly – voted together throughout the session.[76] By July, having committed to increase the council from nine to 19 members and revise the electoral roll, members were unsure whether they were any longer 'a legally constituted Legislative Body'

Above and opposite: Carisbrook, Macandrew's house in the Glen, Caversham, was built in 1853.
56_2-1, Toitū Otago Settlers Museum/ Hocken Collections, Uare Taoka o Hākena, University of Otago

and awaited Governor Browne's permission for dissolution.[77] This came on 26 October 1855 and was followed, uniquely, by a wiping of the official record.[78]

When the council met again in March 1856 there was no objection to a proposal to increase the superintendent's salary from £300 to £400.[79] The council even adopted some of the trimmings of the General Assembly when John Shepherd was appointed sergeant-at-arms to the council; his services were soon required when Speaker Macandrew indicated that unruly behaviour which had occurred in the council sessions must be stopped.[80] Later in 1856 councillors were officially notified of the discovery of gold in Otago, but its significance was discounted by authorities who struggled to envisage the transformation that would eventuate when payable quantities were discovered in 1861.[81] By 1858 so few matters required attention that the superintendent opened Session VII with the words: 'I have been under the necessity of calling you together at this time as the Constitution Act has required you to be assembled, in order to be within one year of your last Session.'[82]

The sale of land occupied all provincial councils throughout the 1850s. The first sitting of the General Assembly had translated Governor Grey's General Land Regulations of March 1853 into the Waste Lands Act 1854, which permitted provincial councils to recommend that the governor issue regulations for the 'sale, letting, disposal and occupation' of the Crown lands in their province; and the Provincial Waste Lands Act 1854, which allowed the governor and the General Assembly to delegate powers to the provinces to make laws for the disposal of their own waste lands.[83] In November 1854 Edward McGlashan proposed that a select committee of the provincial council be appointed to amend Otago's land laws and reduce the sale price.[84] Macandrew anticipated the report of a stacked committee. Committed to the settlement's Free Church ethos, which depended on the continuing income from the sale of land at 40s an acre, he suggested they should wait until the new, larger council had been elected.[85] McGlashan withdrew his motion, but a few days later Macandrew moderated his stance and moved an amendment that would reduce the sale price of bush land, retain pastoral leasing and permit genuine settlers to occupy their land on payment of a deposit. Gillies challenged the executive's refusal to commit firmly to any policy on land and threatened to withhold supply, but his action was aimed at a bigger target than the land laws: Gillies wanted the executive to show leadership.[86]

Factional infighting over executive responsibility and criticism of Macandrew's lackadaisical behaviour saw Macandrew and Reynolds resign from Cargill's Executive Council in November 1854 after only seven sitting days.[87] Macandrew justified their resignations by claiming they had only agreed to be interim members of the Executive Council – although Reynolds, never as independent as Macandrew, quickly rejoined and remained a member until December 1865.[88] With Macandrew and his commitment to a high land price sidelined, Cargill recommended to council that sale prices be lowered and only land in the proclaimed townships and Hundreds be sold. This would ensure that pastoralists continued to lease land and provide the province with income from their rent.[89]

New land regulations were passed on 12 September 1855 that incorporated Cargill's suggestions: town land would be sold by auction; the price of rural land within Hundreds would be 10s per acre; holders of pastoral leases would be entitled to purchase 80 acres (32ha) for their homestead; and all purchasers would be required to spend 40s per acre on improvements within four years.[90] The existing government land commissioner was replaced by a locally appointed Waste Lands Board, which arbitrated purchaser and lessee claims in an open court.[91] The *Otago Witness* approved of the land regulations, calling them 'most simple in construction, and as likely to be most effective in working'. They would, the writer believed, help to control the quality of new settlers, who would require a certain level of capital to become landowners; land-grabbing graziers would be deterred by the requirement for improvement.[92]

Macandrew's contribution to this debate was muted. He did not yet exhibit the self-discipline necessary to belong to the executive and was too much of an opportunist to be a team player. His quirkiness was offset by his lateral thinking and problem-solving skills, however, even if his solutions were not always universally popular. For example, in the debates on the land regulations he suggested the money deposited from land sales be used for loans to settlers. That the state could lend money to its citizens was an idea before its time, and the concept earned the support of only one member.[93] Cutten 'objected to the resolution as erroneous in principle and dangerous in practice … It was a most unwarrantable dealing with the public revenues. It would encourage speculation and encourage the community to invest in lands beyond their means.'[94]

In March 1853 the Macandrews moved to a larger home in a sheltered valley now known as the Glen, which sits below the Mornington ridge in the present suburb of Caversham. The house was built for the expanding family: Jane was born there in 1854, an unnamed infant who died at birth in 1855, James in 1857 and Herbert in 1859. Called Carisbrook, the house was supposedly named after a castle on the Isle of Wight where James and Eliza had honeymooned, and was the hub of a farm that eventually grew to 240 acres (97ha), bounded by what are now Glen and Neidpath roads.[95]

> Carisbrook was a stately home by any standards … The house, with its fine, grey slate tile roof, was a large one, indeed one of the largest in Dunedin when first erected of three levels, having some 20 rooms in all – an imposing panelled hall, a sweeping staircase, a large ballroom with a sprung floor, and the largest fireplace complete with huge iron hobs to hold the logs for burning.[96]

In 1858 Macandrew purchased farmland on Otago Peninsula at Upper Harbour East in a bay called 'The Hundreds' (with reference to the boulders), where his extended family already owned land. The farm was named Colinswood for his intended heir, their first son Colin, and the bay itself was eventually renamed Macandrew Bay. In 1862 the family moved to the farm that was to be Macandrew's home for the rest of his life.

Chapter 5

R arely a good committeeman unless chairman, and eager as ever to be close to the source of power, it is possible that a year on the backbenches following his resignation from the Executive Council in 1854 frustrated Macandrew. In December 1855 he was returned to the House of Representatives for the Town of Dunedin, and in the provincial council elections in the same month he easily won his seat for a second time as one of three Central District members representing the Taieri.[1] Macandrew sat as Speaker on the provincial council for the next four years before relinquishing the position to become superintendent. He displayed no discernible voting pattern in debates about appropriations for the provincial budget, and his previously idiosyncratic behaviour appeared more restrained. He was increasingly engaged in business activities and the expansion of his shipping fleet and immigration agency, sometimes to the detriment of his public duties.[2]

Land sales continued to occupy the provincial council. Sales stagnated in 1856, prompting Cargill to suggest the council consider selling land outside the Otago Block, something that was now possible as a result of financial resolutions adopted by the General Assembly in September 1856.[3] Known as the 'compact of 1856', this arrangement gave provincial councils the authority to manage all waste lands within their province and retain the revenue from sales.[4] Cutten, always conservative when it came to the sale of land, criticised the unwarranted speed with which Cargill was prepared to overturn what had been the fundamental principle of the land regulations: restricted sale at a set price.

The council had divided the original Otago Block into eight Hundreds in August; now, ignoring Cutten's opposition, it moved swiftly to pass the Land Sales and Leases Ordinance 1856.[5] This provided land for farmers at 10s per acre (0.4ha) providing they spent 40s per acre on improvements within four years. A further 600,000 acres (242,811ha) of the province were made available outside the block at 10s per acre in lots of not less than 2000 acres (809ha) with no requirement for improvement.[6] The lower prices led to increased sales and a larger return for the provincial coffers.

While the changes encouraged closer settlement and denser population within the Otago Block, and reassured graziers that lease conditions and access to their large runs would not change, the seeds of rebellion were sown in Murihiku, the part of Otago Province that centred on Invercargill. 'Murihiku' was the Māori name for the southern part of the Middle Island, south of the Waitaki River, but it was used by settlers to refer to the plains between the Mataura and Waiau rivers, the area that became the Province of Southland. That year a scare-mongering Canterbury newspaper reported the sale of 300,000 acres (121,000ha) of land near Bluff (worth £150,000 to the provincial treasury) to 'a well-known capitalist sheep-farmer of the Australias, commonly called "Long Clarke"'. The paper suggested that 'by means of an agency in Melbourne, this sale will be followed by others to the estimated extent of one million acres. We pity the runholders of Murihiku.'[7] Such gossip disquieted those potential Murihiku smallholders who lacked the capital to buy farmland in such large parcels. They were angered by Otago Provincial Council's apparent action of restricting land sales to Dunedin's hinterland, its procrastination in surveying Murihiku, and its refusal to lay out a town at Bluff. Their first petition to the governor for separation, lodged in March 1857, was unsuccessful, but within four years the province of Southland was born.

The first schools are established

Macandrew was passionate about education and debated it vigorously in every session of his first term as a provincial councillor. A product of the rigorous and egalitarian Scottish education system, he was determined that all children in New Zealand should receive the same opportunities that he had been given, and further, that Otago's education system should be the best and most accessible in the colony.

Although the Scottish promoters of Otago had touted the provision of universal Christian schooling, little money had been provided for education in the first five years of the settlement. The Free Church had established a school in Dunedin on arrival in 1848 and by 1853 had allocated further sites in North East Valley, Andersons Bay and Green Island, but teachers had to rely on fees and public subscriptions. The Trust Fund for Religious and Educational Uses provided a little financial assistance, but most of its income was used for the construction of churches and ministers' expenses.[8] Dissatisfaction with the funding of education in Otago simmered until the provincial council intervened, and the recommendations of an education commission were implemented in an Education Ordinance passed in 1856.

Macandrew believed that while education funding should come from the General Assembly, 'the whole apportioning of the money, the management of the schools, and the nature of the education should be under the absolute control of the various Provincial Councils'.[9] Early in the life of the council he introduced a subject to which he would devote a significant investment of time and energy, culminating in the establishment of the University of Otago. On 8 March 1854 Macandrew moved:

> that an Educational Institution, or High School, be established in Dunedin, over which there shall be at least two Teachers, who shall be competent not only to teach all the higher branches of a liberal education, but to train others for the profession of Teachers throughout the rural districts of the Province.[10]

Education was perhaps the sole area in which councillors worked together for the good of the province, and Macandrew's motion was agreed without debate. A select committee convened by Macandrew was appointed 'to consider what provision shall be made, and what steps shall be taken to effect that object'.[11] In December 1854 it recommended 'that provision should be made from the public funds of the Province, or by assessment, for providing a liberal education to the whole children of the Province as far as practicable'. The committee was guarded about what should be taught, however.[12] It added, 'permanent provision for such education should be made by special Ordinance … setting down … the character of the education to be provided, and the mode in which such provision is to be made'. It recommended the establishment of a grammar school to prepare pupils to enter university, staffed by six teachers who would be selected on the recommendation of the government school inspectors for Scotland and the rectors of Free Church Normal Schools in Edinburgh or Glasgow. The province would pay for the teachers' passage to Otago. A scale of teaching salaries was listed.

A year passed, and since no action had eventuated an education commission was appointed and presented an ordinance for consideration on 5 March 1856.[13] It was never popular. The ordinance left the choice of religious instruction to the school committees which, some feared, could be stacked: Cargill's provincial executive controlled the Central Board of Education that would appoint three of each committee's 10 members – and it appointed staunch Presbyterians, who ensured that the Westminster Shorter Catechism was the only text used. Funding for schools would be raised by charging fees and through a one-pound levy to all males over 21 years of age.[14]

Settlers promptly objected – to the board's limited choice of religious instruction; to the poll tax the ordinance imposed; to the lack of local control over school committees; and to the expense to the province. The provincial councillors objected, too, when they realised they had no control over the central board and organisation of the system. Macandrew, returned as Speaker in January 1856 and no longer permitted to promote legislation, supported the ordinance but considered the system too costly. Cutten attempted unsuccessfully in both 1856 and 1857 to amend the Education Ordinance and reduce the powers of the central board, and John Hyde Harris tabled a similar amendment in 1858 that was not accepted, although he did stir Cargill to table an Education Bill in 1859.[15] When this lapsed, Macandrew, now superintendent, bowed to popular demand and in 1860 sponsored a new Education Bill, which received assent in July 1861.

The Education Ordinance 1861 converted the Central Board of Education to a Board of Education responsible to the provincial council. It broadened the options for religious instruction and abolished funding by rating, and eventually launched Dunedin High School (for boys), later renamed Otago Boys' High School.[16] This establishment was opened on 3 August 1863 on the site now occupied by Otago Girls' High School in Tennyson Street, and moved to its present site in Arthur Street in 1885.

It took until 1871 to realise another project that Macandrew backed, although initially in a half-hearted manner: the Dunedin High School for Girls.[17] The primary force behind the establishment of the girls' school, Learmonth Dalrymple, agitated vigorously for at least seven years to win Macandrew and other councillors to her cause.[18] Dalrymple enlisted the support of Eliza Macandrew, who invited her to her home in 1868 to have 'a good long chat' with Macandrew, who had previously fobbed Dalrymple off with the claim that there were no funds to hand.[19] According to the *Otago Daily Times*, Dalrymple said the conversation 'resulted in the Superintendent asking me where I would suggest the school being situated – would the old gaol site do? The subject finished by his saying, "Well, I'll instruct Mr Hislop to sketch proposals." True to his word, these appeared in an appendix to the Education Report of 1868.'[20] The girls' school opened for teaching on 6 February 1871 with 78 students under the leadership of the first principal, Margaret Gordon Burn, in two rooms of the south wing of Dunedin High School.[21]

Although education ceased to be a responsibility of the Trust Fund for Religious and Educational Uses, Macandrew's continued involvement as a trustee indicates his preparedness to use political influence to support his religious beliefs, and he was active in ensuring that the Free Church ethos continued to underpin the settlement. There is no record of Macandrew serving the Free Church in a pastoral or spiritual role until 22 December 1857, when he was appointed as an elder to represent the Kirk Sessions of Dunedin in the Presbytery of Otago.[22] His focus was mainly on the financial side (fundraising was his specialty), and he and John Gillies were named as the deputation to the rural districts of the East Taieri, Waihola, Tokomairiro and Clutha to collect for the Sustentation Fund, which subsidised ministers' salaries, and to attend generally to the interests of the church in their locality.[23] Given the extent of the district and the condition of the few existing roads, this was a sizeable and time-consuming task. When the Presbytery of Otago was inaugurated on 27 June 1854, on the arrival of the Reverends Will and Bannerman, Macandrew was appointed a member of the Sustentation Fund committee, a role he continued in for the rest of the decade.[24] In 1859, following his election as superintendent, he joined a committee appointed to consider the working of the General Sustentation Fund.[25]

While the trustees continued to pursue the general government for their share of land sales money, public agitation to confiscate the trust's assets escalated.[26] The Church Lands Act in 1866 allocated part of the income from the trust's estate to public education through the endowment of chairs at the intended University of Otago, and reserved the remainder for church use. Macandrew's later dealings with the church were from the other side when, as superintendent, he allocated funds for the removal of Bell Hill in order to create a commanding site for the construction of First Church.

Transporting immigrants

Maritime activities began to dominate Macandrew's life. James Macandrew & Co. built, bought and chartered ships, and acted as a shipping and immigration agent. The shipping agency arranged stevedoring and provisioning services, warehoused cargo and marketed freight.[27] It sold passages, loaned money to settlers to bring out friends and families, assembled return consignments, organised insurance cover and recruited crews. One 1856 advertisement announced the dispatch of five ships in one week by the firm.[28] James Macandrew & Co. was also appointed the Otago agent for the coastal steamer *Nelson*, a service funded by Nelson and Wellington provinces with the backing of the General Assembly.

By 1855 a severe shortage of labour in Otago and the availability of unemployed workers in Melbourne persuaded the provincial council to subsidise passages to Dunedin. Appointed as an immigration agent, Reynolds travelled to Victoria, returning in September 1855 with 60 immigrants in 'the splendid fast-sailing packet ship *Gil Blas*', chartered in Melbourne.[29] A second tranche followed soon after, and the council contracted Macandrew and Reynolds to establish a permanent agency to recruit the 'right' sort of immigrant for Otago.[30] The pair purchased the *Gil Blas* for their growing fleet and set about transporting passengers to New Zealand, backloading cargoes of wool on the return journey.[31]

Committed to increasing the number of immigrants to Otago, the provincial council allocated a further £20,000 for this purpose in 1856. It appointed immigration agents in London and Scotland, and called for tenders to transport 2000 migrants from any part of Britain.[32] James Macandrew & Co. won the tender at £16 per adult, to be paid half in cash on landing and half in provincial government debentures in either London or Otago, in 1860, 1865 and 1870.[33] With the debentures earning 10 per cent interest per annum, Macandrew had assured himself of a regular income stream for the next 13 years.

Cutten and Macandrew still held divergent views on land policy and pricing, religious education and immigration, and were obdurate enemies at this time. In his role as editor of the *Otago Witness*, Cutten criticised the contract, claiming, 'Mr. Godley in a letter sent to Canterbury, states that with good management emigrants can be sent out at £10 per head all round.'[34] On the heels of Cutten's critique, Superintendent Cargill attempted to change the conditions of the contract. He accused James Macandrew & Co. of price gouging, and referred to the company as 'parties who would look upon the Revenues as an unknown and inexhaustible quantity, and run the province into an unwarranted amount of debt'.[35] A select committee of the provincial council, appointed to look into the matter and chaired, conveniently, by Reynolds, rebutted the charge but reported sloppy bookkeeping practices.[36]

The contract for 2000 migrants was completed with the arrival of the *Gala* on 23 February 1860.[37] Later that year Macandrew, by then Otago's superintendent, was accused of misappropriating government funds and of 'making temporary use of public funds for your own private purposes' when he took a payment for the passage of migrants on the *Gala* for his own use.[38] A second select committee was appointed, to investigate this affair.[39]

Parliament 1856

Macandrew was active in the first session of the second parliament, which sat from mid-April to mid-August 1856; he was appointed to nine select committees and chaired two of them: both generated Acts of parliament. Throughout his parliamentary career he maintained a special interest in legal and financial matters, and his major contribution to this session was based on his Otago experience and his desire to repeal the existing laws governing banks and the issue of currency.

Macandrew was keen to see uniform banking regulations that would permit the incorporation of banking companies authorised to issue their own banknotes – a predictable desire from a man who had arrived in Dunedin equipped with a suite of banknotes, expecting to establish his own bank. Early in the session he moved that a select committee be appointed to 'take further evidence on the subject of the Bank of Issue';[40] he sat on this committee, which recommended on 2 May that the government 'afford facilities for extending banking operations in this Colony, and that any obstructions now existing be withdrawn as speedily as possible, for which purpose the prohibition of the issue of notes by private banks should be forthwith repealed'.[41] Macandrew held that the effect of the law as it then stood was 'to cramp and paralyse commerce, and to discourage that spirit of enterprise which so largely distinguished the Anglo-Saxon race'. The law, he said, 'enabled one bank to secure a monopoly'.[42] A further committee was appointed on 16 May and submitted its report a week later. This included a proposed bill that became the basis of the Bank Paper Currency Act, passed on 7 July 1856, wherein the governor was authorised to permit banks incorporated by Royal Charter to issue paper money.[43]

Macandrew's second appointment that day, to a select committee on inter-provincial communication charged with considering 'the most efficient mode of maintaining a rapid and frequent communication between all the Provinces of the Colony', might be construed as encouraging the fox to enter the henhouse, given his investment in the maritime trade. Not surprisingly, the report recommended the government offer a subsidy of £8000 for two steamers to maintain 'a communication between the Provinces, including Otago'.[44]

In this session Macandrew crossed swords with the man who would become his nemesis, centralist politician and then premier Edward Stafford, when he criticised the first financial statement of Stafford's ministry.[45] He opposed Stafford's proposal to borrow £500,000 to pay off government debts and buy land from Māori, on the grounds that it would create a national debt that was 'not for the purpose of being expended on public works, or in any way of promoting the progress of the colony, but to be frittered away at the hands of the General Government'.[46] Macandrew also objected to Stafford's idea to retain all customs revenue for central government, even though his quid pro quo was to give all land-sale money to the provinces.

Accompanied by most of the southern members, Macandrew departed Auckland on 9 July, six weeks before the session ended.[47] In his absence the loan was approved and the Waste Lands Act 1856 became law but was disallowed, to reappear as the Waste Lands Act 1858.[48] The Land Compact was agreed: the provinces were to keep three-eighths of their customs and land-sales revenue.

Matters of finance

Macandrew's casual attitude to money, especially that belonging to others, became public when Peter Proudfoot, chief commissioner and treasurer of the Otago Waste Lands Board and factor to the trustees of the Trust Fund for Religious and Educational Uses, died suddenly in Dunedin on 14 October 1857. His successor, William Cutten, requested the key to the board's money chest, but Macandrew, acting as Proudfoot's executor, refused to surrender it. When eventually opened, the chest was found to contain only £705 instead of the anticipated £1929 – a shortfall of some £1200. Coincidentally, over £1000 was found in Proudfoot's house, which Macandrew promptly impounded.[49] The matter was reported in the *Otago Witness*, prompting an aggressive response from Macandrew:

> The money lodged in the Chest, with the cash and other available deposits found in his private cash-box are more than equal to the sum which you state ought to have been in the public Chest.

> … Mr. Proudfoot's habit was to keep the money in his private residence, and that placing it in the Chest at all was the exception, not the rule … His practice in this respect has been so far beneficial that it has given yourself and friends an opportunity of making what you stood much in need of at the time, namely, political capital, and has enabled you so far to divert the public mind from your own and their political delinquencies.[50]

Editor Cutten responded: 'Mr. Macandrew must know that, by affirming that instead of money there are available deposits, he brands his late friend as a defaulter, as no Treasurer has a right to invest the cash of his department in available deposits.'[51] The matter became the focus of a select committee enquiry, as a result of which Superintendent Cargill was reprimanded by the council for exceeding his legal authority by appointing his son-in-law Cutten to be Proudfoot's successor.[52] The committee also reprimanded Macandrew for covering up a discrepancy in Proudfoot's accounts by refusing to hand over the key to the money chest, and demanded the return of a missing sum of money.[53] This particular defalcation had its conclusion in the New Year when it was reported

The cartoon by James Brown has been inscribed by Thomas Morland Hocken: 'Captain Cargill confers the Commissionership of Crown Lands on his son-in-law Mr W.H. Cutten, 1856.'
Acc 7727 Hocken Collections, Uare Taoka o Hākena, University of Otago

that 'the deficiency in the Chest on the 28th of October was £1224. On the 29th of January, just four months afterwards, a sum of £1145.11.1 was paid to Mr. Logie, the Sub-Treasurer of the General Government, leaving a deficiency of nearly £100.'[54] The select committee handed responsibility for retrieving the lost money to the superintendent, but nothing more on this matter is recorded in the council proceedings.

A tolerant view was taken by the broad-minded Hocken, who wrote, 50 years later:

> The evidence showed considerable laxity all round … It seemed probable that the money-chest was a convenient receptacle from which several had an opportunity of withdrawing a little money as occasion arose, to be honestly replaced, of course. Any fault lay in detection.[55]

Macandrew's proclivity for financial risk-taking and fondness for spontaneous and unsupported claims was demonstrated again in November 1858, when the provincial treasurer announced that as the total revenue for the province 'was estimated at £54,000 and the expenditure at £72,000 … there would be a considerable deficiency of funds'.[56] Despite this bleak outlook, Macandrew proposed that 'this large, rich, and beautiful Province might borrow £100,000, or any sum, however great, and he had no fear of the Governor sanctioning their borrowing any reasonable sum'. With some misgivings, the council agreed to introduce a bill to seek 'power to borrow money to meet the deficiency of the revenue during the year'. This bill, however, sank without trace.[57]

In contrast to his willingness to spend up large on public amenities, Macandrew opposed payments to individuals from the public purse, and considered that citizens who undertook civic duties should do so at their own expense.[58] He opposed paying fees to the Waste Lands commissioners, and was against the appointment of provincial surgeons, saying 'everyone should support their own doctor, or, in cases of absolute poverty, the public charity should pay for such humane services'.[59] Naturally enough, he was happy to receive personal rewards from the public.[60] Throughout his career Macandrew attended numerous banquets held in his honour, and accepted many gifts. He was presented with a 'purse of sovereigns' by the Clutha electors in December 1866; he received a testimonial and 1500 sovereigns in July 1877 from the citizens of Otago for his services as superintendent; and he accepted a gold watch and chain in November 1882 for his 'eminent political services'.[61]

Macandrew appears to have been tolerant of late payment by others and willing to provide credit – where it increased patronage of his firm. James Macandrew

& Co. in 1853 offered free grain storage, and advances 'on all descriptions of Produce' between 1854 and 1856.[62] He also used promissory notes effectively to encourage trade.[63] The economy slowed in 1857, however, and Macandrew and his overstretched enterprises gradually ran out of funds. In an advertisement that ran from October to December of that year, 22 Otago businessmen, including James Macandrew & Co., informed their customers of their situation:

> Feeling the injurious effects resulting from the indefinite system of Credit which has hitherto existed in this Province – a system alike injurious to the interests both of the buyer and the seller – [we] hereby give notice, that henceforth [our] terms will be – Quarterly Accounts to be paid in cash within a week of rendering, with non-payers charged 10 per cent per annum for first three months, 15 per cent for the next three and 20 per cent beyond.[64]

Macandrew sued at least one creditor when he summonsed Octavious Harwood of Portobello in 1858 for '£49.2.2 being the balance due to the Plaintiffs upon the annexed items of account'.[65]

Sheep farming was the staple industry of Otago in this decade, and wool, mostly exported to Australia for onward dispatch, generated the majority of the colony's income in 1857.[66] In another first, James Macandrew & Co. chartered a ship to transport wool and general cargo directly to London. The *Strathallan* sailed on 25 May 1858 with 'a cargo of 800 bales of wool, containing 263,258 lbs [119 tonnes]; valued at £19,010.13s'.[67] The venture attracted some criticism, possibly stemming from local rivalry.[68] When Macandrew dispatched a second ship, the *Strathfieldsay*, to Melbourne three weeks later with a cargo of 2757 bags of oats and 59 bales of wool, the criticism resurfaced: 'The charterers were unsupported and unfortunate, as on arrival at Melbourne prices for grain had fallen below the prices paid in Dunedin, so the cargo was stored on shipper's account'.[69] McLintock suggests that this 'unimaginative community, while it applauded Macandrew the man and responded gladly to the warmth of his leadership, and the refreshing vigour of his irrepressible personality, rejected with coldness his schemes for advancing the prosperity of the province'.[70]

Instead of attending parliament in Auckland in 1858, Macandrew focused on his shipping interests and sailed for Melbourne where he bought the steamer *Queen*, with the intention of providing a trans-Tasman service.[71] Its arrival in Dunedin on 27 August 1858 generated great interest: citizens were 'quite taken by surprise at the appearance of a steamer of such dimensions coming so far up the bay – the possibility of which would have been ridiculed but a short time ago'.[72] The proud owner was eulogised in his own newspaper (naturally) as the man who had 'conferred an inestimable benefit upon every interest in the province, political, commercial, and social'.[73] Macandrew had anticipated attracting subsidies for the trans-Tasman service from the governments of Victoria, Wellington and Otago, but was rebuffed by both Victoria and Wellington. The *Queen's* subsequent departure from Dunedin for Melbourne on 15 September 1858 was advertised as under contract to the provincial government of Otago, a deal reputed to have been won by trickery as McLean describes:

> Only by shrewdly announcing a sailing date for the *Queen* and then having colleagues organise a hurried but nonetheless carefully stage-managed public meeting in favour of the ship, did [Macandrew] secure the two-year contract for a monthly service to Melbourne that kept [the *Queen*] in Otago waters.[74]

James Macandrew & Co. was dissolved on 10 September 1858. Acting alone, Macandrew now purchased a larger steamer, the *Pirate*, for the trans-Tasman service, followed by the *William Hyde* in January 1859, which he positioned at Port Chalmers as a floating warehouse.[75] In April that year he invested in a 25-ton steamer, the *Pride of the Yarra*, renamed it *New Era* and launched a council-subsidised service between Port Chalmers and Dunedin.[76] These were his last maritime purchases; the excessive costs of maintenance and coal (imported from Newcastle in New South Wales) would eventually put an end to his commercial shipping career.

The New Provinces Act

In 1858 the General Assembly passed an Act that was to have a major impact on the authority of provincial councils. The New Provinces Act 1858 gave power to the governor 'on certain conditions, but wholly irrespective of the general wishes of any Province … to break up such Province into separate portions'.[77] The same year, in an attempt to control immigration and prevent monopoly land holdings, the General Assembly finally superseded all provincial waste lands legislation. The Waste Lands Act 1858 legitimised the practice in operation since 1856 by authorising the governor to delegate the sale and administration of all Crown lands 'into the hands of any other party'.[78] The Act reduced the maximum size of lots for auction from the existing 2000 acres to 320 acres (809 to 129ha); set an upset price of 5s per acre; forbade the sale of land on credit; and vested responsibility for administration and disposal of waste lands

A small portrait of James Macandrew appears at the bottom left of this 'first photograph take of a New Zealand parliament', 1860. Macandrew did not attend this parliamentary session in Auckland. 1/1-003859-G/23023074, Alexander Turnbull Library, Wellington.

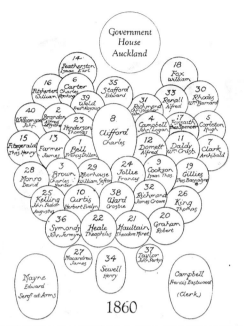

Key to the photograph opposite.

FIRST PHOTOGRAPH TAKEN OF A NEW ZEALAND PARLIAMENT
(AUCKLAND)

throughout the colony in the governor, who could alter the price of land at the request of a provincial council.[79] The two Acts were early ripples of the abolition tsunami that would engulf the provinces 19 years later.

Otago councillors registered their dismay:

> It is with extreme regret that the Provincial Council of Otago finds itself called upon to record its opinion that by the 'Waste Lands Act', and the 'New Provinces Act', principles are established which may possibly in future be attended with injurious consequences to the Provinces.[80]

In his superintendent's address, Cargill expressed wariness of what he called the government's 'desire for centralisation'.[81] Otago councillors responded: 'The Council deems any exercise of the power to raise the price of land in this Province at present unnecessary.'[82]

Despite their declaration, however, the sale of rural land was failing to raise sufficient money for the province's needs. In 1859 the council proposed to amend the Otago Land Regulations by removing the improvement requirement within the Hundreds – but the proposal lapsed.[83] On his election as superintendent in 1860, Macandrew, ever desirous of retaining the distinctive elements of the class settlement, would express his satisfaction with the existing regulations and block further changes.

Macandrew resigned his seat in parliament in 1858 to avoid dismissal for non-attendance at the session of that year. He returned to Dunedin on the *Queen* in 1859 in time to be renominated for the seat. As few citizens could yet afford to attend the Auckland parliament, competition was negligible and voter turnout was poor, and on 15 January 1859 he was re-elected with 40 votes to the three received by his competitor, J.G.S. Grant. The Assembly did not sit again until June 1860, and a timely dissolution of parliament that year avoided his dismissal for further non-attendance.

By 1859 Macandrew was one of the wealthiest men in the province. He is listed as having 3350 sheep in 1860, and was associated with many properties as owner or partner, among them the 'leasehold and joint household' for 'Runs, Nos. 136 and 116, Hokanui [sic], and homestead on Run No. 136'.[84] He may also have held a number of smaller blocks of land throughout the province, since 'Jas. Macandrew & Co.' applied in August 1858 for 200 acres at Tautuku Bush, south of Port Molyneux; and in December 1858 five applications for rural land were made by one James Macandrew.[85] He had certainly made his stamp on the community, and was well placed to take on the leadership of Otago Province.

Chapter 6

William Cargill was too ill to attend the opening of the Otago Provincial Council on 25 October 1859. The clerk read out Cargill's address, which included his official resignation, whereupon Speaker James Macandrew promptly read it to them again.[1] Members of the council, many of whom disliked and distrusted Macandrew, would have been distressed had they realised that this event presaged the next phase in his career: Macandrew would open the next three sessions of the council as superintendent in his own right.

Cargill was now 75 years old and had led the settlement during 11 years of extreme hardship. McLintock describes him as authoritarian, unsympathetic to constitutional government and inclined to favour his family in political matters:

> To those who had the temerity to oppose him, he was a bitter and unforgiving enemy … He had, too, an almost fatal propensity for making enemies. His singularly tactless utterances were little calculated to smooth away the acerbities of party strife and the cold censure of his criticism fell upon friend and foe alike.[2]

Speculation about Cargill's successor began immediately. Macandrew had sufficient enthusiastic supporters to ensure his nomination was promoted well before the next session of council.[3] A committee formed to secure his election was chaired by his erstwhile commercial rival, Johnny Jones, and included his brother-in-law William Reynolds and 13 leading citizens.[4] Macandrew's attributes matched the mood of the times: worldly, devout, popular with working folk, a prosperous entrepreneur and now a proven politician, his personality was the opposite of Cargill's. Rumours of his nomination were greeted with horror by some, however, and one editorial describing Macandrew's behaviour – most likely written by Cutten – was alarmingly prescient:

> … we fail to discover in the whole of that career anything that is deserving of commendation, either in the Provincial Council or the General Assembly. In the first and most important session of the latter body, he supported a weak, miserable faction, under Mr. Wakefield, with no adequate public

motive, and at the last, he was absent when his vote might have been of consequence. In the Provincial Council he has never taken an active or originating part. On political grounds, therefore, we do not see that he has either claim or qualifications to justify his election to the Superintendency. As a Settler, he may have been useful and enterprising, as our contemporary says – speculative and rash we should rather call it – but his qualification on these matters, however, [while they] may occasionally serve for mercantile business, are dangerous characteristics in a Superintendent … The gentleman is also a very large contractor with the Government … some £24,000 of the public money pass through his hands … We have great objections to the gentleman proposed. We believe that in some respects a more unfit person could not be found.[5]

In the following year Macandrew's behaviour, both as a businessman and super-intendent, confirmed this trenchant piece; by 1861 his critics would have been impressed by the accuracy of its forecast.

Superintendent Macandrew

Nomination day on 5 January 1860 was an anticlimax: nominated by Johnny Jones, Macandrew was the only candidate for the superintendency and was declared duly elected.[6] Only then did he expound on his platform, presenting his views on the 'three leading topics – Immigration, Education, and the Price of Land'. He considered that immigration 'should only be limited by the means within ourselves of providing the new comers with food until such time as they could grow sufficient for themselves'. On education, he felt 'it was the duty of the State to see that its youth are all educated, and that the means of education shall be brought within reach of, if not even forced upon all'. He trusted that 'no sectarian prejudice – no niggardly economy – would be brought to bear upon this most vital question'. Regarding the price of land, he was 'perfectly satisfied that the existing Regulations, on the whole, were the best in New Zealand', and promised that one of his first official acts would be 'to get an authoritative opinion as to their validity'. He suggested the province 'had begun at the wrong end in spending so much on metalled roads, when it was clear that railways had been found in all countries to be the cheapest roads that had been made'. As supervisor he planned to spend 'from £50,000 to £100,000 a year for the next four years on public works, such as roads, bridges, and railways' and would 'approve of borrowing money to deepen the harbour, and reclaim it from the Jetty to Grant's Brae'.[7]

Macandrew was 40 years old when elected to the leadership of Otago. He was typical of the first tranche of superintendents who 'went through the whole gamut of the colonist, pioneering, business, journalism and public affairs, and speedily took a leading part in the life of the province'.[8] To all outward appearances he was a highly successful, affluent businessman, the owner of ships, shops, farms, livestock, newspapers and an imposing home for his growing household. He belonged to a prosperous and influential extended family and had been an outspoken and useful voice in Otago politics. His regular appearances as a Justice of the Peace also bolstered his status. Those who dealt with him at close quarters, however, especially those who had financial dealings with him, knew of his unreliability, but few were prepared to criticise him publicly.

Although he had had little impact in colonial politics despite his membership of the General Assembly's brief second ministry, Macandrew was generally viewed as someone with influence in the upper echelons of society. Hocken considered he had 'troops of friends; he was genial, generous, impulsive, ready to assist any one in distress, contributed always and liberally to any object and took an active and principal part in public affairs'.[9] This view is reinforced by a report of Macandrew's meeting with settlers in the Tokomairiro District just a month after his election, when a cavalcade of 50 settlers presented an address describing his place in their affections:

> Many of us cannot forget the kindness you manifested and the assistance you afforded your fellow-settlers in their earlier struggles, when you, as a private merchant, so nobly encouraged private enterprise; while you co-operated in public matters with Capt. Cargill as the head of the settlement; you stimulated and supported the weak but well disposed.[10]

Always ready to share his vision for the province, Macandrew told the gathering of his desire 'to see a railroad from west to north, and … one great trunk line to unite both ends of the Province'. He planned to make Lake Waihola navigable, to appoint a bench of magistrates in the district and establish a troop of yeomanry in the volunteer corps.

His behaviour at this time was unusually subdued, and he surprised many with the moderation and pragmatism of his programme when he opened the ninth session of the provincial council on 11 April 1860. This was held in the capacious wooden courthouse recently constructed on the water's edge in front of Bell Hill, adjacent to the new gaol.[11] His opening words were reassuring:

In 1860 the new Court House was opened on reclaimed land on the seaward side of Bell Hill. The prison where Macandrew was confined is to its right, with the small tower. Photograph by William Meluish, 1862. Album 004, P1910-047-009, Hocken Collections, Uare Taoka o Hākena, University of Otago

> Gentlemen, it is not my intention, nor that of my advisers, to initiate much in the way of legislation during the present session … let us aim at having few laws, and those only of a practical nature … The principal business of the session will be the disposal of the public money.[12]

His proposals were prudent and promising: to reorganise the survey and public works departments, to sell debentures to raise £50,000 for immigration, and to expedite steam navigation on inland waterways. He planned to build a telegraph between Port Chalmers and Dunedin, to impound stray cattle, to regulate the sale of alcohol, enlarge the council, build quarantine facilities at Bluff and lift the salaries of heads of departments. He aimed to fund the harbour master adequately, provide access to an asylum, explore the hinterland of the province, establish a high school, resolve the grievances of southern settlers to avoid a breakup of Otago and, finally, to sort out the land regulations. Even the budget was balanced.

The councillors were supportive, the only criticism coming from Cutten regarding the quality of the bills presented: 'They appear to us to be crude, undigested measures, and the greatest misfortune which could befall the Government would be for the Council to pass them as they stand.'[13] The quality of the bills may have resulted from a lack of cohesion in Macandrew's Executive Council; in a move that demonstrated his disregard for protocol he had appointed merchant Thomas Dick, solicitor John McGlashan and general practitioner William Purdie as his executive – without council approval and before it met.[14] As may be expected, in the absence of common aims and faced with someone as independent as Macandrew, the group did not endure. Within a few weeks he appointed a new Executive Council: Dick, solicitor James Howorth, school teacher William Tarlton, auctioneer Frederick Walker and, surprisingly, his chief critic William Cutten. Townsmen all, none of the appointees could speak for the agricultural sector. Macandrew had, however, demonstrated an unexpectedly cooperative spirit that caught the *Otago Witness* unawares and moved Cutten to comment, 'We were not prepared to find that his Honor would so completely accede to the wishes of the Council as to make so thorough a change, and so far it augurs well of the future.'[15]

The major issue overshadowing Otago in 1860 was the demand for a separate province in the south. Macandrew attended a meeting in Invercargill on 27 February 1860 at which the Southland superintendent-designate James Menzies claimed Murihiku had been treated unfairly in the appropriation and distribution of revenue: money raised by the sale of land in the area had not been spent in the area.[16] Macandrew disputed this, as the *Otago Witness* reported:

> [Macandrew] analysed the statements of the preceding speaker, and apparently proved from official documents signed by heads of departments, that it was an error to suppose that the South had not met with justice at the hands of the Provincial Government – for the expenditure on its behalf bore exactly the same proportion to its contributions that the expenditure of the remainder of the Province did to its portion of the contributions.[17]

Menzies then invoked the New Provinces Act 1858 and announced that the southern region would prefer to manage its own affairs. A vote was taken on the grass outside the courthouse, and 'the Separatists by a bare majority turned the scale in their favour'.[18] A petition was dispatched to the governor and, despite vigorous opposition in Dunedin, Southland became a province by order in council on 25 March 1861; it was inaugurated on 1 April 1861.

In 1863 construction began on a railway to connect Lake Wakatipu with Invercargill and Bluff, so that Southland could cash in on the Arrow River gold rush by transporting and supplying miners.[19] A sense of urgency led to a disastrous decision to use soft-wood rails, and in the end only 13km of line were successfully completed before the rush peaked and the opportunities for revenue tailed off. Crippled by extensive debts incurred in constructing a harbour and the railway, the province of Southland survived only until 5 October 1870 when Macandrew, superintendent once again, had the pleasure of welcoming South-landers back into the Otago fold.[20] On this occasion his fortunes were linked with those of the province:

> Contemporaneous with the separation of the two provinces, Mr. Macandrew himself became separated from the public administration, and throughout the whole of this disseverance the breach between the provinces widened. No sooner does he regain the reigns [sic] of government, than the charm of reunion is drawn around both, and before the first term of his re-election as Superintendent expires, he has the satisfaction of welding the coupling link as firmly as if his warnings and admonitions of 1860 had been duly honored with success.[21]

The grateful Southlanders ensured he was returned in the following year's provincial elections, when many Otago voters rejected him.

Macandrew's fall from grace

Privately, Macandrew borrowed widely and, at times, illicitly. No doubt he was not the only businessman to indulge in this practice in early New Zealand – much speculative activity was funded by the modern equivalent of post-dated cheques, and Macandrew sometimes required cash in a hurry.[22] The deal that reshaped his life, however, was made in 1857, when he took payment for and promised to deliver 1600 sheep to Nathaniel Chalmers by March 1860. By then, however, financial woes had begun to unsettle his hitherto comfortable lifestyle.[23] He can-celled the promise on 20 April 1860 and offered Chalmers a bill of exchange for £3000, to be paid when the sheep were shorn. Macandrew was fast running out of money and options. On 30 July Chalmers presented Macandrew's bill to the Union Bank of Australia, who refused to honour it, and in August Chalmers filed a suit against Macandrew for £3677.14.11.

Macandrew attempted to stall Chalmers by countersuing him over the amount of the claim, which included costs. This failed, and he made a new agree-ment to settle with Chalmers on 28 January 1861.[24] Forced to realise his assets, he mortgaged all his properties and continued to borrow, as Trotter tells us, 'from business associates, from his loyal friends, even from his humble clerks. The streets buzzed with rumours of the financial straits of the new Superintendent.'[25] He even persuaded provincial treasurer John McGlashan to lend him money from the council's petty cash account – although his tardiness in repaying it

Another James Brown cartoon inscribed by Hocken: 'Mr Macandrew whose spare hat was most useful in the case of inconvenient and troublesome visitors. Circa 1855. T.M.H.' Macandrew would disappear out the back door when his creditors came seeking repayment.

The cartoon's legend reads:

> St. Andrew: 'It's no use getting your monkey up, I am very Ca – u – tious.'

Acc 7736 Hocken Collections, Uare Taoka o Hākena, University of Otago

made McGlashan apprehensive about the forthcoming audit.[26] He then allegedly deposited several sizeable payments for provincial services to his own account to maintain an appearance of credit, presumably intending to repay them as soon as he could. This was a serious breach of protocol.

Juggling these business matters kept Macandrew close to home. With his old London debts now also requiring attention, he reneged for a second time on his parliamentary duty and dodged the session that ran from August to November 1860 in Auckland.

Public dissatisfaction with Macandrew's performance as superintendent emerged in September when an editorial, likely written by Cutten – who knew an audit of the public accounts had been undertaken and that council would soon receive an interim report – reiterated the criticism published in July 1859.[27] The writer admonished Macandrew for not attending the General Assembly, saying his presence could have ensured the passage of a bill to suspend the New Provinces Act which had been defeated by a single vote.[28]

Rumours that the province's financial affairs were suspect were sustained by Macandrew's procrastination in calling together the provincial council, and his refusal to announce the results of the audit. Council prevailed, however, and the auditors duly reported on the first day of the eleventh session, 12 December 1860.

Macandrew's opening address to council was impressive. Despite the suspension of land sales for the previous eight months and the consequent reduction in income, he claimed the province's financial position was 'a matter for congratulation' and exhibited 'the healthy and buoyant position of the Province'.[29] He went on to enumerate the number of roads and bridges built or improved since the last session, noted the paddle-steamer service initiated on the Taieri River and the one planned for the Clutha River, detailed the area of land surveyed, and noted the 2532 immigrants whose arrival had brought the population to 13,000. He announced his largest project to date: 'The chief business of the Session will be to consider, and I trust to assent to, propositions on the part of government, involving works of great magnitude, and tending towards the rapid development of the boundless resources of this province.' Macandrew proposed the reclamation of 22 acres (9ha) from the harbour. The estimated cost of £33,000 would be funded by loans, and sale of the land would net £72,000.[30] He argued for the building of a new main road to Central Otago, and suggested the establishment of a Panama route between Britain and the Australian colonies, which he said could be achieved 'without it costing any one a sixpence in the shape of taxation, and without borrowing one single farthing'. It would be paid for by declaring one sheep-run a Hundred, selling the land for intensive farming and constructing three steamers to carry mail, specie and passengers. He also proposed the introduction of salmon into New Zealand rivers and the development of fishing for both local and export markets.[31]

Macandrew's list of 'think big' projects makes him a forerunner of state intervention in the development of infrastructure in New Zealand. Other provinces were investing in large projects – Canterbury in a railway tunnel from Christchurch to Lyttelton, Nelson in civic buildings – but Macandrew's plans exceeded these. His booster schemes would require huge investment by the provincial government; they preceded Julius Vogel's borrow-and-build schemes of the 1870s, and would prefigure his own, later activities as minister of public works in 1877 and 1878.[32] He justified the investment simply: 'If Otago is to be the meridian – the starting point, as it were – the thing must of necessity be started by the Government … as no private company can possibly be found to take the matter up.' He used arguments familiar to modern ears to sell his case: 'If, afterwards, it should be deemed advisable for the Government to relinquish the practical conduct of the undertaking, there will be no lack of private companies ready and willing to take it off our hands at a premium.' In his confident manner, he presented this as fact without identifying any of the private companies waiting to rescue the province.

Macandrew must have known the conservative Otago settlers were unlikely to be impressed by his oratory: this was a speech to inspire potential migrants and distract attention from his financial problems. But having engaged his listeners with his vision, he then announced his exit plan: 'It now only remains for me to say a single word personal to myself, which is, that circumstances will, I fear, render it expedient for me to devote my attention to personal affairs, and that this is probably the last Session of the Provincial Council which will be opened by me.' The flabbergasted council could only reply, 'The various measures suggested by your Honor for the advancement and continuance of that prosperity will receive the most serious attention and consideration of the council, when submitted to it in detail.'[33]

Little did anyone imagine that, with the discovery of gold the following year, Otago would soon be in a position to afford these proposals, and would eventually invest in far greater works than Macandrew envisaged. But while Otago's fortunes were on an upwards trajectory, Macandrew's were heading in the opposite direction.

Chapter 7

A fire at Carisbrook on 17 August 1859 was fortunately extinguished by the women and servants of the house and did little damage to the house, but it was yet another calamity in a trying year.[1] Macandrew's shipping services were proving unprofitable and desperate action was required to stave off mounting debt. On 15 September 1859 he sold his store and auction departments and advised of his intention to confine operations 'to shipping, and to exporting wool, grain, and other produce ... All produce passing through our hands will be stored in our floating hulks, either at Dunedin or Port Chalmers.'[2] On 25 January 1860 the ships and the Melbourne steamship contract were also sold, but the cash raised was insufficient to meet Macandrew's debts. In May 1860 he posted an appeal: 'The Undersigned beg respectfully to request that all DEBTS due to them may be paid forthwith at their Office ... Also, that all CLAIMS against them may be lodged with ... J.S. Douglas, by whom the same will be duly paid. James Macandrew & Co.'[3] By August he had raised £3000 through the mortgaging and sale of various properties, and in September was able to repay most of his borrowings from the council's petty cash.[4] With his estate mortgaged, he was forced to offer Carisbrook and the remainder of his properties for sale on 23 January 1861.[5] His financial woes were exacerbated by the news from London that proceedings against Garden & Macandrew were under way.

On 15 January 1861 Macandrew prepared for voluntary bankruptcy and assigned 'all his Personal Estate and Effects, and all surplus monies to arise from the sale of his Real Estates (after satisfying the debts secured thereon) to "six named trustees" in trust, for the benefit of all and singular the creditors of the said James Macandrew'. But before he could declare himself bankrupt, Nathaniel Chalmers – still awaiting payment – had him arrested as an insolvent debtor.[6]

Incarcerated and dismissed

Macandrew's habits of obfuscation and deceitful dealing were about to land him in strife. The provincial auditor's report, tabled in December 1860, aroused suspicion in the council.[7] The report listed three occasions on which it appeared Macandrew had misused significant sums of money.[8]

For the third time in his council career a select committee enquiry was launched, this one directed 'to examine the state of the Public Accounts, Public funds, and general financial position of the Province, with power to call for persons, papers, books, accounts, and documents'.[9] When called upon to explain himself, however, Macandrew refused to appear. In a letter to the select committee he stated, 'I beg respectfully to decline appearing before the Committee, and most indignantly to deny the allegations referred to … If the Committee chooses to furnish me with a copy of the evidence on which their assertions are founded together with the precise charges themselves, I have no doubt of my ability to disprove them.'[10] He demanded a hearing 'by counsel at the bar of the Provincial Council'. The council retaliated by denying him access to the evidence, and refused his request.[11]

The select committee reported a week later on what it called 'a grave and serious breach of public trust', accusing Macandrew of misappropriating £1712 of passage money for migrants on the *Gala* ('an irregular and improper transaction'), £1000 as payment for railway plant for the Clutha coal field, and £1073.15.4 from the public account.[12] Macandrew responded promptly. He denounced the select committee, 'the sole object of which appears to be to prove that the Superintendent has devoted certain public moneys to his own private purposes'.[13] He then resorted to ad hominem attacks on his critics:

> The Superintendent would only add in conclusion, that assuming the object
> sought by the promoters of the Report to be, to get rid of him officially,
> that object will be attained in due course, without the public business being
> longer suspended, inasmuch as he has firmly decided upon relinquishing the
> office …[14]

The following day the council composed a petition to the governor in which they accused Macandrew of using public funds for private purposes and requested that he be stripped of his post as superintendent. Ironically, the council then had to present an address to Superintendent Macandrew asking him to forward the memorial to the governor.[15]

Macandrew claimed to know nothing about the provenance of the money and tried hard to spread the blame. He accused the provincial treasurer John McGlashan of improperly giving him access to the money, and of confusing and misusing funds from the provincial council, the General Roads Board and his own private accounts.[16] He criticised the council for attempting to 'stigmatise a man (on the eve of his voluntary retirement from office), who has devoted the best ten years of his life to the interests of the Province'.[17]

The council's response summarised their frustration: 'If the allegations against the Provincial Treasurer be true, the Committee considers it was His Honor's duty to the State, irrespective of any considerations of friendship, to have shielded the Province from any chance of injury by the unlawful use of the Public Moneys.'[18] Instead of apologising and going quietly, however, Macandrew further provoked the council by publishing a long, self-justifying appeal titled 'To the People of Otago', in which he lashed out at Dick, Gillies, McGlashan, Speaker John Richardson and the *Otago Colonist*, with passing criticism of the select committee and the council itself.[19]

Richardson was dispatched to Auckland to present the council's petition to the governor.[20] Meanwhile, the council resumed work on 2 January 1861; the agenda included roading, bridge-building, ferries, keeping the Sabbath holy, education and the trans-Tasman steamer subsidy. Despite the bad blood between them, Macandrew continued to communicate with the council as superintendent. In what was to be his final address, on 4 January 1861, he gave his assent to the Appropriations Ordinance 1860–61 and announced his intention to prorogue the council the following day.[21] By the time Richardson returned – accompanied by the government auditor Charles Knight, who was armed with a warrant to enquire into the alleged misuse of funds – Nathaniel Chalmer's claim for the return of payment for the undelivered flock of sheep had been heard. Macandrew had been arrested as a defaulting debtor and imprisoned on 28 January 1861. Although still superintendent, he was now incarcerated and penniless.

Macandrew was familiar with Dunedin Prison, having successfully tendered for its construction in 1855 when its predecessor burnt down.[22] He had been a visiting magistrate there and knew only too well how damp and uncomfortable it was.[23] In a move that is legendary for its brazenness, Macandrew used the authority delegated to superintendents to proclaim any place a common gaol – and declared his own home a prison. He instructed gaoler Henry Monson 'to remove James McAndrew, a debtor in your custody, to Caris Brook house within your jurisdiction which I have this day by proclamation declared to be a prison of the province of Otago'.[24] The gaoler was not happy with this turn of events; he viewed Macandrew as a desperate character and warned his deputy Charles Hunter, who was on duty at Carisbrook: 'I intreat you never to be off your guard, never loose sight of your Charge not for a moment; and see that every night he is locked up; and, if he sleep on the Basement Story, see that the windows etc are all secure.'[25] In another bureaucratic twist, Monson then had to write to Macandrew to request

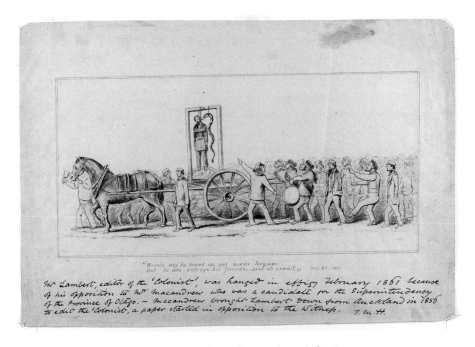

'Wounds may be bound up, and words forgiven
But he who betrays his friends loses all credit' 3 February 1861

According to Hocken's inscription, this cartoon, again by James Brown, shows 'Mr Lambert, editor of the "Colonist", hanged in effigy February 1861 in the main street because of his opposition to Mr Macandrew who was a candidate for the Superintendency of the Province of Otago …' Acc 7731, Hocken Collections, Uare Taoka o Hākena, University of Otago

extra staff for this unusual situation.[26] He also asked the resident magistrate John Hyde Harris for extra assistance, and received a lawyerly reply: 'The Executive Council cannot help you except through his Honor the Superintendent, so that your application to the Executive is practically neither more or less than an application to the Person whose security you wish ensured.'[27]

Lightly guarded, Macandrew continued to administer the province from his home until the governor dismissed him as superintendent on 8 March 1861.[28] He was returned to the public gaol two weeks later.[29]

The election for a new superintendent was held in May 1861 and Macandrew kept himself busy electioneering from behind bars, including publishing a second appeal to the people of Otago in mid-April. When votes were counted he had gathered 189 votes to Richardson's 292, while Alexander McMaster ran a poor third with 106.[30]

Auditor Knight's enquiry ground on until 7 June 1861, when his report was published.[31] He had ascertained that two of the missing sums had indeed been given to Macandrew, as warrants for payment, and these were now misplaced; the third item – an amount of cash – had been given to Macandrew by McGlashan.[32] Knight suggested McGlashan may have been tricked into this action, but when given an opportunity to explain his behaviour the latter was unable to convince the executive of his innocence. Richardson wrote to him on 26 June: 'There is no alternative but to remove you from the position of Treasurer, owing to your having allowed the public moneys entrusted to your care to be employed by the Superintendent for private purposes.'[33]

The matter did not rest there. A reviewing law officer in April 1862 stated:

> Mr. Macandrew is not guilty of embezzlement, for he never was a person entrusted with public money. He has not detained money under false pretences. Nor can I find that he has committed any offence that will come within any of the statutory felonies or misdemeanours. But my mind is clear that he has committed an offence for which he may, and should be indicted. Malfeazance by a public officer to the injury of Her Majesty's subjects or any class of them, is a misdemeanour in the common law.[34]

By May 1862 the government had given up trying to pin the blame on Macandrew. Premier Fox wrote to Superintendent Richardson: 'The Government consider it undesirable to proceed any further in this matter, which is full of difficulty, and the result of any proceedings would be extremely doubtful.'[35] More would be heard of this case in 1867, however, when Macandrew was re-elected as superintendent.

Macandrew was detained in prison for his inability to meet his private debts. After six months, on 23 July 1861, he appeared in the Dunedin Supreme Court seeking a discharge and maintaining his innocence:

> I remember telling several persons the state of my affairs in the beginning of 1860. I then stated that I had a surplus of £25,000 over all liabilities … The balance is now unfortunately on the wrong side to the extent of about £13,000. To account for the loss of the £38,000 in one year, I hand in a statement of the actual losses sustained by me in that time, and which no foresight could have anticipated. (Mr. Macandrew here handed in a document containing the various items which went to make up a total loss of £41,900 within the year 1860.)[36]

He received scant sympathy. The judge commented:

This conduct displayed the greatest recklessness toward his creditors, and his defence to the action by Chalmers was calculated to unnecessary delay … Mr Macandrew seemed to complain of having been ill-treated by every one. He had acted in a most unbusiness-like manner in signing documents without reading them, and this reckless course of conduct must leave an unfavourable impression upon everyone's minds … he saw another reason than revenge or vindictiveness for Mr. Chalmers' conduct. That gentleman had been very badly treated, and he wanted if possible to get his money.[37]

In August a number of Macandrew's creditors petitioned for his release on the grounds that 'without his personal services and exertions – there is little prospect of the Estate being wound up'.[38] One letter to the *Otago Witness* in September, signed 'Mercy', claimed Macandrew had brought his troubles on himself and suggested it was a waste of talent to continue to imprison a man of such 'superior mind and most active temperament':

> I cannot shut my eyes from the fact that this imprisonment is mainly owing to a mean and petty vindictiveness, which nothing can justify, and which is probably defeating its own end, for the retaining creditor is not likely, I believe, to gain anything by it, while to the great body of creditors it may be said to be a certain loss.[39]

Mercy had faith in Macandrew and predicted a bright future for him: 'The dawn of a most extraordinary and unexpected good fortune has just broke upon Otago; rare opportunities are opening for a man of Mr. Macandrew's talent and cleverness. Why not allow him the chance of retrieving his fortune?' The writer was referring of course to the recent discovery of gold in the region.

By October 1861 Macandrew was free and paid a quick trip to Melbourne, possibly to scout out business opportunities.[40] The timing of this suggests he spent no more than nine months in prison before managing to raise enough money to secure his release on probation.[41]

Macandrew's business success was not unique: in the 1850s and 60s many businessmen made large fortunes in New Zealand.[42] Others, such as John Logan Campbell of Auckland, Nathaniel Levin and Barney Rhodes of Wellington, Edward Reece of Canterbury, Johnny Jones and Donald Reid of Otago, had similar experiences: they arrived before or during the establishment of the settlements with capital to invest and earned their money in a variety of ways.[43] Macandrew exploited the booming 1850s. He took excessive risks with both his own and others' money and was immensely successful at grasping investment and logistical opportunities. But where other entrepreneurs weathered the peaks and troughs of the New Zealand economy and hung on to their assets, Macandrew over-reached and lost his capital before withdrawing completely from commercial pursuits.

He was distinguished by what the *Otago Daily Times* called his 'lack of concern about details which would come back to haunt him, often with litigation over payments'.[44] His eventual insolvency and imprisonment for debt had a certain inevitability about them, and it is remarkable that he did not crash and burn much sooner. By the laws of the time he surely deserved to be punished for embezzlement and fraud. That he escaped so lightly is a reflection of the tolerance enjoyed by gentlemen and politicians, and perhaps an indication of his ability to debate any issue convincingly.

It is no surprise that those on the council who knew him well also distrusted him, one contemporary describing him as 'silvery, cunning, and not over-scrupulous'.[45] Many of the settlers, however, responded to his friendliness, his lack of condescension and his readiness to challenge the established order. He appears to have encouraged the growth of trade with personal loans and extended credit – both particularly important at a time when there was little cash in circulation and most business was done on credit. Although his financial collapse seems to have taken the majority of Otago settlers by surprise, many accepted his fall from grace, remembered his generosity in times of plenty, and continued to support him.

Macandrew emerged from these experiences a changed man whose life now took a very different course. His interest in commerce evaporated; instead, in a career move unusual for those times, he committed himself to full-time politics. Just two years later he was once more on the hustings.

PART 3

A fresh start: 1861–67

Chapter 8

With his reputation tarnished, and barred from commercial pursuits as an insolvent debtor on probation, James Macandrew began to rebuild his life. His dismissal from the province's highest office, the loss of his fortune, imprisonment for defaulting on a debt and a near-drowning experience were sufficiently Damascene to produce an enduring change in his behaviour.[1] Despite his record, and to the amazement and horror of the colony, in June 1863 Macandrew again won a seat on Otago Provincial Council and in July 1865 was re-elected to the General Assembly.

By 1863 Otago was booming. Gold, discovered in payable quantities in May 1861 by Gabriel Read in a gully near today's Lawrence, was found in the Dunstan, Arrow and Shotover rivers in August 1862 and throughout Central Otago thereafter. The arrival of a host of miners transformed Dunedin from a straggling, muddy village – 'in wet weather no town ever presented such a miserable appearance of discomfort and utter wretchedness' – to a metropolis.[2] The population grew by 37,000 in 12 months; four new jetties were built, and the demand for supplies and services brought dramatic change:

> shops, stores, warehouses, dwellings, offices, and public and private buildings were run up with marvellous rapidity … There are two theatres, large public gardens, two concert halls, four or five long rooms attached to the leading hotels, capable of accommodating from three hundred to a thousand people; [there are] seven insurance offices … three banks … forty-two hotels and restaurants; two Masons and three Odd Fellows' lodges; there is a Garrick club, debating society, chess club, jockey club, Mechanics' Institution, a Building and Land Society, a chamber of commerce, three daily and three weekly newspapers. The gas is laid on in all the principal streets of the city which are now curbed or paved, or laid down with asphalte.[3]

This was Macandrew's fabulous decade, in which he bounced back from disgrace and directed the richest province in the colony. As outspoken and polarising as ever, he unswervingly promoted a manifesto of continuous immigration, ongoing land sales and settlement, non-stop infrastructure development, and the submission of central government to provincial rule. His views and actions were widely reported throughout New Zealand.

By the end of 1859 Macandrew and Eliza had three sons (Colin, James and Herbert) and two daughters (Marion and Jane). In 1861 following the sale of Carisbrook, and with her husband incarcerated in Dunedin prison, Eliza and the five children moved to a house owned by her mother in Walker Street (now Carroll Street). They were joined by Macandrew on his release from gaol in October 1861, and the couple's fourth son, Hunter, was born on 1 August 1862.[4] The family moved next to Colinswood on the northern side of Otago Peninsula, where Macandrew had previously leased and owned land.

Eliza's will exposes the trail of her husband's financial irresponsibility and explains the ownership of Colinswood. Macandrew had bought a £1000 life assurance policy on himself as a marriage settlement, but the policy had lapsed. In 1851 he acquired 10 acres (4ha) of land for Eliza in Dunedin but sold it in the 1860 liquidation of his assets. Her brother William Reynolds bought it back and initially held it in trust for her, but sold it in 1861 and invested the money in cattle. In 1864 Eliza's trustees purchased part of the land that would become the basis of the Colinswood estate with £1000 from her mother, and the couple built a substantial brick house. In an attempt to place the family home beyond the reach of Macandrew's many creditors, Eliza's will stipulated that it was to be 'free from the debt control or engagements of my present or any future husband'; in the event of her death the property was to pass to her children.[5]

During the 1860s the colony's attention was on settlement and development. More efficient communication, a stagnant economy, wars in the North Island and a growing awareness of the high cost of government stimulated the quest for a better and cheaper model of governance. The battle of provincialism versus centralism was spirited and ongoing, with regular skirmishes at both local and national levels. In the early 1870s a growing number of politicians would attempt to transfer all legislative authority to the General Assembly and leave regional administration in the hands of smaller, local government units. Committed provincialists would resist these changes and offer a variety of increasingly radical plans to preserve the provinces – plans that ranged from federation to secession.

A modern photograph of Colinswood. Kate Wilson Collection

Colinswood, the house Macandrew had built at Macandrew Bay in 1864.
K. Muir & Moodie photograph, from a copy print in Hocken Collections, Uare Taoka o Hākena, University of Otago

The arrival of Julius Vogel

London-born journalist Julius Vogel arrived in Dunedin in 1861 after working for nine years on the Victorian goldfields as a gold assayer, merchant and newspaper editor.[6] With William Cutten, Macandrew's nemesis of old, on 15 November 1861 he launched the colony's first daily newspaper, the *Otago Daily Times*. Aged 28, Vogel was initially strongly opposed to 44-year-old Macandrew's return to politics and wrote of him: 'If ability and genius are other names for consummate cunning and deceit, for trickery and falsehood, for unmeasured audacity and assurance, then is Mr. Macandrew entitled to be dignified with the titles.'[7] Despite this apparent antagonism, Vogel shared many of Macandrew's views on local development and would in the 1860s become Macandrew's closest political colleague.

The pair had much in common. Vogel once claimed:

> Anyone who knows me must recognise in me a member of the working class. I have known what it is to want, and I have always had to depend entirely upon my own personal industry; and those who wish to know what facilities this country affords to working men may be told that whatever position I hold I owe entirely to my own industry.[8]

Both men were newcomers to the educated middle class, and both lacked buttressing inheritances and had to survive on their wits. They were men on the make and openly boosted their new country. Their goal was the optimal exploitation of New Zealand's resources; its governance structures were, to them, a means to that end. Initially in agreement on the need for provinces, as depression bit hard their relationship would become strained, and Vogel, as colonial treasurer in 1869 and premier in 1873, was forced to take radical action to reduce expenditure.

Vogel was politically active and used the *Otago Daily Times* to promote his idea for the complete separation of Otago from the rest of the colony. His views were shaped by his experience in Victoria, which had prospered after its separation from New South Wales.[9] In 1862 he helped to organise a public meeting in Dunedin attended by at least a thousand people, which agreed that separate governments should be established for the North and Middle Islands.[10] In the following year the ambitious Vogel stood for both local and colonial parliaments;[11] as an unknown newcomer challenging long-time residents he was initially unsuccessful, but in June he was elected to the provincial council for a country seat, and in September he won a Dunedin seat in the General Assembly.

'James Macandrew, Esq., M.P.C. Second Superintendent of the Province of Otago, N.Z. From a photograph by Meluish.' Portrait in the *Dunedin Leader*, 24 October 1863

Return to council

In comparison, and despite his critics, on 1 June 1863 Macandrew easily defeated sitting provincial councillor Thomas Tayler by 27 votes to 11.[12] His success provoked outrage throughout the colony. One sarcastic observer in the *Press* was unwittingly prophetic: 'We see no reason why Mr. Macandrew should not again be a member of the General Assembly, a member of the Executive Council of the Colony, and Superintendent of Otago.'[13] Support came from a new weekly newspaper, the *Dunedin Leader*, which published a portrait of Macandrew and a detailed biography emphasising his political activities. As in so many articles published in his lifetime, one may detect Macandrew's hand in this as he laid the groundwork for his re-election as superintendent. A journalist from the *Colonist* was less than complimentary about the portrait, however, contending that it was 'not quite true to nature':

> The copy we have received gives that gentleman a look by no means flattering. There are other modes of libelling a man besides letter-press, and if this portrait were divested of the dress coat, white shirt, and neat neck tie, and a rough blouse and cabbage tree hat represented as the garments, it would be much like the appearance of a man we should not care to meet in a lonely situation in the bush.[14]

Vogel and Macandrew shared a commitment to colonial development and a similar approach to making politics work for their own benefit. Sixteen years Vogel's senior and a risk-taker who readily changed tactics and allegiances, Macandrew was a role model for Vogel, who would later employ Macandrew's template of provincial borrowing to fund development at a colonial level. Vogel acknowledged Macandrew's influence in 1882, saying he had learned 'a very great deal of that which I have put to useful purposes afterwards during the time … when I was his responsible adviser'.[15] When Vogel became colonial treasurer in 1869, however, one pessimistic commentator posted this warning:

> It is true that Mr. Vogel has had the advantage of sitting at the feet of Mr. Macandrew for some years while conducting the provincial business of Otago, but his Government cannot be said to have afforded unmixed satisfaction to the people of that province, the noble resources of which make it so hard to make mis-government acutely felt.[16]

It was predictable that Vogel, the newcomer, and Macandrew, the seasoned 'old identity', should eventually clash.[17] Speaking in Port Chalmers in January 1865, Macandrew presented both sides of the provincial separation case: 'Although the dismemberment of the colony is altogether at variance with my inclination, and subversive to all the aspirations of the past – at the same time, if its integrity is to be maintained at the expense and to the detriment of this Province – then I say, perish the integrity of the Colony.' However, he continued, 'It seems to me that the destiny of Provincial Government is as yet far from being fulfilled, and that until the country is colonised and the land fund exhausted, the Province of Otago, at least, will be committing political suicide if it permits itself to be absorbed in the Middle Island.' He advocated sending strong representatives to the General Assembly to uphold the provincial rights conferred by the Constitution Act.[18]

In an editorial rejoinder Vogel claimed that Macandrew had adopted compromising tactics such as 'a certain smoothness and oiliness of speech, vacillation of purpose, and trimming of opinions to suit both parties'. He commented: 'The truth is the federation of the provinces of New Zealand is one of incongruities – there is no community of interest.'[19] Macandrew acknowledged that the Assembly had 'almost unlimited power to do anything not repugnant to the law of England'.[20] He suggested, however, that it was better to work within the Assembly before considering separation – a demonstration of prag- matism rather than the opportunism suggested by some.[21]

Macandrew did occasionally admit that the provinces could not last forever, and as a leader in the last-ditch battle to prevent abolition, his actions were constrained by this belief.[22] As early as 1866, while campaigning for the Clutha seat in parliament, he commented: 'My idea is that increased population, railways, and electric telegraphs will in due course efface the Provincial system, and my policy is to make the most of Provincial Governments as long as they exist, and until the progress of the Colony shall enable us to dispense with them.'[23] His view of the provincial system throughout his career was inconsistent; at times he supported a federated New Zealand of self-taxing provinces, and at others he advocated a system of provincial governments supporting a strong central administration. When Vogel as colonial treasurer in 1870 launched his public works and immigration programme, to be managed predominantly from Wellington, Macandrew endorsed it enthusiastically as he saw the advantages to the provinces – albeit with the loss of some autonomy.

In October 1863 Macandrew, who at that time supported a decentralisation of power to strengthen the provinces rather than a complete separation, moved in council to vest the 'executive powers of the General Government, so far as their exercise related to Otago, in officials residing within the province'. The motion was defeated on the grounds of giving 'too large powers to the Superintendent'.[24] Its dismissal perhaps suggests that Macandrew's misdemeanours lived on in his colleagues' minds and the prodigal's return was not entirely welcomed. But two years later his experience in government, his political nous, his optimism and his enthusiasm for development were acknowledged: in July 1865 Macandrew was returned to parliament.

Return to parliament

The so-called 'Native question' – colonial shorthand for the costly and bloody campaigns between Māori and European settlers that took place, largely over land, between 1843 and 1872 – stimulated the formation of the Southern Separation League, whose key members were Vogel, Reynolds and James Rattray. It was the first of a series of Middle Island associations committed to provincial autonomy that emerged in early 1865, masterminded by Vogel. Fuelled by resentment at the high cost and perceived poor management of the wars in the North Island, and the perception that the Weld government was treating the Middle Island as a satellite of the North Island, the league was formed for the purpose:

> of obtaining, by strictly constitutional means, the Legislative and Financial
> separation of the two islands of New Zealand, and the erection of the
> Middle Island into a separate and independent colony … the League will
> seek to effect the abolition of the present enormously expensive Provincial

Governments, and the substitution of one strong central Executive, whilst greater local administrative efficiency will be sought in the establishment of local boards and municipalities.[25]

The league organised public meetings in January and February of 1865. At one of these Macandrew displayed his ubiquitous optimism; reported as 'differing from the declared policy of the Separation League of dismembering the colony', he apparently still 'looked upon it as tending to a better day, as he looked upon it as a proof that breath had been infused into the political dry bones of the Province'.[26]

Vogel continued to promote complete separation, and in May 1865 moved in council that it was 'in the interest of both the Northern and Middle Islands of New Zealand to be separated into distinct colonies'. He suggested a meeting of provincial delegates to prepare a request for separation for the General Assembly, but his motion was lost when Macandrew recommended a delay.[27] On 12 May another rising politician, Taieri farmer Donald Reid – who, in the shifting tides of colonial politics was later to be Macandrew's implacable political opponent, and later still his ally – supported Macandrew's motion that it was 'inexpedient to raise the question of separation of the Northern and Middle Islands of New Zealand until the policy of the present General Government shall have a fair and reasonable time to develop itself'.[28] The passage of this motion was a rebuff to Vogel, whose personal popularity at the time was waning. As one journalist commented: 'The Council is growing impatient of that interminable fault-finding which he adopts as a medium for his talking propensities.'[29]

The sale of land engrossed the provinces throughout their existence, with land laws no sooner passed than further amendments were tabled. Governments could be unseated for their land policy, and in April 1865 Macandrew censured the provincial executive for their action, taken without consultation, of remitting a land tax to purchasers in order to encourage land sales and improve the province's financial circumstances. While not rejecting the spirit of their action, he maintained 'that the executive had no right whatever on its own motion to repeal an act of the Legislature, for that practically was what had been done'.[30] The executive resigned and Macandrew was among those asked to form a new one. He declined, a stance that provoked conjecture about his ambitions and led many to surmise 'that he really had some intention of paving his way to an ostensible leadership'.[31]

Superintendent John Hyde Harris indicated his resignation in June 1865, sparking further local speculation that Macandrew might offer himself once again for the post. One writer suggested that 'despite his previous laches', Macandrew had a large amount of support and would 'run any other candidate a hard race'.[32] Macandrew chose instead to run for the General Assembly's two-member seat of Bruce, an electorate with 5828 inhabitants and 500 voters centred on the town of Milton.[33] His view, shared by the editor of the *Bruce Herald*, was that Otago needed strong General Assembly representatives who supported unfettered provincial government. During electioneering Macandrew criticised the growth in central spending and indebtedness, which he blamed on 'the political apathy of the people, and the absence of public opinion on political subjects'. He maintained general government should have nothing to do with land regulations.[34] The *Bruce Herald* was positive: 'The Electors could scarcely find any one who holds sounder or more liberal views as to the disposal of the Waste Lands.'[35] On 26 July 1865 the paper's patronage was rewarded with Macandrew's resounding win: 207 votes to 34 cast for his opponent.[36] His success prompted one editor's wry comment: 'Strange as it may seem, the name [sic] of Mr Macandrew's friends is legion.'[37] After a nine-year absence, Macandrew had been returned to represent Otago interests in the General Assembly.

Wrangling over the provinces

The decision to abolish the provinces was not made in haste. Throughout the next decade parliament debated governance at every session, and the colony came slowly to accept that a central government would be both effective and efficient. Macandrew would play to a national audience as the country moved inexorably towards abolition, salvaging his reputation and confronting Stafford and Vogel in some of the fiercest debates yet seen in the House.

Parliament opened in 1865 in its new location in the Wellington provincial chambers.[38] Macandrew set out on 5 August to attend the fifth and final session of the third New Zealand parliament where, the faithful *Bruce Herald* suggested,

> Otago's influence in the Assembly will be increased by the presence of a sound, far-seeing, and practical statesman, one who has the prosperity of the province thoroughly at heart, and who is able to make himself heard and felt in the Legislature of the Colony.[39]

Vogel also sailed with Macandrew, causing one commentator to note, 'It is not often that two such staunch antagonists are crowded within so narrow a space; and curiosity was raised as to how they would spend their time on the voyage.'[40] But by the time they returned in October the pair were allies, bonded by their opposition to the growing dominance of central government.

Wellington Provincial Council Chambers, 1859. This building became the new capital's first Parliament House in 1865. 1/2-003739-F/22494909, Alexander Turnbull Library, Wellington

In the House, Macandrew contributed to debates on matters ranging from arbitration courts to military pensions, the postal service and scabby sheep. His standing was enhanced by his adroit shepherding through all stages of the New Provinces Act 1865, which safeguarded the original provinces by putting a brake on the establishment of new ones, requiring them to be created henceforth by parliament. He appeared in the media almost daily, his performance drawing favourable comments from the editor of *The Colonist* (Nelson), for one: 'This gentleman has just been returned as member for Bruce, and is now looked upon as one of the leaders of the Opposition.'[41] A correspondent observed:

> He is evidently a shrewd man, and broaches no subject he is not well up in
> … when he does broach it, he brings to bear upon his argument no mean
> flow of studied language, that rises now and then into true eloquence, albeit
> tinged with a north of the Tweed accent.[42]

Another described one of Macandrew's speeches as 'one of the closest, most logical, and most full of hard, practical, common-sense points that has been delivered during the debate'.[43] Vogel meanwhile, elected in 1863 and headed for higher office, provoked reaction of a different kind: 'He may say the best thing possible; he may reason in a manner the most cogent and convincing, yet the House listens with dull ears, or refuses to listen at all'.[44]

Macandrew had no sooner returned to parliament than debate broke out over a report Governor Grey had supposedly sent to the secretary of state in January 1865 regarding the separation of Auckland Province from the rest of the colony.[45] Premier Frederick Weld denied the existence of such a report, and in September the Legislative Council agreed on the necessity of the colony remaining 'one and undivided'.[46] The same day an Auckland member presented a motion to the House suggesting it was time to adjust the colony's liabilities among the provinces: that New Zealand be divided at Cook Strait into two separate colonies; that a deputy-governor be appointed to administer the province of Auckland; and that a bill be introduced to make this happen.[47] Vogel and Macandrew both supported the motion, the latter with some regret, however; he feared 'the breaking-up of the colony would be the breaking-up of all the aspirations which he and others had cherished for many a long year'.[48] In the end, after four days of debate the separationists could raise only 17 votes to the government's 31, and the colony remained united.[49] Vogel did not vote in this division; gossip suggested he was 'drunk & asleep & did not hear the [division] bell' – at one in the morning![50]

Weld's goal of colonial self-reliance in the North Island wars meant greater cost for all settlers when Imperial troops, brought in by the colonial government to mount major campaigns in the land wars, were repatriated and replaced by local soldiery.[51] In an effort to boost the government's income, Colonial Treasurer William Fitzherbert proposed to reduce the parliamentary grant to the provinces from three-eighths to one-quarter of their customs revenue, a move that would make the provinces yet more financially dependent on parliament. A second blow fell when Attorney-General Henry Sewell presented a bill that proposed to introduce death duties and apply stamp duties to various legal processes, as another way of generating revenue. Furious debate followed, in which Macandrew vowed he 'would sooner see the Provincial Governments abolished tomorrow than see them in leading-strings under the General Government'.[52] Weld made the matter into a vote of confidence for his ministry and almost lost the vote to end the debate. A week later, when the proposed stamp duties were again debated, Vogel moved that instead of being retained by central government, the revenue from these could be distributed to the provinces on the same basis as customs revenue. This took the House by surprise and only the Speaker's vote saved the ministry.[53] Weld chose to resign and on 16 October 1865 Edward Stafford – a staunch centralist and seasoned politician, and no friend to either Macandrew or Vogel – was appointed for his second term as premier. He would lead the colony until June 1869.

Otago's dissatisfaction

In November 1865 the newly elected superintendent of Otago, Thomas Dick, welcomed members to the opening of Otago Provincial Council and proceeded to summarise provincial dissatisfaction. He condemned the poor relationship that existed between central and provincial governments, saying, 'on the Provincial authorities rests the onus and responsibility of advancing all the material interests of the Province, and of preserving peace and good order within its bounds, while we are disabled from promptly appropriating, as emergencies arise, the great resources that would otherwise be at our disposal.'[54]

A select committee was appointed to consider how the council might respond to central government on the matter, and reported on 27 November.[55] Macandrew's influence as a member of this was obvious, as he had foreshadowed the committee's 10 recommendations in an address to the electors of Port Chalmers three weeks earlier.[56] The report endorsed a model of government wherein 'the Executive functions of the General Government be confined to matters of purely federal concern, and … the Executive functions of the Provincial Governments be largely increased'. It proposed a repeal of the New Provinces Act 1858; the amalgamation of Taranaki and Auckland provinces; the reduction of the general government to three departments (colonial secretary, treasurer and attorney-general); the delegation of Native affairs to the provinces; and the reallocation of financial liabilities for loans and the cost of government. Councillor Frederick Moss recorded his dissent to five clauses, but the council adopted the report.[57]

When Macandrew's address and the Otago report were both published colony-wide, some residents of the smaller provinces naturally took umbrage at what they considered Macandrew's extreme views. One wrote: 'Mr. Macandrew … looks to the end, without troubling himself greatly about the means.[58] Nor is the end he has in view of a very elevated character; it is narrow and designed for selfish and local means.' A Taranaki resident complained: 'The people of Taranaki are not mentioned, but we suppose they will be handed over as serfs attached to the soil.'[59] It seems Otago politicians had an early talent for upsetting their fellow colonists.

The committee's report reflected Otago demands in the General Assembly made in return for supporting Premier Stafford, who desperately needed all the votes he could muster to remain in power following his unseating of the popular Weld. Stafford, the premier who had sponsored the New Provinces Act in 1858, who had advised the governor to dismiss Macandrew as superintendent in 1861, and who was regarded by some as 'the great enemy to all provincial powers', was now obligated to Macandrew and the ultra-provincialists for his political survival.[60]

Squeezing the provinces

While Macandrew's status in the General Assembly grew from this point, Vogel had to work hard to stay in parliament. His Dunedin seat was disestablished and, after losing in Waikouaiti, he was returned as a Gold Fields member. When parliament was dissolved on 27 January 1866 Macandrew also changed electorates – this time to the other half of the original Bruce electorate, the adjoining, single-member seat of Clutha, which had just 300 voters and was centred on Balclutha. He was elected unopposed on 9 March. In his acceptance speech he announced his goal: 'If the Assembly was to do any good at all, the pruning knife must be applied to the gigantic expenditure of late years.' [61]

On his return for the next sitting of parliament Macandrew moved a number of extreme cost-cutting measures. He opposed the establishment of Hansard as an unaffordable luxury, and a military pensions bill as 'a measure which contemplated the continuance of this miserable war'.[62] He moved that 'the duties on imports be henceforth re-adjusted from year to year, so as to realize a sum not exceeding £800,000 in any one year; the one-half amount of which amount to be legally secured for appropriation by Provincial Councils'; and he advocated that government expenditure should not exceed the other half of the customs revenue and income from other sources.[63] He proposed to do away with 'the whole of the Defence Force, the expenses of the Native Department, and all the Resident Magistrates of the colony'.[64] He criticised the practice of subsidising intercolonial and interprovincial mail services, and complained about the mystery that surrounded New Zealand finance.[65] He suggested that all revenue be made provincial, 'and then let each Province contribute its due proportion to the General Government'.[66] He also opposed a stamp tax on the grounds that retrenchment rather than taxation was required.[67]

Critics mocked him and labelled him an ultra-economist, one claiming that 'he coolly proposes to sweep away the means of giving peace and security to half the colony'.[68] But Macandrew was not entirely dismissed. Some observers saw his tactics for what they were: long-term positioning by Stafford's critics. Come budget time, one editor claimed, 'these malcontents will be augmented' and the ministry would have to be ready to refute them.[69]

The 1866 parliamentary session had opened with uncertain prospects. Fighting in the North Island had eased and rumours were afloat that the Colonial Office would, as the *Nelson Examiner* observed, put 'the veto of the Crown upon any proposal to dismember the colony … separation in its simple form is, for all practical purposes, disposed of for the present.'[70]

This prediction did not stop the Auckland superintendent and parliamentarian Frederick Whitaker from moving on 24 July 1866 that 'temporary provision should be made for the better government of the Province of Auckland'. His proposals included converting Auckland Provincial Council into a provincial assembly with a greater degree of self-government.[71] Whitaker's motion was not welcomed by the Otago contingent: if Auckland were to achieve self-government, then the Middle Island would have to continue to subsidise the remainder of the North Island provinces. Superintendent Dick, by then also a member of the General Assembly, moved an amendment to grant *all* provinces self-government, but the motion was lost.[72] Vogel suggested the provinces would die a natural death when they were no longer necessary but saw no need to cripple them yet: 'When the iron horses ran through the two Islands, then they would have no more need of provinces; but as yet they had only done half their work.'[73] Macandrew voiced a sentiment that would no doubt have upset his neighbours:

> if ultra-provincialism was to encourage the development of the resources of the colony, and to carry out the object of introducing population into the country, then he was an ultra-provincialist and was proud of being so. He desired to see the Province of Otago, for example, having the fullest control over its own affairs, that it might ultimately outshine, and perhaps absorb, the Province of Canterbury.[74]

Whitaker, Dick, Macandrew and Vogel voted together, but Whitaker's original motion was lost by 44 votes to 18.[75]

A week later the provincialists were further distressed by Colonial Treasurer Francis Jollie's financial statement, which reduced the provinces' usual three-eighths share of the customs revenue and introduced a stamp duty to raise urgently needed funds for central government. Stafford elevated the little-changed stamp duty bill to a matter-of-confidence vote and won the debate. This only served to reinstate Stafford with a stronger ministry, and further alienated Otago and Auckland members, who feared that 'an unchecked Stafford might destroy the system for the sake of his obsession with colonial unity'.[76]

Dunedin residents were outraged; a public meeting held on 4 September protested against 'every measure having the effect of diminishing the proportion of the revenue at present locally appropriated'.[77] From this meeting an Otago Association emerged, formed to watch over and promote the interests of the province. It supplanted the Middle Island Association, which had been established earlier along more general lines in order to awaken the public to the threat to Middle Island interests from General Assembly legislation.[78]

When the latest version of the Otago Waste Lands Bill was presented to parliament, Macandrew argued for complete provincial control of waste lands.[79] However, he did not support a call from Otago gold miners to reject the unwieldy and inefficient shared administration of the goldfields, at that time administered by the provinces under delegation from central government.[80] Supported by fellow provincialists, Macandrew requested that the Gold Fields Select Committee consider whether 'the power of legislation might not also with advantage be extended to Provincial Legislatures; or whether the administration as well as the legislation ought not to be in the hands of the General Government'.[81] Whitaker added: 'Give us the whole management or take it yourself.'[82] Somewhat surprisingly, given his views on local self-government, Macandrew favoured central control of the goldfields, whereas Vogel wanted to retain provincial management.[83] The committee recommended retention of the status quo. This unremarked interlude foreshadowed a fearsome dispute that occurred the following year, when control of the goldfields became a political issue of consuming intensity.[84]

Otago stirs

On their return from Wellington in October 1866, Macandrew and Vogel won plaudits for their pro-provincial stance. In Dunedin they were greeted by a cheering mob and paraded through the streets behind a band. The six Otago members who had supported Stafford – James Bradshaw, Arthur Burns, John Cargill, Charles Haughton, Charles O'Neill, James Paterson and John Richardson – were jeered at and their effigies marched through the town before being thrown into the sea.[85]

Otago was on a roll, funded by seemingly inexhaustible supplies of gold and benefiting from an exploding population. Princes Street was now paved

Princes Street, Dunedin, looking north, in 1900. The Otago Provincial Chambers building, by this stage the General Post Office, is on the right, while next to it, the Stock Exchange and its clocktower dominate the Exchange area. 1/2-092614-F/22865659, Alexander Turnbull Library, Wellington

with asphalt, lit by gas, bordered by broad footpaths and lined with substantial buildings. In November 1866 the Otago Provincial Council met for the first time in its new premises, a substantial brick building on land bounded by Princes, Water and Bond streets. The council had spared no cost. One English visitor wrote, 'With their "Sydney cedar fittings" and "chaste" decorations, with Mr. Speaker bewigged and begowned, with reporters' galleries, visitors' galleries, library, smoking and refreshment rooms, the Otago Provincial Buildings stood forth as the embodiment of provincial pride and provincial supremacy.'[86]

Vogel was appointed Otago provincial treasurer in November 1866, his first appointment as a member of an executive council, and his first to a position of responsibility where he could no longer be an unconstrained critic.[87] Firm leadership was expected from Vogel's executive; one scribe caustically suggested, 'they will not regard any question as a Ministerial one, short of a direct want of confidence motion. They will swallow as many leeks as there may be occasion for, but sacrifice power to high principle – never.'[88] It would be a long time before political manifestos were taken seriously in New Zealand.

Vogel's new and more cautious attitude to the place of the provinces was demonstrated when his executive supported financial separation of the islands only. Macandrew wanted more, and responded that on the 'battle field' between the general and provincial governments, 'if there was to be peace in the Colony, one or the other must give way'.[89] Despite assertions that the days of provincialism were numbered, he held that the provinces 'were only on the threshold of their existence'; their mission was 'colonising and settling the country'. In Otago their work had just begun:

> … until every part of the Province was as accessible as the Taieri Plain –
> until all the land had been sold – until all the rivers had been bridged – until
> the country was intersected by railways – until the population could be
> counted by thousands, where there were now hundreds – until then, the
> work of the Province would not be ended; and then the Provincial system
> would die a natural death.[90]

Macandrew and Vogel would now part company over provincial powers. Vogel's political shrewdness was demonstrated in the final days of Session XXII in an episode that also demonstrated how thoroughly Macandrew's pronouncements had polarised his colleagues. The appointment of an Otago emigration agent in Britain was proposed, and following 'a storm such as has not been known before in the by-no-means peaceful annals of the Provincial Councils of Otago', Macandrew's name emerged from a list of 15 contenders.[91] At this, 'a vast amount of vituperation was heaped on the devoted head of Mr. Macandrew'; Speaker John Richardson, who disliked him intensely, resigned rather than taking a vote, with the result that the appointment lapsed.[92] Later reports claimed that Vogel did not intend to make an appointment at all: the bill had simply been a display of activity to suggest his ministry was energetic and worthy of support in the forthcoming election.[93] But the debate had certainly brought Macandrew's name to the fore.

Macandrew had been elected to the council by voters who wanted to benefit from the gold rush; by 1867, firmly re-established in both legislatures and determined to protect Otago's autonomy, he was ready to challenge the sitting superintendent.

Chapter 9

J ames Macandrew's challenge to Superintendent Thomas Dick was first
hinted at in the *Bruce Herald* on 17 January 1867:

> ... it is whispered in town, that there will be no contest, and that Mr. Dick
> will 'walk the course'; but the talk again is, that Macandrew ought to be
> brought forward to contest the highest seat in the Council ...[1]

A private letter from the editor Joseph Mackay to Macandrew, written in August
1866, suggests that Macandrew's return had been planned for some time, albeit
in secret.[2] Mackay thanked Macandew for articles for the paper, and wrote: 'I
regret that you should feel precluded from writing so freely as you would desire,
from being desirous of not showing your hand in the correspondence ... you
may have every confidence in its not being divulged otherwise, as every precau-
tion has been taken to prevent this.'[3]

Macandrew's bid for the superintendency was made official on 31 January
1867 when he announced, modestly, that 'having received numerous signed
requisitions ... I have, although reluctantly and at the last moment, felt it my
duty to comply'.[4] His nomination on 4 February, for the position from which
he had been officially dismissed six years earlier, astonished his opponents and
elated his supporters – and mud soon began to fly. Publications from February
1867 showcase the unvarnished opinions of his critics and followers, and throw
an interesting light on the relationship between Macandrew and Vogel as their
collaboration in both houses of government now began to unravel.

Superintendency beckons

Gold and the influx of thousands of miners had transformed Otago from poor
and conservative to rich and radical, and the injection of unconstrained wealth
into its economy brought rapid development and expansion. Ordinances of the
time resulted in 421 acres (170ha) of reclaimed land being offered for lease,
and the income from this was used to improve harbour facilities. Bell Hill

James Macandrew in his early forties, captured in a studio portrait by Saul Solomon, who owned the Victorian Portrait Rooms in Dunedin 1862–66. Kate Wilson Collection

(also known as Church Hill) was lowered and the rubble used to build up the harbour floor, and a board was established to develop shipping facilities.[5]

But progress was not rapid enough for many citizens. Although devout and honest, Superintendent Dick was viewed as cautious, unimaginative and dull – hardly the leader a booming economy required.[6] Now that the province's coffers were filling and opportunities for growth beckoned, the artisans of Otago wanted an expansionist-minded member to represent them on the provincial council: many wanted Macandrew back.

Not all were welcoming, however, and Vogel in his role as editor of the *Otago Daily Times* led the critics.[7] Although the two shared several political positions, Vogel took a dim view of Macandrew's moral standards and attacked him fiercely during the campaign. His first move was to print, in full, Auditor-General Charles Knight's 1861 report on his enquiry into Macandrew's alleged fraudulent behaviour.[8] Macandrew's downfall, Vogel contended, was 'that he was not proof against temptation, and that, succumbing to it, he went from bad to worse, magnifying his wrong doings by the defence he set up of them':

> His candidature is opposed upon the ground, that he has not cleared up the circumstances which led to his former expulsion, and that in the absence of such exculpation, it is impossible to concede to him the position of the first personage in the Province.[9]

Macandrew's response strained belief. In an eloquent speech at a crowded meeting, he claimed not to have seen the auditor-general's report until its recent publication; his dismissal and disgrace were not a consequence of the report, he announced, but came from his personal financial misfortune.[10] He pronounced himself the victim of a 'diabolical political conspiracy' and even produced tears, excusing himself with the aside, 'Pardon me, but the fact is that these matters bring reminiscences to my mind, somewhat calculated to overcome one.'[11] He made reference to his many achievements, emphasised his experience as superintendent, and made grandiose promises to dredge the harbour, improve the Town Belt, establish a paper mill and develop shipbuilding. The *Bruce Herald* gave its support: 'We fail to perceive what benefit is to be derived from stirring up ... the mud creeks to their lowest depths ...'[12]

Vogel continued to attack Macandrew's morals for the rest of the campaign, repeatedly recalling the events of 1860–61.[13] He reminded readers that Macandrew had 'left the Home country deeply in debt', although evidence for this was not supplied; once in New Zealand, Macandrew had 'sought to purchase political capital with the money of his creditors'. He accused him of taking undeserved credit for agricultural and immigration progress, and claimed that as a member of the Waste Lands Board Macandrew had granted leases illegally and had 'jobbed and trafficked in runs daily'.[14]

Other papers took different tacks, both positive and negative. The *Otago Witness* appealed to its readers' higher principles, saying it was impossible to forget the past and asking what the world would think of New Zealand if Macandrew were to be re-elected.[15] The *Bruce Herald*'s editor, always a staunch supporter, admitted after reading the auditor-general's report:

We do not maintain that Macandrew was guiltless of error or free from irregularities, but we are of opinion that they cannot be deemed so heinous, as to be incapable of explanation or of forgiveness ... he is so well qualified by his energy, comprehensive mind, and consummate tact, to raise this Province from its present humiliating position.[16]

When one city merchant labelled Macandrew's supporters a 'rabble', the *Bruce Herald* responded: 'Never were the mechanics or the laboring class so stigmatised since the passing of the Reform Bill in the British Parliament ... Working men of Otago, Macandrew is your friend, and you know it.'[17]

Macandrew's ability to relate to a wide range of people and his 'hail-fellow-well-met' electioneering style endeared him to many voters. According to the *Bruce Herald*, 'Many old settlers, who have now their own freehold farm, or their business as storekeepers, can testify to the fact ... that their good fortune is attributable to a start, in the land of their adoption, by Mr. James Macandrew.'[18] The loyalty of this cohort was apparent at a rally in Green Island, where the settlers insisted on pulling Macandrew's carriage by hand to the meeting place despite his embarrassed objections. As the paper reported, 'for the first time in Otago, the populace thus exhibited their appreciation of a political leader'.[19] Macandrew had become the complete populist.

This enthusiasm was also evident when Macandrew spoke to constituents throughout the province, sometimes at three meetings a day, and it fizzed when he addressed a fervent crowd of over 2500 at Dunedin's North Recreation Ground on the evening before polling day.[20] Copies of Vogel's *Otago Daily Times* were burnt with mock ceremony before Macandrew delivered a rousing speech – of dubious veracity – in which he defended his response to the 1861 charges of embezzlement. Emphasising the rhetoric of development, he accused his opponents of lethargy. He himself vowed to be proactive – 'I will be no puppet in the hands of any men' – and promised to build railways to all corners of the province. He declared: 'We have two Governments performing the work which one might effect. My policy would be to converge the powers, and ... to carry on the Government for one half of what it now costs.' Once more he promised to 'devote all the influence of my office to accomplish separation between the Northern and the Middle islands'.[21]

The campaign

The tussock-covered hills and arid valleys of Central Otago were home to thousands of rugged miners living in utterly different circumstances to the inhabitants of Dunedin and the coastal plains. Gold mining was a unique industry that required specialised administration, and forceful miners could be a fractious crew.

New Zealand politicians had observed the difficulties in managing goldfields in California and Australia, and were better prepared for the gold rushes at home. The Gold Fields Act 1862 had given the governor responsibility for the issuing of miners' licences, agricultural and business leases, the use of land, local legislation, the administration of justice and matters of revenue. These powers, consolidated in the Gold Fields Act 1866, could also be delegated to the superintendent of the surrounding province.

Recognising that miners had a financial stake in their community but lacked sufficient property to register as voters, parliament granted them political rights. In 1862 the General Assembly electorate of Gold Fields District was overlaid on the existing Otago electorates; all persons holding a miner's licence could now vote for their own two members of parliament. In 1865 another electorate was established, the single-member Gold Field Towns, which was a 'grouping of discontinuous settlements servicing the mining communities of Central Otago': Queenstown, Arrowtown, Cromwell, Clyde, Alexandra, Dunstan Creek (St Bathans), Roxburgh, Hamiltons, Lawrence and Havelock (Waitahuna).[22] Both electorates were abolished in 1870. The Otago Provincial Council Gold Fields electorate, with three members to represent the miners, was also created in 1862; miners in this area voted for their councillors and superintendent at the same time.[23]

Macandrew was in pursuit of miners' votes when he travelled to Central Otago on his first visit to the area. The Alexandra newspaper was dismissive, noting that 'except for the purpose of his election, he has never ventured therein; he knows nothing of the miners or mining'. It attacked his campaign promises:

> the whole of the public works which he would undertake are for the
> benefit of Dunedin and the 'Old Identities' at the Taieri and Tokomairiro.
> A railway for the one – dredging the harbor for the other – and generally
> the improvement of Port Chalmers by means of a dry dock; but not a word
> about roads on the goldfields ...[24]

Despite this, Macandrew's enthusiastic rhetoric pleased sufficient listeners to ensure he gained 62 per cent of the votes cast on 20 February 1867. He won all booths from the Waitaki to the Tokomairiro except Hampden, Dunedin North, Wakari and Portobello, but was unsuccessful in Balclutha, the hub of his Assembly Clutha seat; in the goldfields he won only in the rural centres of

Roxburgh, Alexandra and Cromwell – a portent of future strife.[25] One commentator judged Macandrew's support came from 'the trading classes and ... artisans of Dunedin' and noted: 'This election must be accepted as emphatically a revolt.'[26]

Macandrew's jubilant welcome by the working classes of Otago triggered a storm of protest across New Zealand, and prompted such unprecedented responses that, ironically, the abolition of the provinces may have been hastened. Reaction was swift and disparaging. The *Timaru Herald* observed:

> in electing a man of Mr. Macandrew's character, Otago has signified she
> no longer desires provincial independence, for at that she has now aimed a
> death-blow, and sooner or later provincialism will be an institution of the
> past. Although Mr. Macandrew being again in office is not only a disgrace to
> Otago, but also to the whole of New Zealand, still, being a means to an end –
> the downfall of provincialism – we cannot say we regret his election.[27]

The more cosmopolitan *Wellington Independent* deemed that 'the Otago majority have proved themselves either not very particular, or not very intelligent', and expressed concern about the impact of the election on the reputation of both the province and New Zealand, and on 'Home' money.[28] The *Grey River Argus*, speaking for a county eager for self-government and sensitive to process, claimed: 'This result is the more extraordinary, considering the extreme efforts made by Mr. Dick's party. Not a stone was left unturned to bring Mr. Macandrew into public contempt.'[29] The *Argus* raised the possibility that the governor should veto Macandrew's appointment. Auckland's *Daily Southern Cross*, addressing a large, diverse and class-conscious province, suggested Macandrew's election was 'a sign of the times. He has trampled – or rather the bone and sinew of the province have trampled, through him – on the squatting and moneyed interest, aided and abetted by the Provincial Executive and the leading newspaper.'[30]

The *Taranaki Herald*, whose readers were suffering downturn and war, saw wilfulness in his election:

> We deplore the fact as a dishonor to the whole Middle Island, and as casting
> shame on popular institutions ... the people of Otago may be assured
> that their miserable infatuation will furnish an irresistible weapon to the
> centralists ... [they] have brought provincial institutions throughout the
> colony into disrepute.[31]

Overseas newspapers weighed in also: the *Leeds Mercury* dedicated 1200 words to the story and concluded, disapprovingly, 'it is on record that pecuniary irregularity in office is no bar to reappointment.'[32]

Fallout

Macandrew assumed office on 27 February 1867. Despite his earlier recommendation to the General Assembly in July 1866 – that central government retain complete control of the goldfields – he wrote immediately to Premier Stafford requesting that the governor's powers be delegated to the superintendent as per the Gold Fields Act 1866.[33]

Although perturbed by Macandrew's election, Stafford had hesitated to act against him, knowing that any recommendation to veto the election result would make Macandrew an Otago martyr. Instead, he sought a legal reason for Macandrew's dismissal.[34] He dispatched the auditor-general Charles Knight to Dunedin on 8 March to investigate an item labelled 'Defalcations by James Macandrew, Esquire' – a sum of £1012.14.5 – that had appeared in the Provincial Appropriation Ordinance 1861–62.

Knight's investigation met opposition both from Provincial Treasurer Vogel, who was offended by a breach of official etiquette – Knight had neglected to inform him that he was inspecting the Otago Treasury records – and from Macandrew, who declared that unless the provincial council wanted to reopen its 1860 enquiry, he would not allow the general government to continue its investigation.[35] Knight closed his enquiry immediately, but reported to Stafford that 'some party has secured a pecuniary advantage of £1012 14s 5d at the expense of the Provincial Treasury'.[36] This was sufficient for Stafford to inform Macandrew that the governor's powers would not be delegated to the superintendent as requested: James Bradshaw, MP for the electorate of Gold Field Towns, had been appointed government agent for the goldfields.[37]

Other goldfield regions were appalled by this move. 'It is impossible to exaggerate the evil and confusion that will spring out of this usurpation of authority', raged one Westland newspaper. The writer predicted anger, excitement and the use of language 'savouring a good deal of revolution', and reported talk of seizing the Otago Customs House and mobilising the militia 'for the purpose of resisting the chief authority of the colony!'[38] The *Nelson Examiner* reported the establishment of a vigilante group in Port Chalmers.[39] Even the *Otago Daily Times*, which had earlier pressed for the governor's powers under the Gold Fields Act to be withheld if Macandrew should become superintendent, took offence at Bradshaw's appointment.[40]

The council executive blocked Bradshaw's access to public buildings and records and told goldfields officers to ignore his instructions.[41] Wellington's response was to advise Bradshaw to dismiss any official who refused to obey

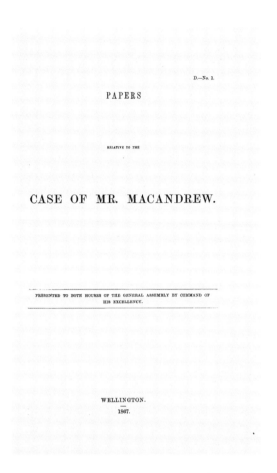

The evidence against James Macandrew: *Papers Relative to the Case of Mr. Macandrew.*
AJHR, D-1, 1867, New Zealand records 20332901, Alexander Turnbull Library, Wellington

his orders; Macandrew countered this by taking complete control of all local government buildings. Seeking to end the impasse, and possibly worried that Wellington might overreact to the mounting disorder, Macandrew wrote to Major-General Chute, the officer commanding the colony's armed forces:

> In the interests of the Empire, as well as of this small but true and loyal portion thereof, I venture to solicit your good offices with the Imperial authorities to the intent that they may be pleased to issue such instructions to His Excellency the Governor as may induce him to comply with what he cannot but know to be the almost unanimous desire of the people of this Province, and thereby to maintain the integrity of the Colony upon the best of all foundations, viz., the allegiance of a free and independent people.[42]

137

Chute did not respond, but Stafford did, dispatching his minister of Native affairs and commissioner of customs to Otago to act as mediator. James Crowe Richmond was an unfortunate choice for this situation. Richmond socialised mainly with the local gentry and was considered somewhat diffident and feeble, a not altogether surprising judgement given his personal view of his role, which he expressed in a letter to Stafford:

> It is a great point not to embarrass these poor people and to show them the difference between gentlemanly usage and factious tyranny … My leading idea is to secure and recover our friends much more than to attack our enemies, then to get on with our business.[43]

Richmond's approach to the crisis was ineffectual. He was ambivalent about the Stafford ministry's stance, and in a letter to his brother commented:

> I do not think, after long and candid meditation that we shd have done wisely in disallowing Macandrew's election, and we shd not have done decently in delegating the Govr's powers to him after Knight's report. To disallow would have made a martyr of him … It may have been that there was an error of older date in not proceeding criminally against him … but it would not have been convenient to paralyse the province by keeping the office vacant as to its higher powers.[44]

He confessed his heart was not in the task: 'I am utterly destitute of pugnacity, and being rich in the smallness of my desires I would gladly retire from a position which jars my sensitiveness at every turn …'[45]

His correspondence provides a counterpoint to the fierce Otago parochialism typified by an editorial in the *Otago Witness*. In response to the government's announcement that Richmond's mission was to smooth over the difficulties that had arisen, the writer claimed the only reconciliation possible was a complete retraction of the policy that the government had initiated:

> if it be doubted whether they [the people of Otago] are capable of managing their own affairs or not, their progress is a sufficient answer … the Executive have shown that instead of hailing the progress of Otago with satisfaction, it is looked upon with aversion, as if the growth of a wealthy, high-spirited, and independent population, was inimical to the course of policy marked out by Mr Stafford and his colleagues.[46]

A dramatic analogy followed and a warning was issued:

> Their conduct reminds one of the supercilious hauteur with which the aristocracy of England looked upon the wealthy manufacturers of the Northern counties, during the early stages of the anti Corn Law agitation.

They could not imagine that education, honor, intelligence, and influence could dwell among spindles and spinning jennies, and they despised the men whose wealth and enterprise gave employment to the multitude of producers by whose efforts Great Britain became wealthy and powerful. Just so do Mr Stafford and his colleagues treat Otago. They seem to imagine that the remote province is to be schooled and punished when it dares to take a step counter to their oligarchic will … there are indications throughout the country, that the conduct of Mr Stafford and his colleagues towards Otago is not approved, and the consequence will, most probably, be the formation of so strong a Provincial party as to … render their retention of office impossible.[47]

Earlier in the year, mounting resentment that Otago taxes were subsidising the wars in the North Island had precipitated a petition requesting the separation of the governments of the two islands. Signed by over 2000 people, this was presented to Governor Grey when he visited Otago in February 1867.[48] Local citizens were outraged when Grey, who was uncertain whether Macandrew's election result would be endorsed or not, refused to meet with the new super-intendent.[49] The people of Otago were now firmly united behind Macandrew; the perception of a deliberate insult to the province, combined with nationwide criticism of their choice of superintendent, strengthened their determination to cut their ties with the rest of the country. The matter also drew Macandrew into partnership with Vogel, as both considered provincial independence was at risk. They were concerned that public works, policing and other services would no longer be provided on the goldfields, and were uneasy about the loss of provincial income should the province be unable to issue grazing licences and collect rents in the area.

Richmond was at a loss to understand the aggressive mistrust that united the residents of Otago, nor could he comprehend their ardent drive for independence. As a consequence he misread the political situation and reported to Stafford:

I shall not be surprised to find in a few days either a breakup of Vogel's Cabinet or a change in the *Daily Times* … On the whole I think things look better than I had expected, and I believe great strength yet may be got out of the crisis, but it must be by cautious movements. I hope you will not think I am too soft for the Emergency. There is really nothing of the character of revolution about the affair, and except in the maintenance of Macandrew as Superintendent I do not believe the majority of the people are keenly interested.[50]

He was not convinced that Bradshaw was the right man to be government agent, did not trust the goldfields secretary Vincent Pyke, and was worried the provincial council was compelling Police Commissioner Branigan to discipline men who had followed Wellington's bidding.[51] Richmond had attempted to sway Reynolds to the government side, and confided to Stafford that he hoped Reynolds would not 'join in the madness of the Council'.[52] He had held several meetings throughout Otago and retrieved various documents, and concluded in a letter to his brother in mid-June that since the goldfields output had peaked, the provincial treasury in Dunedin was earning less: 'a certain languor has crept into the administration … Public works, not public service, have been the specialty of the Provinces and with waning revenues they have not been able to satisfy the goldfields and the city at the same time.'[53] Cold-shouldered by the uncooperative superintendent and council, he admitted: 'It is a grievous effort for me to keep my spirits up to the work before me. My soul loathes the strife I have fallen into.'[54]

The locals judged Richmond sternly on his departure: 'The questionable capacity in which he appears in Otago may have had some little to do with the clumsy, unworkmanlike manner adopted by him to support the General Government.'[55] His visit had simply served to unite the province yet more firmly against the machinations of faraway Wellington.

The plebiscite

When Otago Provincial Council met in May 1867, Macandrew in his address noted the unsatisfactory state of the relations between the general and provincial governments and pressed for the council to assert its position: 'The Provincial system has a great work to perform, and it would be suicidal on the part of the people to relinquish it. It is said that the system has been extravagant and expensive. If so, it has been our own fault, and the remedy is in our own hands.'[56] Perhaps influenced by news of the impending union of the Province of Canada with the colonies of New Brunswick and Nova Scotia on 1 July 1867, he suggested that New Zealand could become a federation: 'The spirit and intention of the Constitution Act evidently is that the General Government should be federal in its action, and the circumstances of the Colony pointed to this as the advisable form of government, otherwise what necessity was there for creating distinct machinery for provincial legislation?' He noted that separation could only be approved by Britain's parliament; in the meantime, Otago had to fight for its rights in the General Assembly.

There was general agreement. Vogel's resolutions from the preceding November were incorporated into a petition to Queen Victoria, urging her to convert the Middle Island into a separate colony and to establish a federal union of the two colonies 'such as has taken place in British North America'.[57] Over 7000 signed the petition. Macandrew, firmly ensconced with Vogel as his 'prime minister', and with his brother-in-law Reynolds now provincial Speaker, demonstrated the new order by presenting the council with the Gold Fields Provincial Management Bill. This made provision for a plebiscite to be held on 1 June, to decide whether the superintendent and his Executive Council should continue to manage the Otago goldfields.

The plebiscite was carried by 8304 votes to 178, but Stafford refused to back down.[58] Thus encouraged and united in their view on the necessity for separation, however, Macandrew, Vogel and Reynolds sailed to Wellington to confront Stafford in the General Assembly, which met on 9 July 1867. There Vogel moved that the governor's powers under the Gold Fields Act should be delegated to superintendents whose provinces contained the fields, a motion which Stafford amended with the addition of 'saving in exceptional cases'.[59] The motion was passed by just 28 to 24 votes.[60] Ten of the 13 Otago members present opposed the amendment, supported by 10 of the 14 Auckland members and three of the seven from Wellington, an alliance that was described as a 'strong provincialist party, now fully alive to the necessity of unified action in withstanding any further inroads upon the rights of the provinces'.[61] Stafford's ministry was rescued by a face-saving compromise: the passage of the Gold Fields Act Amendment Act 1867 and the Governor's Delegations Act 1867, wherein the governor's power of delegation was made over to provincial Executive Councils instead of to superintendents.[62]

In Otago's eyes Macandrew had won another round, but Stafford was not deterred from his mission to remove, or at least reduce, the powers of provinces in order to strengthen central government. Hawke's Bay provincial councillor Joseph Rhodes probably summed up public opinion of the situation when he wrote to Donald McLean, superintendent of his council:

> I hope that no more time will be wasted over McAndrew [sic] & Co., but I quite agree with the remarks of the 'Press' that Stafford's Ministry ought to have disallowed Macandrew's election as Supt. in the first instance – to have taken the 'Bull by the horns' at once instead of beating around the bush.[63]

By now Macandrew had served a dozen years in provincial and colonial politics, and criticism did little to diminish his fervour and forthrightness. One newspaper described him as 'a hard-headed man who can bear abuse, criticism, and denunciation, and yet go on in his course as a public reformer, as if he were immaculate, and his denouncers of marked inferiority'.[64] Macandrew allowed that 'he had become for a long time perfectly case-hardened as to what the newspapers had to say'.[65] However, an unexpected and harsh response to his attack on government policy during an Assembly debate on financial policy late in 1867, demonstrated that he was not completely immune to criticism. Macandrew had repeated his cost-cutting demand to abolish the Native Department and the Defence Office,[66] and condemned the fighting in South Taranaki with Māori led by Riwha Tītokowaru of Ngāti Ruanui, saying he believed it had been 'not only a great blunder, but ... a disgrace to the Colony'. He was referring to reports of atrocities perpetrated by colonial forces – 'atrocities which might make humanity blush':

> We have learned over and over again in this House ... of unarmed men and women having been shot down in cold blood at dead of night by half-intoxicated men – I might rather say demons in human shape. I myself have been told of orgies in the Waikato district.[67]

An uproar ensued, but the Speaker ruled Macandrew's words were not disorderly. The *Evening Post* fulminated:

> It is well for the credit of this colony that the foul aspersions cast last night by Mr. James Macandrew on the colonists of New Zealand emanated from a person whose unfortunate antecedents are such as to warrant a conviction that having gone so far in a career of social and political immorality, it becomes of little moment to him what sort of weapons he uses, provided they be likely to suit his ultimate purposes.[68]

Macandrew refused to retract his statement – with an unexpected consequence: his claims prompted a select committee enquiry into allegations against Lieutenant Colonel Thomas McDonnell, who in August 1866 had led the surprise attack on the Māori village of Pokaikai, inland of Hawera, where the alleged atrocities were said to have occurred. The select committee exonerated McDonnell but recommended that a commission of enquiry further investigate Macandrew's claim.[69] This commission in turn also exonerated McDonnell, although by a narrow margin only.[70]

Major Harry Atkinson of Taranaki, a centralist and future premier, was particularly antagonistic towards Macandrew, possibly because of Atkinson's personal involvement in the Taranaki fighting and Macandrew's resentment of that conflict's financial cost.[71] In an attempt to expel Macandrew, Atkinson now suggested that the 'purity of the House' was insufficiently protected by the Constitution Act. The Act barred felons and those convicted of treason from sitting, but allowed them to return to the House on completion of their sentences; it did not exclude defaulters and defalcators. He introduced the Public Offenders Disqualification Bill, which proposed banning offenders retrospectively from public offices including the Assembly. Naturally this would include Macandrew, who had retained his position only through a lack of parliamentary process.

Vogel protested that the bill was unnecessary: protection already existed and 'it would be a monstrous thing to pass a Bill expressly aimed at a member of several years' standing in the House'. [72] His attempt to postpone the reading for six months was lost and the bill – minus the retrospective clause – became law. Macandrew's position was saved.

During the debate Macandrew was absent, according to the *Hawke's Bay Herald*, 'for once and the first time in his known career. He did not brave the storm that would have burst upon him had he ventured to expose himself to it.' [73] He also did not vote in the division. Although his guilt was commonly accepted as manifest, it had not been proven – yet little was said in his defence. According to the paper, 'Time should have whitewashed him from the consequences of the crimes with which he has been charged, and which he has never even attempted to dispute the truth of.'[74]

Unabashed, Macandrew reported back to his electorate in November that there had been an enormous amount of talk during the Assembly session. A 'perfect crop of ill-natured Acts had been passed', but taxation and expenditure had not been reduced and the financial system was yet to be reformed.[75] He denounced the annual gathering of the General Assembly as wasteful and unnecessary. New Zealand, he said, had five distinct entities – Auckland, Canterbury, Wellington, Nelson and Otago – and in his opinion each should be given 'the five full powers of self-government, and each would work out its own destiny':

> Let there be, in addition, a Federal Council, meeting every two or three years … The General Assembly was a body not adapted to the circumstances of the country. We were just trying to mould together a number of incoherent materials, before they were ripe for fusion; and to do that was an impossibility. [76]

He completed the year by travelling on the paddle steamer *Geelong* to Fiordland, where he investigated the mineral deposits of Preservation Inlet, authorised the naming of the Macandrew Range above Cascade Cove in Dusky Sound, prospected at Milford Sound, and helped release rabbits at Martins Bay, where the site for the future settlement of Jamestown had been selected on the shores of Lake McKerrow.[77]

It had been a turbulent year, both personally and politically. At home, Eliza's father had died as the result of a housefire at Colinswood on 1 January 1867, and the couple's tenth child, Mabel, had been born on 15 December 1867 while Macandrew was in Fiordland. Although in Wellington he was beset by enemies, in Otago, Superintendent Macandrew was riding the waves of success.

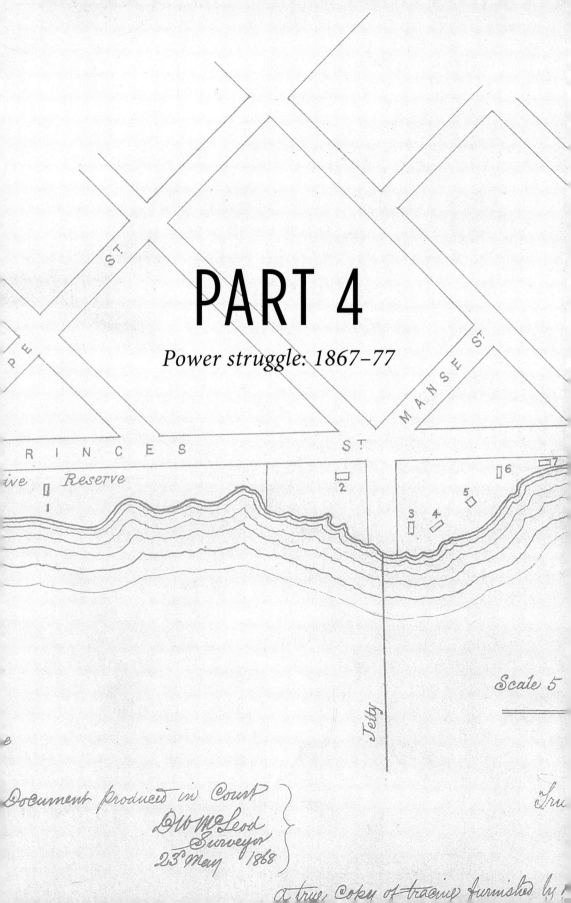

PART 4

Power struggle: 1867–77

Chapter 10

Otago's boom saw out the decade and enabled the province to initiate a hefty building programme. A dry dock at Port Chalmers, a breakwater and wharf at Oamaru, and bridges over the Waitaki, Clutha, Mataura and Shotover rivers were constructed, and railway lines from Port Chalmers to Dunedin and to the north and south of the town were gradually developed.

During his second tenure as superintendent, the province's bursting coffers allowed Macandrew to realise his lifelong commitment to educational matters. A girls' high school, an industrial school for homeless children and a reformatory for delinquents were opened. Under his leadership the School of Art (now part of Otago Polytechnic) and the Otago Normal School, which evolved into the Dunedin College of Education, were launched in the 1870s, and – after many years of intense political wrangling throughout the entire colony – the University of Otago was opened in 1871.[1] These three tertiary institutions owe much to Macandrew's initiative and perseverance.

Otago was one of the original six provinces formed in 1853, of which three were in the South Island. It encompassed some of the most rugged and remote terrain in the colony, much of it accessible only by sea. The province comprised the region south of the Waitaki River, reached from the east to the west coast, and embraced the entire southern coastline of the island. From 1861 to 1870 the province of Southland occupied the plains between the Waiau and the Mataura rivers and Stewart Island, although the latter remained under central control until joining Southland in 1863.

Macandrew advocated persistently for development of the province's unexploited territory, and one of his first actions on becoming superintendent in 1860 had been to place a sum of money on 'the estimates' for exploration of the southwest coast of the province.[2] The council had agreed to the idea, with the proviso that any expedition be accompanied by a competent geologist. This resulted in the appointment of James Hector on 21 December 1861 as Otago's first provincial geologist.[3]

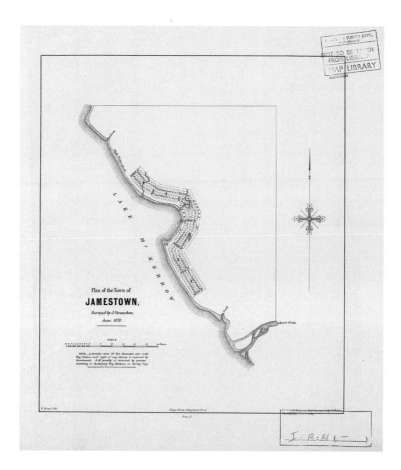

The township of Jamestown, named after James Macandrew, was laid out on Lake McKerrow in Fiordland in 1868. 834.51bje 1870/31940336, Alexander Turnbull Library, Wellington

Hector explored the rugged southwest coast by boat and on foot in 1863. The following year, on the geologist's advice, Superintendent John Hyde Harris reported: 'The character of the entrance to Martin's Bay, and of the surrounding country, do not … appear to justify any immediate steps being taken … to encourage settlement in that direction.'[4] However, the discovery of gold on the West Coast in 1864 renewed interest in the area. Following re-election in 1867 Macandrew visited Fiordland to inspect Martins Bay for himself, to ascertain whether a settlement with a port providing more direct access to Australia might be established.

The council was fired by his enthusiasm for the area and appointed a select committee in April 1867 to 'enquire into the expediency of Settling the West

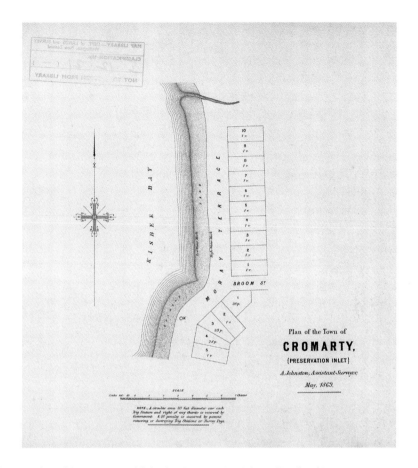

The township of Cromarty, established in Preservation Inlet in Fiordland in 1869.
834.6bje 1869/31864762, Alexander Turnbull Library, Wellington

Coast of the Province, and to report on the best means of doing so.[5] It is not difficult to detect Macandrew's influence on their recommendations. Hector's reservations about the impracticality of settling the location were ignored, the committee even reporting that the 'natural inducements for settlement offered in the district, are not equalled in many portions of the Province'. It suggested a settlement could be initiated at Martins Bay:

> … believing that it is the duty of this Province to endeavor to turn to account its West Coast territory – a territory which presents advantages to certain classes of immigrants, in many respects superior to the East Coast … There is every reason to believe, that were the Government here, empowered to give the like free grants of say 160 acres [65ha] (4 such to the square

mile) to each family of a stipulated number of bona fide settlers … such as
experienced Canadian foresters from the backwoods of Canada, or hardy
and industrious immigrants from Nova Scotia, or the Orkney and Shetland
Isles, whose previous training and occupations have been connected with
shipbuilding, whale or other fisheries; that it would be a means of initiating a
prosperous settlement upon these now valueless shores.[6]

The report recommended an amendment to the Otago Waste Lands Act
1866 to make free land grants, and to make 150,000 acres (60,700ha) available
for purchase. The Otago Settlements Act 1869 subsequently earmarked 100,000
acres (40,468ha) of land in Martins Bay and the same amount in Preservation
Inlet, where the town site of Cromarty was laid out. Although some gold was
found in the vicinity of Cromarty later in the century, nothing came of these
settlements; the few families who settled at Martins Bay departed within three
years, essentially starved out when the province failed to build an access road or
fund a steamer service.

Nothing learned, Macandrew would continue to advocate for settlements in
remote parts of the province, such as one on Stewart Island in 1872 and another
in the Catlins in 1884. These were equally unsuccessful.

The Southern Trunk Line[7]

Intensive settlement required not only migrants but access to land, and public
works were usually discussed at an early stage when provincial councils were
formed. Because initial access to outlying regions was limited to ships only, the
provision of harbour works was given highest priority, followed by the construction of all-weather roads. Settlers from countries with established railway
systems were impatient for the convenience this form of transport provided, and
were quick to press for their construction.

Macandrew was familiar with rail technology from his London days, and the
expansion of a national railway network occupied much of his political energy.
His involvement peaked in 1878 when he was appointed minister of public works
and was able to commission new lines to all corners of the country. Railways
were also responsible for a further blow to his reputation, however; following his
ministerial tenure, the report of the Railway Commission denounced the inept
management and corruption that had occurred during his term in office.[8]

In his nomination speech for the Otago superintendency in 1860 he had
claimed that railways 'had been found in all countries to be the cheapest roads
that had been made'.[9] He spoke further on this matter in his first council address
on 11 April 1860, when he pointed out the need to set aside land for roads and

railroads: 'Unless this is done, we shall have to pay no end of money as compensation to private individuals, as soon as we are in a position to indulge in railroads, which I trust will be at no far distant date.'[10]

In 1863 the provincial council's Select Committee on Roads and their Deviations had reiterated Macandrew's view and suggested that sufficient land should be allocated for the establishment of a railway between Dunedin and the Clutha River via the Taieri Plain and Tokomairiro. The select committee was less interested in a line between Dunedin and Port Chalmers: there was already a macadamised road and good water access, which they considered sufficient.[11] Their advice was ignored, however, and at the next session the council resolved to first build the Port Chalmers to Dunedin line, then to press on south to Balclutha, with proposed extensions further south and to the west. The General Assembly would be asked to pass an enabling Act to encourage a private company to undertake construction of the lines. The Otago Southern Trunk Railway Act 1866 subsequently approved the development of the line from Dunedin to Balclutha and granted the superintendent permission to lease or sell the railway; the council was not permitted to borrow the necessary money for construction, however.[12] Macandrew's re-election in 1867 gave impetus to the project, and a special commissioner was now sent to England to negotiate the formation of a company to build the track to the south.

Macandrew, meanwhile, had to deal with dissension in Otago and answer to the complaint that would eventually undermine the province. As he reported, 'A feeling of jealousy exists in some portions of the Province with respect to the Southern Trunk Line, which is looked upon as conferring an advantage upon the Central portion of the Province at the expense of the extremities.'[13]

The commissioner had little success in England, and it was 1869 before a frustrated Macandrew was able to report that a contractor, David Proudfoot, had been found to build the Port Chalmers to Dunedin section, which would be paid for by 'jetty dues'.[14] Construction began on 30 August 1870 and the line was finally opened on 31 December 1872 by Governor Bowen. Macandrew was thanked profusely and, unburdened by excessive modesty and clearly relaxed in the company of the Queen's representative, he took the opportunity to castigate central government: 'The Colonial Government in its wisdom would neither allow us to borrow money to make our own railways, nor make railways for us; so we had to do the best we could for ourselves.'[15] He was able to report the following year: 'The General Assembly last year authorised the purchase of the railway from the promoters, which purchase has recently been concluded, the line being now in the hands of the Province.'[16]

By 1870 Vogel was colonial treasurer and proceeded to borrow an immense sum of money in London to invest in the construction of railways, roads, bridges and settlements, and to subsidise an influx of migrants to the colony to boost its population. Otago was an early beneficiary of Vogel's building programme when expensive public works became the responsibility of central government, and Macandrew did not hesitate to apply for millions of pounds for Otago projects. The Dunedin to Balclutha railway line was one of the first to be authorised, and eventually opened on 1 September 1875.

Harbour works

Macandrew kept a close eye on his projects.[17] Tenders were called for the building and fitting out of a steam dredge, and the foundation stone for a 100-metre dry dock was laid at Port Chalmers on 18 July 1868 at a ceremony presided over by the superintendent. The dock, the only one in New Zealand and soon to be a profitable earner for the province, opened on 15 March 1872 with a boozy ceremony led once again by Macandrew, now securely enthroned as the local champion and provincial chief.[18]

Oamaru citizens were keen for their share of the investment in infrastructure, and Macandrew put the case for harbour development in the North Otago port at the opening of the provincial council in April 1869:

> You are doubtless aware that a Commission of professional engineers have reported that a suitable dock can be constructed at a cost of £40,000 – a sum which, whether we look at the importance of the district, its large contribution to the revenue of the Province, the vast saving which will be effected in the shipment of its produce, or the stimulus to increased production and exportation which greater facilities for shipment will afford – the Province is bound to expend.[19]

He committed the province to paying half the cost of the development and promised to seek the rest from the General Assembly: the Oamaru Dock Trust Ordinance 1869 was enacted in June that year. Unfortunately the Legislative Council blocked the subsidy, forcing the province to fund the project itself, but in 1875 Macandrew officiated at the opening of both the 130-metre breakwater and Macandrew Wharf, which were connected to the town by a short railway line. Governor Lord Normanby threw a bottle of champagne onto the wharf to christen it and Macandrew declared it now open to public traffic. Macandrew's speech was reported in the *North Otago Times*: 'There was no doubt that Oamaru would become one of the most important ports of the Colony. Bye and bye,

Another first sod is turned – this time for the Riverton to Invercargill railway, 1875.
A.J. Forsyth photograph, P1998-028-09-001, Hocken Collections, Uare Taoka o Hākena, University of Otago

they might see 100 acres enclosed here and docks rivalling the London Docks. (Laughter.) … he hoped they would go on till the wharf was not only 1200, but as many thousand feet long.'[20] At the celebratory luncheon Macandrew eloquently described the difficulties encountered by the planners: 'They had to spread an unlimited quantity of bread with a very limited amount of butter. If their big brother in Wellington would only help them a little they could all be jolly good fellows.' Adept at making spontaneous speeches, he rarely used notes and many of his comments provoked supportive laughter.

A less successful jetty was built at Moeraki during his tenure and was unveiled in late 1873 to muted praise; the residents were soon complaining of its defects.[21]

As superintendent, Macandrew became the statutory chairman of Otago Harbour Board, which first met on 6 July 1874. However, his continual promotion of Port Chalmers as the region's major port over the demands for the development of the upper harbour led to ongoing tension that continued well after the abolition of the province and his departure from the board.[22]

The 1870s were a period of great expansion in Otago, and Macandrew was in demand to turn the first sod for many construction projects. Here he is at the centre of the picture, spade in hand, opening a recreation ground, 1875.

De Maus photograph, from a copy print S17-156a, Hocken Collections, Uare Taoka o Hākena, University of Otago

A university for Otago

In 1878 Macandrew stated, 'There is no other circumstance connected with my public life in New Zealand which I am more disposed to be proud of.'[23] He was referring to the establishment of the university in Dunedin, a saga that demonstrates the particularly Scottish tenacity, single-mindedness and competiveness of the Otago settlers, ably fronted by Macandrew.

Thirty years earlier the *Otago Journal*, the mouthpiece for the Otago Lay Association, had affirmed: 'the [Otago] Scheme embraces provision for religious ordinances, schools and a College'. When the settlers first arrived in Otago the New Zealand Company bought three sections. Dubbed the 'Special Trust' properties, these were gifted to the Presbyterian Church for a church, a school and an institution of higher learning.[24] By the 1860s primary and secondary education (the latter for boys only) had become a provincial council responsibility, and interest now turned to the establishment of a university. In 1861, as trustee of the Special Trust properties, the superintendent assigned the income from one of them towards 'the erection and maintenance of a College or other Educational Institution in Dunedin'. The college fund was launched.[25] Five years later, realising that the provincial council was likely to appropriate all revenue from the Trust Fund for Religious and Educational Uses to pay for public education, the Church sponsored the Presbyterian Church of Otago Lands Act 1866, which provided support for a 'theological chair or chairs' and a 'literary chair or chairs in any college or university which shall be erected or shall exist in the Province of Otago'.[26]

In 1867 the rector of the high school petitioned parliament to establish a number of scholarships to English universities. His request generated debate in both Houses in the General Assembly, and a joint select committee was appointed to report on the provision of higher education in the colony.[27] Fifty-one colonial worthies were consulted and of these, 31 supported the awarding of scholarships for university study abroad, while 16 supported the establishment of a New Zealand university.[28] Macandrew championed the latter. Aware that funds already existed in Otago to support several chairs, he suggested a university could be established in the new Post Office in Dunedin.

Enthusiasm for Macandrew's proposal ran high in Otago, and a public meeting in August agreed that the time had come 'for founding a New Zealand University or College'.[29] But in October the parliamentary select committee released its report: it did not support the notion of a colonial university.

Unperturbed, Macandrew made his own plans for a university in Dunedin, scouted out available lands to reserve as endowments and, backed by the Presbyterian Synod, announced in his opening address to the provincial council in April 1868:

> Measures towards obtaining such an Institution should be commenced, and there is no part of the Colony in a better position to make the commencement than ourselves.

> It is proposed that 100,000 acres [40,400ha] of land should be reserved by way of endowment; the annual revenue from which, together with that which will be derived from other sources, will suffice to provide the living agency which will be required to institute a University worthy of New Zealand. All that is needed now to give effect to this arrangement is your concurrence.[30]

A council select committee formed to examine the proposal was unanimously supportive. It also advised urgency, fearing that 'unless early action is taken by Otago on the subject, some of the other provinces will take the lead in this important matter'.[31] Macandrew appeared before the select committee on 22 April and provided maps of land that the chief surveyor had suggested could be reserved for the endowment. He assured the committee that he would personally approach runholders on the proposed land to request them to cancel their present leases, which were with the province; in exchange, they would receive 'a lease for 21 years from the Education Board or the College Trustees as the case may be'.[32]

The committee's recommendation – that council approve an ordinance to establish the endowment – was not acted on immediately, however, and in the end Otago's ambition to be the home of the University of New Zealand was pre-empted by the government's University Endowment Act 1868. Passed in October to encourage colony-wide development of higher education, the Act provided for the funding of a colonial university.

Otago Provincial Council established the University of Otago on 3 June 1869.[33] A 12-member university council held its first meeting on 10 November 1869, and the official opening was held on 5 July 1871.[34] Teaching began five days later: Professor George Sale offered classes in Latin, Greek, English language and literature; Professor John Shand lectured in junior and senior maths; and Professor Duncan MacGregor presented natural philosophy and mental science. In a first for the empire, all classes were open to both men and women.[35]

A 100,000-acre endowment was secured on 1 June 1870, and Macandrew's hand can be seen in the provincial council's assignment of a second, equally large endowment in May 1872.[36] A third, of 10,000 acres (4046ha) in Southland, would later come into the university's possession after amalgamation with the University of New Zealand, and a fourth in 1877 when Otago Museum and its 11,000-acre (4451ha) reserve came under university control.[37]

Macandrew was ever ambitious; when offering his congratulations to the first meeting of the university council, he suggested:

> Without seeking in any way to obtrude my views upon the Council, perhaps I may be pardoned if I express an opinion that while due provision should be made for classical and metaphysical studies, there should be equal, if not greater, prominence given to the teaching of natural sciences.
>
> I have long thought that a school of Mines and of Agricultural Chemistry would be of great practical importance in this province, and I earnestly hope to find in the University of Otago that, inter alia, provision will be made for these.[38]

The University of Otago building (middle right), in North Dunedin, 1900. St David Street, through the middle of the photo, leads to Lake Logan.

Unknown photographer, private collection, Hocken Collections, Uare Taoka o Hākena, University of Otago

In 1871 Macandrew forwarded a proposal from the provincial council to the colonial secretary, suggesting that income from a University of New Zealand endowment be used to fund a medical school at Otago. This was adopted, and limited medical training commenced in 1875. Law classes began in 1872, a School of Mines was launched in 1879, and Macandrew suggested the development of a School of Agriculture in February 1881. This last provoked a waspish response from a cautious Dunedin businessman, Edward Cargill, a fellow councillor who sat for 34 years and was vice-chancellor of the university for nine. Cargill was 'a little resentful … at a gentleman occupying the very prominent position Mr. Macandrew does, throwing at us extravagant proposals of that sort – proposals to do what is altogether beyond our power'.[39] Macandrew never stopped thinking big!

After initial opposition to Otago's university, a parliamentary select committee in July 1870 recommended the establishment of a colonial university, to be amalgamated with Otago's and based in Dunedin. Initially in support of this idea, Macandrew propounded the potential advantages of increased funding and possible control of the new university council by Otago members.[40]

This proposal, and the implication that the institution would perhaps give Otago undeserved status, heralded what one historian refers to as the 'signs of the gathering storm of controversy, provincial jealousy, and acrimonious debate that characterised all University legislation during this period.'[41]

Disagreement erupted about the authority of the proposed university. Otago's advocates were firmly opposed by a group of Oxbridge-educated parliamentarians – Henry Tancred, William Rolleston, Hugh Carleton and Edward Stafford – who were adamant that a university should be able to examine and to grant degrees, whereas a college should be a teaching institution only. Otago was already performing all these roles. Their view prevailed, and what emerged from the New Zealand University Act 1870 was an examining and degree-granting body entitled to affiliate colleges in New Zealand as they were established, despite Premier Fox's view that 'the idea of an abstract body having no habitation, but only a name, being gathered from time to time for the purposes of holding examinations, framing rules, and conferring degrees, is far too abstract an idea for a matter-of fact colony like ours. Any such institution in this country must have combined with it practical education and a local habitation.'[42] Clause 19 of the Act offered to make Dunedin the home of this body if the University of Otago was dissolved and its endowments transferred to the University of New Zealand within six months.

Discussions stalled, until the government provided assurance that Otago's endowment would be reserved for Dunedin's university only, but finally, after some haggling over the number of Otago members on the new council, the first meeting was held in Dunedin on 31 May 1871. In the meantime Clause 19 had lapsed and the University of Otago, 'with professors and students and the power to award degrees valid only through a Provincial Ordinance, remained confronting the University of New Zealand with no professors, no students, but the power to award degrees and to affiliate colleges.'[43]

Ever reluctant to share Otago's affluence or ownership and control of its affairs, Macandrew was now unhappy with Otago's decision to affiliate with the University of New Zealand:

> It is much to be regretted that the Colony as a whole has prematurely set up a rival University – supported to a large extent out of the revenue of this Province. I trust our representatives in the General Assembly will be unanimous in their endeavours to secure that that portion of the Colonial revenue which is derived from Otago, and applied to University purposes, shall be devoted to the Otago University.[44]

The University of Otago building during construction, 1878. It was ready for the start of classes the following year. Burton Bros photograph, Box-093-002, Hocken Collections, Uare Taoka o Hākena, University of Otago

Two years later he was still dissatisfied:

> I cannot refrain from expressing my regret that the Council and Professors have agreed to relinquish the powers and the status conferred upon the [Otago] University by the Provincial Legislature, for the problematical advantage of being connected with the University of New Zealand. I can only hope that the result of the negotiations now pending between the two bodies may turn out better than may be anticipated.[45]

The New Zealand University Act 1874 repealed the 1870 Act. The University of New Zealand's purpose would be to examine and to grant degrees. It would be composed of affiliated colleges and controlled by a 24-man senate that would meet annually in one of the main centres. Each college would retain its own council, and the Otago institution would retain the right to call itself a university, but without the right to confer its own degrees.[46]

Macandrew joined the senate in 1871 and remained until 1878, when he resigned from both this and the University of Otago council on his appointment

The completed University of Otago building, now known as the Clocktower Building, on the banks of the Water of Leith, c. 1880. The clock was installed in 1931. The professors' houses have been completed, and the building that enclosed the quadrangle housed the Chemical and Anatomical Divisions.

Burton Bros photograph, Box-093-003, Hocken Collections, Uare Taoka o Hākena, University of Otago

as a minister of the Crown. Although the University of New Zealand was granted a Royal Charter in 1876, the University of Otago's lack of a charter always bothered Macandrew, who was keen to see the institution recognised on the world stage. In his letter of resignation from the university council he expressed regret:

> ... that the Otago University ever consented to waive its claim to a Royal Charter. Had it not done so there can be no manner of doubt that ere now such charter would have been granted, and the University would have been saved from the imputation of having sold its birthright for a mess of pottage. In the interests of New Zealand, and in the interests of high class learning, this was, to my mind, a great blunder, and I would venture to urge that no time should be lost in retracing the step.[47]

Petitions requesting a Royal Charter were sent to Queen Victoria in 1872, 1878 and 1887, but all were rejected. At Macandrew's last council meeting on 23 February 1887 his motion – 'That application be again made for an Imperial charter under which the degrees of the Otago University would be recognised throughout the empire' – was carried unanimously and forwarded to the Queen. However, opposition from other colleges, who feared devaluation of their degrees, defeated the application.[48] Autonomy finally came a century later with the passing of the University of Otago Act 1961, which dismantled the University of New Zealand and made each constituent college a university.

As superintendent and Visitor (the university's last Court of Appeal, a position now held by the governor-general), Macandrew ratified the university's annual report and sat on the university council from 1876–78 and from 1884–87.[49] His commitment was recognised on 25 November 1885 when the University of Otago council accepted a portrait of him by Kate Sperry, which now hangs in a public space.[50] However, no building in the institution yet bears his name.

Otago School of Art

On opening the first Fine Arts Exhibition in the new Post Office (later known as the Exchange Building) in Dunedin in February 1869, Macandrew said he hoped this would be 'the commencement of a series of Exhibitions which may become more expansive with the works of native artists'.[51] The city would do well to devote 'this magnificent building to [be] … a temple of science and art'; in time, he felt, 'this City of Dunedin will be distinguished as the Athens of the Southern Hemisphere'.[52] Thanks to Macandrew's sponsorship and provincial council funding, a year later the Otago School of Art was opened under the auspices of the Education Office. It advertised a free class for teachers and pupil teachers on Saturdays, and one-hour classes twice weekly, at a shilling a week, for male high-school pupils and youths who did not attend a government school. Two-hour classes were held on three afternoons of the week for girls at a cost of 15s for 10 weeks.[53] Numbers grew under the tutelage of provincial drawing master David Con Hutton, and evening classes were eventually introduced.[54]

Otago Normal School

The Otago Board of Education had established an effective school system and was offering the highest teacher salaries in New Zealand. For its first decade Otago had an ample supply of teachers, but by 1870, as a result of explosive population growth stimulated by the gold rush, the lack of trained teachers was becoming problematic.[55] Macandrew pushed for improvement, suggesting the province invest in 'the means of turning out a sufficient number of teachers specially trained for the all-important work of Education'.[56]

Otago Normal School, Dunedin's first teachers' college, Moray Place, 1876. The School of Art occupied the top floor. *Otago Daily Times* photograph, P1998-028-03-010, Hocken Collections, Uare Taoka o Hākena, University of Otago

A council commission established to review the performance of the High School for Boys rejected a suggestion that the school should also train teachers, and pressed instead for a separate training institution.[57] At this, former school-teacher-turned-lawyer Robert Stout moved that 'a Normal School, or Training College for Teachers' be established in Dunedin.[58] The council supported the motion, and some £8000 was budgeted for a sizeable building to be erected in Moray Place. Twelve months later in 1876, Otago Normal School, which incorporated a teacher-training department, moved into a suite of eight ground-floor rooms and three large basement playrooms; the School of Art occupied the second floor. Over the next decade, 323 students received teacher training.[59]

Caversham Industrial School

The gold rush turned many conventional behaviours upside down. In 1867 in his first address as superintendent on opening the council, Macandrew raised 'various questions deeply affecting the moral welfare of the community':

> I would allude especially to the serious evil which is growing and festering in our midst, viz., the large number of children – the offspring of profligate parents – who may be said to be homeless, and who are being utterly neglected or trained up to vicious habits. It appears to me that the State must in self-defence take steps to repress this evil.[60]

He proposed the establishment of an industrial and reformatory school – a boarding establishment to house and train homeless children, orphans, and children whose parents were unable to provide them with adequate care. With the support of the superintendent of police for Otago, St John Branigan, Macandrew reported at the end of the council session that he had given his assent to the Neglected and Criminal Children Ordinance 1867. This granted the superintendent the authority to establish, staff and manage industrial and reformatory schools for neglected children.[61]

The term 'neglected' was broad and covered anyone under 15 years of age found begging in a public place, wandering about, sleeping rough, residing in a brothel or associating with a 'thief, prostitute or habitual drunkard'. These children would be cared for in the industrial section of the school. 'Delinquents' – those children convicted of a legal offence – would be sent to the reformatory section. Children could be detained at the school for between one and seven years; rulings on the duration of their terms would be made by a resident magistrate or two justices. Since the powers proposed for a magistrate had to be conferred by an Act of parliament, Macandrew and Vogel swiftly propelled the slightly modified Otago ordinance through the Assembly to create the Neglected and Criminal Children Act 1867.[62]

The project proceeded apace. Premises for the Caversham Industrial School, set on 12 hectares at Lookout Point, were completed within two years, and the first occupants arrived in January 1869.[63] By 1874 Macandrew was demanding the provision of a separate reformatory school, for children who could not be sent to the industrial school 'without contaminating the inmates of that institution, which as a rule consist more of neglected rather than of criminal children. Considerable difficulty has been experienced from the want of the means of separating the two classes.'[64]

In 1878, in his role as minister of public works, he foreshadowed the relocation of Dunedin's lunatic asylum to a site at Seacliff, and his intention to 'erect
upon the same reserve adequate separate buildings for the Otago Reformatory
and Industrial School for boys and girls'.[65] Although the asylum was eventually
built, the school was not.

Life beyond council

Macandrew's membership of social and professional associations expanded
during this period. In 1869 he was one of 80 founding members of the Otago
Institute, an incorporated society affiliated with the New Zealand Institute, a
colonial body established by James Hector and colleagues in 1867 to provide
a forum for the presentation, discussion and publication of scientific papers.[66]
These institutes played an important social role for the settler elite by providing
opportunities for intellectual discussion and keeping abreast with the latest ideas.
They were prominent in the development of both the humanities and creative
arts, and hosted talks covering many fields of intellectual activity.[67]

As well as being president of the Athenaeum and the Mechanics' Institute,
Macandrew was a member of the Freemasons, who had a strong presence in
Otago. Macandrew's admission into the Masons was complicated: having
expressed a wish to join their company, he stood for election in 1867 and was
proposed and seconded for Lodge Kilwinning. Unfortunately one member of
that Lodge carried a grudge against him and threatened to blackball him (i.e.
vote him out) on election night. Macandrew withdrew, and a number of 'Scotch
Freemasons, unattached to any lodge' met and agreed to launch a new lodge in
Dunedin.[68] Macandrew was thus the first initiate of Lodge Celtic at its inaugural
meeting on 17 October 1867 in Wain's Hotel. Other members included Vincent
Pyke, a Goldfields secretary and later a fellow parliamentarian, and journalist
Thomas Bracken, whose poem 'God defend New Zealand' would be adopted as
the national anthem. The lodge attracted a sizeable membership from stevedore
and shipping companies and the railways department, contacts that were no
doubt useful when Macandrew became minister of public works in 1878.

Macandrew was one of 372 Masons in the 2000-strong crowd present when
the foundation stone for the Masonic Hall in Moray Place was laid on 1 June
1868. In his speech he acknowledged the 'presence of much older, and much
more experienced craftsmen than himself' and noted 'the addition to the city
of another handsome building'.[69] At a banquet held by the Scottish Masons to
celebrate St Andrew's Day in November of that year, 'Brother Macandrew' was

toasted as the superintendent of Otago. In his reply he dwelt upon 'the important duty which devolved upon the brethren as Masons and as men, of building up in this colony a social structure, in which the sons of toil in Europe might find a home'.[70]

Macandrew's almost compulsive tendency to join almost every committee, body and society in Dunedin was an effective way of taking control of events, and allowed him to mingle with supportive friends and colleagues. In the 1870s, when the established order of government was demolished and his world fell apart once again, he appears to have surrounded himself with like-minded people. He would need all the support he could muster as he led an ultimately unsuccessful fight to prevent the abolition of his beloved province and battled with rebellion in his council.

Chapter 11

Once the initial resentment over Macandrew's re-election to the Assembly had subsided, he was acknowledged as a member of an increasingly influential parliamentary faction. Wellington life freed him from the everyday administrative tasks of a superintendent and from some of the demands of Otago lobbyists. Little information exists about his life in the capital, however: we do not know where he lived, what his daily routines were or with whom he mixed. One rare reference suggests he enjoyed conventional social events: on 26 August 1867 he attended a benefit concert at the Odd Fellows' Hall in the distinguished company of Governor Grey, Premier Stafford, Speaker of the House David Monro, Speaker of the Council Thomas Bartley and six of the country's nine superintendents.[1] Entries in various shipping columns reveal movements between Dunedin and Wellington of members of his family, all of which coincide with parliamentary sittings, suggesting that from time to time he also enjoyed the company of his family in the capital.[2]

Superintendent Macandrew was now the leading citizen of Otago. In April 1869 he greeted the first member of the royal family to visit New Zealand – the youthful Alfred Ernest Albert, Duke of Edinburgh, fourth child of Queen Victoria and second in line to the throne – when he arrived in Port Chalmers on the steam corvette HMS *Blanche*. They processed through a decorated and illumined city and were greeted by 5000 people at the Caledonian Society's grounds. Over the next five days Dunedin staged elaborate celebrations, including a levee, Caledonian games, a military review, a theatrical performance, a Masonic presentation, a race meeting, a horticultural show and a citizens' ball, where Eliza Macandrew danced with the 25-year-old prince.[3] Macandrew accompanied the royal guest to many events and hosted most of the functions. At the superintendent's dinner for the prince he expounded on loyalty and concluded, 'Engaged as we are here in endeavouring to lay the foundation of a State, we should also endeavour to cherish within ourselves and to instil into the minds of our children, that reverence for constituted authority which … is the chief corner stone of our civil and religious liberty.'[4]

Aged 50 in 1869, Macandrew was at the pinnacle of his political power. Confident in the company of kings and working men, he was popular in Otago for his enthusiastic spending on infrastructure and was considered a powerbroker in Wellington. But all of this was coming under threat. In Wellington Stafford was moving to reduce the power of the provinces, while at home, the council was becoming increasingly disillusioned with his policies and ever more restless with his rule.

Stafford moves on the provinces

The Constitution Act 1852 had provided for the creation of municipalities and granted the provinces authority to establish boroughs and road districts. Dunedin Town Board was the first to be created, in 1855 (it became Dunedin City Council in 1865), after which the general government came under increasing pressure from outlying districts to delegate further, to regulate uniformly, and to fund self-management for ever smaller units of local government.

In August 1867, in an attempt to provide a standardised municipal system for the whole country, Stafford's government introduced a local government bill and a municipal corporations bill. The former provided a process for establishing road boards and district councils throughout the country by petitioning the governor; and it committed the government to providing a £2 subsidy for every pound raised by rates, as well as an endowment from provincial land funds. At the time Otago Province subsidised nine municipalities, and Macandrew described the bill as 'a most expensive and cumbersome machinery for the purpose of performing functions which the Provinces are performing very satisfactorily for themselves'.[5] Removing provincial participation in the process proved to be a step too far for the provincialists, and the local government bill was defeated by 36 votes to 27, a reversal for the government who had denied it was a want-of-confidence vote and so clung to power.[6]

The second bill, the Municipal Corporations Act 1867, survived. This consolidated provincial enactments and allowed towns of over 250 households to petition the governor to become municipalities; these towns could levy rates and administer their own by-laws, which the superintendent could veto. There would be no subsidies. If a superintendent and council objected to a petition, the governor could refuse it. This meant control was shared more favourably, a factor which smoothed the bill's passage.

Stafford's campaign to reduce provincial power had achieved minor success, but the Otago pair of Macandrew and Vogel were now, de facto, leading an effective opposition. This was a fearsome prospect for many, and one editor defended Stafford's retention of power on the grounds that 'to keep out a Ministry led by Mr. Vogel and Mr. Macandrew, is an object which ought to be important to every one who wishes to save our institutions from deserved contempt'.[7] Trust in Macandrew was still not widespread.

Stafford continued his campaign to eliminate the provinces. He responded to Westland's plea for independence from Canterbury with the County of Westland Bill. This created a 'less cumbrous and costly' province, funded by central government, in which the superintendent's powers were retained by the governor but delegated to a county council. Stafford also tabled the Timaru and Gladstone Board of Works Bill, which granted limited local use of provincial revenue for specific public works to a grouping of four road boards and the municipality of Timaru.[8] Both bills were enacted with little fuss in late 1867.

Revolt in the council

The 1868 session of Otago Provincial Council began in April on a harmonious note. In opening the proceedings Macandrew put 'the question in which we are most deeply interested at present … what is to be the future form of government in New Zealand?'[9] He described 'the true meaning of Centralism – one purse for the Colony', but cautioned against rushing into an organic change. He expressed his regret that Otago was continually acting on the defensive in relation to the rest of the colony, but reiterated: 'I am persuaded that nothing is more prejudicial to the real interests of this Colony than a meddling General Government.' His suggested solution was for each province 'to provide for its own peace, order and good government, out of its own resources, as best it may'.[10] Members concurred – after all, Otago Province was financially secure.

Council harmony dissolved in June, however, when a faction led by Donald Reid demanded that new Hundreds be gazetted to encourage closer settlement. Macandrew and Vogel opposed this on the grounds that it was better to maintain council income from the sizeable rents generated by larger pastoral leases.[11]

Macandrew, Vogel and Reid had entered the provincial council together in 1863 and initially shared a commitment to provincialism, and to easy access to land for deserving settlers through a system of deferred payment. Reid had experienced his own hardship as he laboured to become established in the colony, and this made him 'for all his days the friend of the small, and often struggling, agriculturist'; despite his early disputes with Macandrew over land sales, they had become allies in the anti-abolition battle.[12] Now Reid's demands split the council, and he defeated Vogel to become leader of the executive for just two days when he endorsed a council request for a dissolution and new elections. Under the Constitution Act, however, an election for a new council also required an election for the superintendent; since the majority of members did not want to replace their superintendent, the dissolution did not occur.

Macandrew's response to the fracas was to suggest the council request the General Assembly to amend the Constitution Act in order to permit a super-intendent to dissolve a council on a majority request while retaining his own position – an adroit move on his part to make councils more effective. The suggested amendment served to remind the colony yet again of the continuing complexity of running two tiers of government. One Wellington editor wrote, ominously:

> The important measure passed by our Otago friends will, doubtless, prove one of the numerous bones of contention which will be thrown on the floor of the House when it meets next month. The numerous expressions of divers communities in all parts of the country in favor of local government will not fail to be made capital of by the Ministry … As contests there will be, and that of a nature which we prophetise will lead to an appeal to the country.[13]

Macandrew had not met his election promises to cut council costs and run council more efficiently: dismay greeted the superintendent's large salary increase, and council sessions had lengthened rather than being reduced.[14] In his prorogation speech in June 1868 Macandrew lamented the council's disunity, suggesting that councillors had alienated the people and piously censuring them: 'Gentlemen, there can be no question but "an enemy hath done this".'[15]

Vogel had suffered a business reverse and was disenchanted with Otago, and he and Macandrew ended the sitting with a disagreement over the merits of investment in railways versus roads. Their alliance was disintegrating, but it would be seven years before they became absolute parliamentary adversaries.[16]

Meanwhile, in Wellington

Perennial politician and four-time premier William Fox returned to the House of Representatives in 1868, refreshed after a three-year spell abroad.[17] His return galvanised the General Assembly, united opposition to Stafford, revitalised the provincialists, and recharged the alliance between Macandrew and Vogel. Fox's energy rejuvenated a House that was floundering in the face of Māori resistance, economic decline and the deadlock between central and provincial legislatures. Early in the session he accused Stafford's ministry of drifting, and his want-of-confidence motion initiated a fortnight-long debate on Stafford's provincial and Māori policies.[18]

Stafford initially denied any wish to destroy the provinces. Although letting slip that he thought 'some of the Provincial Governments are excrescences', he claimed to have increased their powers. Creeping transformation was under way, however: the road board districts, the creation of the county of Westland and the Timaru and Gladstone Board of Works were evidence of a government intent on change.[19]

A determined Macandrew now emerged to sway the House. Claiming he had heard a minister 18 months earlier mention that the government's aim was to gradually undermine the provinces, he now suggested that policy to subvert the constitution was being introduced 'insidiously, and by a side wind'.[20] In his opinion, the country could pull itself out of recession by increasing immigration and investment in infrastructure; progress would be achieved when there were 'two millions of people in the country instead of two hundred thousand', at which time the provinces would have 'fulfilled their mission'. The government should leave the provinces 'free and unfettered to carry out the great colonizing work which they, and they alone, have hitherto undertaken, and which they alone are capable of carrying on'. He suggested each province should be permitted to keep any revenue raised, and pay a levy to maintain a federal government. He considered it absurd to have two bodies to do one thing, and challenged Stafford's strategy: 'If the General Assembly is to legislate for the peace, order, and good government of the Provinces, what necessity is there for keeping up the Provincial Legislatures? … If the Provincial Legislatures are to be abolished, give them their quietus at once.'[21] He suggested appealing to the population to decide, but warned that the General Assembly could in fact end up being the body abolished.

Fox's want-of-confidence motion was lost by just nine votes on 12 August 1868, but was a warning to Stafford.[22] As a peace gesture to the provincialists, Stafford supported Vogel's motion to allow the provinces to spend their own land revenue and make their own arrangements for immigration. Macandrew also supported this, claiming the motion was based on an Otago Provincial Council proposal to 'land from 25,000 to 30,000 immigrants on these shores within the next few years'.[23]

Fox promptly attacked Stafford again and moved another want-of-confidence division. Macandrew could not resist making a contribution and once more addressed the partnership between the general and provincial governments. This time, however, he admitted that his view was 'somewhat peculiar': he recommended the provinces retain all their revenue and each province pay its own debts.[24] As head of the province that paid nearly one-third of the colony's taxes, he commented again on the 'Native question' – the ongoing conflicts in the north – saying that 'the indefinite liability of the Middle Island for native purposes must cease'. In his opinion, 'a fraction of the money which had been expended on gunpowder would have acquired the whole Northern Island by purchase, had the settlers been left to deal with the subject'. It was an unlikely solution to the 20 years of interracial fighting that had occupied the colony to date, and few listeners would have believed that the individual provinces could now end the war.

Although Fox could not persuade his colleagues to support his motion, time was running out for Stafford's government. Stafford was not prepared to admit defeat, however: 'I shall … urge our friends to take every possible opportunity of pointing out how miserably insufficient the present provincial system is … whatever little efficiency it once possessed has, as a rule, died out.'[25]

Macandrew and Vogel were now counted among the leaders of the opposition bloc, labelled the 'Constitutional Party' by correspondents, although editorial reaction to their assuming the ministry was mixed. To stress his importance in Otago and his indifference to Wellington, Macandrew abandoned the assembly for its last four weeks and headed south to open a substantial bridge across the Clutha River at Balclutha.[26]

The rift between Macandrew and the provincial councillors continued to grow. In his opening address in April 1869 Macandrew made his usual lament about central government's policies, noting gloomily that whereas before the provinces were able to raise loans, these were now forbidden.[27] Since taxes were likely to be spent on maintaining a standing army in the North Island, development would likely be halted.[28] He announced that, while in Wellington, he and Vogel had omitted to request the council's change to the Constitution Act seeking authority to dissolve a council without re-electing the superintendent, and he now declined to call a new election. All of this simply added to the council's existing dissatisfaction with both Macandrew and Vogel.[29]

Agitation increased when the session commenced without an Executive Council because several members had resigned without notice, leaving the province with no responsible governance. Vogel was criticised for his poor management, and for his expedient but dubious method of funding the proposed southern trunk railway by creating a private company.[30] When censured for depressing land prices by releasing too much land for sale, he seized the chance to resign. Turning his back on Otago, Vogel departed for Auckland in May 1869 to edit the *Daily Southern Cross* and continue his political career in the north. Following his appointment as colonial treasurer in June, he rapidly lost sympathy with Otago's apparently selfish grievances, and by the time he secured the premiership in 1873, Vogel had determined that the greater good of the country came before the prolonging of provincial privileges.

Without Vogel's support, and considered pro-squatter by his Clutha farmer constituents who were now demanding his resignation from parliament, Macandrew was attacked for his role in the passing of the Otago Hundreds Regulation Act 1869 with its high compensation rates for grazing lessees, and for his application for an earlier £50,000 loan – both seen as primarily benefiting the pastoralists.[31] The provincial council was divided over the issue of land use and was now ignoring wider issues, but despite the continuing deadlock Macandrew refused to dissolve the council.[32] His concluding remarks for the 1869 session were mildly hypocritical in the light of his usual party-politicking in the General Assembly: 'It is a matter of deepest regret that there does not appear to be this unity of action among us ... Gentlemen, let each and all of us strive to be influenced less by party spirit, and more by enlightened patriotism.'[33]

The council convened again in December 1869 with a full agenda of local matters and was remarkably productive: they ratified the reunion of Otago and Southland, endorsed the construction of the Port Chalmers to Dunedin railway, and agreed to build the southern trunk railway. They agreed to gazette new Hundreds, and to release land at Martins Bay and Preservation Inlet for settlement in order to encourage further immigration.

National politics

Dissatisfaction with Stafford's administration wrought change in Wellington. On 9 June 1869 the General Assembly supported Fox's want-of-confidence motion regarding Stafford's management of the land wars.[34]

The land wars were initially triggered in the 1840s by tensions over disputed land purchases. By the 1860s, as settler numbers rose and Europeans came to exceed the Māori population, there was increasing pressure 'to obtain more land under Māori control'.[35] Widespread and sustained clashes followed in Taranaki, Waikato, the East Coast and central North Island.[36] One besieged Taranaki settler expounded his view of the wars in a letter to his son in England. He deplored the separation proposal that appeared to be gaining support, and laid the blame for the fighting entirely on Māori:

> The troubles with the Rebel Moaries [sic] – instead of decreasing are on the increase. Many of us are expecting a fearful crisis – if we were but a united people – we could meet our difficulties and subdue our enemies. The settlers in the Southern Island are getting up a combination to grant no more money to carry on the War – a most dastardly proceeding – this seems to be paving the way for a separation of the two Islands … The Rebel Moaries seem bent upon bringing about a War of Races – our efforts to prevent this have failed – we have exhausted every means – we shall I believe be compelled – surely against our wishes – to meet the Moari – and try our strength – There can be only one result – it is very sad to think of it – No savage race in my opinion ever had so good a chance of raising themselves to a high state of civilization – they have everything to gain and absolutely nothing to lose – I can truly say from my own experience and observation – that the settlers of New Zealand have done all they could do to place the Moaries on a perfect equality with themselves – we have wanted but one law for both races – we have been desirous that our privileges should be shared alike – as well as our responsibilities – we have met with every opposition in carrying this out by the Humanity Mongers who professing to be the Friends of the Moaries in practice have been their greatest enemies – and our base calumniators.[37]

Fox was now premier, and his anti-centralist ministry, with Vogel as colonial treasurer, had an opportunity to calm these fears and revitalise the provincial system. However, they were challenged on 14 July by Edward C.J. Stevens, the member for Selwyn, an electorate to the south of Christchurch. Stevens, a land and commission agent, a director of the Christchurch Press Company and a close friend of Stafford, considered that the piecemeal creation of counties was creating weak provinces; all legislation could be done by the General Assembly instead, which would save around £10,000 a year. He resurrected an 1868 Assembly motion that no more provinces should be created, and moved that any further constitutional changes should incorporate eight principles. These included curbing taxation, allocating loan repayments from provincial land funds, and immediately increasing colonisation.[38]

Stevens' third principle was the most radical: 'that Provincial Government should cease to exist, and a system of local government be established throughout the Colony'. He proposed the devolution of 'full powers for management of local affairs' and funding to the new organisations. These changes, he believed, 'would unite the colony in a strong nationality'.[39]

In a week-long debate most speakers – including members of Fox's 'provincial' ministry – agreed that change was necessary, but the majority were unsure of what they wanted.[40] A cautious motion to postpone further change was accepted on 20 July: it was agreed that 'in the present condition of the colony, it is inopportune to decide questions involving great constitutional changes; that such should more properly be left for the consideration of the next parliament.'[41]

Otago benefited immediately from the change of government. Macandrew presented his Otago Settlements Bill, which aimed to promote settlement on the West Coast by offering land at a lower price than had been permitted by the Otago land regulations. It was passed with no discussion: the Legislative Council made two minor adjustments and it became law in record time.[42]

In August Macandrew successfully shepherded the Otago Loan Bill through the House.[43] This sought to overturn the ban on provincial borrowing, and included a request that Otago be permitted to raise a loan of £50,000 for public works. In a debate that would have infuriated members from other provinces, Macandrew catalogued Otago's assets: the estimated revenue for 1869 was £301,000; the value of unsold land £3.1million; main roads and bridges £1.2million; public buildings £90,000; school buildings £50,000; the dredge £10,000; wharves and harbour £187,000. Total debt stood at £650,000. He claimed to feel 'ashamed almost, at asking for a paltry loan of £50,000'.[44]

Treasurer Vogel was supportive: providing that the loan was 'a strictly local one, raised by trustees, to be met out of pastoral revenue, the government would make no objection.'[45] Stafford, however, was opposed to the provinces competing in the money markets, 'depreciating each other's stock' while using their unreserved land as security. He suggested that larger loans at lower rates could be obtained if the colony as a whole borrowed for a cohesive programme of public works. The Legislative Council concurred. They agreed with the member for Mataura, Francis Dillon Bell – a long-term partner with Stafford, C.W. Richmond and William Steward in the extensive Central Otago Idaburn run, and a man with unassailable pastoralist credentials – that 'to mortgage the pastoral rents is tantamount to saying that there shall be no more legislation on the land question.'[46] Macandrew's bill was rejected.[47] Stafford had enunciated an important principle: the colony could achieve more by acting in unity. His advice bore fruit within the year.

The noose of centralism was slowly tightening. Stevens' motion to abolish the provinces, although lost, provoked council defensiveness and a shift in stance.

The following year Otago councillors responded in their own forum with the motion 'that it is expedient that steps should be taken with a view to uniting the Province of Otago with the Province of Canterbury'.[48] Then, following an extraordinary financial statement from Vogel in which he proposed to borrow £6 million to invest in colonial migration and infrastructure in the next decade, the Otago councillors asked the superintendent to request the union of Otago and Canterbury, to be decided by three members of each council and ratified by all members.[49]

The prickly council next demonstrated its independence, shocking even arch-separationist Macandrew with its refusal to accept a loan for public works from the General Assembly under the just-passed Immigration and Public Works Act 1870, unless this was 'modified in such a way as will leave the Middle Island free to deal with its own finances for the promotion of Public Works and Immigration'.[50] Councillors claimed the only way to achieve such a result was 'by financial separation of the two Islands'. Macandrew, closely attuned to the realpolitik, knew the provinces' powers were now irretrievably trimmed and responded, saying: 'If Provincial Government is to stand in the way of peopling the province, developing its mineral resources and intersecting it with Railways, then perish Provincial Government!' This comment likely cost him his Clutha seat three months later.[51]

Relations between the superintendent and the council worsened. Just two weeks later the council formally sought 'Insular and Financial Separation between the North and Middle Islands'.[52] Macandrew and his council were at loggerheads. Over the next six years he would propose increasingly radical solutions to avoid abolition in an effort to retain their support, but to no avail: by 1876 the provinces were finished.

Chapter 12

Macandrew had always promoted immigration with a passion, and it had been one of three leading topics of his election platform when he was nominated as superintendent in 1860. In 1868 he wrote, 'The great want of the Province now is population; and one of the duties to which the Government is earnestly devoting itself is, that of influencing an adequate stream of immigration of a suitable class from the Mother Country.'[1] In 1870 he was more outspoken. Never afraid of planning on a grand scale, he claimed in his address to council:

> Instead of 65,000 – the present population of Otago and Southland – I
> believe that several millions of industrious people might find the means of
> comfort and independence within our borders ... There can be no doubt
> that there are in the overgrown countries of Europe thousands of industrious
> people, possessed, more or less, of a means of their own, whose condition
> would be greatly bettered by coming here.[2]

Although he favoured English-speaking immigrants for the colony, particularly Scottish ones, unlike some Otago citizens Macandrew was not opposed to other races coming to New Zealand. For example, he welcomed the arrival of Chinese gold miners in the Otago goldfields. His dealings with Ngāi Tahu in Otago were, however, inconsistent and at times destructive.

Like many settlers, Macandrew was insensitive to Māori cultural practices and impatient with their traditional allocation of rights to land, fishing grounds and other resources. As historian Jonathan West notes, 'The subtlety of ... property rights would have been hard for British settlers to understand even if they had wanted to, which they seldom did other then in the context of buying land from Māori.'[3] As a member of both the provincial council and the General Assembly, and particularly as superintendent, Macandrew's input to the controversy surrounding the Princes Street reserve in Dunedin probably did as much to shape his reputation in Otago as did his incarceration. Both events generated strong responses that linger to the present day.

Chinese miners come to Otago

By 1865 the easy pickings of alluvial gold had been garnered and the gold rush peaked. The number of miners in the district fell from over 18,000 to around 6000.[4] The Otago Chamber of Commerce was eager to attract workers from Victoria to Otago and, having sought assurance from the provincial secretary that 'the persons and properties of any Chinese coming here would be protected', began negotiations with 'a leading Chinese merchant in Melbourne … on the subject of the introduction of Chinese to this Province'.[5] 'There were particular reasons for choosing Chinese people: they were thought to be hardworking, inoffensive and willing to rework abandoned claims, and they preferred to return eventually to their homeland.'[6]

Some Otago miners were swift to oppose this move. A gathering of 200 at Mt Ida composed a memorandum to Superintendent Dick:

> The assertion of the Dunedin Chamber of Commerce that the Chinese
> will be content to work ground which the Europeans would not consider
> remunerative, shows that they are ignorant of the nature of the Otago Gold
> Fields, the poorest of which have been made remunerative by the investment
> of capital. It would be a great injustice to the hard-working and enterprising
> European miner, to allow the product of his enterprise and toil to be usurped
> by the Mongolians, whose dishonest propensities are notorious, and whose
> immorality would seriously injure the social character of Otago.[7]

Their views were not universally shared. The *Otago Daily Times* described a miners' meeting at the Dunstan goldfield, where it was felt that 'the introduction of Chinese into this Province would be productive of most beneficial results, especially in this district, which affords an almost unlimited field for the profitable employment of Chinese labor, and without interference with the European miner'.[8]

Chinese miners began to arrive on the goldfields, and by 1871 it was reported that 3561 were at work in Otago.[9] Anti-Chinese prejudice soon surfaced, and there were so many reports of harassment and physical assaults that Macandrew was moved to issue a proclamation in 1868:

> Notice is hereby given that, the Chinese having come to Otago under
> promises made by successive Superintendents that those who came would
> be fully protected, the Provincial Government is determined to fulfil that
> promise; and the Police are strictly enjoined to keep a protective watch over
> the Chinese population in their respective districts; and in case of their being
> made aware of any injury having been illegally inflicted on any of the Chinese
> population, to lose no time in bringing the perpetrators thereof to justice.

The Superintendent relies upon the assistance of all right thinking, well disposed people, to aid him in affording that protection to the Chinese, which
every person residing within a British settlement has a right to count upon.[10]

In 1870 the *Otago Witness* editor noted, 'Nearly every steamer from Melbourne brings some 15 or 20 of them [Chinese immigrants] to our shores, and
on one occasion they have come hither in hundreds.'[11] He suggested that recent
harassment of Chinese miners in California could lead to increased numbers
moving to New Zealand, and raised questions about the consequences of such an
influx. In California it was reported that the Chinese had 'cut out' the Caucasian
workman in many trades, greatly reducing the rates of wages', while in Victoria
'there has been no little outcry regarding the immorality of the Chinese camps'. If
employed in preference to European labour, he felt, 'disturbances would ensue'.[12]
This concern was sufficient to be considered by a select committee of Otago Provincial Council in 1871, which resolved 'that for the best interests of the country
it is desirable that no Chinese shall be permitted to come into this colony'. The
committee recommended to the council 'the advisability of passing an Act to
close the auriferous mines of the Colony from being worked by Chinese arriving
in the Colony after the passing of the Act'. Their report stated:

> The subject of Chinese immigration is a matter which ought to receive
> consideration from the legislature, involving as it does, grave political and
> social questions. The presence of a limited number in the Colony is not
> a matter of great importance, although not beneficial, as they eventually
> leave the Colony, taking with them all the money they may have saved, and
> rarely settle as colonists. But if no check be imposed, they may come in such
> numbers as may lead to serious difficulty, and check the influx of European
> immigrants. On these grounds your Commissioners desire to call the
> attention of the legislature to the subject.[13]

Macandrew was unmoved by the committee's advice and that year sat on a
parliamentary select committee appointed to consider a petition signed by 155
gold miners at Switzers in Central Otago. The petition demanded bans on both
'the further influx of Chinese' and the granting of miners' rights to Chinese, and
claimed that 'unless the most stringent measures are taken, the result will be
bloodshed and anarchy'.[14] After examining 13 witnesses and quizzing goldfields
wardens and numerous police officials, the committee declared Chinese immigrants were 'industrious and frugal ... as orderly citizens as Europeans'. Their
presence appeared to pose no threat to the morality or security of the community: they were unlikely to introduce disease and 'were well adapted for menial

and light mechanical and for agricultural occupations'. As a rule they turned to good account ground that would not pay the European miner, and their presence had not 'entailed any additional police expenditure'. Macandrew voted in favour of all clauses of the report, but opposed an amendment that sought to impose heavy import duties on rice and opium, and a poll tax of at least £2 per person. The amendment was defeated and the committee concluded that there were 'no sufficient grounds shown for the exclusion of the Chinese'.[15] Their place in New Zealand society was consolidated when large numbers were employed on railway building projects in the 1870s, alongside a new wave of European immigrants.

The Princes Street Reserve

In 1844 during negotiations over the purchase of the Otago Block, Māori requested that:

> there should be made … and guaranteed to them, certain small reserves, including two at Otepoti, now known as Dunedin … one near the stream which crosses Princes Street, near Rattray Street, and the other fronting a small sandy cove to the eastward of the site afterwards occupied by the manse and the land adjoining.[16]

At the time the company agent had refused the request and the chiefs had departed. However, they had returned a few days later on the assurance that the land would be set aside for them. During the early days of European settlement, Otakou Māori, dependent on access to Dunedin markets for income, had used the reserves as places to land fish for sale, beach their waka and camp overnight. By 1858, however, any records of Māori entitlement to the reserves appeared to have been lost.

Although originally waterfront land, by the mid-1800s reclamation work had removed the second reserve some distance from the shoreline, and it now fronted Dunedin's main street and was considered valuable real estate. The area had become the site of various public buildings, including a hospital and 'immigrants' barracks and stores for luggage, constabulary depot, &c., &c.'[17] During the gold rush, commissioners had let the sections, and the commissioner of Crown lands had retained the rental income, which now amounted to a considerable sum.

In 1867 a legal battle erupted over ownership of the Princes Street Reserve and entitlement to the rent.[18] In August Ngāi Tahu chief Teone (John) Topi Patuki, of Ruapuke Island in Foveaux Strait, petitioned Queen Victoria to instruct the governor of the colony not to endorse a bill that was likely to be submitted to him for royal assent, 'whose object may be to decide by legislation on rights

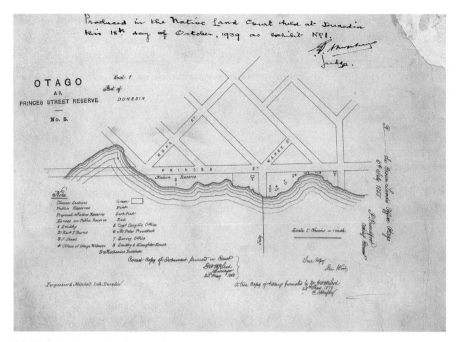

The Princes Street Reserve was originally on the harbour foreshore, but reclamation moved the shoreline approximately one kilometre. DAHG D497/22/e – Otago A.2, Princes Street Reserve No.8, 1939. ANZ, Dunedin

which are capable of being tested judicially'.[19] He also sent the petition to parliament, asking that the government 'refrain from passing a Bill relative to the Dunedin Princes Street Reserve or its rents, now or presently to be submitted to the General Assembly of New Zealand, or any other law of similar principle and tendency'.[20]

In his preamble to the Queen, Patuki noted that the bill was likely to be passed by a legislature in which his people had no representative:

[They] are thereby subjected to the control of a popularly elected body, not only not representing their interest, but in many respects having interests altogether opposed to theirs; whose deliberations are conducted in a language of which very few Maoris have any knowledge, and whose laws, affecting as they do all races of Her Majesty's subjects in the Colony, are rarely published in the only language known to the Maori ... questions affecting their rights should upon no account be submitted to a political body wherein they are not represented, but, on the contrary, referred to and left to the decision of Her Majesty's courts of law and equity.[21]

If passed, he said, the bill would deprive his people of the rent that had accrued from letting of the reserve and 'render nugatory any effort which he, on their behalf, is making, or may hereafter make, in the Supreme Court of the colony, or elsewhere to recover possession of the land itself'.[22]

Rights to the land had become confusing. When approached by Patuki, Walter Mantell – a Grey appointee who had replaced Cargill in 1851 and was now commissioner of Crown lands for Otago – could find no record of any town reserves for Māori.[23] The bodies responsible for the sale and allocation of land in the first days of the settlement – the New Zealand Company and the Otago Lay Association – no longer existed. Mantell recommended in April 1853 that Governor Grey reserve a strip of foreshore between Princes Street and the harbour, extending from the manse site in Jetty Street to Hope Street, as a place for Māori to stay when they visited Dunedin.[24] In June he had received the governor's approval. He was unaware that Cargill had reserved all waterfront sections for public use in 1848; following the passing of the Constitution Act, the provincial council had placed land reserved for the public under the 'Board of Commissioners for the Management of the Public Lands of Dunedin'.[25] Grey's staff had failed to gazette the reserve, however, and the absence of records following Mantell's departure from Dunedin meant the competing claims were not revealed until 1858.

When central government sought to clarify ownership of the reserve in April 1865, an Otago Provincial Council select committee reported that Mantell's 1853 recommendation to set apart the land in question 'was made and sanctioned without the knowledge or concurrence of the several parties interested, to wit, the Provincial Government and the land purchasers whose rights were invaded by such a reserve'.[26] The committee demanded that 'the money which has been derived from the same [the rent from the Princes Street Reserve] will be restored to the Province as its rightful owner'.[27]

The Weld ministry, in which Mantell was minister for Native affairs, disagreed with the provincial council findings and launched its own enquiry, and later that year Macandrew was called before a select committee in Wellington.[28] Chaired by its sole Otago member, his brother-in-law William Reynolds, it too was attempting to establish the ownership of the Princes Street Reserve.[29] Macandrew's contribution was slight but definite: 'I do not remember ever having seen in the Town of Dunedin a plan with this specific object marked on it, but I was well aware that the water frontage had been reserved for public purposes subsequent to its having been laid off in one-quarter acre sections'.[30]

The committee concluded that 'the land forming the Dunedin Reserves, having been reserved from sale for a specific public purpose, was wrongly set aside for the use of the Natives'. It recommended that 'a Crown grant be issued in favour of the Municipality of Dunedin, as trustees and representatives of the local public, as was evidently the intention of the New Zealand Company, conveyed in the instructions of Mr. T.C. Harington to Colonel Wakefield'.[31]

With that, the House passed a resolution, 29 to 17, that the reserve set aside in 1846 'should be vested in the Superintendent of Otago in trust for the municipality of Dunedin, as originally intended' – with, as Reynolds noted, 'the whole of the members of the [Weld] Government giving it their most strenuous opposition'.[32]

The subsequent Stafford ministry accepted the House ruling and issued the province with a Crown grant for the land on 11 January 1866, which Grey signed – although 10 months later he would claim that he had not intended to approve it, but had endorsed it at a rushed meeting of the Executive Council 'in ignorance of what I was doing'.[33] Grey actually supported the Ngāi Tahu claim. (Professor Alan Ward, in evidence given to the Waitangi Tribunal in 1991 during its investigation of the Ngāi Tahu claim, suggested a political reason for the signing: the unpopular Stafford government, having displaced the well-liked Weld ministry, was dependent on the support of Otago members. The quid pro quo was their promise to give the Otago Provincial Council a grant for the reserve.)[34]

A bill was introduced to remit the accrued rent to the superintendent, but was narrowly lost in the Legislative Council in September 1866. It was resurrected in 1867, at which point the House passed it again, but was allowed to lapse in the Legislative Council.[35]

Despite having granted the reserve to provincial ownership, the government reversed its stance in August 1866 on receipt of a letter to the governor from Hori Kerei Taiaroa, son of the Ōtākau chief Te Matenga Taiaroa.[36] Taiaroa wrote, 'I request you to make clear to us the case in respect of [the Princes Street Reserve]. I have heard that it is being taken away by the Pakehas of the town.' He claimed the reserve for the 'Natives of Otago', or payment for it.[37] In a move that surprised the province, Stafford backed Taiaroa and told Superintendent Dick in October that 'the Government is of opinion that the question of the validity of the grant should be submitted to a proper judicial tribunal ... the Supreme Court'.[38] Dick initially declined this proposal, but had no choice when Stafford withheld assent for an ordinance, passed to vest the Princes Street Reserve in the Dunedin City Council, until the validity of the Crown grant was tested in the Supreme Court.[39]

In February 1867, following Macandrew's re-election as superintendent and the commencement of the auditor-general's enquiry into his earlier misdemeanours, and with the scrap over the goldfields management looming, antagonism between Wellington and Dunedin created a serious impediment to any negotiated settlement.

Grey and Stafford were operating on a larger stage: deadly skirmishing with some North Island Māori had continued throughout the decade, and any conflict with South Island tribes was to be avoided. Politics aside, their sympathies lay with Taiaroa, not the querulous Otagoites. Ten years later Grey would state: 'I believed they [Ngāi Tahu] had a right that these reserves should be made, and under these circumstances I should have reserved the land … I should have carried out what I believed to be the agreement … I regarded the promise to make reserves for the Natives as part of the purchase-money of the block.'[40]

Macandrew was one of 16 Otago parliamentarians who signed a letter to Stafford in July 1867 claiming the land in question 'was and is quite unsuitable for the use of the Natives for … landing and encampment … and that it has never been used by them for such purposes.'[41] The letter reiterated the province's right to the reserve and asked that the £6000 in accumulated rent be paid to the superintendent: the city council had commissioned public works in expectation of receipt of the sum and urgently needed to pay for them. In yet another policy reversal, Stafford replied that the government was 'of the opinion that the payment requested should be made, and will consider in what manner this can be legally effected.'[42] The money would be paid, but on condition that Macandrew would refund it should Otago lose the forthcoming case in the Supreme Court.[43]

Macandrew declined: agreement to the condition would have implied 'a doubt on my part as to the rightful ownership of this money, and because it appears to me to be inexpedient to expend money to which there is not an absolute right.'[44] Convinced the Supreme Court would find in Otago's favour, he suggested letting the Assembly decide on ownership by reviving the bill to remit the rents to the province, which had been passed by the Lower House the previous year but lost by one vote at its second reading in the Upper House. Stafford agreed, unexpectedly, and reintroduced the bill to the House on 7 August, where it passed its readings and went to the Upper House on 12 September. Uncertain whether it would become law, Macandrew caved in and assured Stafford he would refund the rents to the government if they were paid to the province and it lost the case. He now suggested, 'On this being done, I see no object to pressing the Bill now before the Legislative Council.'[45] With this offer, Stafford allowed the bill to lapse. On behalf of the province, Macandrew accepted £6031.18.9 from the colonial treasurer on 24 September 1867.

That was not the end of the matter. The following year the payment was challenged in the House; another select committee was appointed to discover why the bill had been defeated in two consecutive sessions of the Assembly, and to investigate the 'manner in which the money was finally paid to the Provincial Council'.[46] This select committee found that the petitions committee had upheld Patuki's petition because the Supreme Court case was pending, and considered this was 'practically a rejection of the Bill', which had been allowed to lapse. It noted also that Macandrew had offered to repay the rents if Otago lost in court, and that despite a 'technical irregularity' in the manner of its payment, the province had kept the grant.

During these negotiations Macandrew had written to Native Minister James Richmond with a counter-offer: to set aside a piece of land at Pelichet Bay on the north side of Otago Harbour, and to spend £1000 on a 'Native hostelry' 'made solely with a desire to benefit the natives, and to prevent much useless and expensive litigation'.[47] This would replace a Māori hostelry built with colonial funds in 1860 beside the Toitū Stream, in an area now known as the Exchange. Once a popular marketplace, it had been demolished in 1865 when Princes Street was widened.[48] However, the offer was withdrawn when the province decided to defend the Supreme Court proceedings.

Taiaroa's letter and Topi Patuki's petition bore fruit. In October 1867 Grey signed an Order in Council directing that £400 be allocated to the 'Natives claiming to be interested in the Princes Street Reserve, Dunedin, in prosecuting a suit to test the validity of the grant of the said reserve made on the eleventh day of January, 1866'.[49] Reynolds, well after the event, suspected a conspiracy:

> from some cause or other, which I cannot account for without imputing motives which would be unworthy of any Government, the Stafford Ministry supplied Mr Mantell with some £400 of colonial funds, to enable him to take action against the Otago Provincial Government for the cancellation of the Crown grant. This proceeding on the part of Mr Stafford is all the more strange, seeing that he was not only a member of the Select Committee, but also spoke in favour of the resolution in the House and voted for it.[50]

Two years later on 27 September 1869, the Supreme Court delivered judgment in Regina v. Macandrew; it found for the province and declared: 'This reserve being shown on the record to be illegal and void, did not come within the scope of [the Public Reserves Act, 1864]'.[51] Six weeks later, when the Appeal Court upheld the judgement, one journalist commented: 'It would seem that their Honours have not a very favourable opinion of the merits of the case.'[52]

Despite the outcome, Mantell, a legislative councillor since 1866, advised the Māori plaintiffs to take their case to the Privy Council, a move that prevented the provincial council transferring the land and all back-rent to the city council.[53] In November 1872, with the Privy Council appeal looming, Macandrew suggested that Colonial Treasurer Vogel and Mantell, as representatives of the two sides, should meet to find a compromise:

> I may observe that, in agreeing to the course indicated, I am influenced by a desire that a reasonable sum shall be paid to the natives rather than be thrown away on litigation, and not because I think there is the shadow of a claim. In fact, as I am advised, the claim on the part of the Maoris has not a leg to stand upon.[54]

Vogel and Mantell negotiated an agreement to buy the land from Ngāi Tahu to discontinue the case, and the city council took ownership of the reserve when the Dunedin Reserves Management Ordinance 1873 received the governor's assent. The payment was made on 22 January 1874. As one journalist recorded: 'We proceeded to a house where Mr Watt was distributing the purchase money for the Princes Street reserve. About £5000 was paid away, in sums ranging from £850 to £2 10s.'[55]

Ngāi Tahu were not satisfied. Taiaroa made a further petition to Native Minister McLean: 'The amount of rent owing to us is £6000; I desire that you should pay it at the present time, as money has already been paid on the land to the extent of £5000, having been discovered that it was Maori land.'[56] Macandrew's reaction to the petition was sharp: 'If the Superintendent and Provincial Government (of Otago) had not understood that the money then paid was to be a full settlement of all demands, they would never have agreed to pay the £5000 – money to which … the Natives were not entitled, either in law or equity; but they agreed to pay the money and have done with all these so-called claims.'[57] Taiaroa's petition was heard by the Native Affairs Committee of the General Assembly, to whom he vowed, 'The question of the ownership of the land we gave up at the time we accepted the £5000. I shall not stop urging for the £6000.'[58]

The committee presented its report on 21 November 1877, by which time the provinces had been abolished. It concluded:

> it is highly desirable to remove all further grounds of complaint; and the Committee is of opinion that a further payment should be made to the

> Natives of the rents which had accrued prior to the issue of the Crown grant, or a reserve should be made of land to that value, for the benefit of the Natives interested.[59]

William Fox entered a dissenting opinion, in which he claimed that the original payment was intended by Vogel and Macandrew to be final; Macandrew signed Fox's opinion.

Two weeks later Macandrew made a last-ditch attempt to block the payment. In Committee of Supply, fellow Dunedin member Arthur Burns moved that the item "'Final settlement of Native claims to the Dunedin Princes Street Reserves, £5,000" be struck out'.[60] Macandrew reiterated that the original payment of £5000 had been a final payment: 'That was the condition upon which the money was paid, and that was the condition on which it was received. It would only encourage a bad state of feeling among the Natives, and tend to demoralise them, if these claims were to be brought up year after year.'[61] He accused the Native Affairs Committee of knowing nothing about the issue, and suggested 'some of the members of the Committee thought Otago would have to pay the money and not the colony, or they would have voted differently'.[62] As the *Evening Star* reported, 'He was surprised beyond measure at the action of the honorable member for Avon (William Rolleston) in this matter. That honorable gentleman was actuated by mere sentiment in pandering to the Natives, as in this case he had done.'[63] The motion was lost by a narrow margin of 23 to 28. A second payment of £5000 was made on 4 May 1880.

Ngāi Tahu continued to argue that they had been wrongfully deprived of their land. Their grievances were eventually heard over a century later in 1987 by the Waitangi Tribunal, which was 'not satisfied that the [New Zealand] company or Crown representatives made any such promises for the two reserves at the upper harbour foreshore'.[64] The tribunal rejected the claim that the governor was entitled to create the reserve (in 1853) and the further claim that only 'administrative bungling' prevented it being done. It noted the reserve was 'by all accounts unsuitable for the purpose for which it was ostensibly created', and concluded: 'We find it somewhat incongruous to be asked to hold that it was a breach of the Treaty by the Crown, to fail effectively to create a reserve which was not suitable for the purpose to which it was needed.' The tribunal was 'unable to find that the Treaty imposed any obligation on the Crown to provide a permanent hostelry [on the reserve] vested in Ngāi Tahu, to meet a temporary need'. The report ended: 'Regrettably, but understandably, this money was not invested by Ngāi Tahu in a property of their own in Dunedin, but was, as we have seen, distributed quite widely among the tribe. Had it been so invested, and the property retained, almost certainly we would never have heard of this.'[65]

Macandrew was equally unsympathetic to a parallel land claim by Otago Māori for the 'Otago Tenths'. In 1840 the New Zealand Company had agreed that one-tenth of all sections offered in the blocks of land made available for European settlement would be reserved for local tangata whenua. Governor Fitzroy had reiterated this commitment in 1844, but Governor Grey had ignored it when he confirmed the company's title to the Otago Block in 1846.[66] The Native Land Court, established in 1865 to expedite the transfer of collectively owned Māori land to settlers, sat in Dunedin in May 1868 and adjudicated on the Otago Tenths. It awarded 2100 acres (850ha) to 35 Ngāi Tahu claimants, but because most land fit for habitation was now occupied, Māori were offered just 400ha of land at Tautuku on the remote south-east coast of Otago. Macandrew bitterly opposed even this, 'on the grounds that the Otago Province had not been heard in court'.[67]

The Maori prisoners

On the day that Mr Justice Ward delivered his judgment on the Princes Street Reserve in the Dunedin Supreme Court, 27 September 1869, 94 Pakakohe men – a hapū (subtribe) of Ngāti Ruanui – appeared at a special session of the Supreme Court in Wellington. They were charged with high treason under the hastily passed Disturbed Districts Act 1869, which suspended habeas corpus in conflicted districts along with other usual legal protections.[68] The men had been captured inland of Patea in June during the final days of the second Taranaki war, and incarcerated in a hulk on Wellington Harbour. On 12 October, 74 of them were found guilty and sentenced to three years' hard labour.[69] The government now had to find a prison that would take the large group. Macandrew, apparently without consultation and to the surprise of many Otago citizens, offered to accommodate them in Dunedin.

The editor of the *Otago Daily Times* foresaw numerous problems: the men would 'naturally be insubordinate'; it would 'not be safe to rely implicitly on their good behaviour', it would be hard to 'infuse energy into them', and 'the discipline of the gaol' would be endangered.[70] He noted that Canterbury had declined to take them because 'the expense and responsibility attending them would outweigh the value of their labour … and they would probably succeed in escaping.' He could only conclude that 'the Provincial Government was moved by a purely patriotic desire to assist the General government in a dilemma, and that the warmth of its patriotism led it to overlook those practical considerations by which it ought to have been guided.'[71] It is more likely that Macandrew was playing a longer game: he suspected the Princes Street Reserve decision would be appealed and saw an opportunity to curry favour with Wellington and demonstrate his generosity.

The 74 prisoners arrived by sea on 6 November 1869 and were housed in Dunedin gaol. For two and a half years they laboured on the city's roads and recreation fields and shaped the Botanic Gardens. By and large the Dunedin community took them to heart – several citizens were prosecuted for throwing tobacco to the working prisoners – and their conduct was praised by the prison staff. However, the unhealthy accommodation, cold weather and ill health resulted in the deaths of many of the men, who were then buried in unmarked paupers' graves in the Southern Cemetery.[72] The 51 survivors departed for Wellington on the government steamer *Luna* on 10 March 1872 escorted by Donald McLean, the Native minister and minister for colonial defence, and by Macandrew, a firm friend of the ruling Fox ministry. Macandrew's address to the departing Māori revealed his Eurocentric values and was translated by McLean:

> My friends, depend upon it, if the Maories [sic] desire to become rich, prosperous and powerful like the Europeans, they must do as the Europeans do – that is to say they must respect and obey the Queen's laws ... I should have been glad had you sent for your wives and families and remained in the Province. We have here plenty land, plenty gold, and plenty hard work, all of which, I am sure, we should be willing to share with our Maori fellow subjects. Indeed, I had suggested to Mr McLean that the country around Lake Hawea would be well adapted for you: plenty fish, plenty bush, and good land for cultivation ...[73]

In his response, rangatira Ngawaka Taurua promised to be obedient to the Queen's laws and live in peace and harmony with Europeans, but was sceptical about the Lake Hawea offer 'unless the soil was suitable'. Macandrew 'was then landed at his own residence [on the peninsula] amid the hearty cheers of the Maories'.[74]

The affair is a clear example of Macandrew's by now predictable behaviour: the decision to accommodate the prisoners appears to have been his alone and made with little regard for cost, the main incentive likely being his own political gain; he made a spontaneous offer of land, which he knew he would not have to honour; and he grasped the opportunity to play to an appreciative audience. His attitude to Ngāi Tahu's claims for the reserve and the Otago Tenths, and to the Pakakohe prisoners, is a clear example of European colonial thinking of the day.

This can also be seen in the words of one journalist who, in response to a Ngāi Tahu complaint about the unfair treatment of their claim, in 1874 wrote:

> His charge against our Courts of favouring the European cause is one which is not infrequently made by natives who fail to understand the system under which their lands have been, and are being, transferred to European hands.[75]

Macandrew's views on the matter were probably representative of most Otago settlers. Indeed, the provincial council, the city council and the media supported him every time the matter of reserves was raised. However, as the superintendent and provincial figurehead of the time, he has often been cited as the one responsible for depriving Ngāi Tahu of their land within Dunedin and Otago.

Chapter 13

From 1870–76 the General Assembly and Otago Provincial Council were occupied by 'questions involving great Constitutional changes', as economic conditions fluctuated, political views evolved, and fledgling parties in both bodies confirmed their approaches to governing the country.[1] Stafford, premier from 1865–69, had been faced with a determined and well-organised provincialist opposition, and although he had been able to modify the Constitution Act, without firm commitment from his supporters he was unable to make the major change that he wanted: the abolition of the provinces.

Transformation began to emerge when Vogel became responsible for the colony's sagging economy in 1869, but it took dire financial straits to hasten major change. As colonial treasurer, then as premier from April 1873, Vogel drove the political agenda and shaped the government of the colony, forcing Macandrew and his Otago supporters into a defensive stance. In 1875, abandoned by their allies, the provincialists were outvoted: after 24 years the provinces were abolished, and Macandrew's beloved Otago ceased to exist.

The New Zealand gold rushes had produced a surge in population that boosted the demand for imports. The resulting injection of money into the economy led to increased inflation and rising prices, followed by growing unemployment as the rushes wound down. The slump that ensued was exacerbated by a worldwide depression that followed the American Civil War and the Austro–Prussian War, which in turn led to reduced earnings for the colony's major exports of wool and livestock, and the collapse of emerging industries such as flax processing. Demands for government intervention were inevitable and not original: in 1863 Premier Alfred Domett had proposed to borrow £4 million to build infrastructure in the North Island frontier districts and to introduce 20,000 settlers to the country; in 1864 Colonial Treasurer Reader Wood had proposed raising £3 million for a land settlement scheme; and in 1868 the treasurer William Fitzherbert had recommended a scheme of immigration and public works. All had failed to eventuate.[2]

This was a demanding period of Macandrew's personal life. In 1870 his nine children ranged in age from one to 21, and Eliza was in poor health. While his superintendent's salary enabled the family to live in comfort at Colinswood, the time he spent with his wife and children was greatly limited by his frequent trips around the province and the need to be in Wellington, where the House sat for upwards of four months each year.[3] Politically, his stance shifted from an acceptance of central government intervention in provincial affairs to a fervent resistance to abolition.

Vogel's immigration and public works policy

Fighting in the North Island was winding down but had left a substantial defence debt. Vogel used this to launch his proposal for increased immigration and substantial public works on 28 June 1870:

> Last year, we had in this Assembly many evidences that the colonizing spirit
> was re-awakening. During the recess, from all parts of the country, these
> evidences have been repeated, in the anxious desires expressed for a renewal
> of immigration and public works … we must set ourselves afresh to the task
> of actively promoting the settlement of the country.[4]

Vogel amazed the General Assembly, and the electorate, when he presented his financial statement: estimated receipts £1.05 million; estimated expenditure £903,523. The statement included a spectacular proposal to borrow £6 million, and to invest a total of £10 million over 10 years in a North Island trunk road, Middle Island railways, goldfield improvements, immigration, a North Island land bank, the discharge of past and future defence costs, and payments to some of the provinces.[5] He proposed the appointment of a minister of works to supervise the scheme – a role that would figure largely in Macandrew's future.

Reactions to the statement were varied. Wood was outraged, calling the scheme 'so wild, so unpractical, and so impracticable'.[6] Macandrew on the other hand was enthusiastic: 'I see in these proposals the realization of a day dream, of aspirations I have cherished for the last twenty years.'[7]

Backing came from unexpected quarters as Stafford and his supporters, including Edward Stevens and J.C. Richmond, gave Vogel's Immigration and Public Works Bill their blessing. Although critical of details, Stafford felt the proposal 'was one to which the mind of the country generally has been for some time directed'.[8] In his crusade for fiscal responsibility and effective administration, he saw it as a precursor to the abolition of the provinces:

> … if it is matured …into a great and at the same time, safe and
> prudent scheme … in a few years' time, we shall hear very little more
> about provincial administration, provincial land laws, and provincial
> mismanagement. That is one of the great merits of the scheme in my eyes,
> and one of the reasons why I have been anxious not to see it jeopardized.[9]

William Reynolds responded with predictable resolutions: the government
should divide the colony into two provinces; restrict the colonial government
to three departments and give it responsibility for colonial debt; and make all
revenue provincial, with a capitation grant to the colonial government and for
interest payments.[10] Vogel fobbed him off, saying that if the need should arise,
'there is nothing to prevent our adopting, at some future time, some such
proposals as those'.[11]

In pursuit of members' support and constituency backing in the election
scheduled for January 1871, Vogel had been careful to avoid any extreme
positions, stating that he felt it desirable 'to avoid as much as possible mixing
up organic political changes with the great colonizing question …'.[12]

Vogel's financial statement formed the basis of four Acts, passed on 12 and 13
September, to borrow and allocate funds for the various projects – which he kept
firmly in the hands of central government.[13] The provinces were to be charged
interest on the cost of their projects, but could exchange land for the repayments
if they wished.

One of the Acts was the Immigration and Public Works Act. Otago provincial
councillors were unimpressed by the restrictions it placed on their autonomy,
but the opportunistic Macandrew was prepared to accept the largesse that flowed
from it. Anticipating that provinces might be replaced by smaller bodies, and
knowing that roads boards would be entitled to a share of the funding, he presented a bill to validate an Otago ordinance to consolidate its 110 road boards
into 35 boards, each with the capacity to make bylaws and charge rates.[14] On
presenting his bill – of over 200 clauses – he claimed it had been approved by
his provincial council, and confidently stated that he did not intend to debate it
if the House would not 'validate it in its entirety'. This was provocation indeed.
Macandrew was mocked for his about-face on centralism and the Legislative
Council rejected the bill.[15] Unfazed and playing to Otago voters, his next move
on 29 August had a predictable outcome. He requested permission to raise a
loan of £650,000 for Otago public works projects. This time he received short
shrift from Vogel, who pointed out that it was inconsistent with the government's
policy of not allowing the provinces to borrow independently.[16]

A Burton Brothers portrait of Macandrew, 1870s. Presbyterian Church Archives, Knox College, Dunedin

These were typical demonstrations of Macandrew's parliamentary tactics – his blithe self-confidence, his clever use of parliamentary procedure, and his pragmatic ability to adapt to change and exploit unexpected opportunities.

Elections 1871

The political landscape had altered considerably during Macandrew's first four-year term as superintendent. Southland and Otago had reunited on 5 October 1870, peace was returning in the north, and immigration and settlement now received a mighty boost from Vogel's public works programme. Yet despite these positive events, Macandrew was forced into a vigorous defence of his stance on the provinces when the election campaigns for the superintendency, council and Assembly began in the spring of 1870.

Agitation for his resignation as the member for Clutha first surfaced in 1869 as a result of his apparent bias towards the pastoralists and his support of Premier William Fox, who had succeeded Stafford. Macandrew's critics claimed he had prevented working men from acquiring their own land, and he was attacked for undermining provincial authority through his support for Vogel's public works programme. Nor was Macandrew helped when Vogel visited Dunedin in 1870 to explain his policy and bolster Macandrew's campaign. A hostile audience ensured the rally was 'unequalled by any scene which had before occurred at a public meeting in New Zealand'. Vogel rebuked them.[17] In his opinion, they were not aiding the cause of provincialism 'by endeavouring sullenly to stand in opposition to the determination of the Assembly, that there are certain works – the work of settlement – in which it should aid the provinces, the provinces not being strong enough to carry out the work themselves'.[18] Many Otago residents thought the opposite.

Vogel's scheme offered a way to fund the proposal Macandrew presented in January 1871 to a raucous Dunedin audience of 700, during his campaign to continue as the province's leader. In his speech he admitted that he held 'strong opinions in regard to immigration, and he was not going to shirk them, even at the risk of exciting unpleasant demonstrations'.[19] He read a memorandum he had submitted to the provincial Executive Council, in which he had suggested 'that the Governor be requested to provide for the selection and transport of immigrants to this province'. He envisaged welcoming a total of 16,000 new settlers over the next 10 years: 200 families from Orkney, Shetland and the Western Isles, 50 families from the coalmining districts of the United Kingdom, and 50 families of miners from Cornwall could be settled at Preservation and Chalky inlets on the southwest coast, where he believed there was 'a splendid coal field … and we were sending away hundreds and thousands of pounds for coal at Newcastle [in New South Wales] when if we had people capable of working our own fields, we might keep this money in the country'.[20] As well, 500 Scandinavian families could be settled on Stewart Island and 200 from North America on the Catlins coast, along with 20 families each of flannel-makers and stocking-makers from Wales. Families could each be granted 20 acres (8ha) of land. Migration to the colony on this huge scale did in fact follow: over 5000 landed in Dunedin in 1876 alone, although none of Macandrew's special settlements ever took root.

It was ironic that Macandrew, once a supporter of complete separation, was now seen as a moderate provincialist and out-flanked by the ultra-separationist critics who dominated the provincial council. His changed stance emerged in a parliamentary debate on the Otago and Southland Union Bill on 22 July 1870, which he supported:

> As one who desired to see the number of the Provinces gradually reduced
> – as one who desired to see them gradually merging into each other, so that
> ultimately they might have one great and united Province in each Island
> … he looked upon [the union] as the first step towards further and more
> important amalgamations.[21]

Six months later he explained his views in an electioneering speech:

Provincialism was on its last legs, and although he had always been an ultra-provincialist, he did not see how to avert the impending change which must, in the case of Otago, come about within a few years … it was rather odd for him, as an ultra-provincialist, to go in for the centralism involved in the Public Works Scheme; but much as he was attached to the provincial system, he would not let a mere abstract idea stand in the way of public works.[22]

It was no wonder voters had trouble keeping up with Macandrew's policy shifts. His style of politics perplexed and infuriated his listeners. One asked:

How does it come about that the tide of popular opinion invariably turns in Mr. Macandrew's favor on the eve of some political change? … The great secret is, he has got diplomatic skill, and his character will never be fully revealed until that great day when he occupies a chair of diplomatic economy in the future New Zealand University.[23]

Others referred to his 'wheedling ways' and called him 'the Charmer'.[24] One Invercargill correspondent commented, 'Oh doesn't he know how to lay on the butter! So nicely and smoothly, and withal so thickly; and then doesn't he rub it in!'[25] Another was openly critical: 'The affairs of the province generally are pretty much in the same condition in which he found them. He cannot be said to have improved his position; on the other hand no serious objection can be raised against his administration.'[26] He was still 'the dreaming, speculative, scheming mortal he ever was'.[27] One writer felt Macandrew had 'proved a helpless tool in the hands of Mr. Vogel and his friends … If the electors desire to see the ruin of Otago completed, they should again return Mr. Macandrew as their Superintendent.'[28]

The election for superintendent on 20 February 1871 was a close-run race between Macandrew and Donald Reid who, it was claimed, 'is not under General Government influence – he is believed to be a thoroughly independent man.'[29] Reid wanted no truck with Vogel's grand plan and warned, accurately, that provincial lands would eventually be taken by central government to pay for public works. He did not excite everybody, however, as the *Otago Witness* reported: 'Like his opponent, he cannot boast of intellectual ability.'[30] One attendee at an election meeting in Naseby compared the two: 'Reid, as keenly alive to the interests of Otago as Macandrew, but with more limited vision … sincere enough but always unimpeachably straight … carping and personally critical.' Macandrew was 'off on his theme – the present, and the future, of his beloved Otago.'[31] Macandrew's popularity in Otago was waning. He was criticised as 'the only man who will go to the Assembly from Otago who will blindly support the present Ministry in this obnoxious policy'.[32]

Macandrew narrowly won the superintendency for a third time with just 52 per cent of the vote – Reid beat him by 140 votes in Otago, but Macandrew was saved by the people of Southland, where he outstripped Reid by 408 votes.[33] In contrast to his 1867 win, Macandrew retained his urban support but was thoroughly rejected by rural Otago – although he did manage to claw back support in Central Otago, to the bemusement of one editor: 'Mr. Macandrew has altogether been such an extraordinary man, and the people of Otago have behaved in so strange a manner towards him, that nothing which he or they could do with reference to each other would excite astonishment.'[34]

In one of only two defeats in his career, Macandrew was decisively rejected by the Clutha farmers in his bid for a General Assembly seat on 31 January 1871. He was replaced by James Thompson, who won three times as many votes. Macandrew's place in the Assembly was only secured by the voters of Port Chalmers, whom he had represented as a provincial councillor until 1867.[35] In Wellington, following an election that saw the first use of the secret ballot, the House of Representatives had a 50 per cent turnover with 39 new members out of the 78. One journalist suggested that nearly all of the new Middle Island members were separationists.[36] However, Premier Fox was reluctant to honour his August 1869 promise to consider questions involving fundamental constitutional changes until Vogel, on official business overseas from January to August 1871, should return.

Change in council

When Otago Provincial Council met in May its composition was also considerably altered, to Macandrew's detriment. The 46-member council had 17 new members, most of whom supported Reid's view of provincialism, giving him a 12-member majority.[37] According to the *North Otago Times*, the council had lost 'many "Macandrew-worshippers" – men who vote as their chieftain bids, and load him with fulsome gratitude for telling them what to say and how to act'.[38] Deadlock soon emerged, as Macandrew became increasingly estranged from his own council. In this power vacuum, the council – encouraged by the return of Southland, resentful still of subsidising the North Island peacemaking efforts, and ever hopeful that the Middle Island might win autonomy – supported a motion 'that the Province of Otago protests against the further waste of its revenues in the North Island; and ... requests the co-operation of the other

Middle Island Provinces, and especially of our powerful neighbour, Canterbury, to put a stop to it'.[39] A range of isolationist and Eurocentric attitudes is apparent in the various iterations of this motion as it evolved: 'further waste of its revenues in Maori Wars in the North Island' was amended to 'further waste of its revenues on the Maoris in the North Island', before settling on the less inflammatory final version, 'further waste of its revenues in the North Island'.

The council further demonstrated its disapproval of the government's behaviour by punishing its supporters: Reynolds, who had held portfolios continuously in the four ministries from 1872 to 1876, was dismissed as council Speaker, and the superintendent's salary was reduced from £1000 to £900. (It was reduced to £800 the following year, then reinstated at £1000 in 1873.) Macandrew now had to deal with a stone-walling council who would reject his usual techniques for seeking compromise.

Vogel moves on the provinces

The House resumed in August 1871 on Vogel's return from abroad. The public works policy had been the salient vehicle of his campaign to restart development of the colony's infrastructure, while matters of provincial versus central powers and the possibility of separation had been carefully avoided. Vogel could now count on the support of half the members, while 24 opposed his scheme and 15 were doubtful.[40]

Macandrew was a strong supporter of retrenchment, and during the regular debate on adjusting the parliamentary honorarium he suggested dispensing with it altogether. While acknowledging that, without it, few members would be able to remain in Wellington for the three-month parliamentary session, he suggested the solution to the problem might be found in increased efficiency: in his opinion, 'the legislative business of the country could be got through in one-third of the time'.[41] His next proposal still resounds with all governments: 'The cost of the Civil Service has assumed dimensions altogether beyond the circumstances and requirements of the colony, and must needs be curtailed.' He requested the government 'to amalgamate offices in every direction, where such can be effected without serious detriment to the public service', and to reduce all salaries over £400 a year by 25 per cent.[42] The motion was carried but no action followed. The severity of these suggestions contrasts with his extravagant spending as minister of the Crown six years later, although he would continue to oppose spending on anything that would not generate further wealth, and always felt public service should be a virtue in itself.

The debate on a liquor licensing bill for the colony during this session casts further light on Macandrew's libertarian views. He opposed the bill, as '[he] did not think drunkenness would be put down by legislation, unless licences were abolished altogether'; the best way to tackle the evils of alcohol would be to allow 'complete free trade of liquor'.[43] He advocated punishment for anyone who supplied intoxicated people with alcohol, and the removal of political rights for confirmed drunkards. Macandrew himself was no wowser: regular drinking was part of his lifestyle, a fact borne out by tolerant newspaper references to his alcohol consumption. He once joked that his 'mellifluous eloquence' was 'nurtured by the genial influence of "five or six tumblers of toddy"';[44] and when turning the first sod of the Dunedin, Peninsula and Ocean Beach Railway in December 1874, he would be ribbed by Reynolds about his drinking habits: 'His Honour has been boasting that he could not make a speech until he had half a dozen bottles of toddy – (laughter) – or rather glasses.'[45]

Macandrew was impatient for a resolution of the uncertainties surrounding the future of the provinces, and eager to exert provincial influence over the new colonial loan. In an attempt to mollify his increasingly reactionary provincial council, he was quick to present an Otago motion to the General Assembly. On 14 September he presented 13 resolutions that called for the amalgamation of the Middle Island provinces and its one county (Westland) into one provincial legislature, to be overseen by a lieutenant-governor. It would be financially independent, would administer waste lands consistently, and would be responsible for its share of the funds arising from the Immigration and Public Works Act 1870. The change, he said, would bring uniformity of laws, economy of administration, and local knowledge to the inevitable promulgation of counties. He deliberately excluded the North Island from his scheme, claiming it was not ready for 'provincial fusion'.[46]

Reaction, as usual, was mixed. The *Auckland Morning News* suggested Macandrew had another agenda:

> It is a difficult game the Superintendent is playing; but if he succeeds, he will have achieved a double triumph. He will have humiliated the Otago country members, who hate him most cordially, and compel them to become joints in his tail; and what is of far greater consequence to the country, he will have postponed any solid reform for a twelvemonth, and rendered the tenure of office by the Government more likely than it otherwise would be.[47]

Wellington's *Evening Post* saw uncontrolled ambition in the resolutions and depicted 'Governor Macandrew at the helm of such a very composite confederation, Mr. Reynolds vice, and the body of very disinterested Otago members as whippers-in'. The writer expressed the hope that if the resolutions came to a division, 'the good sense of the House will administer a lesson that a gentleman possessed of even his pachydermatous qualities must inevitably wince under'.[48]

In a letter to Stafford, Edward Stevens described Macandrew's resolutions as 'perfectly insane and impossible as it ignores … any of the governmental requirements or at least many most important ones, of one half of the country':

> I can hardly think it possible that Ministers can have consented to entertain such proposals, nor do I think that Vogel, although I do not consider him as having even the germ of a statesman in him, could be so perfectly stupid as to waste public time in thinking about the resolutions.[49]

Premier Fox dismissed the resolutions as incompatible with government policy, and noted that choosing the seat for a Middle Island legislature would be problematic – to which Macandrew responded: 'Cromwell would be a very good site.'[50]

Vogel's contribution to the constitutional debate was a Provincial Governments Bill that was given its second reading on 12 October 1871. It was designed, he said, to reduce 'the dimensions of the machinery and the expenditure of the provincial system … [and] to make the provincial body much more intimately related to the Superintendent'.[51] He proposed to reduce grants to the provinces; that superintendents become ex officio members of their councils; that the same electoral districts be used for both Houses, thus reducing the number of council members; and that councils be permitted to be dissolved without dismissing the superintendent and vice versa. Faced with strong opposition, however, he withdrew his bill.

Vogel's 'nibbling' technique would have reduced the role of the provincial governments in the forthcoming immigration and railways programme. Biographer Raewyn Dalziel suggests he was 'slowly but surely strangling the provincial governments', but does not see evidence of a cohesive plan.[52] It is likely, however, that Vogel was now finding the operation of two levels of government unnecessarily demanding; the removal of one layer must have looked highly attractive.

The separationists were not prepared to let the matter lie. Not content with 'the puerile attempt of the government with regard to constitutional reform', and in the absence of any attempt to discuss the matter apart from Macandrew's resolutions, an Otago dissident – William Murray, the member for Bruce – presented yet another variation of local government organisation.[53] He proposed that the country be divided into counties, these to be grouped into two North Island provinces and three Middle Island ones 'for purposes of revenue and co-operation'.[54] He was ignored. William Steward, member for Waitaki, took the opposite approach, requesting the ministry prepare a bill during the recess 'for the simplification of the form of provincial institutions by the withdrawal of their legislative powers, or for the entire abolition of such institutions at a fixed date, and the substitution therefor [sic] of a system of local administration under county and district Boards'.[55] He too was ignored.

Wood of Auckland ambushed the General Assembly on 26 October 1871 with an intriguing motion to hold the next session of the Assembly in Dunedin. He suggested that, in light of the large amount of public works about to be undertaken throughout the colony, the move would help legislators to develop local knowledge. Auckland and Middle Island members naturally combined to pass the motion by 40 votes to 20, but later editorials suggested the move would cause loss, inconvenience and delay, and applauded the Legislative Council's prompt veto.[56] Closer examination indicated a conspiracy may have been at work, especially after Macandrew was quoted as having told a Dunedin meeting that he had 'no expectation that the Assembly will be in Dunedin permanently as yet; but this is the first step'.[57] He suggested the Post Office and provincial council chamber could be a suitable venue; colonial architect William Clayton, earlier dispatched to Dunedin to plan accommodation, had proposed linking the two buildings with a bridge over Water Street.[58]

In the face of mounting suspicion that his grand plan for New Zealand's economic salvation had run into difficulties, Vogel ended the 1871 session with a promise of a new Constitution Act. It was slow to eventuate. Over a year later, his suggestion of a need for centralised management of the colony drew a frustrated group of 'Superintendents and their tail' into a caucus, described by an observer as one that could 'raise the party of opposition into one of active obstructiveness to the real business of the session, and by the banding together of dangerous and disaffected adherents under the leadership of a Fitzherbert or a Macandrew, retard the beneficial working of a policy of colonisation'.[59]

The group's pursuit of provincial control of public works and immigration ensured a tumultuous session of the Assembly in 1872, during which there were three changes of ministry: Fox was defeated; Stafford was reinstated for just 32 days for his third term as premier; and George Waterhouse was installed as the leader of a ministry in which Vogel was the real power. Little progress was made on either public works or immigration, but constitutional change was a recurring theme. Vogel denied that his government had overlooked its promise 'to deal comprehensively with the whole subject of provincial institutions and to define the functions of Provincial Councils', claiming it was now unnecessary.[60] Central and provincial governments had worked much more harmoniously during the year, he said, and this had reduced the pressure on the government to force change. The ministry 'should interfere as little as possible with the existing institutions of the Colony'. 'I think it quite possible that we shall see – perhaps after … some considerable time – the establishment of a single Province in each Island, exercising larger provincial legislative powers than those which at present exist.'[61] Nelson superintendent Oswald Curtis was of the view that 'hasty changes in the boundaries of Provinces, and especially the establishment of new Provinces, tend to uncertainty and confusion in government, and to needless increase in departmental expenditure'. He put a motion for a 'definite and permanent scheme applicable to the whole Colony'.[62] Macandrew retorted that this motion was 'a self-evident proposition which could not be gainsaid'; if it had been acted upon years ago it would have saved 'hundreds of thousands of pounds'.[63]

Reynolds was next to offer a 'definite and permanent scheme' in the form of 15 resolutions, which called for each island to become a separate province and for the establishment of a federal government for New Zealand. In a move reminiscent of his brother-in-law, he suggested Akaroa could be the seat of government for the Middle Island, and reminded the House that Fox and Vogel had promoted a similar scheme in 1863 and 1870.[64]

While Fox prevaricated, Stafford sprang to Reynolds' defence and vigorously attacked the premier – a foretaste of the want-of-confidence debate that began two weeks later and ousted the Fox ministry on 5 September 1872. Stafford alleged that Fox's administration of the public works and immigration policy had been unsatisfactory; ministers were too often away from Wellington, and this had led to insufficient consultation, inefficient management and extra cost. He proposed that 'the colonial Government should retain full responsibility for the proper conduct of all works authorised and the sole control of all sums voted by Parliament'; where possible, it should use existing provincial machinery to do the job.[65]

In this debate Macandrew supported Fox. He was blunt: with such a new policy and a lack of experience, 'the Colonial Legislature has made a grand blunder in undertaking the practical administration of the public works and immigration policy at all … it would have been far better administered by the respective local Legislatures.'[66] He argued that ministers needed to travel around the country to stay informed. The House was closely divided and Fox resigned.[67]

Stafford's ministry lasted a month. On 4 October 1872, following a snap want-of-confidence debate won by two votes, Vogel orchestrated the appointment of an experienced newcomer, the legislative councillor and former chief secretary of South Australia, George Waterhouse. Waterhouse met parliament on 11 October in the unique position of a premier without portfolio, without salary and without a seat in the popular chamber.[68]

At this juncture Macandrew might have expected to be offered a ministerial appointment – after all, Vogel controlled the ministry, and although they disagreed about the place and powers of the provinces, until this time Macandrew and Vogel had remained close colleagues.

An *Otago Daily Times* reporter described Macandrew in 1874 as:

> a man in whom the possession of no real genius, no startling attainments or exceptionally superior qualities of mind and intellect, is counterbalanced by an unusually liberal allowance of sound and solid common sense … with the canniness and craftiness of the true Scot …[69]

Faint praise indeed. Macandrew was not a charismatic parliamentarian, despite his popularity in Otago, but his political career had been long and varied, and his parliamentary faction was in the ascendant. He was energetic in parliament: Henry Sewell reported that 'Macandrew may be seen at all times and all places – passant and fumant.'[70] Nor was he completely single-minded on provincial matters: he surprised many by supporting the construction of a railway from Wellington to Masterton, the beginning of a trunk line between Wellington and Auckland that would open up 'an enormous tract of land', and which had the potential to recoup the cost of construction. According to Macandrew, accelerated European settlement was the 'only effectual way of settling the Maori difficulty'.[71] Wellingtonians were loud in their praise of his broad-mindedness and viewed him as a powerbroker par excellence.

Perhaps Macandrew's allegiance to his family and Otago caused him to refuse an offer of appointment. He may have felt he could not give the two jobs his full attention, or that his record would be held against him, or that he was still vulnerable to earlier creditors. Whatever the reasons, he appeared to carry no grudge for his lack of ministerial appointment, and entertained Vogel in Dunedin during the summer recess of 1872–73.[72]

Opposite: Members of parliament, 1874. Macandrew is number 31, second from the right in the third full row. 1/1-018642-G/22807221, Alexander Turnbull Library, Wellington

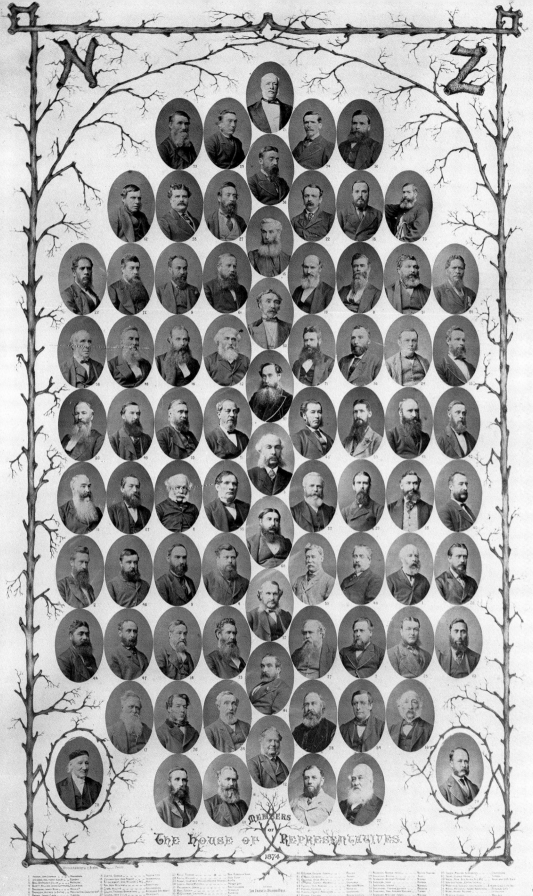

MEMBERS OF THE HOUSE OF REPRESENTATIVES.

1874

Council reshuffled

The independence of a superintendent was a consequence of the vague definition of a superintendent's powers in the Constitution Act, a situation which the New Provinces Act had attempted to improve in 1858. According to the latter, super-intendents of new provinces would no longer be separately elected; they would be chosen by their council and could opt to sit on the council. However, one community's desire to choose its leader saw Marlborough residents regain the right to elect their superintendent in 1872, and similar legislation was passed for Taranaki and Hawke's Bay the following year.[73] When the province of Westland was created in 1873, Premier Vogel reduced the popularly elected superinten-dent's role to that of a chairman bound by the decisions of the council. In Otago, though, the superintendent continued to be elected by the people.

Donald Reid had been provincial secretary for Macandrew since May 1869. His constant opposition, especially to the sale of waste lands, had angered Macandrew, who was further vexed when Reid incited a council revolt against implementing the public works scheme in Otago. On his reappointment as premier in September 1872, Stafford appointed Reid as minister of public works, the position established in 1870 to oversee the implementation of Vogel's public works scheme. Macandrew responded by going to considerable lengths to get rid of Reid from the provincial council: he made two voyages to Dunedin during House sittings in September 1872 to dismiss Reid as provincial secretary, claim-ing the two positions were incompatible.[74]

A stalemate was inevitable when superintendent and council disagreed. In 1873 in the address-in-reply, the vengeful Reid referred to Macandrew's attempts to appoint an Executive Council without council support as 'unconstitutional', after which the provincial council refused to reply to any of Macandrew's messages and twice rejected his nominations for the Executive Council.[75] In frus-tration Macandrew wrote that 'the majority of the Council, by seeking to force upon his acceptance advisers, who … entertain entirely opposite views from the Superintendent, are seeking to place him in a false position – a position which he refuses to accept'.[76] The relationship between Otago Provincial Council and Superintendent Macandrew had deteriorated to the point that he dismissed the council after nine sitting days and called for fresh elections. His gamble paid off. On 18 June 1873 he defeated John Gillies, the only other contender for the super-intendency. It was the fourth time Macandrew had been elected superintendent of Otago, and his 59 per cent share of the vote was a 7 per cent improvement on his 1871 result.

A cartoon showing Macandrew dancing over swords labelled Radicalism and Toryism, intended to suggest that he was a 'rail-sitter' who was not committed to any political party, in a period when he was at odds with his provincial council. It appeared in the *Otago Witness* jubilee supplement, 31 March 1898, and used a Punch cartoon of the British Liberal Prime Minister William Gladstone with Macandrew's face superimposed. W.B. Gibbs photograph, Box 267-003, Hocken Collections, Uare Taoka o Hākena, University of Otago

With 19 of the 46 councillors replaced, the two opposing sides were now almost evenly balanced and Macandrew expressed a wish to bury the hatchet.[77] Gillies was elected Speaker when council met in July 1873, and despite a shaky start and an unsuccessful want-of-confidence motion within the first week, on closing the session Macandrew expressed satisfaction with the amount of business disposed of in a comparatively short space of time.[78]

Vogel's New Zealand Forests Bill

Extensive railway construction had created a huge demand for timber, and Otago possessed in its forests 'a mine of wealth' that would need to be protected.[79] In his opening address to council the following year Macandrew remarked on the importance of conservation, a subject that he said was 'engaging the attention of the Colonial Government, with a view to legislation by the General Assembly'.

Macandrew and Vogel would now part company as their perspectives on the role of government diverged: Vogel's responsibility for the wellbeing of the whole colony led him to back a central government, while Macandrew grew increasingly vigorous in his defence of the provinces, in particular of Otago.

Vogel had likely been influenced, during his 1873 visit to the south, by Macandrew's descriptions of Otago's successful forestry activities. With the introduction of his New Zealand Forests Bill on 14 July 1874, Vogel instigated a series of events that finally brought down the provincial structure. The bill proposed to establish state forests by requisitioning three per cent of the land in each province in return for suspension of the repayment of loans for building railways.

Reid had returned for another term as provincial secretary on 6 May 1874, now prepared to sell land and raise loans to fund local public works. This presaged a period of co-operation with Macandrew during which they formed a close alliance to fight Vogel. Macandrew believed the state's role should be limited to guidance and the funding of major projects that private capital was unable to afford. In opposing Vogel's forestry bill in August 1874, he noted that he agreed with the importance of forest conservation, but objected to the proposed means:

> I cannot see what necessity there is for removing the control from the
> hands of those who have hitherto been administering these forests … the
> authorities on the spot are far more likely to preserve timber from waste
> than any Ministers sitting here in Wellington … if the State goes in for
> growing timber, I do not see why it should not go in for growing flax, corn,
> or any other commodity … there is a very great danger of the State usurping
> individual functions.[80]

Vogel noted that many of the speeches opposing the forests bill had 'resolved themselves into questions not affecting the Bill, or its objects, but affecting other matters relating to the question of provincialism'.[81] The bill was 'proposed in the interests of the colony as a whole'. He denied that the state would take over working forests.[82]

Superintendent James Macandrew.
Otago Witness, 17 March 1893

The responses to his bill unleashed Vogel's frustrations with the opposing members and with the continuing demands of the impoverished North Island provinces. He now declared the time had come for central government to exercise responsibility and control over public works and immigration.

The end of the provinces

On 13 August 1874, conceding that his actions would likely end political alliances and 'alienate … support which has been most generously and ungrudgingly given in the past', Vogel presented three resolutions to the House: that the provincial form of government in the North Island should be abolished; that Wellington should be the permanent seat of government; and for continuation of 'the localization of the land revenue with what is known as the compact of 1856'.[83] The government would decide on the best model to replace the provinces over the coming recess.

Vogel won the division on his resolutions by 41 votes to 16, a clear indication that he had read the country correctly.[84] The die-hard provincialists in the House could be dealt with at leisure. In committee, Vogel reminded listeners of his 1870 criticisms of the provinces. In response to Macandrew's demand for consultation, he pointed out that in 1871 Macandrew himself had proposed to destroy all the provinces of the Middle Island without going to the country.[85]

Given his previous public statements about the inevitable passage of the provinces, Macandrew cannot have been surprised by the turn of events. As one newspaper commented, 'Though the storm has apparently gathered rapidly and broken on us suddenly, the elements of it have in fact been gathering in the political atmosphere for years.'[86] On 18 August 1874 he spoke at length about the 'spoliation of the Middle Island land revenue' to support the North Island, and said he felt the government was unwise to 'nip in the bud that dawning spirit of self-reliance which is at the present moment coming over the North Island'.[87] In this debate he made his memorable assertion: 'Sir, the Colonial Government is the upas tree beneath whose pestiferous shade all life dies, and death lives.'

Vogel and Macandrew's alliance was over. Gossip that suggested Stafford might join Vogel's cabinet was the final straw for Macandrew; from then on he would vote consistently with the Opposition.[88] The final showdown had arrived, but Vogel would produce one more surprise: not only would he dispose of the North Island provinces – he would actually abolish them all.

Chapter 14

Eliza Macandrew died on 1 March 1875 at the age of 48, after a long battle with ovarian cancer, and the demands on Macandrew's time and energy mounted. He was 55 years old, and his five younger children, aged six to 16, were now his sole responsibility. His parents-in-law were dead, Thomas Reynolds in a house fire in 1867 and Marion in 1869, and he now relied on the older girls to organise the household. As the campaign to defeat abolition intensified, he spent increasing amounts of time away from home.

Macandrew was convinced that Vogel's successful 1874 Assembly resolutions would result in abolition of all the provinces, and his pessimism showed when he opened the council on 3 May 1875.[1] He predicted that central government would soon take all revenue and probably all land reserves, and asked: 'Why should the people of Otago submit to their resources being still further swallowed up in the maelstrom of Colonial finance?' Far better, he thought, to retain the provinces, adopt a federal system and aim for financial separation of the two islands. He warned against renouncing the local self-government system they now enjoyed. The council was noncommittal, but supported Macandrew by passing a motion that called for the proposed changes to the system of government to be tested by general election.

Macandrew's policy swings were condemned in the press – from his 1871 resolutions to his 1875 solutions; from advocating for one Middle Island province to suggesting retention of the existing provinces; from reducing administration costs by abolishing provinces to curbing departmental expenditure; from supporting county boards to abhorring their costs. One ambivalent editor wrote, 'We are disciples of Mr. Macandrew, but not the Mr. Macandrew of today. We want such principles as he once avowed to be triumphant, and we put him forward as our best advocate.'[2] Macandrew answered his critics in a speech to his Port Chalmers constituents in July 1875, where he defined himself as a 'thorough Separationist'. If the government should try to change the constitution, he vowed to be 'found in the opposition lobby upon every question affecting the existence of the Ministry.'[3] For the next 18 months he was true to his word.

In Otago his detractors bridled at his apparent single-mindedness. The *Bruce Herald* now turned on him and wrote: 'For New Zealand as a colony, for a country to which in its entirety, he owes allegiance, gratitude, and respect, he has not a word.' According to the writer, provincial government was the worst sort of centralism for rural areas: 'it agglomerates in a city the influence and the revenue which should be at the disposal of separate districts.'[4]

When parliament opened on 20 July 1875, Macandrew's suspicions were confirmed. Governor Sir James Fergusson announced that the ministry, with Premier Daniel Pollen standing in while Vogel was on business in London, had prepared measures for the abolition of the North Island provinces. Members would be asked to decide whether or not the process should be applied to the whole country.[5]

The 88 members elected to the first session of the sixth parliament consisted of 53 pro-abolitionists, 26 anti-abolitionists – mostly from Auckland and Otago – and nine fence-sitters.[6] When the Abolition of the Provinces Bill was introduced by Colonial Treasurer Harry Atkinson 10 days later, Macandrew was one of a 'small but compact phalanx' of superintendents who opposed it. The others were Sir George Grey (Auckland), William Fitzherbert (Wellington) and William Rolleston (Canterbury).[7] Donald Reid supported Macandrew and the pair voted together on all divisions, but they were completely routed when the bill was read for a second time and affirmed by 52 votes to 17. It was a clear message that both the Assembly and the country were impatient for change.[8]

The debate on the bill was Macandrew's final opportunity to sway his parliamentary colleagues on the subject, and he failed. In the certain knowledge that abolition would now be approved, he worked hard to influence the final shape of the Act during the second reading.[9] His arguments were familiar: he agreed it was time to modify the existing expensive system of government, but considered Assembly members ill-equipped to legislate for provincial matters. How would they deal with Otago's 59 bills of local interest, for example? Macandrew called for proof of the desire for change:

> We are told that the people from one end of the colony to the other are
> demanding that their local administration shall be handed over to the
> Central Government; but I ask, where is the evidence of this? Where are the
> petitions?[10]

Rather than making New Zealand 'a great and united colony', he felt the bill would position the country under 'the despotism of a Government apparently but not really responsible to the people'.[11] He read out resolutions passed by

Otago Provincial Council that deplored the changes and sought consultation, and accused the ministry of acting too quickly.

The second reading took three weeks, and its opponents were so obstructive that Atkinson realised he might not achieve his goal of passing the bill that session. In order to speed its progress he compromised on the Act's implementation date.[12] It was agreed that this would be 'the day next after the last day of the first Session of the next or sixth Parliament of New Zealand' – in other words, at least a year hence. The date finally agreed on was 1 November 1876, which allowed New Zealanders to have their say in the December 1875–January 1876 election.[13] It was a small victory for Atkinson's opponents.

The ministry accepted more changes during the committee stage in September. Macandrew moved several amendments. One – to establish an Otago Board of Works to undertake public works – was lost when the responsibility was given to local governing bodies, which were yet to be defined. His amendment to establish an Otago Education Board to manage educational matters, including the education land reserves, became the model for the country, and he persuaded the government to add provincial museums to the list of institutions to be beneficiaries of the consolidated fund.[14] He fired his last salvo on 29 September, when he denounced the proceedings as 'unreasonable, tyrannical, and utterly unworthy of any representative assembly':

> This Act will evoke a spirit of resentment which, I believe, will result in this Assembly being crushed into the dust. I feel very strongly upon the subject, and I can hardly trust myself to say what I should like to say, in case I should indulge in unparliamentary language.[15]

The third reading passed by 40 votes to 21 and the bill finally became law on 12 October 1875. It repealed Section Two of the Constitution Act, replacing the provinces with provincial districts. The remainder of the Act specified procedures for the changeover, which would take until 1 January 1877. Provincial councils were instructed not to meet in the interim.

Endgame

Accompanied by the superintendents of Auckland, Wellington and Canterbury, Macandrew returned to Dunedin on 27 October 1875 to launch his next parliamentary election campaign and continue the fight against abolition. His efforts were recognised at a banquet where he was fêted by more than 400 diners. According to the *Otago Witness*, he had 'gone through as many ups and downs of popularity and disapproval as would content some twenty ordinary men.

Just now, he is at the very tip-top of prosperity, and a more substantial token of approval would not be amiss than a mere banquet.'[16] The *Otago Daily Times* was of the opinion 'that a more popular man than James Macandrew does not exist just now in New Zealand'.[17] Macandrew had spread the province's largesse widely, and the miners – forgetting their frosty reaction in 1867 when he first ventured into Central Otago – also praised him for his substantial efforts on their behalf: 'To the Goldfields, Mr. Macandrew has been a constant friend … Blot out the names of Mr. Macandrew and Sir Julius Vogel during the last five years, and where would the Goldfields interest be?'[18]

Macandrew responded fulsomely to the banqueters. In his speech he claimed that policy makers had committed three blunders 'to which most of the political evils to which New Zealand has been heir may be attributed, and but for which the Colony might have been a political paradise'.[19] These were the failure to define the functions of the colonial and provincial parliaments; the fact that the Legislative Council was not nominated or elected by provincial councils; and 'the anomaly of responsible Government in the Provinces, without the power of appeal to the people'.[20] An escape from 'despotic Centralism' was urgently required, he said. How different would New Zealand politics be today if Macandrew had been successful in securing his ideal – an Upper House elected by the provinces?

In November Macandew distributed a privately printed pamphlet titled 'Address to the People of Otago' in which he took some 32,000 words to put his usual arguments for provincialism.[21] Not all of his audience were impressed, however, and one Otago detractor voiced the opinion of many New Zealanders:

> If there were a James Macandrew in every one of the nine Provinces, and each had his own way, New Zealand … would inevitably become a land whose people would be divided against themselves, cursed with petty jealousies, and growing up in narrow-mindedness and selfishness.[22]

It was a rare opponent who appreciated Macandrew's ability to rebound from defeat. Edward McGlashan, lately the member for Roslyn, reported to Vogel's Native minister Sir Donald McLean:

> today I happened to meet with our friend Macandrew – I find him still to be as bitter as gall – I cannot well make him out … I twitted him with the statement that he must have considered himself like a victorious Roman warrior dragging at his chariot wheels Sir George Grey & Sir John Richardson [the latter now a supporter of insular separation] at the demonstration seeing their determined hostility to him in days of yore. He seemed to chuckle over the idea as something good, remarking however that

it was wonderful when the State was in danger, how extremes did meet – It was pure patriotism he said, to which I replied it was pure humbug and he knew it.[23]

While McGlashan made fun of Macandrews' alliance with Grey and Richardson, he would never have guessed that Macandrew and Grey would be the nucleus of a future ministry.

The finale

Otago's voters returned a majority of anti-abolitionists in that summer's parliamentary election. This time Macandrew withdrew from Port Chalmers and stood successfully for the three-member Dunedin City seat, which also returned William Larnach and Robert Stout. This was retribution on his brother-in-law William Reynolds, a sitting member for Dunedin City and former separationist who had recently become a Vogel minister. Macandrew's attempt to oust Reynolds did not work, however. Due to the drawn-out election period, Reynolds was able to recover from his defeat and win Macandrew's old seat of Port Chalmers.

The new House was evenly balanced on the abolition issue. With the administrative structures to replace the provinces yet to be defined, the provincialists did not go quietly into the night; instead they mounted a vigorous campaign in the papers and the House to prevent ratification of the Abolition Act.[24] They generated substantial hostility from most of New Zealand in the process, but were strongly supported in Auckland and Otago – to the wonderment of some observers. Jane Maria Atkinson, sister of the ineffectual James Richmond and sister-in-law of Premier Harry Atkinson, was a close observer of the political scene. Her views, voiced in a letter to a second brother, were possibly influenced by Macandrew's rough treatment of her brother 10 years earlier:

> … that the abolition of the provinces is a fait accompli is hardly denied now by even the hottest Provincialist, but how can Auckland and Otago work together harmoniously now the Provincialist war cry cannot be used to rally them? Sir G.G., Rolleston and Macandrew cannot have the same objects to obtain, and could hardly form a Government together if they do turn out the Vogel Ministry … both Otago and Auckland are sending up some dreadful specimens of human nature.[25]

Vogel resumed the premiership on his return in February 1876. He inadvertantly reinvigorated the abolition campaign by dispatching three commissioners to the provinces, tasked with collecting information for the provision of government services following the changeover. Macandrew considered Vogel's action premature and refused to assist the commissioners. In a public exchange of letters with Vogel he wrote, 'it will be time enough to take such action after the parliament has determined ... the specific form of Government for the future'.[26]

The letters reviewed the various arguments and, although icily polite, highlighted the breakdown in their relationship. Macandrew blamed Vogel for Otago's difficulties in dealing with waste lands: 'I ... attribute them chiefly to the action taken by yourself in granting a renewal of so many pastoral leases in 1866–7'.[27] Vogel's reply was equally acerbic:

> I continued to aid the Provinces, and to believe they might be enabled
> to survive, long after that belief was dead in the minds of some of the
> most acute men in New Zealand. No Province has, in my opinion, more
> contributed to make Abolition necessary than has Otago – for it has refused
> to accept any limit to its desire to expend money.[28]

The publication of this correspondence allowed supporters on either side to keep score – Vogel was considered to have come off second best – and ensured that members of the General Assembly were well informed when they met on 15 July 1876 for the final round of implementing abolition.[29]

Although forbidden by law from assembling Otago Provincial Council in 1876, Macandrew filed a final superintendent's report in which he predicted that the concentration of power in Wellington would be the prelude to 'years of departmental extravagance, political turmoil, and well founded local discontent which cannot fail to exercise a most baneful influence upon the advancement of the Colony in general and of Otago in particular'.[30] He painted a glowing picture of Otago as a province at its peak. Public revenue for the year stood at £1,058,104. There had been 1573 births, 5132 immigrants had landed and 162 public schools were operating. Some 108,791 ounces of gold had been recovered, 102,094 acres (41,316ha) of rural land had been sold, and 202 miles (325km) of railways were operating at a profit.[31] He questioned the 'preposterous' logic of abolishing such a successful province.[32]

The anti-abolitionists continued their efforts. On 3 August Grey moved an eight-part resolution in the House that called for a reconsideration of the colony's financial and constitutional affairs; for the colony to remain united; for the establishment of a local government for each island and a redistribution of charges for the colonial debt; and for local government to control its own affairs and keep its own revenue. He advocated for Auckland to be the seat of local government in the North Island and Christchurch in the south, and for central government to remain in Wellington.[33]

Grey's resolution was another variation on the separationist resolutions that Reynolds had put in 1870 and 1872, and Macandrew and Murray in 1871, and it triggered a two-week debate in which all the old arguments were rehearsed yet again. In the end all parts were lost by majorities of between 14 and 17 votes, except the last: to retain Wellington as the seat of government.[34]

With a decisive majority and the provincialist party seemingly beaten, Vogel introduced his Counties Bill: 63 counties would be authorised to levy rates, with limited overdraft rights and responsibility for county roads, public works and aid to charitable institutions.[35] Macandrew was dismissive, and claimed there was 'not one district throughout the colony which will avail itself of its provisions'.[36] He presented resolutions passed by the South Otago Roads Board that called the bill 'cumbrous and utterly unworkable', and accused the House of 'a recklessness and a tyranny repugnant to the spirit of free institutions … inconsistent with the idea of this colony becoming a great and a united country'.[37]

The London agent-general's position became vacant when Featherston died in June, and Macandrew was among those named as contenders for the post.[38] Perhaps this prominence, along with a series of well-attended meetings throughout Otago protesting against the demise of the provinces, stimulated him to present yet another resolution in the House.[39] Members' patience must have been sorely tried when he moved that the governor be asked to dissolve Otago Provincial Council and call fresh elections in order to give the voters a voice in the choice of suitable self-government. With Vogel now posted to London as agent-general, the new premier Harry Atkinson responded brusquely, saying Macandrew seemed 'unable to recognize the fact that his cause is the cause of the past'. The resolution was defeated by 37 votes to 24 – numbers that indicate that Macandrew was clearly not alone in his stance.

Macandrew decamped to Dunedin to agitate further against the Abolition Act and missed Grey's next stonewalling effort, the Provincial Abolition Permissive Bill, which called for each province to be able to choose its own time of dissolution. This was smartly voted out.[40]

Macandrew's final acts of resistance included mailing a petition to Queen Victoria seeking Otago's secession from New Zealand. He addressed a rally of around 2000 protestors in Dunedin on 27 September 1876, and brought the house down with his suggestion that isolation was now the way forward: 'the only way to save Otago is to erect into a separate Colony … by having recourse to the Imperial Parliament'.[41] In a telegram to the governor he indicated Otago's strong opposition to abolition and asked him to refrain from assenting to the

Act, warning that it would result 'in a dismemberment of the Colony'.[42] Otago Provincial Council, he said, was being urged to hold a plebiscite and would send the result to the imperial government, 'who, it is confidently hoped, will not turn a deaf ear to what I believe will undoubtedly be … the deliberate and unmistakeable desire of an overwhelming majority of the settlers of Otago'.[43] In a memorandum to the governor, Premier Atkinson commented that Macandrew 'appears to forget that the Abolition Act is now law, has been left to its operation by Her Majesty, and will come into force without further legislative action'.

As usual, Macandrew opted to have the last word. He responded, enclosing a copy of a telegram he had sent to the British secretary of state for the colonies: 'Have honor suggest said Act be referred to her Majesty's Attorney General with view disallowance if void. Deep feeling wrong pervades Province.'[44] Grey, his staunch but erratic ally, had also telegraphed the secretary of state warning of a likely uproar: 'Disturbances imminent. Some threaten employment Queen's ships. I earnestly pray telegraph to prevent disturbance.'[45] Lord Carnarvon's prompt reply endorsed the Act and was dismissive of the risk of 'unconstitutional disturbances'.[46]

The Abolition of Provinces Act became law on 1 November 1876, with few regrets and little rejoicing throughout the land. It came into force on 1 January 1877, 24 years and six months after the passing of the 1852 Act to Grant a Representative Constitution to the Colony of New Zealand.

Macandrew had become a separationist zealot. On 8 November 1876 he opened a two-day conference in Dunedin for members of the House of Representatives, the provincial council, mayors of municipalities and chairmen of district road boards and local education committees, to 'determine the best means of extricating the Province of Otago from the evil results involved in the "Abolition of Provinces Act"'. Over 100 attended and heard him declare:

> The only panacea for the great wrong which is being inflicted upon Otago
> is that it should be proclaimed an independent Colony, with a supreme
> legislature of its own and the absolute control over its own revenues.[47]

Resolutions were passed to petition the Queen once again, this time to proclaim Otago a separate and independent colony; and for Grey, Macandrew and Captain Thomas Fraser MLC to sail to England to deliver the petition in person. Although Macandrew was willing to make the journey the other two were not and, somewhat carelessly, the petition was sent by ordinary mail instead of official channels, with the result that it could not be presented to Her Majesty.

London's rebuff, which did not arrive until the following June, quashed all hopes of reversal for the provincialists.

The demise of provincial government was inevitable. The provinces were a necessity at their creation when settlements were separated by distance, time and culture, but within 20 years, technological progress had reduced many of these barriers. A unified country was possible, and a growing majority of settlers were now prepared to see their taxes spent for the good of the entire colony. The cost of a combined system of provincial and central government had become unwieldy, as Vogel asserted: 'the system … was beyond the strength of the colony to continue. It was the finance question … which made the change necessary'.[48] He acknowledged the toll of the process on his friendship with Macandrew:

> I had not from the time when I took office any stronger supporter or firmer personal friend than the Superintendent of Otago, Mr. Macandrew – I felt for him … an esteem founded on the conviction that there was no man in the colony more disinterested or public-spirited than he was – and yes, I knew, so strong were his feelings in favor of provincialism that his support was likely to be lost to me.[49]

In an era of robust characters Macandrew was conspicuous, a man notable for his passion, persistence and parochialism. His somewhat manic obsession with Otago's survival, based on a belief that the province's wealth should be used to improve local conditions rather than shared with the remainder of the colony, distinguished him from his peers. It is somewhat surprising that he chose to ignore the problems faced by the other provinces, however. Although his loyalty to Otago was indisputable, his modest Scottish origins offended some of his colleagues who considered him not quite 'a gentleman'. In a letter to a colleague, one superintendent and member of parliament asked, 'Are you going to join the University Council with Macandrew upon it? I have given no answer yet as I wish to hear whether the other members would protest against such an enormity'.[50] Some took offence at his behaviours, including one correspondent who noted:

> I for one am not sorry that that big rascal is at last meeting with his deserts, and that at the hands of those through whose assistance he climbed into power. Honest conscientious men who have hitherto been driven out of any say in public affairs will now have a chance of letting their voice and influence be felt without coming under the wing and patronage of 'slippery Jim'.[51]

Macandrew's earnest defence of the provinces as a practicable form of government saw him cast as a reactionary, a label that was to haunt him for the rest of his career in politics. He was comfortable in the House, however, and was an affable member who used its procedures to his advantage, even though he lost his major battle. Macandrew was a kingmaker: influential in dethroning Stafford and promoting Fox in 1869, he worked to remove Stafford again in 1872 and replace him with Waterhouse, then supported Vogel's successful bid for premier in 1873. Parliament provided a national platform for his views and a place where he could answer the attacks he suffered on his home territory.

With the end of the provinces he was well positioned for a larger role in national politics. In the second period of his parliamentary membership, Macandrew moved from spurned bankrupt to leader of a substantial opposition bloc.

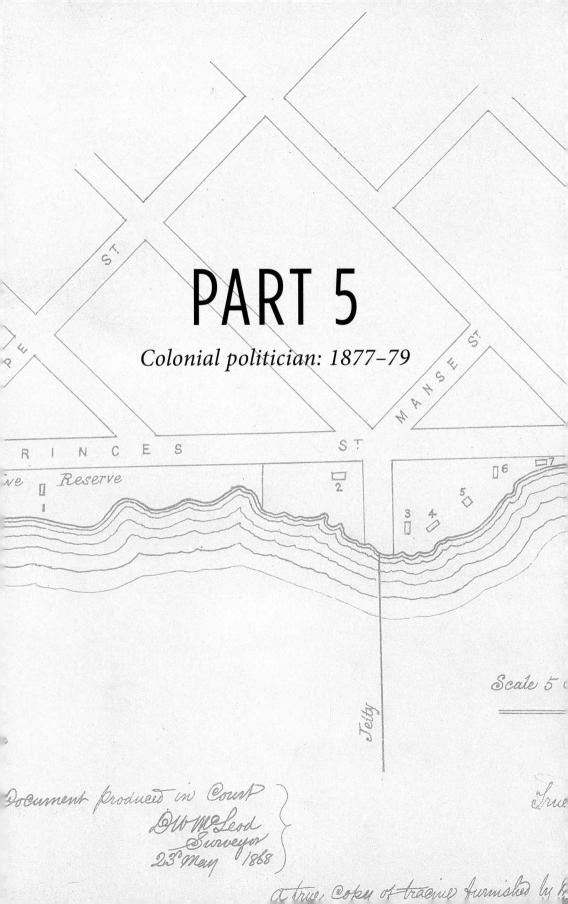

PART 5

Colonial politician: 1877–79

Chapter 15

In 1871 Edward Stevens predicted the course of events that would drive the colonial parliament for the next 20 years:

> There will be a so called 'party of progress' and a 'prudent' party. Whilst there is money to spend the latter will be regarded as do-nothings and obstructive, when the money is spent the party of prudence will be invited to come in and restore solvency. Before they have accomplished this, they will be railed at as torpid and slow, and they will soon after be ejected to let the gamblers and thimble-riggers in again.[1]

The boom-and-bust cycle was a consequence of the unstable economic conditions that afflicted New Zealand from the mid-1860s until the 1890s, as consecutive governments struggled to escape the unavoidable depression. A parliamentarian needed considerable faith in himself to believe he could influence the seemingly uncontrollable economy.

Macandrew had such faith. During the 1877–79 tenure of George Grey's erratic government of conservative provincialists and liberal reformers, he served as secretary for Crown lands and minister of immigration for nine months, and minister of public works for 18 months.[2] Where before he had been a pruner of government expenditure, he now became an outrageous spendthrift. After Grey's defeat on 3 October 1879 he was judged the only politician capable of attracting sufficient votes to defeat the Hall ministry and was chosen to lead the opposition, a position he held for three years.[3]

As a minister of the Crown Macandrew could finally give free rein to his belief in deliverance through 'roads, population, bridges, capital'.[4] Although in his early days he had advocated a high price for land to control the flow of 'acceptable' immigrants, he now wanted every deserving man to have access to land at the cheapest price and on the easiest of terms.

Macandrew's two years as a minister reveal his values, drive and unorthodox style of work. His performance in this role has been strongly criticised, but this biography contends that he was the mainstay of Grey's ministry. He worked

The Government Building in Lambton Quay, Wellington, was opened in December 1876 to house the Cabinet offices and all of the public service. It is seen here immediately after its opening. 1/1-039911-G/23527492, Alexander Turnbull Library, Wellington

collaboratively when required and had the vision and personality needed to drive a radical programme. Although his idiosyncratic behaviour often antagonised his opponents, he performed well in difficult circumstances – before eventually being unsaddled by events beyond his control.

The new Government Building was opened in December 1876, and Grey's ministers were among its first occupants.[5] With 143 rooms spread over four floors, it was the largest building in the country and stood on land reclaimed from Wellington Harbour for the purpose. The executive and legislative branches of government were now separated: ministers met in the Cabinet office on the first floor and occupied rooms surrounded by their departmental staff. The expanded public service required to administer Vogel's public works and immigration programme was now housed in one place, and soon became one of the largest departments, occupying most of the building.[6] In Grey's words, parliament could now avoid 'the din, confusion, and worry that arose from mixing the public departments and members of the General Legislature together'. The relocation had one unfortunate effect: that of insulating ministers from daily interaction with members except when the House sat, a factor that made them easier targets for criticism.

The Wellington Government Quarter about 1880 viewed from the harbour reclamation. The Supreme Court is on the left, Government House is in the centre and the Government Building is on the right. 1/2-005775/F/23064651, Alexander Turnbull Library, Wellington

Depression

The impetus of Vogel's public works scheme had faded by 1875, but full employment generated by a heady investment in the expansion of the country's infrastructure had led to inflation and encouraged the anticipation of giddy profits for landowners. Land sales shrank and prices rose, and many new immigrants found themselves unable to afford land or become self-sufficient.[7] The gold bonanza had waned, export prices had fallen, and public debt in 1875 stood at £17,388,000.[8] When Premier Vogel resigned in 1876 to become the New Zealand agent-general in London, loan repayments were almost crippling the country, and various forms of fundraising were being explored to repay the national debt.[9] Through his borrowing Vogel had avoided imposing new taxes, but the country was now so poor that parliament needed to find new forms of direct taxation that would shift a greater share of the burden from poor workers to wealthy landowners.[10]

Taxation and the most effective methods of collecting taxes became major points of difference among politicians of this period, and the balance between

Looking down on Wellington's Bolton Street, 1881, with, from left, St Mary's Cathedral, Parliament House, Government House and the Government Building. 1/2-110651/F/22836322, Alexander Turnbull Library, Wellington

indirect and direct taxation began to shift. Ex-governor Grey, elected to parliament in 1875 to fight abolition and strongly influenced by political economist John Stuart Mill, was intent on taxing the 'unearned increment' of land – the increase in value that occurred without any owner input.[11] Grey's first call for the introduction of income and land taxes came in 1876: he and his bloc of reformers were prepared to increase death duties, and to make the wealthy carry a larger share of the cost of government.[12]

As superintendents and outspoken defenders of provincialism, Grey and Macandrew had formed a close friendship. Cecil de Lautour, member for Mount Ida from 1876 to 1884, observed that 'they shared a passionate devotion to New Zealand and her people'.[13] This friendship would be severely tested in the next decade.

Backed by conservative landowners, Atkinson became premier on 1 September 1876. His opposition consisted of the radical-leaning Aucklanders headed by Grey, the provincialist Otagoites led by Macandrew, and the middle party,

which was predominantly composed of liberal-minded Middle Island runholders led by William Montgomery.[14] After sitting for three months, by September
1877 parliament had enacted only one bill: the Education Act. When Atkinson
presented his first financial statement he commented: 'for the immediate future,
the government believe that the need of the country is political rest' – a sentiment
that hastened the search for a more effective ministry.[15]

Grey opposed Atkinson's financial policy and moved instead for taxation of
income and property to 'relieve the people of the colony from some onerous
Customs duties now paid'.[16] In supporting Grey's motion, Macandrew displayed
his impatience with parliamentary convention and paraded a new liberal stance:
'Let us at once adopt a proposal which is calculated so greatly to promote the
interests and add to the comfort of every man, woman and child throughout
the length and breadth of the colony.'[17] Atkinson's supporters rejected what they
saw as a land tax that would cost rural landowners more than town dwellers. But
although Grey's motion was lost, the concept was launched in the public arena.

Grey's ministry

Grey emerged as premier on 15 October 1877, his appointment possibly
engineered by William Larnach, John Ballance and Robert Stout in a bid to help
them sell their jointly owned tracts of adjacent and worthless land on the Waimea
Plains in Southland.[18] It may be that Larnach's want-of-confidence motion on
8 October 1877 attracted frustrated members who wanted to break an impasse.[19]
Alternatively, the dissatisfied principals of the Middle Group, which included
members opposed to the political separation of the islands as well as Grey
opponents, may have encouraged one of its more obscure members to put the
motion in an attempt to oust Atkinson.[20] When Lanarch was unable to assemble
a ministry, however, he approached the opposition grouping led by Grey, who
eventually emerged as premier.

Grey's liberal manifesto of parliamentary reform included male suffrage, an
equal distribution of seats, the abolition of plural voting, payment of members,
triennial parliaments, the substitution of land and income taxes for customs
duties, and land reforms to promote the interests of the small-holder against
speculators and run-holders.[21] Support for these policies came from an expanding urban population concerned by increasing unemployment and the lethargy
of Atkinson's do-nothing government.

Boosted by the energy of the frustrated provincialists, Sir George Grey's charismatic personality and radical proposals sparked a movement that flared, then

fizzled and smouldered. He had mobilised a pressure group to fight abolition and produced a cohesive political manifesto – something that was unusual in that period.[22] His programme of radical political reform, which easily surpassed Atkinson's bland vision for economic recovery, generated colony-wide support. Once elected, however, Grey had to balance a parochial parliament, combative colleagues and conflict in the electorate, all exacerbated by a worsening economy. Without the support of a constituency prepared to fight wholeheartedly for his agenda, he was unable to enact his programme during the three sessions in which he controlled parliament. But although his premiership has been described as 'one of the most desultory and least edifying in our political history', his programme did lay the foundations for the politicians who won the Liberal victory in 1891.[23]

Grey was attempting to administer a major change in governance without the support of effective administrative systems.[24] Following the abolition of the provinces, so many local issues had to be resolved at a national level that one contemporary protested:

> The House of Representatives, since 1875, has been a monster Board of Works for every part of the colony; and has been unable, at least for ten years, to relieve itself of a burden which it should not properly bear; from a task which it cannot satisfactorily fulfil.[25]

Grey set the tenor of his office in his first ministerial statement, in which he claimed that 'every possible retrenchment was necessary'.[26] Ministers' salaries would be the first items reduced, followed by cutbacks in the civil service – although it was noted that, as the recipient of a British pension, Grey did not draw a salary and so was unaffected by this move.[27] He also called for administrative change, set to be his greatest challenge as premier:

> Two great systems had been running concurrently – the General and Provincial. These two were never merged into one … [The ministry's] great effort should be to devise a system by which the public affairs of the colony would be grasped by one government.[28]

It soon became apparent that Grey did not have the skills to work with his ministers to establish the new system. He was not a team player, and was known for his irascible nature and inability to compromise with his able associates. Editors in the smaller provinces, the political bases of the now opposing faction, were quick to criticise. One considered Grey to be 'the last man in New Zealand to administer public affairs under a sense of Ministerial responsibility'.[29] Aucklanders took an opposing view, however. One correspondent wrote, 'The great – the very great – majority of people in this province rejoice in no measured way at [Grey's] accession to power. They have implicit faith in his independence, ability, and unselfish purpose, that he will command supporters from every Auckland constituency if a dissolution should occur.'[30]

In what was judged to be a bizarre mix of personalities, Grey's ministry comprised William Larnach, John Sheehan, James Fisher, George Whitmore and Macandrew, a combination that both amazed and appalled commentators. The editor of the *New Zealand Tablet* wrote, 'In our present Cabinet are met a cluster of men differing as widely from each other as it is well possible for men to differ.'[31] The *Marlborough Express* was alarmed: 'How can the country have faith in a Ministry which has so many elements of disunion? How can Mr. Sheehan and Sir Geo. Grey on the one hand, and Mr. Macandrew and Mr. Larnach on the other, agree that the Land fund of Otago is sacred, and not to become Colonial Revenue?'[32] In Otago the editor of the *Bruce Herald* was reserved: 'Despite the presence in the Ministry of two able administrators, in the presence of Sir George and Mr. Macandrew, and a promising one in Mr. Sheehan, we cannot regard the ministry as a strong one.'[33] A London correspondent expressed puzzlement: 'I was amazed to hear of a Ministry comprised of Sir G Grey, McAndrew [sic], Sheehan, &c, &c. I remember the time when Sir G Grey declined a banquet at Otago because he would have to sit at the same table with McAndrew as Superintendent.'[34]

Politician and historian Alfred Saunders recalled, 20 years later:

No public man ever committed a more evident and unmistakable act of political suicide than Sir George Grey committed, when he declared his willingness to be held responsible, as Premier, for the actions of five colleagues, who had never willingly committed an act of self-denial in their whole lives, and who had, each in his own way, proved himself to be so remarkably untrustworthy.[35]

Governor Lord Normanby was highly critical of Grey's policies and reported to the secretary of state for the colonies that Grey was 'a dangerous & unscrupulous man who would shirk at nothing which would advance his own ends, provided he could do it with safety to himself'. Of the others he wrote:

Mr. Larnach is a sick man but a wild speculator & getter up of companies. Mr Shean [sic] is a pettifogging lawyer the son of a Public house keeper in Auckland. Mr. Macandrew's character has been found not to bear very strict interrogation & Mr. Fisher two or three years ago was a common labourer.[36]

In the face of a barrage of criticism, Grey advanced a radical political agenda that was hailed as the remedy for the country's problems: an amalgam of

Premier George Grey's Cabinet, 1878. A-051-009/23173463, Alexander Turnbull Library, Wellington

retrenchment, daring taxation and substantial spending to fire up the economy, and expansion of the franchise.

Treasurer Larnach, who was charged with executing Grey's agenda, took the country by surprise when he presented his first financial statement on 20 November 1877. He announced the reversal of a plank of the Immigration and Public Works Act of 1870 that had allowed the provinces to keep the income from land sales after paying central government for public works.[37] Now, all land revenue was to become 'colonial revenue', although Larnach was prepared to rebate 20 per cent for works to the counties that had replaced the provinces. He proposed to increase government borrowing in London to £4 million for investment in major projects – twice what Atkinson had intended to borrow – and foreshadowed a rise in taxes: 'we should be prepared to submit to heavier burdens, to meet our obligations to the outside creditors, and conduct the business of the country'.[38] Grey's chances of survival were not rated highly; three weeks later, a want-of-confidence vote required the Speaker's support to rescue his ministry from defeat.[39]

Minister Macandrew

Macandrew's ministerial tenure was distinguished by his ability to identify important issues, his capacity to publicise solutions before others did, and his propensity to use public money to buy support. As a minister he reverted to the extravagant behaviours exhibited in his years as superintendent, and his performance has been judged severely by some historians. According to Erik Olssen, Macandrew 'retained his faith in expansion; however, through his persistence he did more than any other man to bring about the rejection of Vogelite policies and to create a climate for retrenchment'.[40] Macandrew's Cabinet colleague William Gisborne was a more sympathetic commentator. Macandrew, he explained, held strong and 'apparently strange' views, and 'was often looked upon as speculative and unsafe':

> He generally saw a great object afar off, and wished to reach it per saltum; he did not usually give himself time to reach it by sure, though slow, degrees to overcome difficulties, and to carry with him public opinion … though too sanguine, [he is] a farseeing and sensible man. His mind has often conceived the idea which it has been the fortune of others to make a great fact.[41]

Macandrew took responsibility for the Crown lands portfolio from Donald Reid, his ally in the anti-abolition debates. The timing was fortunate. Reid had held the portfolio for 13 months in the Atkinson ministry and spent most of that time preparing a Lands Bill, which Macandrew inherited after its second reading and shepherded, unaltered, through the House in late 1877. The Lands Act 1877 consolidated the 'confused mass of colonial land laws, the heritage of provincialism', established 10 land districts – each with a commissioner of Crown lands and a land board – and repealed 56 acts, ordinances and regulations.[42] Its passage marked the end of the 'old, unfettered freedom of enterprise', and demonstrated concern for working men who wanted to buy their own smallholding, by introducing a system of deferred-payment tenure for the whole country.[43] That a ministry should adopt and pass unchanged legislation prepared by its predecessor indicates the fluidity of politics and the absence of consistent party policies at that time.

Macandrew handed the lands and immigration portfolios to Robert Stout in July 1878, a move that allowed him to undertake a number of inspection tours to investigate the many public works projects the government had been asked to implement. In February of that year he had joined Grey and his entourage on one such tour to the West Coast before going south to Bluff and overland to Dunedin.[44] Disaster struck: on 20 February 1878 when the party was boarding the government steamer *Hinemoa* off Westport, Macandrew lost his grip and 'had a narrow escape from drowning, as the sea was very lumpy and the night somewhat dark'.[45] When the party had to land by boat at Greymouth the next day Macandrew declined to join them and proceeded alone to Hokitika, where he disembarked by tugboat and resumed the tour. He inspected the gaol, a lunatic asylum, the hospital, the river and harbour works, public offices and other public places.[46]

The local newspapers greeted Macandrew obsequiously, and one suggested: 'There is probably no man in the Colony better fitted for presiding over the Public Works Department than the late Superintendent of Otago, the vigor of whose administration has raised that part of the Colony to its premier position.'[47] Macandrew responded predictably and generously: he approved the immediate building of bridges at Kumara and Kanieri and committed money for the construction of a road southward to Haast.[48] He then proceeded to Jackson Bay, the first minister of the Crown to visit this isolated settlement. The *West Coast Times* was full of praise: 'It is a cause of public congratulation that a member of the Government should see this much-vexed settlement for himself, and especially that that member should be a person of such colonising experience and natural ability, as Mr. Macandrew.'[49] In contrast, the editor of the *New Zealand Tablet* had a low opinion of Macandrew's morals, describing him as 'canny and Presbyterian, orthodox to the heart's core, but like the orthodox of his class, keen and accommodating where accommodation pays'.[50]

Macandrew continued his tours and his handouts: to the Waikato to inspect a railway, a wharf and a coal mine; and to Blenheim, where he bestowed a railway and a bridge on the community and promised more.[51] He reassured the Greymouth County Council that their harbour works would receive further funding when parliament resumed, saying he considered the work 'a national undertaking, which having been so far commenced, must be proceeded with'.[52] His interest in technology and the development of New Zealand's resources led him to sponsor the use of Taranaki iron sands for industry, and he had his office issue a call for tenders in British newspapers in March 1879, for 100,000 tons of steel rails to be manufactured from New Zealand ores.[53] He presented the Titanic Steel Company of New Plymouth with an order for railway wheels to test the iron, promising the company that if they could 'turn out a quantity … the Government would give them an order for 5000 wheels to start with'.[54] Two railway carriage wheels inscribed 'The Hon. James Macandrew, Minister of Public Works. From Taranaki iron sand' were dispatched to the 1879 Sydney Exhibition, but in the end the company was unable to solve technical problems involved with smelting, and the fledgling New Zealand steel industry died at birth.[55]

Macandrew won an unexpected accolade from the founding provincialist and former Canterbury superintendent William Moorhouse, who reported to his Christchurch constituents on 'the spirit of moderation that had come over the new Ministers. He bore testimony, from his own daily knowledge at Wellington, to their undoubtedly able powers of administration, and was especially forcible on the point that Mr Macandrew, since taking office, was not guided by the belief that Otago was all New Zealand.'[56] Macandrew would have derived immense satisfaction from such praise after his 25 years of political battles in New Zealand.

On his relinquishment of the Crown lands portfolio, Macandrew's service to Otago was recognised by the Vincent County Council, who renamed a bridge over the Kawarau River 'Macandrew Bridge' as 'a deserving tribute to the hon. Minister of Lands in recognition of the valuable aid he had given in obtaining assistance from Government towards purchasing this and other bridges in the County.'[57] This river crossing mirrored Macandrew's turbulent life somewhat: one bridge was washed away in 1874, and its replacement was destroyed by fire in 1896.

Chapter 16

The planning and construction of railways dominated Macandrew's Cabinet career and were the major focus of his first public works statement, presented on 27 August 1878. Having met the previous year's commitments for roads and bridges, Macandrew proposed 'to confine Public Works operations entirely to railway construction'.[1] Small amounts only would be reserved in order to prepare land for settlement before sale, for roads in Native districts and for public buildings. The five-year budget included the £2 million remaining from Larnach's 1877 borrowing, combined with an estimated ordinary revenue of £3.5 million to be generated by the railways for that period, plus a new loan of £3 million. Macandrew proposed to fund these projects with enormous loans supplemented by income calculated on a somewhat irresponsible scale. Nevertheless, Cabinet approved this spending.[2]

The statement discussed the introduction of separate management systems: one for working railways and one for those lines under construction. The move would require a complete reorganisation of the Public Works Department and the appointment of a commissioner of railways for each island.[3] For the North Island he listed six lines under construction and suggested a further eight for development over the next five years.[4] The Middle Island had nine lines under completion and 15 more planned. All in all this would entail 'an expenditure for railways in the North Island of £3,733,000, and in the Middle Island of £4,612,000' – a sum of £8.3 million.[5] This was an immense increase on the £1,370,100 that his predecessor John Ormond had proposed in his 1877 public works statement, and it marked a return to borrowing and spending on a Vogelian scale.[6]

Macandrew itemised the large areas of land in the districts of Thames, Piako, Bay of Plenty, Poverty Bay and Wellington that would be opened up for sale by 10 of the proposed rail lines, and dazzled his audience with his bold calculations for the Middle Island:

> … an area of nearly 4,000,000 acres [1.6m ha] of Crown land in the Middle Island will be affected by the proposed lines. Much of this land if accessible

by rail, and in the market now, would realise £5 an acre and upwards. Probably we shall not be beyond the mark in estimating that it will realise to the State … little short of the whole estimated cost of the railways – viz., £4,650,000 – now proposed to be made in the Middle Island.[7]

Taranaki County was scheduled to receive 20 per cent of the sale price of land around Parihaka on the Waimate Plains, which the government had confiscated from Māori as war reparations, and Macandrew proposed to levy 15 per cent of this sum to build a railway through the district.

Macandrew's public works statement was received with almost universal acclaim. The colonial press were admiring and many of his opponents 'discovered' his hitherto unrecognised talents. The partisan *Evening Post* offered this encomium:

> Every thoughtful politician who reads the Statement with attention cannot fail to recognise a sound statesmanlike ability, and power of dealing with colonial affairs on a broad basis, which will add not a little to the already well-earned reputation of James Macandrew.[8]

The *Lyttelton Times* was enthusiastic:

> The Statement more than justifies the reputation Mr Macandrew has long enjoyed as one of the ablest public men of the colony … Vigorous, far-reaching, and comprehensive, his policy recommends itself to the country, which will not be slow to share the enthusiasm which animates every line of his Public Works Statement. And it will not be forgotten that Mr. Macandrew is an organiser and administrator of a high order.[9]

The *Press* was also positive, saying the proposals were 'of so comprehensive a character as to practically embrace all consideration of railway construction, either required or possible for the colony to undertake, for many years to come'.[10] Even the *New Zealand Tablet*, which regularly criticised Macandrew for his opposition to funding of the Catholic school system, was moved to claim the project was 'so wise, that we feel assured it will at once recommend itself to the approbation and acceptance of the overwhelming majority of New Zealanders'.[11]

This was populism at its best – the 'coming man' had arrived. Macandrew's elevation was complete when, on 6 September 1878, he escorted an official party of dignitaries – including the governor, ministers and members of both Houses, local mayors and councillors – on the first through-train from Christchurch to a rejoicing and decorated Dunedin.[12] The opening of the line, a major Vogel public works project, reminded the country of the benefits of borrowing to build. Thomas Hirst of New Plymouth was on the journey – 'a most exciting affair'

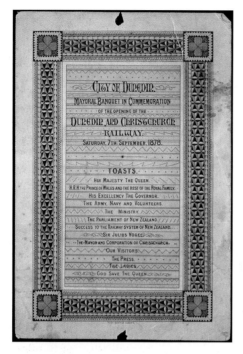

The 'toast list' for the huge banquet held after the first train travelled on the South Island Main Trunk Railway from Christchurch to Dunedin on 6 September 1878. Vogel was toasted and the absent Macandrew was not, even though this event may have been the high point of his career as minister of public works.
Eph-A-RAIL-1878-01/22300473, Alexander Turnbull Library, Wellington

– and was well impressed: 'Truly New Zealand is a wonderful place – Britain may well be proud of her Colonies – what a refuge they have been and are to the tired middle class of England – but more so if possible to the working man.'[13] Macandrew's sentiments entirely.

In October 1878 Macandrew again demonstrated his gift for devising grand visions when he presented a bill to ratify his public works statement. The Railways Construction Act 1878 listed the eight lines to be built in the North Island and, now, 17 in the Middle Island – two more than in his original statement. It included a line from Amberley in North Canterbury to Cook Strait, manifestly added to win the votes of the Nelson–Marlborough members.[14] The Act contained a five-year programme in which each line would be funded separately rather than through parliament's usual annual budgetary allocation.

This time, however, members were more cautious, and many voiced their opposition to his bill. Some were daunted by the scale of the proposed expenditure, and one declared he was 'amazed at any Government proposing that such sums of money should be spent upon works of which we know so little'.[15] Another condemned the bill as 'the most ill-considered, ill-advised, impolitic, and unjustifiable measure that has ever been laid before a reasonable House of Parliament'.[16] A third was shocked by the request to 'confer powers on a

Government which no constitutional Government ought to seek or ought to accept; and we are asked to give up powers which, if we have any proper sense of our own responsibility, we cannot and we dare not give up'.[17] Atkinson was appalled by a bill which, once enacted, would give the government 'the absolute and uncontrolled power of spending six and a half millions of money exactly as they please'; he warned of 'the enormous pressure to which any Government possessing such power must be immediately subjected'.[18] Some members, quite legitimately, accused Macandrew of favouring Otago over the North Island: after all, 10 of the 17 Middle Island lines were to be built in Otago, including a line from Dunedin via Central Otago to the West Coast.[19] Macandrew ended the debate by claiming that he was best qualified to sponsor this bill: 'I do not think there is any public man in New Zealand whose idiosyncrasies are more cosmopolitan than my own.'[20]

The bill passed its second reading with a majority of 34 votes.[21] Macandrew had vastly expanded the country's railway building programme and went on to sponsor two further railway Acts at this time. His amendment to the District Railways Act 1877 permitted the government to buy private lines; and an amendment to the Public Works Act 1876 granted the government power to take land for railways, authorised the appointment of a 'commissioner of railways' and an 'engineer in charge of railways' in both islands, and regularised a number of procedures. The latter stirred little debate and passed its second reading by 38 votes to 2.[22]

Parihaka

In 1884 an interviewer would report that Macandrew never wanted to discuss 'Native affairs' because 'he had never lived in a land overrun with Maoris; knew nothing of their ways and wants, and wanted to know nothing of them'.[23] Macandrew had opposed Stafford's land seizure and war policy in 1868, but beyond that there are few records of his interaction with tangata whenua, with the exception of the long-running saga of Dunedin's Princes Street Reserve (see chapter 12), which took over three decades to settle.[24]

The Weld government had intended to survey confiscated land on the Waimate Plains for settlement purposes. In 1866 the Taranaki spiritual leader and prophet Te Whiti-o-Rongomai established the village of Parihaka there in an attempt to 'end the slaughter without surrendering the land'.[25] Parihaka became the centre of a campaign of nonviolent resistance to European occupation of land in the area.

The government was wary of provoking further conflict, and a decade later the plains still had not been surveyed. On 22 May 1878 Macandrew presented a Cabinet minute that revealed his hard-nosed attitude to the pursuit of money, and his antagonistic approach to any show of Māori political independence:

> I desire to submit to the Cabinet the expediency of there being no further delay in taking the necessary action towards surveying for settlement and disposing of the Waimate Block. In my opinion the Government has shown great remissness in not having had this land in the market now. It would have placed us in funds to a very large extent, and enabled public works to be carried on, so far, irrespective of loan … I would suggest that a strong detachment of Armed Constabulary should be located in the neighbourhood, and surveyors started on the block at once: and that the native minister be apprised that such is the intention of the Government unless he is of opinion that good policy absolutely forbids it.[26]

His minute was approved by Cabinet and work commenced on 10 August of that year. By March 1879, 16,000 acres (6500ha) of the plains had been surveyed. Local Māori, led by Te Whiti and the Ngāruahine leader Riwha Tītokowaru, responded with a series of nonviolent campaigns to halt the work, and a battle of wills ensued. Mapping ceased when the surveyors attempted to move onto land cultivated by the villagers, who in turn disrupted the surveyors' work by removing their pegs. John Ballance, who had inherited the financial portfolio in January and was now colonial treasurer, immediately requested the Taranaki Land Board to arrange for the disposal of the surveyed area.[27] However, uncertainty about the designation of Native reserves led the government to halt and then cancel the sale; Grey was not prepared to risk a fight to eject the owners of the land. The Hall government would infamously adopt Macandrew's suggestion in 1881, a move that resulted in the exile in Dunedin of another tranche of Māori political prisoners.[28]

Macandrew's public works statement included a proposed railway line from Te Awamutu to Inglewood as part of the link between Wellington and Auckland, but the Māori king Tūkāroto Matutaera Pōtatau Te Wherowhero Tāwhiao was adamant he would not open the King Country to European settlement.[29] Macandrew was at a loss to understand Tāwhiao's refusal:

> If those natives have a just conception of the vast revenue which will accrue to them after parting with sufficient land whereby to construct this railway, they will not hesitate for a moment to enter heartily into a transaction which is bound to increase the value of the land which will be left to them very

many fold. Moreover, they may earn a large amount of money by devoting their labour to the construction of the line.[30]

In the event, the North Island main trunk railway was not started until 1885, and was completed in 1908; the Taranaki connection, from Okahukura to Stratford, finally opened in 1932.

A dysfunctional Cabinet

Treasurer Ballance presented his first budget on 6 August. It did not deliver the savings Grey had promised; rather, his 'estimated expenditure for 1878–9 (£4,193,500) exceeded that of the previous year by £224,000'.[31] His generous gift to voters, 'a free breakfast table', would be created by reducing customs duties on grain, flour, tea and sugar, to be offset by the introduction of a land tax of a halfpenny in the pound on the unimproved value of properties worth more than £500.[32] He also proposed two new taxes, on company profits and beer, but Grey, in the face of fierce opposition, withdrew them without consultation.[33] This so incensed Ballance that he threatened to resign, and although he did not follow through on this occasion, it confirmed the Cabinet's volatility as members struggled to work with Grey.

The City of Glasgow Bank failed in October 1878, and the repercussions shook the empire. The bank had made large loans on inadequate security to investors in land, farming and mining in Australasia and America, and its collapse sent numerous businesses and shareholders to the wall. A rapid retrenchment of credit and a slump in land and export prices ensued; in New Zealand, bankruptcies proliferated and unemployment soared.[34] The poorly performing economy was one factor in the downfall of Grey's ministry.

But there were others. Grey's Cabinet began to unravel in early October as a result of his unpredictable, autocratic behaviour and interpersonal tensions within the team. William Russell, member for Napier, described the Cabinet:

a more disconnected, disunited, ill-assorted party than those honorable gentlemen who call themselves Ministerial supporters never sat within this House before. It reminds me of a comet. They have a great, brilliant, erratic head, but their body tails off, diminishing in light, until it vanishes into nothing at all.[35]

Grey did not manage to deliver on his vision of sweeping electoral reform. The Electoral Bill presented on 1 August did not include the triennial parliaments, the redistribution of electorates and the franchise for all men that he had promised, although it offered the vote to those men who had resided in New Zealand for a year, lived in one electorate for six months and who owned freehold property worth £25. In a world first, it extended the franchise to female ratepayers. But frustrated by the Legislative Council's amendment to remove the voting rights of Māori ratepayers, in a fit of pique Grey withdrew this bill also.[36] Women would have to wait another 15 years for suffrage.

The Agricultural Company

The drawn-out collapse of Grey's government was also linked to the involvement of some of its ministers in a complicated and devious business deal to sell land on the rabbit-infested Waimea Plains in Southland. Faced with poor returns and falling land values brought about by the vermin, run-holders were desperate to sell their farms; Larnach, who owned Middle Dome Run on the plains, devised a scheme to sell the land to British investors without revealing its true condition. This involved the launches of the Waimea Plains Railway Company in June 1878 to open up the district, the New Zealand Land and Loan Company in October 1878 to lend money to prospective farmers, and the London-based Agricultural Company, which bought eight runs totalling 309,000 acres (12,5050ha) in December 1878 to onsell to English investors. The presence of ministers as company directors bestowed the scheme with a veneer of respectability: Larnach was director of the railway board, Stout and Ballance of the loan company board, and Larnach and Vogel of the Agricultural Company. [37]

In February 1879 Macandrew was honoured by the naming of Macandrew Township, a new settlement to be sited on the west bank of the Mataura River at one of the few safe crossings on the route between Gore and the Waikaia (Switzers) gold diggings. The timing of this is noteworthy. It was gazetted by Macandrew's successor as minister for lands, Robert Stout, at the same time that Ballance turned the preliminary sod of the Waimea Plains Railway, the first line to be built under Macandrew's District Railways Act 1878.[38] In London, Vogel advertised the commencement of the railway's construction and reassured English investors that the estate would be accessible and land values would increase. Investors subscribed enthusiastically to a scheme that appeared to be backed by the New Zealand government.[39]

When Grey realised what Ballance and Stout had done, he insisted they either resign their directorships or leave the Cabinet. The pair chose to stay in government, but the resulting loss of trust brought any effective functioning of the Cabinet to an end, and both resigned their portfolios later in the year.

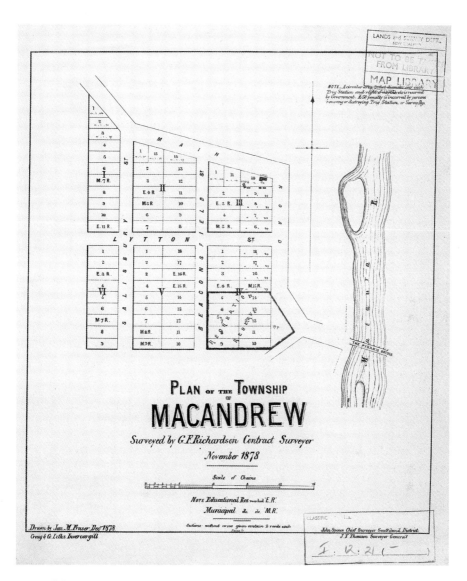

A map of the proposed Macandrew Township in Southland. It was laid out in 1878 but never built. 31946889, Alexander Turnbull Library, Wellington

Vogel attempted to justify his simultaneous directorship of the Agricultural Company and employment as agent-general, something that was contrary to official policy. He claimed that Ballance, Stout and Macandrew knew of his activities, and this he had conveniently interpreted to mean that he had government approval to continue as a director.[40] Vogel refused to give up either position until his hand was forced by Grey's successor, John Hall, who demanded he resign as agent-general – which Vogel did on 6 October 1880.[41]

It is difficult to imagine that Macandrew did not have some inkling of his colleagues' plans, although his earlier experience of prison would presumably have made him wary of involvement in such dubious machinations. A note in the Grey Papers held by the Auckland Council Libraries suggests he was unaware of the matter: 'Macandrew denied to Rees – and Dignan – that he knew of it – also to Sir G. Grey himself.'[42] On 14 October 1884 during the debate for the second reading of the District Railways Leasing and Purchasing Bill (which would allow the government to buy the Waimea Plains Railway, among others, and rescue the Agricultural Company from its debts), Macandrew fiercely opposed the purchase of the line, saying, 'it is not the duty of the State to relieve those who have entered into bad speculations'.[43] This was not the stance of an expectant investor. His later behaviour adds to the puzzle, however: he abstained from voting for the bill's third reading after the Speaker stated that members with a pecuniary interest were not entitled to vote. Ballance, Stout and Vogel also abstained, although Larnach did not.[44] (Of course, it is possible Macandrew may have invested in another railway.)

The disharmony in the Cabinet was exacerbated in February 1879 when, in the face of objection by Grey, Ballance appointed David Luckie as government insurance commissioner on a salary four times higher than the official rate. Although the salary was later reduced, ill feeling ran high, and in April the Cabinet stopped meeting altogether. Before long, 'Grey was issuing decrees as though he had no ministers and no such institution as Cabinet even existed'.[45] Stout resigned in June, ostensibly to focus on his legal career, and Ballance departed in July after a confrontation in Grey's office that almost came to blows; Macandrew threatened to resign also, but Grey managed to talk him out of it.[46] In this poisonous atmosphere parliament met again on 11 July.

Despite their collective antagonism towards the government, some members of the press continued to speak well of Macandrew. A reporter for the *Southland Times* acknowledged his skill as a 'go-between' but held out little hope for the government as a whole:

> Sir George Grey is really much beholden to Mr Macandrew; the latter has
> stuck to him with unswerving fidelity, and should the Ministry by any
> chance tide over the present difficulty, they will owe a great deal to Mr
> Macandrew's buoyancy, sagacity, and shrewd common sense. However, we
> do not think it is possible for even 'Old Mac' to save his party; discontent
> is chronic, and there is such very much better men waiting, and ready to
> supplant the present occupants of the Ministerial benches.[47]

His opponents were less complimentary. The *Wanganui Chronicle* accused
Macandrew of malfeasance based on an incident in the House. Edward
Richardson, member for City of Christchurch and a previous minister of public
works, requested a copy of a map showing the proposed North Island railway
lines.[48] When it was presented, Richardson claimed that an extension of the
Thames railway from Te Aroha to Grahamstown had been added 'under
instructions from the Hon. the Minister for Public Works'.[49] Construction had
commenced, seemingly without the permission of the House, and electoral
bribery with public money was suggested. A select committee appointed to
investigate the affair found that the wrong map had been supplied. Whether this
was another example of Macandrew's impatience with procedure or a recurrence
of his lifelong pattern of carelessness, he maintained that permission to build
the line had been given by a previous minister in 1873. The inquiry committee
was directed to reconvene with a different membership.[50] Although the second
committee agreed with its predecessor, parliament adjourned on 11 August
and Macandrew avoided penalty.[51] His judgement was condemned by a royal
commission in 1880, which considered the Te Aroha–Grahamstown line
to be extravagant and ordered for it to be discontinued. It was eventually
recommended and reached Thames in 1898.[52]

Aware that his party was unlikely to win the forthcoming election, Macandrew was subdued when he presented his second public works statement on
7 August 1879 in the final days of the session:

> I have carefully abstained from saying anything debateable; and shall
> conclude by expressing a hope that, into whatever hands the future
> administration of the Public Works Department may fall, the Railway
> policy which I had the honor to enunciate last session may be earnestly and
> vigorously prosecuted.[53]

Grey's efforts to impose a radical manifesto on New Zealand politics had been
'ineffectual, inefficient, and extravagant', the government's land tax 'extremely
unpopular', and he was accused of stirring up further conflict with Māori in his

attempt to open up land in the region of Parihaka.[54] He was defeated twice in the House before succumbing to a want-of-confidence motion on 29 July.[55] Grey requested a dissolution, expecting to have it denied, but the new governor, Sir Hercules Robinson, called his bluff and sent him, unwillingly, to the polls.[56] In August 1879, Grey went to the country for an election triggered by greed and fuelled by animosity.

Macandrew's political philosophy

Macandrew returned home to stand again for Port Chalmers, the seat he had won in 1871 but deserted for Dunedin City in 1875. During the election campaign in September 1879 he expounded on his economic philosophy of decentralisation, self-interest and self-reliance. He opposed any increase in taxation since most of it would be used to subsidise local bodies, which he believed should raise their own funds. To address the colony's appalling debt of £20 million he proposed reducing expenditure, and he repeated his unwavering belief that population expansion would ease New Zealand's economic problems:

> If this Colony is to prosper, its population must be greatly increased … instead of supporting 400,000 people I believe it will take many millions of people to beneficially occupy this country … every facility should be given for the acquisition of moderately-sized farms, not by the thousand but by the hundreds of thousands … and I, for one, say that we could afford to plant 200,000 families – aye, twice 200,000 – upon 50-acre farms without interfering with those men who desire to occupy more extensive holdings and are in a position to acquire them.[57]

His speech included the revolutionary proposal that New Zealand should adopt a paper currency that was not gold-based:

> he could see no great difficulty in the way of the State paying for its public works in its own bonds, bearing interest … But why should not these bonds be issued in small amounts and made legal tender in New Zealand? … they would bear interest, and as such would speedily supplant bank notes.[58]

He confirmed his commitment to the utilitarianism of Jeremy Bentham and John Stuart Mill:[59]

> the greatest possible happiness to the greatest possible number had been his pole-star all along. Progress, whether in opening up the country by roads and bridges, in extending the means of education throughout its length and breadth, in promoting intercourse by steam with the neighbouring provinces and colonies and with the Mother Country, in the construction of railroads

and docks, the encouragement of manufactures, the introduction of immigrants, the suppression of crime and the nipping it in the bud; – these and many other things had been his watchword, not in word but in deed, for he could point to each and all as realities which it had been his lot chiefly to influence.[60]

His belief in independent local government was still strong. He now advocated for a reduction of local bodies, and for them to be given 'the administrative powers which were exercised by the Provinces, with power to borrow under certain conditions … all local railways and other works should then devolve upon the counties'.[61] The colony should collect taxes only 'for the protection of the public creditor, for the protection of life and property, and for the maintenance of peace, order, and good government throughout the Colony'.[62]

Macandrew's activity in parliament in late 1879 mirrored his behaviour as superintendent of Otago in 1860, when he spent a great deal of time and energy defending his actions in debates of excruciatingly minor detail. As a minister he may have been lulled by media praise; certainly he appeared unaware that many of the public held negative views of his tendency to ignore established protocol.

Macandrew was 60 by this time, and the life of a politician may have begun to lose its gloss. His stress was apparent in a letter to his daughter Mabel, aged 13, in which he apologised for a tardy reply:

> I have had so much to do and to think about that days and weeks slip away before I know where I am hence the delay. You may rest assured that I do not forget my dear little girl and that your letters as well as those from Arthur, Alice and all of you afford me very great pleasure and satisfaction.[63]

Macandrew won the Port Chalmers seat on 6 September 1879 with 363 of 630 votes cast, defeating sitting member James Green who had opposed Grey in the House, and went on to retain the seat, unchallenged, in both the 1881 and 1884 elections.[64] From this victory he morphed effortlessly into the role of elder statesman of the country, and on his return to Wellington he was elected leader of the opposition, a position he would hold for the next three years.

Chapter 17

I the last few weeks of the 1879 parliamentary session there was a close-run race for the premiership. Macandrew failed to win the post by a mere four votes.

Grey appeared to have won the general election, but before the House could confirm the election result, John Hall, member for Selwyn and the new leader of the opposition grouping, moved a want-of-confidence vote that was carried 43:41.[1] Edward Stevens' prediction of 1871 had come to pass: on 3 October 1879 the 'gamblers and thimble-riggers' were ejected.

Wellington's Provincial Chambers were modified several times after 1870. This is the more spacious Parliament House in 1880. 1/2-018471/F/23167253, Alexander Turnbull Library, Wellington

Hall's 'prudent' party, which included the returning Stevens, was a combination of land and property owners and businessmen, who were keen to abolish the land tax and halt the extravagant spending on public works. It was installed to restore solvency, but no politician could defeat the deepening economic crisis – only Vogel's and Grey's enthusiastic borrowing had prevented the colony from suffering 'unrelieved depression for thirty years, 1865–95'.[2] Successive ministries had attempted to avoid deficits by rearranging customs duties and introducing direct taxes on property and beer, but the country's income – earned predominantly from the export of primary produce – continued to fall.

Leader of the opposition

Grey immediately handed leadership to Macandrew of what was now the opposition party, who accepted it as a compromise candidate, rather than out of ambition or with the approbation of his colleagues. As the *Otago Daily Times* editor noted, 'Mr. Macandrew is not, we believe, anxious for the post of Premier, but his acceptance of the task of forming a new Government would probably lead to a successful result, as of all the members of the Ministry, he has the fewest personal enemies in the house.'[3] Macandrew tried, unsuccessfully, to emerge from his predecessor's shadow, but Grey continued to act as the putative leader of the Liberal faction and refused to support its political programme.[4] Macandrew was forced onto the defensive, his leadership subverted also by Harry Atkinson, his successor as colonial treasurer, who justified his own economic austerity programme by relentlessly assailing Macandrew's performance as a minister. The *West Coast Times* later reported that 'the Hall party had the gratification of seeing their only dangerous opponent ignominiously deposed through the stupidity of his professed friends and supporters'.[5]

Although Grey had been evicted from the treasury benches, Hall's majority was insecure. When Macandrew moved his own want-of-confidence motion on 10 October 1879, Hall stalled debate on it for two weeks while he worked to consolidate his majority. Macandrew's motion lapsed on 28 October.

Few philosophical differences divided the politicians of the day, something that became apparent when the supposedly 'conservative' Hall introduced his remarkably un-conservative triennial parliaments and franchise bills, which granted all male New Zealanders over 21 the right to vote.[6] Male suffrage had been a mainstay of the liberal reform programme, but Grey had not enacted it during his term. In introducing these bills, Hall hoped to force Macandrew to oppose his own principles.[7] Macandrew responded by challenging every

William Brickell Gibbs' cartoon, in the *Otago Witness* jubilee supplement of 31 March 1898, illustrates Macandrew's solution to the financial crisis after John Hall had replaced George Grey as premier, and highlights Macandrew's next motion of no confidence, moved and lost on 24 November 1879.

'Sir I move "That the Financial proposals of the Government are unsatisfactory."
I have got my pruning knife and I shall cut off County subsidies
and make them support the Police and Educate all the Children.
And then I shall write a history of what I have done. Thomson says so!'

([Above the hanging figures on the left:]
'I should also propose to consolidate departmental offices thus')

Box-267-002, Hocken Collections, Uare Taoka o Hākena, University of Otago

government motion in order to force his want-of-confidence motion to the top of the order paper.[8]

Members of the Grey, Ballance and middle party factions coalesced behind Macandrew to position him as premier.[9] With the clear support of a majority, his success was assumed; the press even went so far as to forecast his Cabinet: 'The proposed Macandrew Government will probably consist of Macandrew, Premier and Colonial Secretary; Ballance, Treasurer and Customs; Montgomery, Public Works; Stewart, Attorney General; Sheehan, Native Minister; Pyke, Lands and Mines; and Shepherd, Postmaster General.'[10]

But it was not to be. In an action that resonates yet in New Zealand political lore, four Auckland members – William Colbeck, William Hurst, William Swanson and Reader Wood, ostensible Grey supporters who were expected to vote for Macandrew and who were labelled ever after as the 'Auckland rats' – gave their votes to Hall in return for commitments to their province, including more money for public works.[11] The *Waikato Times* described the situation:

> A section of the Auckland members at Wellington, awakened to the danger
> of allowing a Macandrew Ministry to perpetuate a reign of financial terror
> over the colony, have used their position … to secure for the Auckland
> district some equitable redress for the wrongs done to it in the unjust
> allocation of the loans under the Public Works and Immigration Policy.[12]

Although it was not uncommon for hometown allegiance to trump party loyalty, it was a sorry outcome for Macandrew. Swanson had been a minister and colleague in the Grey Cabinet for its final three months; Wood, a Liberal party executive committee member, had actually nominated Macandrew as leader of the party.[13] It may have been a small comfort to Macandrew that loyal Otago voters returned him unopposed in the 1881 election, when Auckland jettisoned Wood and Colbeck, and returned him again in 1884 when Swanson lost his seat.

With the severe downturn in the economy, public opinion turned against the Greyites and erstwhile supporters now voiced scathing criticism.[14] The *Evening Post* proclaimed:

> The Grey Ministry … promised vast retrenchment in the public expenditure
> and a general lightening of the public burdens … [They] not only inherited a
> large surplus and a million of unexpended loan, but they also borrowed two
> millions and a half more during their two years of official life. All these large
> sums they have spent, much of it, we fear, utterly thrown away and wasted.[15]

In a letter to Sir James Hector, James Farmer was particularly acerbic: 'It will take years to undo the mischief they have done the Colony.'[16] Farmer's prediction would prove accurate.

Members of the new government were critical of what they regarded as past gross extravagance in the depressed economic climate. Atkinson commented, 'The colony is … in a state of complete darkness as to our real financial position.'[17] He noted that the Grey ministry had committed almost half of a proposed loan of £5 million to projects without having received 'the slightest news from Home as to whether it is likely we shall get the money.'[18] A month later he pointed the finger at the Public Works scheme:

> When we remember that the Public Works scheme of 1878 was to take five years to complete, that the expenditure from loan was only to be at the rate of some £900,000 a year, and that by a special provision of 'The Loan Act, 1879', no money raised under it was to be spent without appropriation by Parliament, we … have come to the conclusion that Parliament has not been treated with frankness in this matter, and that its authority has been disregarded.[19]

In December Atkinson described New Zealand as 'the most heavily indebted and the most heavily taxed country in the whole world … It is attributable solely to excessive borrowing.' He proposed a strict rule for the future: 'Not one shilling of borrowed money shall be expended except on works which will at once yield a profit at least equal to the annual interest upon their cost.'[20]

While Grey's men challenged Atkinson's figures, Premier Hall wrote to Vogel who, in London, was confidante of both sides of the House:

> If [New Zealand's] finances had remained for another 6 months under their old management, I do not believe that all our & your exertions would have averted a smash. Macandrew still refuses to believe in the liabilities we found; and Grey told FitzGerald that with an additional £80,000 a year he would be satisfied.[21]

In an attempt to pinpoint the blame for the sluggish economy, in 1880 Hall launched four royal commissions to review the performance of the Grey government. Although Grey's entire Cabinet had been responsible for the expensive construction programmes, Macandrew's casual management style and reputation for corner-cutting made him a convenient scapegoat. Two of the enquiries examined Macandrew's conduct as a minister; one considered the organisation of the Civil Service and whether its costs could be reduced without impairing its efficiency, and another examined the cost and value of completing railway lines already under construction.[22] Macandrew was fortunate to escape a reckoning, but his credibility was further undermined when the commissions censured the Grey regime and its management of the Public Works Department. While not identified by name, Macandrew's many ad hoc decisions and the careless administration of his department were criticised. The Commission on the Civil Service in New Zealand reported: 'We ... have come to the very painful conviction that New Zealand has not received good value for the large sums that have been expended.'[23]

The commission also accused Macandrew of inadequate oversight of William Conyers, commissioner of railways for the Middle Island, who, it was later reported, 'has capital invested in a firm contracting with the department of which he is head ... his receipts from this capital depend on the success of that firm.'[24] Further accusations of cronyism and fraud, tabled in parliament, claimed that a Dunedin locomotive engineer, Alex Armstrong, had not only improperly bought material from the firm of Guthrie & Larnach, but had replaced it with inferior stock to assemble wagons.[25]

The accompanying report from the Railways Commission described what it considered to be a 'fatal' error of judgement: 'the making of railways in some parts of the colony far in advance of existing settlement, and consequently of an amount of traffic adequate to their support'.[26] It is clear today that Macandrew's plans for railways were strategically astute, as nearly all of his proposed lines were eventually built: his problem lay in the timing.[27]

Macandrew's ambitions constantly outstripped available resources, but despite his irresponsible spending:

> He at one time commanded a far greater amount of popularity and applause than has ever been given by the New Zealand public to men of a far higher stamp, to far more unselfish patriots, to men of more self-control, of greater ability, or more reliable judgment, and more trustworthy integrity.[28]

It was Macandrew's misfortune to be a minister at a time of severe economic downturn. Vogel's borrow-and-spend policy had been appealing as an economic stimulator; on becoming minister of public works, Macandrew had persisted with it in response to the public's demand for government intervention in the economy, and spent without restraint. Given his earlier record for retrenchment, it is surprising that he did not support Atkinson in 1876, and that he was prepared to launch a spending round in 1877. Nor did he support Hall's severe cutbacks from 1879 onwards; instead he continued to advocate for ongoing government investment to solve the country's woes, even after his return to the backbenches.

There are few clues to explain his inconsistent attitude to government spending, but he appears to have followed a similar path to Vogel. Both men discovered that leadership involving responsibility for the welfare of citizens could change a politician's values.

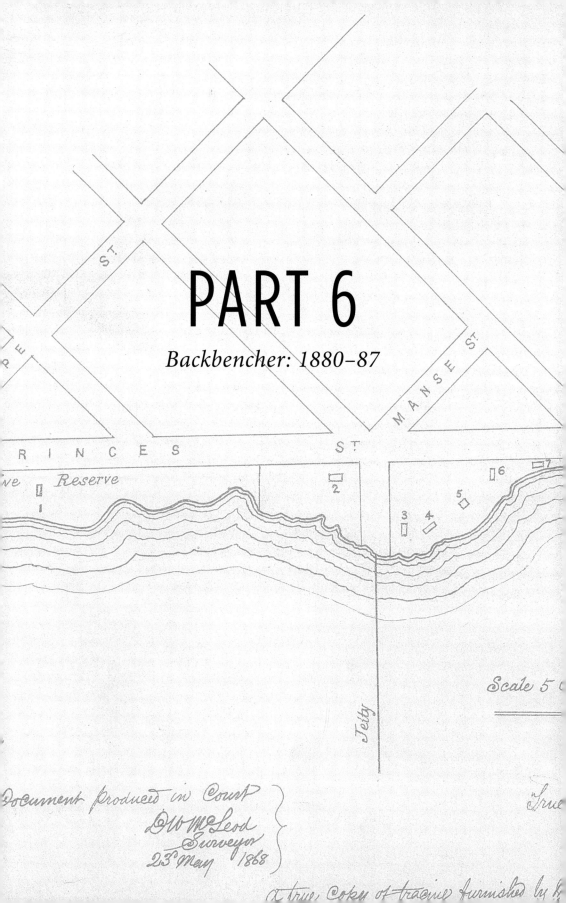

PART 6

Backbencher: 1880–87

Chapter 18

Over the next seven years in parliament, as leader of the opposition party and father of the House, Macandrew continued to demonstrate his commitment to settlement, development and improving social conditions in New Zealand.[1] He was indulged by many, but treated seriously by few. Criticism of Macandrew's leadership must be treated cautiously, however – after all, he led the opposition for three years of the long depression, during which time no other politician challenged him for the position, and during which George Grey, the Liberals' *éminence grise*, continued to destabilise the party.[2]

From the opposition benches Macandrew regularly aired his complaint about Atkinson's calculation of the public works expenditure during the Grey administration. Macandrew denied his responsibility for these costs, claiming that the figures Atkinson had presented included expenses incurred by other portfolios.[3] His protests did nothing to enhance his reputation, or to lessen the accusations of extravagance in the Grey ministry.

Although Macandrew espoused frugality in many areas, despite the faltering economy and the downturn in railway revenue he continued to promote his railway building programme, and he was eager for Hall's government to maintain railway investment at the same rate as the Grey government had done. Averse to the concept of money sitting around unused, he suggested, 'Surely we could not do better … than to devote a portion of this money, while it is lying idle in the bank, towards the finishing of these railways?'[4] Small wonder his financial opinions often invited attack: to most people his views were too progressive and suspect.

In an address to his Port Chalmers constituents in 1880 he referred again to the concept of a colonial currency. The *Press* reported: 'Mr. Macandrew, again, is understood to have some nostrum or another for the manufacture of wealth as fast as greenbacks can be turned out of our Government printing office.'[5] Wellington's *Evening Post* considered him 'still the reckless and speculative visionary as of old': 'Mr. Macandrew opined that a bale of paper and a printing

It was unclear to the public whether Macandrew, Montgomery or Grey was the leader of members opposed to the Hall ministry. The *Observer* of 23 June 1883 ran this cartoon with the accompanying text:

TWO RICHMONDS IN THE FIELD: The Government whip has set aside one of the Committee rooms on the upper floor of the Parliamentary Buildings, and inscribed over it the words 'Leader of the Opposition.' In looking over the new buildings, Sir George Grey and Mr Montgomery arrived at the door simultaneously, and the two having glanced at the inscription, Sir George Grey, with his never-failing tact, began to speak of the weather and the indications of a storm.

press were all the colony needed – excepting perhaps a little ink – to overcome any possible financial difficulties, by the wholesale issue of paper money.'[6] Although Macandrew denied making the comment, the mockery was accepted as fact and the *Evening Post*'s label stuck.[7]

As the depression worsened, Macandrew continued to promote a liberal economic programme. In a want-of-confidence speech in June 1880, one of the few occasions on which he spoke at length as leader of the opposition, he made his position on governance and taxation clear:

> I quite agree as to the expediency of changing the incidence of taxation, so as to distribute it more equitably, but I can be no party to increasing the aggregate of the present taxation upon the country … this Legislature should leave the localities to tax themselves for all their local requirements.[8]

In a statement reminiscent of Atkinson's earlier call for a 'political rest', Macandrew asserted that 'the Opposition … is not bidding for office now'.[9] This was scarcely the fighting talk that voters who were eager to unseat Hall wanted to hear. One journalist's blunt judgement probably represented a widely held view: 'The speech was not brilliant nor very effective.'[10]

In May 1881 Macandrew announced a nine-point legislative programme that included plans to complete his 1878 railway policy, to repeal property tax and to resume immigration. He promised to reduce education spending by lifting the school starting-age and increasing local control and levies. He wished to reform the law courts, to establish a direct steamer service with England, to readjust parliamentary representation, to return 20 per cent of the land fund to local bodies, and finally – his old favourite – to enable the 'transfer of such business to local bodies, as nearly as may be analogous to Provincial councils as they were intended to be'.[11] Most of these points were adopted the following year by his opponents as a 'liberal political programme for New Zealand'. This also supported a property tax and proposed that the Legislative Council be partly elected by local bodies.[12]

Insular separation – code for provincialism – was one of Macandrew's *idées fixes*, and the country would not have been surprised when he released what he called an 'insular manifesto' in October 1881. In it he suggested that each island should revert to provincial status, elect a president, and establish a legislature responsible for all laws – with 12 exceptions that would be the responsibility of the General Assembly, which would have its powers of taxation curtailed.[13] Although Macandrew did not acknowledge his source, older settlers may have recognised this as a modified Clause 19 of the Constitution Act 1852.[14] His proposal was dismissed, however, as 'more pretentious but less efficient' than existing plans to devolve powers to the counties.[15] In his 1885 constituency report, he returned once again to his concerns about the imbalance of power between central and local governments. Good government was not possible in New Zealand, he believed, 'so long as Centralism, not content with confining itself to its proper sphere, insists upon exercising all the functions of localism as well'.[16] That year he also moved that a royal commission be established to consider turning the two islands into separate provinces. Members may have agreed with him about the imbalance of power, but they were not prepared to return to provincialism to solve the problem, and this motion was also dismissed.[17]

The proposed Australasian federation

By the 1880s New Zealand enjoyed limited self-government, along with five of Australia's six colonies, Newfoundland, the Cape Colony and most of modern Canada. Prompted by concerns about the future of the empire if all colonies were to become completely independent, the Imperial Federation League was formed and held its first meeting in London on 29 July 1884. The league proposed that the countries of the British Empire federate, establish an imperial parliament in London to oversee federal interests, and make arrangements to share the costs of defending the realm. A federation of South Pacific colonies had already been considered. Representatives from the Australian colonies, concerned about European expansion in the Pacific, had met with New Zealand and Fijian politicians in Sydney on 28 November 1883 and formed the Federal Council of Australasia. The council discussed joint action to counter German and French incursions into New Guinea and the New Hebrides (now Vanuatu), and the establishment of a body to legislate for issues common to all their colonies.

The council's resolutions may have provoked a strong sense of déjà vu for Macandrew, as they had the potential to recreate the saga of the writing of the New Zealand Constitution Act, and the problems experienced in agreeing on a workable governance structure. To his constituents he suggested it would be 'the greatest possible blunder for New Zealand to enter into any such confederation upon the lines laid down by the Conference in Sydney, and that we had better remain as we are, on our own hook'.[18]

In November 1884 the General Assembly was requested to ratify an Australasian Federal Council Bill for presentation in the House of Commons. Premier Stout moved that the establishment of a federal council with legislative authority over a number of areas such as extradition, fisheries, patents and copyright would be premature.[19] Members agreed the matter required more consideration, and it was deferred until the next session. When it was raised again in September 1885, Stout moved: 'It is inadvisable for this House to join the Federal Council of Australasia under the existing Federal Council Act.'[20] Macandrew immediately moved a protracted, alternative motion:

> That ... the time has come when efforts should be made to unite the whole English-speaking people throughout the world in one grand political confederation or alliance, having for its object mutual defence against foreign aggression, the maintenance of peace, and the promotion of the brotherhood of nations. That a respectful address be presented to His Excellency the Governor, requesting that he may be pleased to transmit this resolution to the Queen, in the hope that Her Majesty may still further distinguish her illustrious reign by endeavouring to bring about a Conference that shall represent the whole of the British dominions and the United States of America, to meet either at London or Washington ...[21]

He spoke at length of 'the unspeakable benefits that would be derived therefrom, not only by the whole English-speaking people, but by the whole human race ... The mere manifestation of such a sentiment by the most powerful, wealthy, and important race on the earth would produce results that it would be impossible to overestimate.' He quoted from pamphlets of the London-based Imperial Federation League, and from historian Edward Freeman; he reminded listeners of the Greek Achaean League, the Swiss cantons, the United Provinces of the Netherlands and the Dominion of Canada; he presented population figures, measures of national wealth and travel times, and ended with a verse by Robert Burns. Although subsequent speakers expressed concern at the possibility of losing control over national issues, Macandrew's motion was agreed. Atkinson, however, defused the debate with the time-honoured technique: he moved to defer consideration of the bill until the next session.

The country was struggling to cope with an intense depression alongside political instability as ministries rotated rapidly – in September 1883, twice in August 1884 and again in September 1884. Few could see any advantage in federation. There appeared to be little economic gain for the country, as by now the majority of exports were going to Britain. Many present had endured the prolonged effort to achieve self-government; others, aware that central government had achieved abolition by removing provincial powers, feared that a wider federal government might do the same to New Zealand.[22]

The Australasian Federal Council Bill lapsed. By 1886 there was still no reply from the Queen regarding the request for a conference to establish 'an alliance of all English-speaking nations throughout the world'.[23] The question of federation did not occupy the House again until 1891, by which time the drive for it had diminished, and New Zealand turned its back on political union with its nearest neighbour.[24]

Further immigration proposals

Although no longer the party leader, Macandrew maintained his push for immigration and settlement. In an amendment to the Land Act 1877, passed in 1884 by the re-elected Vogel ministry, he instigated the inclusion of a clause that reserved 10,000 acres (4046ha) of land between the Catlins River and Mataura, to be offered to crofters from the Highlands and islands of Scotland.[25] Each would be given 10 acres (4ha) and could apply to purchase a further 20, figures that reappeared in a more comprehensive Land Act passed the following year.[26]

There was some resistance to this perceived preferential treatment: one protester asked why the Scots should be selected over evicted Irish peasants; another predicted that crofters 'would land ... as absolute paupers, and have to be maintained at the public expense until they could make a living for themselves'.[27] Macandrew justified this project in a letter to emigration agent George Vesey Stewart in London, later published in *The Times*.[28] His sole desire, he wrote, was 'to be instrumental in transplanting as many of my fellow-countrymen as may be from poverty and serfdom to independence and plenty'.[29] Robert Stout, premier from 1884–87, encouraged Macandrew to return to Scotland to 'promote an exodus of crofters to New Zealand' to develop the fishing industry, but the *Auckland Evening Star* reported that Macandrew displayed 'great reluctance to accept the mission, his diffidence being heightened by his inability to converse in Gaelic, a very important qualification in dealing with inhabitants of the Isles of Scotland'.[30] The item's faint whiff of scepticism reflects the growing attitude many now displayed, for a man considered past his time who was not yet prepared to retire.

Macandrew persisted with his project, despite the abject failure of settlements he had earlier promoted for Scottish migrants: Jamestown in South Westland in 1868, Cromarty in Preservation Inlet in 1869, and Port William on Stewart Island in 1872 – where Shetland fishing families had endured only 18 months. He appeared blind to the realities of poor soils, challenging climates, remote locations, distant markets and inadequate shipping services. Fortunately for the prospective settlers, however, a lack of enthusiasm and funds in Britain spelled an end to the scheme.

Macandrew had held executive positions almost continuously since 1867 but was now forced to share the tables in the General Assembly library. Although a despondent air surrounded him in these years as his influence declined, he could still raise a laugh with his seemingly outrageous predictions – at Port Chalmers in 1883 he quipped, 'the time will come when Port Chalmers and Dunedin will be all one … that either Dunedin will swallow up Port Chalmers, or Port Chalmers will swallow up Dunedin.'[31]

There is no doubt that he missed his family during his Wellington sojourns; in a letter dated July 1881 he chided Mabel: 'I expected to have received letters from you or Arthur by the mail which came in this morning – but have been disappointed. I thought that you all promised to write every Saturday. But as yet your performances have come much short of your promises …'[32] He could have retired and returned to Dunedin, but the long depression and an active social conscience drove him on.

A minister once more

Julius Vogel made a brief return visit to economically stagnant New Zealand in December 1882 and was welcomed enthusiastically as 'the man who had once brought prosperity to the country and whose policies might work again.'[33] Macandrew lionised him at a Dunedin banquet, where they resumed their friendship: 'Sir Julius Vogel may be said to have matriculated in Otago, and therefore Otago is entitled to regard him as one of her sons, and as such to feel proud of … any distinction that he may have acquired since he went out from among us.'[34]

On his next return, in April 1884, Vogel decided to stand for parliament in the July election; the Ashburton voters returned him. Stout successfully challenged Atkinson for the premiership, and his Cabinet – announced on 16 August 1884 – included the unlikely combination of Ballance, Macandrew, William Montgomery, George Morris, Edward Richardson, Vogel and George Whitmore. Macandrew's inclusion provoked scathing criticism from the *Timaru Herald*:

> Mr. Macandrew belongs to a prehistoric generation of New Zealand politicians, and to present him as a member of the powerful, vigorous, enlightened Ministry who are to give the Colony new life and a fresh impulse towards prosperity is like putting a fossil megatherium in harness to help to perform a fast coach journey. [35]

The *New Zealand Herald* resurrected Macandrew's transgressions of old and opined: 'He goes far beyond even Sir Julius Vogel in his enthusiasm for getting into debt, and would create wealth with a printing press and a bale of paper.'[36]

In 1884 Stout appointed Macandrew to three portfolios: lands, immigration and mines. Macandrew had not expected to fill a ministerial position again, and was pessimistic about his survival in office. In a letter to Mabel he reflected on the uncertain times:

> I was constrained by my friends very much against my will to form the New Government, knowing well all the time it was not likely to stand, – as to this, my prognostications proved true and we now hold office only until our successors are appointed. When that may be it is hard to say – as things are in a very unsettled condition and there may probably be several changes before any permanent Govt can be formed. I am being strongly urged to join another Government. I think however that I shall keep out of it and prefer to spend my time at home during the recess.[37]

The preponderance of South Islanders made Stout's first ministry unpopular, and it survived for just 12 days. Ministers resigned on 28 August 1884 and Macandrew withdrew from office. A typical nineteenth-century parliamentary shuffle followed: Atkinson resumed power for seven days but was unable to establish a viable government; and Stout and Vogel resumed command on 3 September and governed for the next three years. Their restructured ministry included William Larnach and, ironically, Reynolds – Macandrew's brother-in-law and some-time political rival. Stout considered appointing Macandrew as New Zealand's agent-general in London, and wrote to Vogel: 'The more I see of Macandrew's desire for the good of the colony … his fairness & his unselfishness I must say I feel unable to express my appreciation of his conduct. It is our duty not to forget him. We have none so loyal.'[38] Nothing came of this proposal, however.

Macandrew promoted a variety of increasingly liberal causes in his last years in parliament. In 1855 he had suggested the state make loans to settlers to facilitate their purchase of land, a concept he resurrected in the election campaign of 1884.[39] Now he proposed the establishment of a state bank:

> … whose sole business it would be to make advances upon land at a low rate of interest … any person should be entitled as a matter of right – not of favor – to produce certificate of title under the Land Transfer Act, together with certificate of value under the Property Assessment Act, and … obtain advances not exceeding a certain proportion of the assessed value, which would be fixed by the Legislature at such a rate as would leave margin sufficient to cover contingencies.[40]

As usual he was snubbed: the country was not ready for such a radical concept.

Speaking in the House later in 1884, Macandrew put the suggestion of a royal commission to investigate changes to the currency law, and the establishment of 'a Government land bank' similar to one used by the government of India. Treasurer Vogel promptly dismissed the ideas.[41] In 1885, however, Macandrew's perseverance resulted in the appointment of a select committee, which he chaired, to investigate state loans to settlers. The committee recommended 'that the public credit of New Zealand might with advantage be applied towards enabling settlers, on the security of their land, to acquire advances at a comparatively low rate of interest'.[42] Loans could be administered by the Land Transfer Office and payment could be in interest-bearing New Zealand government debentures, which could be used as currency. The committee proposed that a bill incorporating its recommendations be prepared for the next session.

Since Vogel would not adopt the committee's submission, Macandrew prepared his own Public Advances on Land Bill that summer and moved its second reading in July 1886. The bill reflects his shift in values from laissez faire to populist liberalism, and he was determined to be heard: 'The objects sought by this Bill ... are so vastly important in relation to the future welfare and progress of this colony that I shall be content to stand any amount of adverse criticism if I can only induce the House to seriously consider the matter'.[43] He suggested land was the only security that offered a perfect guarantee to the state: 'Whatever tends to make the pastoral and agricultural industries more profitable, whatever tends to the beneficial occupation of the country – that is a benefit to every class in the community.' He reminded members that 'many of our best settlers, now merely in nominal possession of the land ... will find the utmost difficulty to face the tax-gatherer and make ends meet'. His solution to breaking the grip of the depression was to minimise interest rates and the cost of borrowing. Having dispensed with the idea of a state bank, Macandrew suggested it was the duty of the state to use its credit to make loans to landowners at rates lower than those obtainable commercially. His bill would allow advances on the security of the land to be made at moderate terms through the Land Transfer Department:

> Under this Bill, the borrower gets rid of all this [commissions and fees]. He has nothing but the interest to pay; he goes to the Land Transfer Office with his certificate of title in one hand and his certificate of assessed value in the other, and asks for a loan, not as a matter of favour, but as a matter of legal right, of any sum that he may want, from £50 up to £2,000, for which he will pay interest to the amount of £2.5s up to £50, according to the amount that he requires.[44]

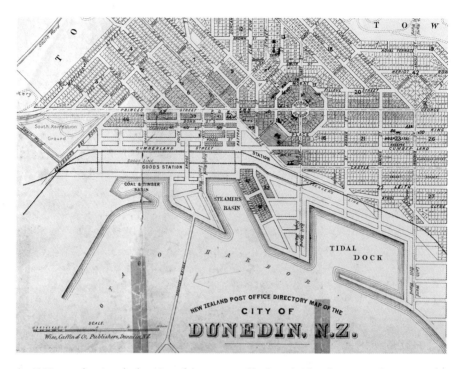

An 1886 map showing the location of the proposed harbour bridge that Macandrew sponsored. Misc-MS-0489, Hocken Collections, Uare Taoka o Hākena, University of Otago

He pointed out that most mortgages held in New Zealand depended on British investors; the bulk of the interest paid – money that could be retained and reinvested – actually left the country. He proposed to fund the loans by issuing debentures, but admitted this concept involved 'the whole question of the bullionist theory … a question upon which so-called political economists can talk a thousand miles over the heads of ordinary mortals'. He now reiterated the economic philosophy that had estranged him from the establishment for most of his life:

> For my own part, I am rather disposed to disregard the political economy
> that is enshrouded in the cobwebs of the past, which may have applied to the
> circumstances of the world a century ago, but does not apply now. I am very
> much inclined to throw all the theorists and theories to the winds. I frankly
> admit it; and the sooner this House comes to the same mind the better.[45]

In this debate, Stout spoke for the fiscally conservative when he expressed concern about the state issuing paper money. He doubted whether the bill would give relief to the neediest, and considered it the first misguided step of many that could result in the ruin of the country. As he said, 'it is the people who have already borrowed on their land far beyond 50 per cent of its value, who ask for relief':

> I think there is already too much tendency in the colony to ask the State to do every possible thing for the people … if you train the people to believe that the State will do everything for them – will be their banker, their money-lender, do everything for them – then you do much to destroy individualism, and, in fact, you are introducing the wildest kind of Socialism … If the State functions are increased, and the State is doing everything for everybody, you may call it a democracy, but you are creating a despotism.[46]

One outraged editor spluttered:

> the absurdity of the whole business is so manifest, so ludicrous, that discussing it would be thought a waste of time were it not that the second reading of the Bill was carried by 31 to 18 … as long as Mr. Macandrew lives to adorn the House, the question will come up.[47]

This view was not held by a majority of parliamentarians. One quarter of the members were absent, but Vogel, Ballance, Grey, Larnach and the future Liberal minister of lands, John McKenzie, supported Macandrew's scheme; Stout, Seddon and Montgomery opposed it. The Liberal's votes point to their steady re-evaluation of the role of government and their acceptance of state intervention in the economy.

Macandrew's bill was interrupted by the end of the session. It should have progressed the following year, but his untimely death in early 1887 would leave it without a sponsor. The proposal did eventually bear fruit, however, when Joseph Ward's Government Advances to Settlers Act, which incorporated Macandrew's suggestions, was passed in 1894. According to historian Michael Bassett, the State then 'took upon itself the task of acting as broker between overseas lenders and domestic borrowers.'[48]

Macandrew's solutions for the country's widespread poverty grew more radical as the depression deepened. The *Otago Daily Times* quoted his idea that the unemployed be driven from the towns and compelled 'to support themselves upon land of their own, for which they should pay nothing to the State.'[49] To that end Macandrew brought six propositions before the House. These included the recommendation that 'every man who is able and willing to work' be granted 'an adequate area of land, on the sole condition of beneficial occupation'. Blocks of land could be administered by local government bodies 'to be by them assigned, in small allotments, to the able-bodied poor'.[50] (This recommendation was an extension of the Village Settlement clauses of the Lands Act 1877 Amendment Act 1879, which had enabled working-class men and their families to live on the land by encouraging groups of prospective farmers to each buy up to 20ha of land on deferred payment and form a community.[51]) He proposed the appointment of 'a separate Minister of the Crown [whose time and attention] might be devoted exclusively to land administration in each Island'. Unfortunately, the arrival of Black Rod with the prorogation message meant the propositions were not debated.[52]

Macandrew was ill for two weeks in the winter of 1884 and wrote to Mabel that 'a straw would have knocked me over'.[53] Failing health and the cost of supporting his large family were taking their toll. A year later he admitted to his fourth son, Hunter:

> I have been very much on my beam ends since coming here from a pain in one of my knees … and the prospect of increased taxation does not render the prospect brighter. I wish I had taken possession of Cod Fish Island [off Stewart Island] with its 3000 acres which I could have had for £500 and £25 a year rent. It would have been a standby run which would have enabled the family to live in comparative affluence and independence.[54]

In May 1885 Macandrew, now aged 65, informed his constituents of his intention to retire at the end of the session.[55]

But weary or not, he was still a force in local affairs. In 1886 he sponsored an Act authorising the construction of a bridge across the upper reaches of Otago Harbour.[56] Land speculators, eager to encourage settlement on the sunny but remote side of the harbour, were pushing for the structure, and local residents – of which Macandrew was one – were keen to have their journey to and from Dunedin shortened. The planned bridge was over 1500 yards (1.4km) long and would span the harbour from the Jetty Street wharf almost to Portobello Road, where it would fork; one arm would lead towards Andersons Bay and the other down-harbour, the two enclosing a swimming pool.[57] The Act made allowance for the Portobello Road Board to install mooring places, davits and any other additions that would be 'not inconsistent with its use as a public highway'.[58] According to the *Otago Daily Times*, the bill was expected to pass as it was 'warmly promoted by Mr Macandrew, who enjoys great popularity in the House'.[59]

The proposal generated vigorous debate around cost, the lack of consultation, and the fact that the bill was sponsored by Macandrew rather than the local member. The Otago Harbour Board predicted problems with silting, and fretted over shipping access to their proposed wharves. In the end the board's parliamentary supporters inserted a requirement for an expensive drawbridge to be included in the plan; they removed the road board's proposed rating powers, which would have paid for the structure, and gave the city council and the harbour board authority to approve the maps, plans and specifications for the bridge. The bill became law, but paralysed by its unworkable terms it was heard of no more.

Macandrew's long service to local and colonial government was recognised in several ways. He was re-appointed to the University of Otago council in 1884, and in November 1885 the council received a portrait of him by Kate Sperry, a copy of which would later be hung in the General Assembly Library.[60] He was also elected president of the Otago Early History Society (now the Otago Settlers' Association) at its inaugural meeting in May 1884.[61] A contemporary publication summed up his contribution to the province:

> It has almost passed into a proverb that Otago is Macandrew and
> Macandrew is Otago. So much has he been associated with almost every
> important event, and connected with every institution, that no history of
> the province would be correct or complete without his name being brought
> prominently and repeatedly to the front.[62]

He was the only serving parliamentary survivor of the first Assembly and was now considered an 'old identity'. His longevity earned him special treatment, although many critics were distracted by his reputation. One newspaper announced: 'Mr. James Macandrew is a privileged person in the House. He would be the last man to make any pretension to eloquence, yet he is always listened to.'[63] The editor was amazed that Macandrew's Public Advances on Land Bill had been supported by such a generous majority, saying: 'It is not on the grounds of his long experience so much as from a vague superstition that he is a practical man, a title that once acquired, no matter how, is a sufficient cloak for the wildest vagaries.'

Chapter 19

Shipping services to and from New Zealand were essential for transporting mail, supplies and a steady supply of new migrants, and were a matter of constant concern. In the 1850s only sailing ships could tackle the route from Britain to New Zealand, as refuelling stations were too widely separated for the coal-driven steamships of the time. From Britain, ships steered south through the Atlantic to the Cape of Good Hope, where they caught the roaring forties, strong westerly winds that propelled them south of Australia to make New Zealand landfall at Bluff. On the return journey they sailed east to Cape Horn then north through the Atlantic. Conditions on board were often miserable and uncomfortable, especially in the tropics and the ice-strewn Southern Ocean. As well, voyages took 75–120 days, and many ships were lost to storms or wrecked on inhospitable coastlines.[1] The quest for a reliable service was finally solved in 1876 with the inauguration of a regular steamer service to San Francisco.

Macandrew had a strong interest in shipping and was an early exporter of produce to Britain. He ventured into coastal and intercolonial trade in the 1850s, and his bankruptcy later that decade stemmed in part from his over-investment in a trans-Tasman steamer service. In 1856 he sat on a parliamentary select committee on interprovincial communication that urged the government of the day to subsidise a steamer service between the provinces; and he continued to agitate, in both the provincial and Assembly chambers, for the provision of swift and efficient shipping between Britain and the colony.[2]

A service from New Zealand to Britain via Panama, which included an overland crossing of the isthmus, was introduced in June 1866. Subsidised by the governments of New South Wales and New Zealand, it collapsed in 1869, leaving travellers dependent on the Suez–Australia–New Zealand route. This was some 3200km longer and, until the Suez Canal was opened in 1869, had included an overland leg from the Red Sea.

In 1869 a House select committee on postal communication calculated that shipping mail via San Francisco would be 21 days faster than sending it via Suez.

The committee recommended the government investigate the shorter service and explore whether the Australian colonies would contribute to the cost.[3] The government had contracted the Intercolonial Royal Mail Service to provide a mail service to all New Zealand ports and to Australia in 1858. Macandrew now put two motions to the House: first, that subsidies for interprovincial and inter-colonial maritime postal services be withdrawn, because there was now enough regular shipping to compete for the business; and second, that the government advertise 'for a monthly steam service' to San Francisco, and cease contributing towards the Suez service, which it had done for six years.[4] Both motions were carried, although some members considered the moves too experimental. Their doubts were vindicated when mail deliveries throughout the colony became unpredictable following the removal of the subsidies. A Taranaki editor observed:

> To announce to our readers that no mail arrived by the steamer on Sunday last, may appear very like telling them the historical fact that Queen Anne is dead, for, practically, one announcement is about as much news as the other … It is not much that persons in this Province will suffer by the alteration, further than vexation and disappointment at not getting their letters regularly, but in large commercial centres where, to business men, the arrival and departure of an English mail is a matter of importance, where the missing of a mail for home may be the means of ruining their credit, that this disorganisation of mail communication will be felt.[5]

On the basis of Macandrew's second motion, a contract was signed for the San Francisco route. The first ship departed New Zealand in April 1870, but by August the service was struggling; the New South Wales and Victorian governments then reneged on their proposed subsidies and by November 1870 it had collapsed completely.

In August 1870 the General Assembly again debated the future of the service to North America, and concluded that New Zealand should now act independently. A new service using slow and inefficient American paddle steamers began in April 1871 but lasted only until April 1873. Yet another service was inaugurated, this time in conjunction with New South Wales, but this in turn folded in June 1874.[6] Finally, a contract was proposed between the governments of New Zealand and New South Wales and an American company, which was subsidised by the American government to carry mail to Hawai`i. In the debate to ratify the contract Macandrew demurred, saying he believed 'it would be much better to have a direct line connecting with South America through Magellan Straits.'[7]

This was a return to the thrust of his 1850 circular letter, in which he had boosted the potential markets on the Pacific Rim and predicted steamer services to Panama and San Francisco.[8] In the adjourned debate four days later, he let his imagination go wild:

> It is sufficient to say that it would bring us into direct commercial communication with the millions of inhabitants of South America, and would afford a market not only for our wool, but for our preserved meats, potatoes, beer, and other commodities which the people of South America would be glad to take, giving us in return sugar, coffee, guano, and so on.[9]

Nevertheless, a 10-year contract was signed in July 1875 and the service ran until 1885.

Migration drove Macandrew's determination to establish fast, direct shipping routes from Britain. Passenger services were routed through Australian ports, where travellers were forced to transfer to other lines; migrants tended to travel on chartered sailing ships. In 1870 in his address to Otago Provincial Council, Macandrew suggested the council could establish direct steam communication with Europe: '[If] we were to set apart £25,000 a year for Immigration for three years, arrangements may be made whereby a direct steam line can be secured, and our immigrants brought out in 50 days at the same rates as are now being paid to sailing vessels.'[10] Nothing eventuated from this, as by this time provincial borrowing for public works had become a central government prerogative.

His appointment as minister of immigration in 1877 gave Macandrew the opportunity and authority to further pursue direct steam maritime communication with Britain. In a letter to Vogel, who at that time was agent-general in London, Macandrew commented that he thought the government ought to have 'applied the large sum now paid annually towards the Californian line to the now subsidizing of a direct line of steamers of sufficient power and capacity to have combined both a postal and emigration service'.[11] Accurately predicting the future of the colony's trade and emergent Victorian-era prosperity, he continued, 'in the course of a very few years, the colony ... will supply the market of the world with food to an extent unequalled by any other country of similar area and population'.

> In estimating the prospect of a steam line to New Zealand it is not so much the carrying of cargo that may be reckoned on, as that of passengers, a very large proportion of whom would be of what may be termed the 'paying class'. You may rely on it that, as surely as New Zealand is brought within forty days' sail of England, by means of floating hotels, the attractions of the

Hot Springs in the North, and grandeur of the scenery in the Middle Island, will lead to an enormous passenger traffic to and from Europe; in point of fact, New Zealand must inevitably become an essential portion of the 'grand tour'.[12]

Vogel replied that he recognised the immense value to New Zealand of a direct line: 'I quite agree with you that the value of the Pacific service has been much impaired by its ceasing to do more than merely call at Auckland en route to Australia. As a mail line it is excellent, but it has lost its character as a New Zealand service.'[13] He reported that several shipping firms had suggested that steamers of at least 5000 tons would have to be built for such a service, which would make the enterprise too expensive.

This message drove Macandrew to further action. In July 1878, when Lord Normanby opened parliament, Macandrew made sure his proposal to establish direct shipping lines between New Zealand and the United Kingdom was inserted in the Speech from the Throne.[14] But his poorly timed motion, put to the House at the stub-end of the session – that the government be authorised to establish a 'direct monthly steam service between New Zealand and the mother-country' – had to be shelved as he was unable to provide the information necessary to justify his request.[15] As with so many of his schemes, his enthusiasm had outstripped his planning.

This endeavour did win support outside the House though, and one erstwhile critic was moved to write that he had 'invested the subject with rare attractiveness when he associated it with a steady and liberal stream of immigration'.[16] The following year Macandrew resubmitted his motion and requested a select committee be appointed to study the matter, but despite his efforts the committee failed to eventuate. When the Grey ministry fell in early October 1879, Macandrew returned to the back benches and his mission faltered.

Undeterred, he returned to the matter in 1881, knowing that the government contract for the North American service would end in 1885 and that support for a direct route was growing. He suggested an even shorter voyage time was possible, and proceeded to gild the lily:

… thousands upon thousands of settlers of the right stamp with money would be induced to come to the country if they could get comfortable communication and a voyage not extending over thirty-five or forty days: not to speak of the thousands of tourists who would visit New Zealand, and drop money into the country in all directions. And there would be the great advantage of getting our produce – grain in bulk, frozen meat, eggs, and butter carried Home to England within thirty-five days … before five years had passed over there would be a weekly steam service between New Zealand and the Mother-country, and Auckland and every other large port would share in the immense advantages.[17]

He then moved the appointment of a select committee to consider the best means of establishing a direct service to Britain. The resultant Direct Steam Service Committee, which Macandrew chaired, met on 11 August 1881 and submitted its report, the very model of a useful document, on 30 August.[18] It suggested that six ships of specific tonnage, draught and speed were required for a monthly service, the cost of which 'would not exceed one million sterling'; the government should be empowered to tender for the service for seven years. The report provided details of interest and earnings, and suggested preference be given to a New Zealand contractor. It cited financial figures to justify the investment, and recommended the government be advised to take action before the Session ended, since it could take up to two years to initiate the service.

Members declared the service beyond the means of the country, but agreed that the establishment of a direct monthly service with Europe 'would very materially promote the interests and develop the resources of the colony'. They suggested the government could 'make inquiry as to the terms on which a direct steam service with Great Britain could be arranged, and report the same to the next Parliament' – which the government duly did in 1882, but only after Macandrew had asked for the report three times during the session.[19] The steam service saga inched forward.

Postmaster Walter Johnston presented the government's seven recommendations on 28 August 1882, and a lengthy debate ensued.[20] It was considered 'not expedient ... for the present to establish a direct steam postal service to England, as the large subsidy required would more than counterbalance the advantages'; the San Francisco service should be extended for two or three years if costs did not increase. There should be 'a monthly passenger and mercantile steam service established between England and New Zealand by suitable steam vessels'; the voyage each way should not exceed 50 days, and the contract should not exceed three years. Agreement was reached: the subsidy would be £20,000 annually and the government, after public tendering, was authorised 'to take the necessary measures to give effect to these resolutions'.

Impatient with the debate and the cautious commitment of funds, Macandrew was abrupt: 'Delay, delay; inquire, inquire. It is five years now ... since this question was brought before the House ... The question of subsidy is of no importance. It is a mere drop in the bucket as compared with the advantages which flow, directly and indirectly, from the service.' Richard Seddon, a zealous defender of the rights of working people and certainly not a supporter of free trade, counterattacked in language that Macandrew himself might have used earlier in his life:

> I have no hesitation in saying that the proposal now before the House is not in the interest of the majority of the taxpayers of the colony, but is simply to play into the hands of those who raise sheep and cattle in this country, and at the same time to hold out to a shipping company belonging to this colony a certain inducement, while I believe, in the interests of their shareholders, they would undertake the service without any subsidy at all.[21]

Despite the barbs, Macandrew had finally converted the unbelievers and a House majority backed his suggestion.

In his 1883 Speech on Opening Parliament, Governor William Jervois announced: 'I have been able to give effect to the wishes of the Legislature by arranging for the continuation of the San Francisco mail service for a period of two years ... Tenders for the establishment of a direct line of steamships between Great Britain and the colony were advertised for here, as well as in the United Kingdom; but neither the Agent-General nor the Postmaster-General received any offer.'[22] This setback disappeared in August when the Minister of Immigration, William Rolleston, sought parliamentary approval for the government to sign a one-year contract with the New Zealand Shipping Company to trial the transport of freight and migrants from Britain to New Zealand, departing monthly and taking no more than 50 days. The Shaw, Savill and Albion Steamship Company had made a similar offer.[23]

Macandrew's response was cautious. He noted that daily improvements were being made in steam communication, and questioned 'how far it would be prudent to tie up our hands for even the very shortest time as against a possible thirty days' service'. Seddon listed the adverse consequences which he thought could eventuate from this service: 'We are to take the money from the people of this country, and use it in bringing persons from the Old Country to compete against them and bring down the price of labour. Then, the beef and mutton that we live on is to be taken away, and the price increased to consumers.' Members could not agree, and the matter was referred to yet another select committee.[24]

Macandrew was a member of the Joint Committee on Direct Steam Services that reported within a week and recommended that no contract for a direct steam service should be entered into before the next session of the General Assembly.

The government should make arrangements that were the 'least burdensome on the public revenue'; the New Zealand Shipping Company was to be looked upon favourably and preference given to 'unsinkable ships'; and Bluff should be a port of arrival and departure. Members were losing interest, however. They agreed to print the report but to take no further action, leaving it to the government to work out a suitable deal.

The New Zealand Shipping Company completed a trial run and, in November 1884, Treasurer Vogel asked the House to ratify a five-year contract with them for a fortnightly service. Macandrew's response, typically, was to want more: 'I should have been glad if it were possible to put some provision in the contract by which the company would be compelled, for example, to use New Zealand coal … There might be a condition that they should use New Zealand mutton, beef, potatoes, and all the rest.'[25]

He then basked in the fulsome praise conferred on him by Vogel, who considered 'there is no one more entitled than the honourable member to be considered the father of steam services in this colony for a very long period past. There is no doubt that it is to the honourable gentleman's action that we owe the San Francisco service. Then, again, in 1878, he pointed out how urgently it was needed that the colony should have a direct steam service with England.'

All had now come to pass.

Chapter 20

Suddenly he was gone. On 23 February 1887 at the age of 67, James Macandrew was travelling home from a university council meeting with his 17-year-old son Arthur, who dismounted at Waverley to adjust the horse's harness. The horse bolted, and at the gateway to Colinswood the buggy overturned and Macandrew was thrown out.[1] Although at first his injuries were not considered serious, hes died the following afternoon from 'shock and laceration or rupture of internal organs'.

His death came as a huge shock to many, and his funeral at Macandrew Bay on 28 February was enormous. Premier Stout, ex-Premier Hall, five members of the Legislative Council and 15 members of the House of Representatives were joined by a crowd of 1500 mourners, who arrived by road and aboard steamers, steam launches and the Port Chalmers Naval Brigade's pinnace. Indisposed by their health, Vogel and Reynolds sent their apologies from Wellington.[2] Reynolds offered Colin Macandrew practical advice: 'He should be buried beside your grandfather and grandmother as in the event of selling the property your mother would have to be lifted.'[3] Many shops and businesses in Dunedin closed while a service was held at Colinswood, after which 'the coffin was borne by the mayor and councillors of Port Chalmers and settlers on the Peninsula' to the private cemetery on the hilltop behind the residence, 'where Mrs. Macandrew was buried some 12 years since'.[4]

Most obituaries were effusive. They ignored his faults, laboured his virtues and personal qualities, and were circumspect about the events which had seen him imprisoned so many years before. His commitment to Otago featured in many:

> Otago had no truer friend; New Zealand no more faithful servant, and if he seemed to place the Province first and the Colony second, it could scarcely be his fault, for his whole heart and soul were bound up in the place and people where, and amongst whom, he passed the greatest portion of his useful and vigorous existence.[5]

Another writer recalled his energy and unceasing activity: 'He never paused nor rested satisfied with what was already done. Every achievement was only a stepping stone to him.'[6] The personal qualities that had enabled him to convince so many were also remarked on:

> Members felt that when he addressed them, whether the views he advocated met with their approval or not, he was honest in their advocacy; and so they often listened without impatience to his exposition of theories on many subjects which were far from being in accord with their own views and opinions. Much of the kindly feeling evinced towards him was also due to his unfailing geniality, and to the remarkable absence of satirical comment and of all bitterness, by which his speeches were characterised.[7]

The *Otago Daily Times* dwelt on his flaws but acknowledged his redeeming qualities:

> Mr. Macandrew's public character had grave defects. He never could understand the importance of details, and his absolute lack of what is termed business capacity led him into errors which made him a mischievous administrator, and would have terminated the political career of any ordinary man. But James Macandrew was no ordinary man … He has long been the David to the people of Otago, the man after their own heart, in spite of faults which it is impossible to defend or even entirely to forget.[8]

The University of Otago Council acknowledged its loss: 'To him very specially as Superintendent of the province of Otago, and to those that worked with him, the colony is indebted for the very existence of the university and for the wise foresight which provided its endowments … it is gratifying to record that the very last public act of his life was an endeavour to raise the status of the University which he loved.'[9]

Macandrew's life was celebrated in verse. Fellow Mason Thomas Bracken penned a 13-stanza ode that referenced Canaan, Commerce, Industry and Edina.[10] Alexander Stewart's 'In Memoriam: James Macandrew M.H.R.', published in March, consisted of eight tercets with such memorable lines as 'The Ocean Beach is white with sobbing seas!' and 'Otago's Champion, doughty Chieftain true / Grand, genial "Mac," whom all New Zealand knew.'[11] They were not universally appreciated. One columnist noted, acerbically, 'Scarcely had the last sod been laid on his grave when the press is inundated with the pukings, dismal bleatings and rasping doggerel of the hundred and one poetasters who are scattered like a plague over this fair province.'[12] Not to be outdone, another writer 'discovered' three, singular coincidences in Macandrew's life. He had been elevated to the superintendency on 28 February 1867; his wife Eliza had died on 28 February 1875; and he was buried on 28 February 1887.[13] (The first two dates were actually incorrect.)

Distance lent enchantment. The *Aberdeen Weekly Journal* wrote: 'It is in great part due to his indomitable perseverance and fertile brain that New Zealand is so well supplied with railways … As a statesman and a public benefactor, Mr. Macandrew had few equals in the colony, and his loss will be mourned throughout its length and breadth.'[14] *The Times* of London condensed the Aberdeen item into a muted 125 words and concluded: 'Both as a statesman and a public benefactor the deceased was held in high esteem through the colony.'[15] The ambitious young settler who had sailed from London in 1850 would have been satisfied with this epitaph and doubtless taken it as his due.

The need for a suitable monument to his memory was discussed within days of his interment. The *Otago Daily Times* planned to establish a scholarship in his name, tenable at the University of Otago, and a public statue was also suggested.[16] A meeting called by Mayor Richard Leary a week after his death attracted 140 people, who agreed to raise money for both a statue and a scholarship.[17] But as in life, so in death: an event involving Macandrew soon generated dissension and discord. One school committee wanted each child to contribute sixpence, a plan that did not meet with widespread approval.[18] Oamaru citizens, having discovered that Macandrew's family was not very well off, suggested provision be made for them instead.[19] The Gore School committee decided to start a collection for a Macandrew prize at their school instead.[20] Then, in true Otago style, the memorial committee was sundered: scholarship supporters versus those favouring a statue.[21] One meeting of the committee was described as 'most disorderly … a large amount of recrimination was indulged in'.[22] The *Evening Post* reported that 'strong personalities were used and for a few moments it seemed likely that something stronger than argument would be resorted to'.[23] 'It would seem characteristic of Dunedin men to undignify their most serious concerns,' wrote another.[24]

The Dunedin committee raised £650 and, since his family expressed no desire 'to have anything to do with the money collected', agreed to allocate a portion to erecting a memorial tablet and the remainder to a scholarship.[25] The university accepted £500 and created the Macandrew Scholarship in Political Economy.[26] The Sir Robert Stout Scholarship in Economics was instituted in 1930 and, eventually, the two were combined to create the present-day Macandrew–Stout Postgraduate Scholarship in Economics, which is awarded to master's and doctoral students. It was an appropriate union of two political giants who dominated the political landscape for 50 years.

The final act was played out on 4 July 1891 in the northern corner of the Triangle (now known as Queens Gardens). Mayor Charles Chapman, Sir Robert Stout and the Rev Dr Donald Stuart made speeches 'eulogistic of the departed, his patriotism and great public service', and a bust of Macandrew – 'life size and a half ... executed by Messrs George Munro and Sons, in their studio at Canova' – was unveiled.[27] It was inscribed:

> In memory of James Macandrew, late member of the House of
> Representatives, and formerly Superintendent of the Province of Otago.
> Born 1819, died 1887. Erected by public subscription in recognition of his
> public services.

Reaction was mixed and focused on the monument's proportions: '15ft of base, surmounted by 3ft of bust,' the *Otago Daily Times* reported, and asked, 'Why, oh! why, is there so very much of pedestal and so very little of Macandrew?' The reporter claimed it looked like 'a white cockatoo perched on an exaggerated tombstone'.[28] The *Evening Star* described it as 'a gigantic extinguisher, with a big knob'.[29] The *Clutha Leader* expressed the hope that when the early history of the colony was written, the 'long, many and varied public services' rendered by Macandrew would have a prominent place, and suggested such a record would 'form a far more lasting and appropriate memorial of the man than the somewhat incongruous erection in the triangle, Dunedin'.[30] These days the bust stands on a properly proportioned pedestal in front of Toitū Otago Settlers Museum, from where the old 'Otago Chieftain' can mark the progress of commerce in the centre of his city.

Careless about details to the end, Macandrew died intestate, and the Dunedin Supreme Court appointed his sons Colin and James to administer his estate.[31] The final reckoning showed him to be somewhat impecunious, with assets worth £1485; after debts were paid only £643 remained – little enough to show for the vast amounts of money that had passed through his hands in his lifetime. He had signed an informal will in January 1877 that left the proceeds of his life insurance policy of £1042 to his daughters, but this had been used as security against a Bank of New Zealand overdraft that stood at £456 at his death; a codicil signed in June 1881 directed that the remainder of the policy be supplemented by the sale of his sheep. In the event these fetched just £9.10/-, leaving the four young women to share £576 between them. Farm assets valued at £80 and crops valued at £51 were divided between his five sons, and his personal effects were left to James. Eliza in her will had instructed that the land at Colinswood was to be shared by their children; the house was left to Jane, and a cottage their father had built on the property with money bequeathed by his mother was left to Marion. It was a meagre estate for a man once worth thousands of pounds and the owner of myriad properties.

In 1887 his nine surviving children were adults; the older boys and Marion had left home, and it is likely that his other three daughters and Arthur were still living at Colinswood. The boys had all attended Otago Boys' High School, were well educated and could provide for themselves; of the girls, only Alice and Mabel had received secondary education.[32] None of his offspring engaged in national political activities, and none of his daughters ever married.

In 1889 Larnach, member for the Peninsula since 1883, noting that Macandrew's sudden death had left his large family insufficiently provided for, requested that the General Assembly grant £500 to each of the daughters, 'who do not always enjoy very good health, and who are consequently unable to battle with this world and much of its selfishness'.[33] It was not agreed to without debate. Ballance denied the commonly held view that Macandrew worked more for Otago than New Zealand, reminding listeners that 'when he came to occupy a higher position ... he devoted his services and his time with entire devotion to the welfare of the colony'.[34] An Auckland Member, in referring to Macandrew's unconventional financial views, was delicately circumlocutory: 'The gentleman referred to had some qualities which in private life led to bankruptcy, and in public life to incurring burdens and liabilities greater than ought to be imposed upon the people'.[35] Sir Maurice O'Rorke, who claimed friendship with Macandrew since the first sitting of parliament in Auckland and throughout his parliamentary career, sprang to his defence:

> he had never met any gentleman who was so completely imbued with the colonial spirit, combined with warm love of his native country and an ardent patriotism towards the Empire ... If only for these two important services, – the introduction of higher education into the colony, and the establishment of steam communication between Australia, England, and America, – the late James Macandrew had done that which entitled him as a public man to public recognition at our hands of those who inherited his name.[36]

The grant was approved and was paid later that year.[37] Despite their purported ill-health, the daughters all lived for at least 35 years more; Mabel survived for another 77.

Following their father's death, the family sold the house and 300-acre (121ha) farm at Colinswood and moved from the bay. Colin bought the original homestead again in 1910 and disposed of sections along Marion, Jane and Featherstone streets in 1911.[38] Hunter and Arthur also bought land nearby.

Macandrew's legacy

Accounts of Macandrew were shaped by the social rank, economic standing and political views of the observer. He clashed with social superiors such as Governor Grey and Henry Valpy, he vied with equals like William Cutten and Johnny Jones, and while he was seen as 'silvery, cunning, and not over-scrupulous' by one contemporary, he was also considered an esteemed friend of the working class.[39] His appeal to Otago voters is demonstrated by his total of 17 successes in the 19 elections he contested: he won three elections to Otago Provincial Council, 10 of his 11 parliamentary races, and stood for the Otago superintendency on five occasions and was elected on four.

Many felt that his empathy offset his character flaws. One colleague wrote that although Macandrew's ideas were 'eminently visionary, and his speeches … curiously illogical and unconvincing',

> [y]et he could carry a bill or a motion which nobody else in the House could have carried. And all because his nature was extraordinarily sympathetic. He could get men to vote with him against their judgment, simply by enlisting their feelings.[40]

His strong Christian faith endured throughout his lifetime. The Rev Dr Donald Stuart said of him, 'Mr Macandrew was intimately acquainted with the scriptures and held that their acceptance as the guide of life is indispensable to the production of that "righteousness which exalteth a nation and the glory of any people".'[41] His everyday language was laced with Old Testament references, and his beliefs are apparent in the letters he wrote to his children and in his parliamentary speeches, in which he frequently invoked God and Christian values. Others identified with his faith, which was described by the Rev Alexander Greig:

> Mr. Macandrew was a truly religious man – one who feared God, and who respected and honoured every ordinance of God. He was one who did not act from impulse, but from principle, and who was never ashamed to show where his heart was. He was not given to speak of his faith, or his feelings, or his hopes, but he was constantly giving evidence that all of these were of the right kind.[42]

Land ownership in New Zealand conferred independence, prosperity and political power, to the extent that one Taranaki settler was able to declare in 1862, 'we were now free from the injurious conventionalities of English life'.[43] Macandrew was a perfect example of the 'explosive coloniser': an exploiter of resources and a fervent supporter of intensive settlement and easy access to land. As the financial position of the colony improved then faltered, his economic philosophy and 'pragmatic interventionism' evolved.[44] An isolated settlement like Dunedin had few communal resources to support the needy and every man had to pay his own way. With the demise of the provinces and the advent of the long depression, Macandrew was forced to acknowledge that individual responsibility was insufficient in the face of poverty: settlers needed state support to help them survive. And if the state could invest in infrastructure, then the state could invest in its people.

He is best remembered for his belief in a distinct division of responsibilities between central and local bodies: provincial government should provide the essential community services of education, law and order, and public works; central government should take responsibility for matters affecting the entire country. He once observed: 'The Provincial Councils, which some among us nowadays in their ignorance affect to despise, were no shams. What would the people of Ireland and Scotland give for such Councils?'[45] The current reorganisation of local government in New Zealand supports his view, as attempts are made to amalgamate local bodies into regions that look remarkably like the old provinces, and to delegate certain central governmental powers to these.

While Morrell provides a comprehensive and compelling set of explanations for the demise of the provinces, he does not acknowledge the influence of personal relationships on the timing and outcomes of the debates.[46] If Macandrew's passionate defence of the provinces had not so infuriated Vogel and led to a sequence of widely published recriminations, abolition might not have been absolute.[47] If Macandrew had been less reactionary and had supported the passage of the New Zealand Forests Bill in 1874, Vogel might have been restrained to transform the North and the Middle islands into two separate provinces. A less obstinate Macandrew might also have ensured that the provinces survived as the units of local government, with fewer areas of responsibility but modelled on the English counties – as intended by the drafters of the Constitution Act of 1852.

By the 1880s Vogel's prediction – that 'when the iron horses ran through the two Islands, then they would have no more need of provinces' – had eventuated and political stability in New Zealand was secure.[48] With a responsible and representative central government and the nation at peace, the rapid development of infrastructure unified the country. According to historian Ron Palenski, 'the telegraph, the railways, shipping and other enterprises which were national rather than local all transformed New Zealand, all led to a sense of "oneness", to a recognisable and recognised national identity'.[49] In addition, the Education Act 1877 created a nationalising movement by replacing 'provincial variety' with 'a colony-wide system of primary education, thus reducing if not eliminating regional disparity'.[50] In this period Macandrew articulated his concerns for all New Zealanders and launched his suggestions for economic deliverance, including state loans for settlers, crofter immigration and free land for the unemployed. Although recognised foremost as a promoter of Otago, Macandrew's parliamentary record demonstrates that he always had the interests of the entire country at heart.

The Scots were a large and disproportionately successful minority of early settlers who shaped New Zealand's modern culture, and Macandrew was prominent among them. He retained his Scottish brogue all his life, attended Caledonian games and Presbyterian services and epitomised Scottishness, although no record exists of his wearing Highland garb: in the few existing photographs he is dressed in the sombre black typical of the period. His meritocratic world view was the wellspring for the time and energy he invested in education at all levels.

James Belich's depiction of Lowlanders as 'archetypically egalitarian, competent, undemonstrative and somewhat dour', the prototype of the emerging New Zealander, does not apply to this effusive Highlander.[51] However, to make a provocative generalisation, modern New Zealanders do exhibit many Macandrew-like traits: his risk-taking, boldness, enjoyment of gambling, social drinking and loyalty to family; his propensity to find quick (and often unsuitable) solutions to complex problems; his disdain for ceremony, proclivity for joining groups, and his sense of ownership and responsibility for his home territory. Macandrew would probably be comfortable in many clubs and societies in New Zealand today, and quite in tune with most of their members. He would also be at home in our present parliament, with its mixed member proportional representation system of government, its scope for negotiation and its voting coalitions – all closer in style to his more freewheeling General Assembly than to the subsequent, party-dominated twentieth-century model.

The new library wing (on the right-hand side of the entrance) at Parliament House was opened for the 1899 session, but all of the building to the left of the entrance was destroyed by fire in 1907, together with Kate Sperry's second portrait of Macandrew, which had been presented to the General Assembly after his death. 1/2-106917/F/22591856, Alexander Turnbull Library, Wellington

Macandrew was a man of regular habits, and throughout his parliamentary career pressed regularly for changes to House proceedings. In May 1885 he cited parliamentary procedure as the reason for his intended retirement, saying, 'the absurd and unnatural system which the House has adopted of turning night into day, and of continuing its sittings long into the small hours in the morning … does not suit my constitution'.[52] He had advocated for changes to the sitting hours from the start: in 1872 he suggested the House sit from 10am to 5pm; in 1879 he moved that the House 'should be compelled to adjourn at half-past 12 o'clock every night';[53] and in 1883 he advocated for sitting hours from 10.30 to 5.30 with committees sitting in the evening. His fellow parliamentarians declined to back him then or in 1885, when he sought similar hours.[54]

Macandrew was an avid reader, and like many early members of parliament he had a substantial library of his own.[55] His literary tastes were catholic and he always had a book to hand, often from the Assembly library, where loans were recorded by the borrower in a register.[56] This rule was regularly disregarded, and Macandrew admitted he had taken books home during the recess for many years. After his death the librarian wrote to his son James to ask for the return of his father's loans.[57] Macandrew took a keen interest in the establishment of libraries: the Dunedin Mechanics' Institute and Athenaeum, the University of Otago Library and the General Assembly Library all benefitted from his interest and support. In 1872, on behalf of the Library Committee, he moved in the House that the expanding parliamentary library appropriate the smoking room. Macandrew, a virtuous non-smoker, agreed it would involve 'considerable self-sacrifice on the part of honourable members who were shortening their lives by their narcotic proclivities'.[58] It was an unpopular move in a time when most members smoked, and resistance was stiff, but a division supported his proposal by 35 to 26 votes.

He had an intimate knowledge of classical history, which he displayed tellingly. At a banquet in Palmerston in October 1882 for his good friend John McKenzie, a member of Otago Provincial Council who had recently been elected as member for Waihemo, Macandrew adapted the words of a malevolent editorial to praise the guest of honour.[59] The *Otago Daily Times* had suggested that McKenzie's addition of Clause 67 to the Land Act 1877 Amendment Act 1882, which set a limit on the stockholdings of large runholders and thus on the size of their runs, introduced 'cramping measures associated with a system of commercial restriction'. This, the paper said, would ensure that McKenzie's career would be as brief and unsuccessful as that of Tiberius Gracchus, who had attempted to limit the size of Roman landholdings and was subsequently murdered.[60] Macandrew announced that McKenzie had 'inherited the mantle of the Gracchi', and challenged him to not only 'break the monopoly of the landed nobility' but to avoid Gracchus' fate.[61] Macandrew moved in liberal circles and was increasingly supportive of efforts to make land available for men with little capital.

Macandrew's commitment to the British Empire and its underlying values were strong. In 1886 he presented the report of the Joint Jubilee Committee, which included an address from New Zealand's parliament to Queen Victoria for her Golden Jubilee. In his speech to the House he reflected: 'Perhaps there are few things that have exercised a greater influence for good upon the destinies of the Empire than the sentiment of loyalty. Respect for the throne, or, in other

The Macandrew Effect

Otago Provincial Council appointed three select committees to investigate aspects of Macandrew's behaviour:
- V&P, OPC, Session VI, 16 November 1857, Appendix: Report, Select Committee on the State of the Land Office
- V&P, OPC, Session VII, 11 November 1858, Appendix: Report, Select Committee on Immigration Correspondence
- V&P, OPC, Session XI, 18 December 1860, Appendix: Report, Select Committee on the State of the Public Accounts, Public funds, &c.

AJHR, 1867, D–1, 'Papers relative to the case of Mr. Macandrew' contains two items by the auditor-general:
- 'The Report of the Commissioner Appointed to Examine the Public Accounts of the Province of Otago, 1861', 17–21
- Letter: Dr C. Knight/E.W. Stafford, 18 March 1867, printed as Enclosure 2 to Paper 19, 41

Macandrew's behaviour precipitated six Acts of parliament:
- Superintendents' Elections Disallowance Signification Act 1866, no. 58 (passed to give the governor sole right to dismiss a superintendent)
- Gold Fields Act Amendment Act 1867, no. 68
- Gold Fields Act Amendment Act 1867 (no. 2) 1867, no. 69
- Otago Gold Fields Judicial Officers Act 1867, no. 70
- Governor's Delegations Act 1867, no. 74
- Public Offenders Disqualification Act 1867, no. 49 (which prevented felons and bankrupts taking elective office)

AJHR 1879 contains the reports of two select committees appointed to investigate a map supposedly altered by Macandrew:
- I–2: Report of the Railway Map Inquiry Committee, 23 July 1879
- I–2A: Report of the Railway Map Inquiry Committee (Revived), 8 August 1879

AJHR 1880 contains the reports of two royal commissions on Macandrew's performance as a minister:
- E–3: Report of the Railways Commission
- H–2: Report of the royal commission on the Civil Service of New Zealand

words, respect for constituted authority, has been a distinguishing feature of our forefathers for many generations; … in no part of the Empire does the flame of loyalty burn more brightly than in these distant islands of the sea.'[62] These were interesting sentiments from the man who had challenged the system many times since he arrived in the colony. But age had not reduced his flair for a rhetorical flourish, and before he sat down he offered this advice:

I say that probably the world is now on the eve of greater changes than we have any conception of. Events, so to speak, are travelling with lightning speed ... 'Old things are passing away, and all things are becoming new.' Let us hope ... that, wherever the British flag is unfurled, there the sentiment of loyalty will continue to flourish; let us hope that wherever that flag is unfurled, it will be the emblem of protection to life and property, the symbol of law and order, and the guardian angel of civil and religious liberty ... I hope that each one of us, as patriotic and representative men, will cherish within ourselves this feeling of loyalty, and instil that feeling into the minds of our children and our children's children.[63]

Settlers looked to Macandrew for leadership, and his knowledge of parliamentary procedure made him a valuable, if contrarian, member in the fledgling provincial council where, over the years, he occupied most of the leadership positions as member, executive councillor, treasurer, Speaker and superintendent. Macandrew took advantage of his positions, however, sometimes using them as a means of salvaging his personal financial position. He used his own assets, his wife's inheritance, money held in trust for other colonists and public money to rescue his unviable business ventures. But political activism and impatience with detailed planning and accounting led to the collapse of his business world, which he never attempted to rejuvenate.[64] His political life was characterised by his obsession with promoting major projects and a similar disregard for details, and despite his persuasiveness he was often unable to garner support for his goals: the provinces were abolished despite his desperate opposition, and his tenure as a minister ended in disarray. Ultimately he trusted too much, borrowed too casually and was a diffident manager of men.

His career earned him few accolades. While many other ministers of the Crown were knighted, Macandrew was not.[65] And because Grey's ministry did not survive for a full term, he did not earn the right to retain the title 'Honourable' for his two years of Cabinet service, whereas his Otago colleagues did: Vogel in 1871, Reynolds in 1876, Oliver and Dick in 1884, Larnach and Stout in 1887, and Pyke in 1893.[66]

Today his monuments are few and far-flung and most are insignificant. His bust stands in front of Dunedin's Toitū Otago Settlers Museum, a full-length portrait commissioned in 1885 hangs in the University of Otago's Clocktower Building, and there is an eponymous bay on Otago Peninsula where he lived for much of his life. Macandrew Wharf still serves Oamaru, and a number of streets bear his name: Macandrew Road can be found in both South Dunedin and

Careys Bay, and Otautau, Milton and Owaka in the South Island and Woodville in the north all have a Macandrew Street.[67] Less obvious reminders of his enterprise are the sites of Jamestown on the shores of Lake McKerrow in Westland, Cromarty in Preservation Inlet in Fiordland and Macandrew Township near the present Riversdale in Southland. Macandrew Intermediate School in Dunedin was renamed in 2015, and all traces of Macandrew Bridge over the Kawarau River at Bannockburn, erected in 1878 and rebuilt in 1897, were lost when Lake Dunstan was filled in 1992.[68]

James Macandrew was 'a leader staunch and true' who enthused people with his vision and plans, and relied on stirring speeches to carry his audiences with him. He was sufficiently audacious to lead the development of a new and richly endowed province, emotionally resilient, and ready to engage any man as an equal. Had he become premier of New Zealand with the assistance of a responsible treasurer, who knows what visions might have eventuated?

Appendix 1

Circular Letter from Garden & Macandrew to Oliver & Boyd, 15 August 1850

Messrs Oliver & Boyd Publishers
Tweeddale Court
High Street
Edinburgh
London 15 Augt 1850

Sir

We beg respectfully to advise you that we have established a house in New Zealand for the purpose of trading there, as well as in the countries adjacent in which our colonies are so flourishing, and also with the numerous islands of the Pacific and the Indian Oceans.

To those who are acquainted with New Zealand, there can be no doubt that from its locality, climate & capability, it is fitted and destined to become the Great Britain of the south, it has a good soil with vast plains suited for immediate pasturage, a climate more closely resembling Britain than any other, a long line of coast with fine harbours, which will always make it a maritime country.

The sources of wealth in New Zealand are its flocks, agricultural products, Fisheries and Minerals, and as markets must be found for these – a constant communication will be kept up with the Australian and Indian Colonies, China, California and the West Coast of South America.

As all these markets are most readily accessible to New Zealand, we are of opinion that the latter is well fitted to become a depot for British goods.

Intelligence from most of the markets to the South of the Cape of Good Hope and Cape Horn, as well as from those situated between the Eastern Coast of Africa and Western Coast of America will reach New Zealand in less than half the time which will be required to reach England, for example take San Francisco in California, the most remote point to which there is any probability of sending British Goods from New Zealand.

The voyage at present from Sydney & New Zealand to Panama may be estimated at six weeks. When steamers are established it will probably take not more than half that time. So that goods could be ordered from New Zealand & delivered in San Francisco, in three months at most from date of order, whereas the same goods ordered from England and sent round by Cape Horn, could not possibly be delivered in less than six to seven months.

Should you feel inclined to give any of these markets a trial, we shall be glad to take charge of any consignments with which you may favour us, in the meantime however, we would not recommend you to send more than the smallest possible assortment, by way of sample, unless it were a staple article, in which case a considerable shipment would not hurt.

('Business letters Oliver & Boyd, Booksellers of Edinburgh/Garden & Macandrew', National Library of Scotland, MSS, Acc 5000/vol. 207)

Appendix 2

Last Will and Testament of James Macandrew (d. 28 February 1887)

'A'

This is the Copy informal Testamentary Disposition marked with the letter 'A' referred to in the annexed Affidavit of Colin Macandrew and James Macandrew severally sworn this ninth day of March One thousand eight hundred and eighty seven before me A. Finch

This is the last Will and disposition of James Macandrew of Colinswood in the Province of Otago

I James Macandrew aforesaid do hereby in the event of my death will and bequeath as follows that is to say

1st The proceeds of my life policy One thousand pounds (at present lodged in the Bank of New Zealand Dunedin as collateral security in respect of a Cash Credit in my favour for Four Hundred Pounds) after deducting any balance which may be due in respect of such Cash Credit and after defraying the Cost of my funeral which I desire shall not exceed Ten pounds at most – to be divided equally between my four daughters – Marion Jane Alice and Mabel – or so many of them as shall survive after my death – or rather at the time thereof the money to be invested to the best advantage and the principal and interest secured to each of them so as that in the event of the marriage of either or all of them such investment shall be held in their own right and shall be beyond the control of their respective husbands –

2 The whole of the Household Furniture Books maps pictures + plate belonging to me to be taken possession of and held by my eldest second Son Colin James and in the event of his death without lawful issue shall descend in like manner to my other surviving Sons in order of their seniority – and failing the survival of any of my sons with lawful offspring then the said Articles shall revert to my eldest surviving daughter and her descendants if any

3rd all sheep Cattle Horses Pigs and other live stock as also all carriages Carts Harness ploughs and other agricultural dairy and gardening implements and tools belonging to me at the time of my decease to be sold by public auction and the proceeds equally divided between and among my five sons Colin James Herbert Hunter and Arthur – or the survivors of them

4th The Cottage recently erected by me on this property (near the steam boat jetty) partly out of the legacy left to her by my late mother I bequeath absolutely and solely to my eldest daughter Marion and the adjoining House on the same property which has been built and renewed, entirely at my expense I bequeathe in like manner to my next daughter Jane and in the event of either or both of them dying without offspring unmarried and childless I desire that the said tenements may belong to my daughters Alice and Mabel

5th and I do hereby nominate and appoint my brother in law Mr Thomas Reynolds together with my two sons Colin and James their respective heirs and administrators as my joint Executors to give effect to the foregoing provisions
Dated at Colinswood this ninth day of January One thousand Eight hundred and Seventy Seven
J Macandrew

Since writing the foregoing I have erased the name of my Son Colin as Legatee of personal effects and substituted my Son James instead
J Macandrew 26.5.80
Signed in the presence of Marion Fyfe Cochrane

Macandrew Bay 26 May
1880
To the Commissioner
New Zealand Gvt. Assurance Department
Wellington

Sir
In the event of my decease without making any subsequent disposal of the One thousand pounds payable on my death by the Government of New Zealand I have the honor to request that you will be good enough to pay the amount (less any sum that may be owing by me to the Bank of New Zealand) to the trustees named in the annexed will in trust for my daughters as therein directed
I have the honor to be
Sir
Your most obt
J Macandrew

Codicil
In the event of my Cash Credit at the Bank of New Zealand being drawn upon at the time of my death thereby reducing the amount of my life policy to be divided as heretofor directed among my four daughters I desire that the amount by which the said policy may be reduced shall be made up out of sheep to be sold so as that the full sum of one thousand pounds may be available for my four daughters as aforesaid
J Macandrew
7 June 1881

(Archives New Zealand, Dunedin, DAAC D239 9074 251 A917)

Appendix 3

James and Eliza Macandrew's family

Colin (1849–1928) was born in London on 7 August 1848 and sailed to New Zealand with his parents on the *Titan*. He was 38 at his father's death, had married Alice Browne in 1878 and was father of two sons and a daughter (James 1879, Alice 1881, Colin 1891) – the only grandchildren Macandrew would have known.[1] Colin senior was employed, variously, by an investment company, the Bank of Otago and the Government Stamp Office. He was a partner in Bouman, Macandrew, and Co., a firm of ship brokers and customs agents, and was secretary to the High Schools' Board and clerk of the Portobello Road Board. He was a member of the North East Valley Borough Council for five years and, as a Mason, rose to become Right Worshipful Master of Lodge Celtic No. 477 of the Scottish Constitution, his father's Lodge, in 1886. He was also its secretary and treasurer. He remained in Dunedin for the rest of his life.

Marion Hunter (1851–1925), known as Marnie, was 36 at Macandrew's death and was born on 16 May 1851, five months after the *Titan* reached Dunedin. She trained as a nurse at Wellington Hospital and was initially employed at Grey River Hospital. She also worked as head nurse at Dunedin Hospital for four years, as matron at Kumara Hospital for four years, and as matron at Ashburton Hospital from 1906.[2] During World War I she served with the Joint Red Cross and St John's Society as an acting matron and nursing sister in various hospitals in England. On her return she resumed duties as a nursing sister of the St John's Guild. In 1925 she received the long-service medal of the Order of St John, and was later made an honorary nursing sister of St John of Jerusalem.

Jane (1854–1940) was born at Carisbrook on 26 May 1854, and was 33 and living at Colinswood when her father died. She later lived with Marion in Wellington.

James (1857–1927) was born at Carisbrook on 31 May 1857 and was 30 on his father's death. On leaving school he joined the Bank of New Zealand before managing his father's farms on the Otago Peninsula. He then bought his own farm at Wickliffe Bay. He married Martha Nicol in 1889 and served for many years on the Portobello Board, the Otago A&P Association, and as a Justice of the Peace and a manager of the Otago Peninsula Presbyterian Church.

Herbert (1859–1917) was born at Carisbrook on 17 September 1859 and was 28 when his father died. He trained as a medical doctor in Otago and Edinburgh, graduating in 1883.[3] In 1889 he married Lissie Rich, granddaughter of Sir John Richardson, and had three children (Gladys 1890, Marion 1897, Herbert 1903). After working in Britain, in 1889 he was appointed assistant medical officer at Seaview Mental Hospital in Hokitika where he worked until his death aged 57. He was a Hokitika borough councillor, president of the Acclimatisation and Tourists' Society, and a surgeon-captain of the Volunteer forces.[4]

Hunter (1862–1952) was born at his grandmother's house in Walker Street on 1 August 1862, during or just after his father's imprisonment. He was 25 when Macandrew died and had joined the Public Works Department in Dunedin in 1879, where he trained as an engineer. He was appointed assistant engineer on the Central Otago, Catlins and Seawoods Bush railways, then was in charge of construction of the Te Aroha–Paeroa railway from 1894. He transferred to Invercargill in 1897 and became district engineer in Christchurch in 1904.[5] He married Ethel Roberts in 1894 and had four children (Majorie 1894, Dorothy 1896, James 1898, Alister 1900).

Alice (1864–1927) was 23 at her father's death, and was born at Colinswood on 31 July 1864. She was enrolled at the girls' school in 1876. She spent several months in the Straits Settlement in 1915 and lived with Jane for some time in Wallaceville. Little else is known about her life.[6]

Mabel Featherstone (1867–1957), known as Mavie, was 20 at the time of her father's death. She was also born at Colinswood on 15 December 1867, and was enrolled at the girls' school in 1882 where she won the Mrs Holmes' Prize for steady and satisfactory work in the lower school in 1883, and a prize for class work throughout the year. She travelled overseas after Macandrew's death and settled in Wellington about 1900, where she owned a fancy goods shop on Lambton Quay that was later relocated to Manners Street.[7]

Arthur William (1869–1950) was born at Monticello, the home of his uncle William Reynolds, on 11 August 1869, and was 17 at his father's death. He was a government electrician in 1917, and later an orchardist and a civil servant.[8] He was noted as a singer and married musician Jennie West in 1901.

Notes

Abbreviations

AES—*Auckland Evening Star*
AJHR—*Appendices to the Journals of the House of Representatives*
ANZ—Archives New Zealand
ATL—Alexander Turnbull Library
AWJ—*Aberdeen Weekly Journal*
BH—*Bruce Herald*
BoPT—*Bay of Plenty Times*
CB—Companion of the Order of the Bath
CL—*Clutha Leader*
CMG—Companion of the Order of St Michael and St George
DN—*Daily News* (London)
DNB—*Dictionary of National Biography*
DSC—*Daily Southern Cross* (Auckland)
EP—*Evening Post* (Wellington)
ES—*Evening Star* (Dunedin)
F&J—Flotsam and Jetsam, a collection within the papers of Thomas Hocken, HC
GCMG—Knight Grand Cross of the Order of St Michael and St George
GH—*Glasgow Herald*
GOC—General Officer Commanding
GRA—*Grey River Argus*
HBH—*Hawke's Bay Herald*
HC—Hocken Collection Uare Taoka o Hākena, University of Otago, Dunedin
KWMSS—Kate Wilson Manuscript Collection of Macandrew Family Correspondence
JP—Justice of the Peace
KB—Knight Bachelor
KCB—Knight Commander of the Order of the Bath
KCMG—Knight Commander of the Order of St Michael and St George
LC—Legislative Council
LT—*Lyttelton Times*
ME—*Mataura Ensign*
MHR—Member of the House of Representatives
MLC—Member of the Legislative Council
NE—*Nelson Examiner and New Zealand Chronicle* (later *Nelson Examiner*)
NEM—*Nelson Evening Mail*
NLS—National Library of Scotland
NOT—*North Otago Times*
NZH—*New Zealand Herald*
NZJ—*New Zealand Journal* (London)
NZ—*New Zealander* (Auckland)
NZJH—*New Zealand Journal of History*

NZPD—New Zealand Parliamentary Debates
NZT—New Zealand Tablet
OC—Otago Colonist
ODT—Otago Daily Times
OEC—Otago Executive Council
OPC—Otago Provincial Council
OW —Otago Witness
SC—Southern Cross (became the *Daily Southern Cross* in 1862)
ST—Southland Times
TarH—Taranaki Herald
TimH —Timaru Herald
TA—Thames Advertiser
*TT—Tuapeka Time*s
V&P, OPC—Votes and Proceedings, Otago Provincial Council
WC—Wanganui Chronicle
WCT—West Coast Times
WH—Wanganui Herald
WI—Wellington Independent
WT—Waikato Times

Introduction

1. Three different arrival dates are recorded by Dunedin scribes; *Otago Witness*, 22 February 1851, 'Table of the weather at Dunedin, for January, 1851'.
2. Rev. Thomas Burns: 'increasing our population … from the 260 souls first landed, to about 1450, our present population, as nearly as may be': *OW*, 8 March 1851.
3. K.C. McDonald, *City of Dunedin: A century of civic enterprise*, Dunedin: Dunedin City Corporation, 1965, 5–15.
4. http://en.wikipedia.org/wiki/George_Street,_Dunedin. Olive Trotter, *Dunedin's Spiteful Socrates: J.G.S. Grant*, Dunedin: Olive Trotter, 2005, 12. Most of the buildings were wooden: the Royal Hotel in Princes Street was prefabricated and brought out on the *John Wickliffe*, and some prefabricated houses had been imported from Britain. 'A few brick and stone buildings have been erected, but the inferior quality of the bricks made in the settlement render them unfit for outside use': *Nelson Examiner and New Zealand Chronicle*, 11 May 1850.
5. John R. Godley, ed., *Letters from Early New Zealand by Charlotte Godley* 1850–1853, Christchurch: Whitcombe & Tombs, 1951, 44. The mud was being tamed when Macandrew arrived. Charlotte Godley recorded in May 1850: 'In one of our first walks about Wellington we almost shed tears of sentimental admiration at coming suddenly in sight of bits of flat, well-macadamized road.'
6. *ODT*, 29 April 1887. Auckland had a population of 57,048.
7. Appendix 1, Letter: James Macandrew/unnamed recipients, 27 July 1850, KWMSS. A copy, with a business card listing two Macandrew companies, one each in London and New Zealand, dated 15 August 1850, is held by the National Library of Scotland, MSS, Acc 5000/vol. 207: 'Business letters Oliver & Boyd, Booksellers of Edinburgh/Garden & Macandrew'. In it, Macandrew predicted that New Zealand's future was assured because 'there can be no doubt that from its locality, climate & capability, it is fitted and destined to become the Great Britain of the south'.

8. John Dunmore, *Wild Cards: Eccentric characters from New Zealand's past*, Auckland: New Holland, 2006, 34.

9. Guy Scholefield, *New Zealand Parliamentary Record*, Wellington: Government Printer, 1950. Of the first 17 premiers (if FitzGerald and Forsaith are counted), FitzGerald, Grey, Stafford and Whitaker were superintendents, while Atkinson, Domett, FitzGerald, Forsaith, Fox, Hall, Pollen, Seddon, Sewell, Stout, Vogel and Whitaker were provincial councillors. Only Ballance, Waterhouse and Weld were not associated with a provincial council. Thirty-eight of the 44 provincial superintendents were either members of the House of Representatives or members of the Legislative Council at some stage of their political careers (eight were in both); 33 served at provincial and colonial levels simultaneously.

10. Edmund Bohan, *Edward Stafford: New Zealand's first statesman*, Christchurch: Hazard Press, 1994, 9.

11. Scholefield, *New Zealand Parliamentary Record*, 121.

12. *ST*, 26 February 1887.

13. *BoPT*, 28 May 1887.

14. Ibid.

15. A.H. McLintock, *The History of Otago*, Dunedin: Centennial Historical Publications, 1949; Christchurch: Capper Press, 1975, 623–24; W.P. Morrell, *The Provincial System in New Zealand: 1852–76*, Christchurch, Whitcombe & Tombs, 1964 (2nd edn), 131, 190; Erik Olssen, *A History of Otago*, Dunedin: John McIndoe, 1984, 48; Erik Olssen, 'Macandrew, James 1819?–1887', from the Dictionary of New Zealand Biography: www.teara.govt.nz/en/biographies/1m1/macandrew-james

16. Thomas Bracken, *Musings in Maoriland*, Dunedin: Arthur T. Keirle, 1890, 323; McLintock, *The History of Otago*, 495; David Hall, 'Macandrew, James', Te Ara – the Encyclopedia of New Zealand: www.TeAra.govt.nz/1966/M/MacandrewJames/en;
    Stuart W. Greif and Hardwicke Knight, *Cutten: Letters revealing the life and times of William Henry Cutten the forgotten pioneer*, Dunedin: Stuart Greif and Hardwicke Knight, 1979, 73. William Cutten, 1822–1883, b. England, landed New Zealand 1848. Son-in-law of William Cargill, Dunedin merchant, emigration agent, editor then owner of *OW* and *ODT*; member OPC 1853–63, 1871–73; OEC 1854, 1857, 1860–61, 1871–72; MHR 1853–55, 1878–79.

17. Brian Fitzpatrick, *The British Empire in Australia: An economic history 1834–1939*, Melbourne: Melbourne University Press, 1941, xxiv. Fitzpatrick suggests that 'an intellectually drunken conception of the "illimitable" resources of the principal colonies was fashionable' in late nineteenth-century Australia; this was equally true of New Zealand at the same time.

18. *ST*, 3 March 1887.

19. *OW*, 18 September 1875.

Chapter 1

1. Erik Olssen, 'Mr. Wakefield and New Zealand as an experiment in post-enlightenment experimental practice', NZJH 31, 1997, no. 2, 197–218.

2. Arthur Herman, *How the Scots Invented the Modern World*, New York: Crown Publishers, 2001, 19.

3. R.J. Morris, *Men, Women and Property in England, 1780–1870: A social and economic history of family strategies amongst the Leeds middle classes*, Cambridge: Cambridge University Press, 2005, 369–71.

4. Lenore Davidoff & Catherine Hall, *Family Fortunes: Men and women of the English middle class, 1780–1850*, London: Hutchinson, 1987, 13.

5. McLintock quotes J.G.S. Grant, that Macandrew was born in Fortrose, which is incorrect. He was born in Aberdeen. A.H. McLintock, *The History of Otago*, Dunedin: Centennial Historical Publications, 1949; Christchurch: Capper Press, 1975, 323.
    James Gordon Stuart Grant, 1832?–1902, b. Scotland, educated Kings College, Aberdeen and St Andrew's University, landed Melbourne 1851? Persuaded by William Reynolds to emigrate to Dunedin 1855 expecting to become the rector of the new high school; when not appointed, he began his long career challenging Otago authority figures. Public speaker, educator, agitator. Produced *Saturday Review* 1864–71, *Delphic Oracle* 1866–70 and *Stoic* in the 1870s (13 issues); published 60+ pamphlets 1870s–80s. Member OPC 1865–67; opposed Macandrew in elections for the General Assembly 1858 (won 3 votes) and the superintendency 1867 (won 2 votes). Unsuccessful candidate for Dunedin mayoralty 1868 and stood in many parliamentary elections thereafter.

6. 'Headstone flat in the Fortrose (Black Isle) Cathedral grounds is inscribed: "Sacred to the memory of John McAndrew and his spouse Mary Bisset and of their son Donald McAndrew and his spouse Helen Munroe and of their son Colin McAndrew, all respected inhabitants of this burgh. Erected by John McAndrew and Robert McAndrew of Edinburgh, surviving children of the said Donald McAndrew and Helen Munroe 1842."' Letter: Marsha Donaldson/Tom Brooking, 11 June 1984.

7. International Genealogical Index: www.myheritage.com/research/collection-1/myheritage-family-trees?s=361122641&itemId=212630361-1-8009&action=showRecord. Digest of Quaker births, marriage and burials in Scotland, MS–2703, University of Aberdeen Library.

8. 'Colin McAndrew Shoemaker, Summer Street and his Spouse Barbara Johnston had a son born named James, baptised by the Rev. Professor Kidd. Witnesses were James and Samuel Johnston.' Baptismal Register, Old Machar Parish Church, Aberdeen, 18 May 1819, McAndrew, James [o.p.r. Births 168/b00 0050 0610 Old Machar]: www.scotlandspeople.gov. uk/. The Macandrew family Bible, held in Toitū Otago Settlers Museum, Dunedin, lists 1820 as Macandrew's birth year (in his own handwriting). His age, recorded in the same Bible after his death in 1887, suggests 1819 as his birth year.

9. London 1841 census, 0bbba32d01db8027d3a224b2464d608e.pdf: www.ukcensusonline.com/ search/index.php?fn=james&sn=macandrew&phonetic_mode=1&event=1841L

10. 'Mr. Macandrew is a native of Aberdeen, where he was born in 1819. He was educated at Fortrose Academy in Ross-shire and subsequently at Aberdeen': *Dunedin Leader*, vol. 1, no. 2, 24 October 1863. His three siblings were christened in Rosemarkie. Another link is suggested by the naming of settlements in New Zealand after Fortrose and Cromarty on the Black Isle.

11. Eliza's brother William Reynolds was the other witness at their wedding and became Macandrew's business partner in New Zealand.

12. Daniel Macandrew, 1821–1899, b. Rosemarkie 1821, architect, emigrated NZ 1850; resident Dunedin 1850–54; practised Aberdeen 1855–87. *Aberdeen Press and Journal*, Obituary, Daniel Macandrew, 28 March 1899.

13. Charles Waddy, 2016, 'A Casa Reynolds: The personal, commercial and political adventures of one generation of a British family in Great Britain, Spain, Portugal and New Zealand', unpublished history of the Reynolds family, 42.

14. Exercise book inscribed 'James Macandrews book 18 Septr 1832' on the inside front cover, and 'James Macandrews Book 11th Jany 1833' on the inside back cover, Misc–MS–0619, HC. It contains 44 pages filled with arithmetic exercises written in a regular copperplate script. The exercises include topics such as compound interest, discount, and profit and loss.

15. 'Macandrew, James', from A.H. McLintock, (ed.), *An Encyclopaedia of New Zealand*: www.teara.govt.nz/en/1966/macandrew-james. Letter: David Walton, Asst. Registrar, Ayr

Academy/Tom Brooking, 30 April 1985. The school could not confirm that Macandrew had ever attended.

16. *AWJ*, 22 August 1891.

17. Letter: James McLean Macandrew/James Macandrew, January 1836, MS–00–111/2, HC.

18. Letter: John Macandrew/James Macandrew, 22 March 1838, KWMSS.

19. *CL*, 4 March 1887.

20. J.N. Hay, *Epidemics and pandemics: Their impacts on human history*, Santa Barbara, Cal: ABC–CLIO, 2005, 230.

21. James Adam, *Twenty Five Years of Emigrant Life in the South of New Zealand*, Edinburgh: Bell and Bradfute, 1876, 63. Adam is quoting Macandrew so his words should be treated with caution.

22. Waddy, 'A Casa Reynolds', 44. The 1841 London census shows Robert Garden, clerk, aged 22 and James Macandrew, clerk, aged 21, living with Isaac and Eliza Pitman at St Georges Terrace, Wells St (now Wells Way), Camberwell: www.ukcensusonline.com/search/index. php?fn=james&sn=macandrew&phonetic_mode=1&event=1841L. Business letters: Oliver & Boyd, Booksellers of Edinburgh/Robert Garden, then Garden & Macandrew of London 1841–50, MSS, Acc 5000/vols. 201, 203, 204–07, NLS.

23. George Cameron, *The Scots Kirk in London*, Oxford: Becket Publications, 1979, 29: 'The Scots who came south with the Stewarts colonised the area to the east of Westminster. Jacobean London quickly became used to the sight – than which, as a Scot of this century observed, few are more impressive – of "the Scotsman on the make". And the records show that London and Westminster, no less than the Scot himself, reaped the benefit of his enterprising, independent spirit.' Letter: Robert Reynolds/James Macandrew, 23 December 1848, Toitū Otago Settlers Museum. The firms were at 43 Watling St, London.

24. Letter: Donald Macandrew/James Macandrew, 9 September 1847, KWMSS.

25. *WH*, 25 October 1882.

26. Guildhall Communion Records, London.

27. Cameron, *The Scots Kirk in London*, 26.

28. Phillida Macdonald, *Eliza's Journal*, Christchurch: P. Macdonald, 2000, 4. The older sons Thomas and Robert were living in Portugal at this time. Thomas Reynolds (1783–1867) married Marion Hunter (1786–1869); Their children were Thomas William (1811–1898); Robert Hunter (1820–1872); William Hunter (1822–1899); Eliza Hunter (1827–1875). William Hunter Reynolds migrated NZ 1851, merchant, m. Rachel Pinkerton 1856. Member OPC 1853–76; OEC 1854–60, 1862–63, 1865; MHR 1863–78; minister of customs (Waterhouse ministry) 1872–73; minister of customs (Fox ministry) 1873; colonial secretary and minister of customs (Vogel ministry) 1873–75; minister of customs (Pollen ministry) 1875–76; member of executive council (Stout ministry) 1884–85, 1886–87; MLC 1878–99.

29. *OW*, 6 April 1899. 'Obituary: William Hunter Reynolds'. This obituary is incorrect: the plantations were in Portugal and William grew up in Oporto.

30. *OW*, 6 April 1899. £180,000 is approximately equivalent to £14,230,000 in 2016. Waddy challenges this amount, and claims that cork exports from Portugal to England were around £50,000 annually during the 1840s (Waddy, 'A Casa Reynolds', 41).

31. Eliza was aged 21 and Macandrew was 29. Perhaps he changed his age to lessen the gap.

32. Tom Devine, *To the Ends of the Earth: Scotland's global diaspora, 1750–2010*, London: Penguin, 2012, 289.

33. Marjory Harper, *Adventurers and Exiles: The great Scottish exodus*, London: Profile, 2003, 3.

34. Jock Phillips & Terry Hearn, *Settlers: New Zealand immigrants from England, Ireland & Scotland 1800–1945*, Auckland: Auckland University Press, 2008, 53, Table 4. The data is from the 1871 New Zealand census.

35. James Belich, *Paradise Reforged: A history of the New Zealanders from the 1880s to the year 2000*, Auckland: Allen Lane, 2001, 221; Marjory Harper, 'A century of Scottish emigration to New Zealand', Immigrants & Minorities, 29:2, 2011, 222, estimates 75 per cent of the Scots were Lowlanders.

36. Tanja Bueltmann, *Scottish Ethnicity and the Making of New Zealand Society 1850–1930*, Scottish Historical Review Monographs Series no. 19, Edinburgh: Edinburgh University Press, 2011, 207.

Chapter 2

1. Philip Temple, *A Sort of Conscience: The Wakefields*, Auckland: Auckland University Press, 2003, 223–39.

2. Edward Gibbon Wakefield, 1796–1862, b. England. Employed British Diplomatic Service, imprisoned for abduction, adviser to Lord Durham on Canadian government. Designed colonising model for South Australia where income from artificially high land prices subsidised the passage of labourers. Director New Zealand Co., 1839; member Canadian House of Assembly 1842–44; emigrated New Zealand 1853; member Wellington PC 1853–55; MHR for Hutt 1853–55.

3. *Colonial Gazette*, 17 August 1842; *NZJ*, 20 August 1842.

4. *NZJ*, 8 July 1843, 178. William Cargill, 1784–1860, b. Scotland. Nonconformist upbringing, veteran Napoleonic Wars. He had banking experience before he sailed, aged 64, with five of his 17 children, as chief administrator of the Otago Settlement. First superintendent Otago Province; MHR 1855–59. He countered Macandrew's more extreme proposals in the OPC of the 1850s.

5. T.M. Hocken, *Contributions to the Early History of New Zealand (Settlement of Otago)*, London: Sampson, Low, Marston and Co, 1898, 20; A.H. McLintock, The History of Otago: *The origins and growth of a Wakefield class settlement*. Dunedin: Otago Centennial Historical Publications, 1949; reprint, Christchurch: Capper Press, 1975, 174; E.N. Merrington, *A Great Coloniser: Rev Dr Thomas Burns*, Dunedin: Otago Daily Times and Witness Newspapers, 1929, 78.

6. McLintock, *The History of Otago*, 174. Rev Dr Thomas Burns, 1796–1871, b. Scotland. Nephew of Robert Burns; minister Church of Scotland then Free Church from 1843. Emigrated to New Zealand on the *Philip Laing* 1847; first minister of the Presbyterian congregation in Otago, initial minister First Church Dunedin; first chancellor University of Otago 1869–71.

7 Roderick Bunce, 'The Trust Funds for Religious and Educational Uses at Otago 1842 to 1866', MA thesis, University of Otago, 1982.

8. Letter: Rev. Dr Candlish/William Cargill, 9 September 1847, MSS–0075, HC.

9. McLintock, *The History of Otago*, 201.

10. Letter: Thomas Burns/William Cargill, 2 May 1845, MSS–0076, HC, quoted in McLintock, *The History of Otago*, 201.

11. McLintock, *The History of Otago*, 142.

12. Ibid., 208.

13. Terms of Purchase of Land in the Settlement of Otago, June 1847, MSS–Pam 124/2, HC.

14. Letter: Secretary of Otago Lay Association John McGlashan/Secretary of the New Zealand

Company T.C. Harington, 15 May 1849, MSS–0077, HC, describes the impressive marketing activities undertaken by the association, which revitalised the Otago project: 12,000 copies of an address, 10,000 copies of the *Otago Journal*, 800 copies of a circular and 8000 copies of a handbill were distributed in Scotland, and 1000 newspaper advertisements were run.

John McGlashan, 1802–1864, b. Scotland. Solicitor, full-time secretary of the Otago Lay Association in Edinburgh from 1846–52, leading campaigner for the settlement of Otago. Member OPC 1855–63; OEC 1855–60, 1862–63; OPC treasurer 1854–61. Worked closely with Macandrew in Britain and Otago, especially in the provincial council. Macandrew turned on him in 1860 and accused him of dishonesty when Macandrew himself was caught misusing official funds. McGlashan was dismissed as provincial treasurer for allowing Macandrew to access public money for his private use.

15. McLintock, *The History of Otago*, 235.
16. Hocken, *Contributions*, 286–96.
17. A Report of the Edinburgh Committee of the Otago Lay Association to the Special General Meeting of the Association, 25 May 1850, MSS–0077, HC.
18. T.C. Smout, *A Century of the Scottish People 1830-1950*, London: Collins, 1986, 110.
19. Letter: Harington/John McGlashan, 3 May 1850, MSS–0077, HC.
20. Letter: Macandrew/McGlashan, 14 June 1850, MSS–0078, HC.
21. Ibid.
22. Letter: Macandrew/McGlashan, 17 July 1850, MSS–0078, HC.
23. Ibid.
24. Letter: McGlashan/Cargill, 14 June 1850, MSS–0077, HC.
25. Letter: McGlashan/Harington, 19 June 1950, MSS–0077, HC.
26. Letter: McGlashan/Cargill, 28 June 1850, MSS–0077, HC.
27. Letter: Macandrew/McGlashan, 28 June 1850, MSS–0078, HC. The college was to train Free Church ministers for the colony. McGlashan offered employment at it when trying to recruit an editor for the Lay Association's newspaper.
28. McLintock, *The History of Otago*, 313.
29. Letter: Macandrew/McGlashan, 11 July 1850, MSS–0078, HC.
30. Letter: W.H. Reynolds/McGlashan, 12 July 1850, MSS–0078, HC.
31. Letter: Macandrew/McGlashan, 12 July 1850, MSS–0078, HC.
32. Letter: W.H. Reynolds/McGlashan, 15 July 1850, MSS–0078, HC.
33. Letter: Macandrew/McGlashan, 17 July 1850, MSS–0078, HC.
34. Letter: McGlashan/Earl Grey, 8 August 1850, MSS–0078, HC.
35. *OW*, 8 February 1851.
36. Letter: McGlashan/James Watson, chairman of the London committee of the Otago Lay Association, 14 September 1850, MSS–0078, HC: 'In your absence I was aided by Mr James Macandrew now on his way to Otago, his partner Mr Crane, Mr Robert Roxburgh, Mr Anderson and Mr W Cargill a son of Captain Cargill.'
37. Letter: Benjamin Hawes, under-secretary of state/Cargill, 29 August 1850, MSS–0080, HC. This is different to one sent to Macandrew on 2 September 1850, which had raised the expectations of the Otago Lay Association committee.
38. Letter: Benjamin Hawes/Macandrew, 2 September 1850, MSS–0081, HC.
39. *ST*, 26 February 1887.
40. James Belich, *Replenishing the Earth: The settler revolution and the rise of the Anglo world 1783-1939*, Oxford: Oxford University Press, 2009, 21.
41. Ibid., 184.

42. Letter: Macandrew/unnamed recipients, 27 July 1850, KWMSS. Just how widely this letter circulated is unknown, but two copies have been found during research for this book

43. John M. McKenzie (ed.), *The Victorian Vision: Inventing New Britain*, London: V.&A. Publications, 2004, 154.

44. New Zealand Company Tender to Provide Steam Communication in New Zealand, 10 November 1849, MSS–0079, HC.

45. Belich, *Replenishing the Earth*, 311: 'Victoria, then the Port Phillip District, had shared the later half of Australia's first boom of 1828–42, and busted with it. But a second boom began around 1847 … the population more than doubled in the five years between 1846 and 1851, from 32,000 to 77,000.' This was before their gold rush.

46. Ian Farquhar, 'Letter to the editor', *ODT*, 30 January 2001.

47. Charles Waddy, 2016, 'A Casa Reynolds: The personal, commercial and political adventures of one generation of a British family in Great Britain, Spain, Portugal and New Zealand', unpublished history of the Reynolds family, 52–54.

48. 'NEW ZEALAND – FOR WELLINGTON and OTAGO, to sail on the 25th of August next, the splendid new clipper-built schooner TITAN, 350 tons burden, GEORGE CRAIG, Commander; to load at the Jetty, London Docks. Has excellent accommodation for passengers; has all her dead weight engaged, and room only for a limited quantity of measurement goods, for which immediate application should be made. For terms of freight or passage apply to Messrs Garden and Macandrew, 34, Dowgate-hill; or to Joseph Stayner, 110, Fenchurch-street': *The Times* of London, 25 July 1850.

49. *Aberdeen Journal*, 31 July 1850.

50. 'The Little Enemy' was a group of largely English settlers with capital, mostly Episcopalian by inclination, who were not prepared to accept conditions imposed on the community by the Free Presbyterian Church. The core members appear to have been John Carnegie, David Garrick, Henry Graham, John Hyde Harris, Henry Manning, Walter Mantell, Alfred Chetham Strode and Dr Robert Williams. They individually and collectively challenged many of the decisions made in early Dunedin.

51. Letter: McGlashan/I. Langmuir, 10 September 1850, HC, MSS–0078.

52. Hocken, *Contributions*, 323, records *Titan*'s voyage dates as 5 September 1850 to 15 January 1851.

53. Letter: Cargill/McGlashan, 21 January 1851, MSS–0081, HC.

54. Hocken, *Contributions*, 323; NZ, 15 February 1851.

55. 'Obituary, James Scott', *BH*, 12 August 1887.

56. Speech: Tom Brooking to Rich and Macandrew families' descendants, 15 February 2001, Dunedin.

Chapter 3

1. T.M. Hocken, *Contributions to the Early History of New Zealand (Settlement of Otago)*, London: Sampson, Low, Marston and Co, 1898, 298.

2. 'As a class settlement, Otago appears rather to have failed, for the religious returns only give 392 as followers of the Free Church, out of 1182, whose professing creed is stated. There is, however, 423 of the Church of Scotland, and the remainder are made up chiefly of members of the Church of England, and of the various dissenting bodies': *Nelson Examiner and New Zealand Chronicle*, 11 May 1850.

3. Letter: McGlashan/John Hall Maxwell, 11 October 1851, MS–0078, HC.

4. One exception was the establishment of a Mechanics' Institute in 1851, for which the Scottish and English settlers cooperated closely.

5. *NZ*, 27 December 1851.
6. A.H. McLintock, *The History of Otago: The origins and growth of a Wakefield class settlement*, Dunedin: Otago Centennial Historical Publications, 1949; reprint, Christchurch: Capper Press, 1975, 324.
7. 'Reports of Meetings 14 March & 5 April 1851', *OW*, 22 March 1851.
8. *OW*, 3 May 1851.
9. *NZH*, 27 March 1884, quoted in the *ODT*, 3 April 1884.
10. The cartoonist was James Brown. The cartoon appears in McLintock, *The History of Otago*, facing p. 360.
11. *OW*, 9 October 1858.
12. Letter: Macandrew/Cargill, commissioner of Crown lands, Otago District, 1 October 1851, MS–1751–001, HC. Macandrew owned a quarter-acre (0.1 ha) town allotment, a suburban allotment of 10 acres (4ha) and a rural allotment of 50 acres (20ha); Letter: James Macandrew/William Cargill, commissioner of Crown lands, Otago District, 1 October 1851, Wm Cargill Receipts for Payment in Otago Settlement, Cargill, William Walter, Captain, Papers relating to the New Zealand Company and the early settlement of Otago, MS-1751-001, HC. Although Macandrew's town and suburban allotments have not been identified, his rural allotments were identified in his application for a depasturage licence: 'The run now claimed is situated behind and immediately adjoining the two rural allotments held by us, East Taieri, and that we now have a number of cattle depastured there.' He may not have kept his town and suburban allotments for long, as an advertisement in the *Otago Witness* on 13 December 1851 stated on behalf of James Macandrew & Co., 'The Undersigned wish to dispose of a Suburban and Town Choice for which they are willing to take a Rural Choice in payment.'
13. 'Register of Rural & Town Allotments pre-1850', Cargill, William Walter, Captain, Papers relating to the New Zealand Company and the early settlement of Otago, MS-0209/001, HC. These were Sections 30 and 34 in Block 6.
14. *OW*, 8 February 1851; *NZ*, 15 February 1851; *LT*, 22 February 1851; *OW*, 8 March 1851. F&J, no. 5, Letter 38, James Macandrew/William Cargill, 26 February 1851: 'I agree to rent from you the English Barracks near the jail and now unoccupied at the rent of fifteen shillings p week.' *OW*, 22 March 1851: 'To Storekeepers. The undersigned are Importers of every description of British and Colonial Produce, which they will be glad to supply at Wholesale Prices. JAMES MACANDREW, & Co.'
15. *OW*, 17 May 1852: 'THE UNDERSIGNED have now OPENED their NEW STORE, Opposite the Jetty where they purpose to keep a regular Stock of such articles of British and Colonial Produce as are in general demand. And as their Stock will be supplied direct from the first Market, they will be enabled to sell at fair and moderate prices.'
16. *OW*, 24 May 1856: 'Mr J.B. Clarke appointed to manage Clutha store'; ST, 25 October 1884; 'In November (6 November 1856) the *Star* arrived (in Invercargill) with … James Macandrew, with a quantity of merchandise and building materials for a store': F.G. Hall-Jones, *Historical Southland*, Southland Historical Committee, Invercargill, 1945, 125; *OW*, 11 September 1858 :'Firm of JAMES MACANDREW AND COMPANY has been this day DISSOLVED by mutual consent'; Hocken, *Contributions*, 192.
17. *OW*, 5 April 1851.
18. *OW*, 21 June 1851: Reynolds returned via Otago (berthing 26 May 1851) with a cargo of two hogsheads of brandy, 100 tons of potatoes, 96 bags of sugar, 62 bags of flour, 54 boxes of onions, 38 boxes of apples, 16 cases of jams, and lesser quantities of turpentine, French

polish, wheat, fruits, live plants and other sundries. He loaded another six tons of potatoes and some 290 bushels of barley and departed for North America.

19. *OW*, 10 January 1852.
20. *OW*, 6 April 1899: 'The death of the Hon W.H. Reynolds'.
21. *OW*, 12 February 1852, 6 April 1899. £9000 is equivalent to around $1 million today, a large return for a year's investment of time and money. Calculated on Reserve Bank of New Zealand website: www.rbnz.govt.nz/monetary-policy/inflation-calculator
22. In his publicity, 'alcohol' came between 'gun powder' and 'window glass': clearly Macandrew had no qualms about supplying settlers with that commodity. OW, 12 August 1854: James Macandrew & Co. advertised: 'Now Landing ex "Thetis" from London … Trueman's XX Stout, in hhds. Bass No. 3 Ale, in barrels. Whitbread and Marzetti's Bottled Ale and Stout. Geneva, Brandy, Rum, Whisky, Port and Sherry Wine, in cases. Geneva and Gin, in cases. Kent Hops.'
23. McLintock, *The History of Otago*, 344.
24. Charles Waddy, 2016, 'A Casa Reynolds': 70–72. I wish to thank Charles Waddy for the use of his detailed research which informs much of this chapter; William Downie Stewart, ed., *The Journal of George Hepburn*, Dunedin: Coulls Somerville Wilkie and A.H. Reed, 1934.
25. *DN*, 29 October 1851.
26. *GH*, 10 November 1851.
27. Waddy, 'A Casa Reynolds', 59.
28. *DN*, London, 11 and 14 August 1860; *The Times* of London, 15 August 1860.
29. *OW*, 27 July 1861.
30. The tale of Garden & Macandrew's misfortunes is in Waddy, 'A Casa Reynolds', 117.
31. Letter: McGlashan/Cargill, 21 February 1853, MSS–0078, HC: 'I am this morning in receipt of … your letters dated 25 September and 14th October 1852, the former enclosing Bill of Exchange for £115 by Frederick Brock Holinshead upon Messrs Twining & Co. endorsed by James Macandrew & Co. and payable to me, in lieu of the unaccepted Bills for £90 and £25 formerly transmitted.'
32. Letter: McGlashan/Cargill, 12 April 1853, MSS–0078, HC; Letter: Cargill/McGlashan, 20 November 1852, MS–463/028, HC.
33. *OW*, 8 March 1851.
34. Letter: Grey/Cargill, 12 February 1851, MS–0080, HC: 'I have appointed Mr. Macandrew a Justice of the Peace.' Sir George Grey, 1812–1898, b. Portugal. Served in British army 1826–40; government resident, King George's Sound, Western Australia 1839–40; governor, South Australia 1841–45; lieutenant-governor NZ 1845–47; governor-in-chief NZ 1848–53; governor of NZ 1853–54; governor Cape Colony 1854–60; governor NZ 1861–68, Auckland superintendent 1875–76, MHR 1875–95, premier 1877–79, KCB 1848, PC 1894.
35. *OW*, 15 November 1851. His assailant, the coroner Dr Robert Williams, was found guilty and fined 30s and costs.
36. *OW*, 7 February 1852.
37. 'To the end he remained a devoted member of the free church, walking up the steep hill to Pukehiki for divine service each Sabbath when he was at home, and resisting with all his domineering magnetism the introduction of such papist practices as hymns': Erik Olssen, 'Macandrew, James', from the Dictionary of New Zealand Biography: www.teara.govt.nz/en/biographies/1m1/macandrew-james
38. 'Minute Book of the Trustees', Trust Fund for Religious and Educational Uses, Dunedin, 1848–67, held at the office of the Otago Foundation Trust Board, Dunedin. Macandrew

joined trustees Thomas Burns, William Cargill and Edward McGlashan on 24 March 1851, replacing Edward Lee, and served until 1854 and again in 1858–59.

39. Clause 6 of the Terms of Purchase allocated 100 of the 2400 Otago properties offered (6025 acres/2438ha) to the estate of the Trust Fund for Religious and Educational Uses. The trustees anticipated collecting £36,150 (one-eighth of the sale price of the 144,600 acres of land at 40s an acre) and spending £12,050 to buy their 100 properties, leaving £24,100 to pay for the establishment of churches and schools. In reality, land sales were slower than expected in the six years until the establishment of the Presbytery of Otago, by which time the estate owned only 1325.5 acres (536ha). Their income was never sufficient to pay for the planned institutions.

40. McLintock, *The History of Otago*, 348.

41. *OW*, 9 April 1853.

42. *OW*, 25 June 1859.

43. *OW*, 5 July 1851.

44. *OW*, 5 and 19 July 1851. Patrons Valpy, Lee, Wakefield, Jones, Turner and chairman Macandrew were titled 'Esq.'; 16 other office holders were either 'Mr' or without title. Macandrew was rarely titled 'Mr' in any publicity.

45. *OW*, 15 November 1851, 8 January 1853.

46. Hocken, *Contributions*, 131.

47. It was eventually moved to Carroll Street in 1872 and supplanted by the Cargill monument, the latter relocated from the Octagon. In October 1858 Macandrew offered to relinquish his lease of a section on the corner of Manse and High streets to allow a combined Athenaeum and Mechanics' Institute to be built, and this second building was opened on 2 June 1862. In 1869 a site in the Octagon was chosen as a permanent home for the institute and the foundation stone was laid on 12 November. *OW*, 13 November 1869.

48. W.P. Morrell, *British Colonial Policy in the Age of Peel and Russell*, Oxford: Clarendon Press, 1930, 105.

49. The first colony in the British Empire to gain responsible government was Nova Scotia in 1848, followed by the Province of Canada in the same year, Prince Edward Island in 1851, New Brunswick in 1854 and Newfoundland in 1855. New South Wales and Victoria achieved that status in 1855 and New Zealand in 1856.

50. 'An Act to make further provision for the Government of the New Zealand Islands', dated 28 December 1846, printed in the *London Gazette*, 29 December 1846.

51. William P. Morrell, *The Provincial System in New Zealand: 1852–76*, 2nd edn, Christchurch: Whitcombe & Tombs, 1964.

52. William Lee & Lily Rees, *The Life and Times of Sir George Grey, KCB*, Auckland: H. Brett, 1892, 115.

53. Dispatch: George Grey to Lord Stanley, 27 January 1846, quoted in Morrell, *The Provincial System*, 35.

54. A.H. McLintock, *Crown Colony Government in New Zealand*, Wellington: Government Printer, 1958, 297–301. Opposition to nomineeism was a major plank of the constitutional societies; the British Colonial Reform Society, on which the settlers' associations were modelled, aimed at obtaining for each colony 'the real and sole management of all local affairs … including the disposal of waste lands, and the right to frame and alter its local constitutions at pleasure' (304).

55. Ibid., 305.

56. Minute Book no. 1, 1851, 20, Otago Settlers' Association, MS 0032, HC; 'Report of a public meeting and a petition: 3 December 1850', includes a cutting from *OW*, 5 July 1851; On 16

February 1852 the Otago Settlers' Association proposed a governance model that included a lord-lieutenant, an elected senate, a House of Representatives and municipal charters, with a mayor and aldermen for Otago (and other districts). *OW*, 21 February 1852.

57. *OW*, 24 May 1851.
58. Guy Scholefield, *A Dictionary of New Zealand Biography*, Wellington: Department of Internal Affairs, 1940, vol. 2, 414.
59. *OW*, 24 May 1851.
60. 'Petition', *OW*, 8 February 1851; A petition forwarded by Grey to the colonial secretary protested: 'The very name of Class Settlement engenders endless disputes between the different professing parties of Christian settlers, which your Petitioners cannot but regret.' It had about 186 signatures. McLintock, *The History of Otago*, 317.
61. Minute Book No. 1, 1851.
62. Ibid., 3.
63. *OW*, 19 July 1851; Minute Book No. 1, 1851, 12.
64. Minute Book No. 1, 1851, Minutes of a Meeting, 31 May 1851, 10.
65. Ibid., 43.
66. Letter: Burns/Macandrew, 14 April 1854, MSS–0076, HC. Fellow Trustee Thomas Burns intimated there was dissatisfaction with the trust deed.
67. *OW*, 21 February 1852, reported Macandrew's comments from the chair of a general meeting of the Otago Settlers' Association held on 16 February 1852: 'It was difficult to estimate the influence which the resolutions of a meeting like the present at this peculiar juncture of the affairs of New Zealand might have upon the future prospects of themselves and their prosperity. They would reach home in time for debate which would take place in the ensuing Session of Parliament upon the proposed Constitution for New Zealand and would no doubt be of material service to the friends of the colony.'
68. Letter: Macandrew/Cargill, Pasturage Application, Application no. 15, 1 October 1851, MSS–1571/001, HC.
69. Depasturage Licences Applications, Applications nos 24 and 45, MS–0209/006, HC.
70. Ibid., Application nos. 30, 34 and 47.
71. The bricks were advertised in the *OW*, 21 February 1852; 'The Patent Wedge Shingle … as durable as ordinary English slates, and cover the same surface at half the expense', *OW*, 5 & 19 April 1851; lime was advertised at 4½d a bushel in the *OW*, 1 November 1851, compared to Captain Blackie's 9d a bushel advertised in the *OW*, 18 October 1851; Letter: William Cargill/John McGlashan, 29 July 1851, MS-0080, HC.
72. *OW*, 15 May 1852: 'LIME The Undersigned … are now erecting a shed on the top of the ridge above the Kaikarai [sic] Lime Kiln, where there will shortly be a large stock of Lime constantly at hand, and from where there is easy access for carts in all weathers to all the suburban districts … JAMES MACANDREW & Co.' *OW*, 13 October 1855. The kiln was offered for sale and would have been a valuable asset, as 'the party working the Kilne will also secure the right to Cut Timber over 20 acres Bush land in the neighbourhood. J. Macandrew & Co.'
73. *OW*, 20 & 27 August 1953. Section 14 in Block 17 in the Town of Dunedin, Ratesbook of the Dunedin Town Board (established 1857), Dunedin City Council, vol. 4/1.
74. Letter: Macandrew/Superintendent, 16 March 1859, ANZ, Dunedin, AAAC 707 D500 130/c 118; OW, 10 December 1859 & 28 April 1860.
75. *OW*, 17 May 1851, James Macandrew & Co. intimated 'that they have been empowered by Mr. William Hunter Reynolds, Lloyd's Agent at Otago … to act for him as such … during his

temporary absence from the Colony'; *OW*, 20 May 1854. Reynold's licence was issued by John McGlashan, who was by then provincial treasurer of Otago; *OW*, 26 August 1854.

76. *OW*, 16 August 1856, 'House and Estate Agency – JAMES MACANDREW & CO.'; Olive Trotter, *Dunedin's Spiteful Socrates, J.G.S. Grant*, Dunedin: Olive Trotter, 2005, 22. In 1855 Grant 'was visited by James Macandrew as manager of Captain Cargill's estate'.

77. Section 2 in Block 15 in the Town of Dunedin, Ratesbook of the Dunedin Town Board, Dunedin City Council, vol. 4/1. This section had a house on it which Macandrew let to Charles Bentley from 1857 to 1860 and possibly longer.

78. *OW*, 24 January 1852.

79. *OW*, 13 March 1852.

80. *OW*, 27 November 1852; McLintock, *The History of Otago*, 274–85. All of the proprietors supervised the editor, then a subcommittee of two directed him, then the editor ran the business at arm's length.

81. *OW*, 27 November 1852.

82. *OW*, 27 July 1861: the *Otago Colonist* became the *Colonist* in 1862 and was incorporated into the *Daily Telegraph* in 1863, which folded in April 1864. Macandrew is reported to have said, 'I lost £700 in establishing the "Colonist" newspaper. Altogether I spent £1800 or £1900 in establishing this paper, but when in 1860 I came to settle accounts with Mr. Lambert, he only paid me £100, and repudiated the remainder and denied his liability for it.' McLintock, *The History of Otago*, 434.

83. Hocken, *Contributions*, 136; *OW*, 18 September 1875: James Macandrew, 'the young Aberdonian … drew up a prospectus for the Bank of Otago, and when shares were taken up to the extent of £7000, a preliminary meeting was called, directors appointed, and, to the astonishment of the shareholders, a handful of beautifully engraved notes of the Bank of Otago were laid on the table, and the design submitted for approval.'

84. *OW*, 19 April 1851.

85. Bank Charters Act 1851, Sect. 2 (3).

86. James Barr, *The Old Identities*, Dunedin: Mills, Dick & Co., 1879, 100.

87. Hocken, *Contributions*, 136.

88. *OW*, 30 October 1852.

89. *OW*, 20 August 1853.

90. *OW*, 3 January 1857. The Bank Paper Currency Act 1856 allowed the Union Bank of Australia to issue and redeem their own notes and Otago gained its first bank (a branch office only).

91. Johnny Jones, 1809–1869, b. Australia. Hocken, *Contributions*, 137.

92. *OW*, 4 October 1851: Eliza Macandrew of Stafford Street advertised for a servant.

93. Colin was born in 1849; Marion in 1851; Thomas in 1852; Jane in 1854; an unnamed child in 1855; James in 1857; Herbert in 1859; Hunter in 1862; Alice in 1864; Mabel in 1867; and Arthur in 1869. Macandrew was survived by nine of his children.

94. Letter: Eliza Macandrew/Thomas Reynolds, 19 February 1852, MSS–00 111/2, HC.

95. Some of Macandrew's donations recorded in the *Otago Witness* were:
    - 19 July 1851: £21 to the Mechanics' Institute plus 'all the lime, which was more than twice as generous as the next listed donor'
    - 30 April 1853: £1 plus all the nails for a bridge over the Water of Leith
    - 25 June 1853: The chairman of the Otago Settlers' Association noted at the second annual general meeting in 1853: 'The treasurer, Mr. Macandrew, has with great liberality supplied whatever funds have been deficient; he is consequently £8 out of pocket.'
    - 25 February 1854: £5 to the collection for 'the purpose of raising a Sum of Money sufficient

to defray the expenses of the Outfit and Passage of two additional Ministers for the colony of Otago'

- 14 July 1855: £25 to the patriotic fund 'for the Relief of the Widows and Orphans of the Soldiers and Sailors who may fall in the War with Russia'
- 26 July 1856: 'Subscriptions in Land ... *Promised* ... ¼-Acre at Dunedin' for the Church of England
- 31 January 1857: £100 to the sustentation fund of the Free Church at Dunedin
- 15 August 1857: a contribution for the metalling of Stafford Street
- 1 May 1858: a contribution to victims of the mutiny in India
- 4 June 1859: £12 to the parsonage building fund for the Church of England.

Chapter 4

1. An Act to Grant a Representative Constitution to the Colony of New Zealand, 1852.
2. 'Waste lands' referred to all land without title.
3. *OW*, 21 August 1852. Macandrew was a hands-on proprietor of the newspaper; cf. A.H. McLintock, *The History of Otago: The origins and growth of a Wakefield class settlement*, Dunedin: Otago Centennial Historical Publications, 1949; reprint, Christchurch: Capper Press, 1975, 284, fn. 3: 'It is easy to detect the editorials written by Macandrew and Burns as the style of each was so distinctive.'
4. Ibid.
5. *OW*, 13 November 1852.
6. R.J. Polaschek (ed.) *Local Government in New Zealand*, Wellington and London: New Zealand Institute of Public Administration and Oxford University Press, 1956, 18.
7. House of Commons Debates, vol. 121, col. 922, 21 May 1852. 'Blue Books' became the official government statistics volumes.
8. Ibid.
9. Gavin McLean, *The Governors: New Zealand's governors and governors-general*, Dunedin: Otago University Press, 2006, 56. Governor Browne suggested to the Colonial Office in November 1855: 'The head start given to the provincial councils by Grey had enabled them to get the better men. Few settlers, he believed, could afford to serve outside their province.'
10. D.G. Herron, 'The circumstances and effects of Sir George Grey's delay in summoning the first New Zealand General Assembly', *Historical Studies Australia and New Zealand* 8(32), 1959, 364–82; W.P. Morrell, *The Provincial System in New Zealand: 1852–76*, 2nd edn, Christchurch: Whitcombe & Tombs, 1964, 72–79. Herron (364) suggests J.C. Beaglehole, *New Zealand: A short history*, 1936, 33 and A.H. McLintock, *Crown Colony Government in New Zealand*, Wellington: Government Printer, 1958, 361–88 support this view.
11. McLintock, *Crown Colony*, 367. But Grey's decision made in March 1853 deserves criticism, when he appropriated a responsibility of the General Assembly and issued new regulations for the sale of waste lands, reducing the price already set in some of the fledgling provinces. Grey claimed he was entitled to use the authority delegated to the governor under the Act, but this was not the case.
12. Morrell, *The Provincial System*, 64; Guy Scholefield, *New Zealand Parliamentary Record*, Wellington: Government Printer, 1950, 73. Life did mean life! William Bailey from Marlborough was appointed to the LC in 1861 and served until 1922.
13. McLintock, *Crown Colony*, 347.
14. McLintock, *The History of Otago*, 351, fn. 1, cites J.S. Marais, *The Colonisation of New Zealand* (Oxford: Oxford University Press, 1927, 297). J. Milne, *Sir George Grey: The romance of a proconsul* (London: Chatto & Windus, 1899, 116) states that Governor Grey acknowledged

he was inspired by 'many hints from the United States constitution' when composing his contribution to the Constitution Act 1852. Forty years later Grey was still resentful of this change to his version, when he complained about 'the dictation of a single man' that prevented the election of members to the Legislative Council by the provincial councils. *Australasian Federation Convention Debates*, 1891, 617, cited in Brett, *Acknowledge No Frontier: The creation and demise of New Zealand's provinces, 1853–76* (Dunedin: Otago University Press, 2016, 282, fn. 41).

15. Morrell, *The Provincial System*, 70.
16. McLintock, *Crown Colony*, 345, fn. 1. David Herron, 'The franchise and New Zealand politics, 1853–8, *Political Science*, 1960 12(28), 28–44 provides a detailed analysis of the reach of the franchise in this period. Herron suggests: 'A franchise which was virtually universal did not automatically produce a high percentage of enrolments … Interest, or lack of it, affected enrolments.'
17. Molesworth, in the same Commons speech in which he opposed the nomination of superintendents, claimed: 'Generally speaking, they [the nominated superintendents] would be jacks in office of the most odious description, unless constantly kept in control by being frequently subjected to popular election.' Macandrew may well not have been nominated to be a superintendent!
18. Clause 19 of the Constitution Act listed the 13 areas the provincial councils were not permitted to handle: customs duties; courts of justice; coinage and currency; weights and measures; Post Office; bankruptcy and insolvency; beacons and lighthouses; dues or other charges on shipping; marriage; Crown lands, native lands (explicitly no sales); laws 'inflicting any disabilities or restrictions on persons of the native race to which persons of European birth or descent would not also be subjected'; criminal law except summary punishments; inheritance and wills.
19. McLintock, *Crown Colony*, 334: 'Pakington … had his own ideas on the relative importance of the General Legislature and the Provincial Councils, and firmly rejected the theory that the provinces be regarded as independent colonies.'
20. *NZPD*, 29 April 1856, 32.
21. Morrell, *The Provincial System*, 59; Brett, *Acknowledge No Frontier*, 52, says 'many immodestly saw themselves as lieutenants to the colonial governor in Auckland'.
22. Morrell, *The Provincial System*, 61.
23. Dispatches: Robert Wynyard/Sir Henry Labouchere, no. 63, 25 May 1855, ANZ, Wellington, ACHK 16585, G 30/25.
24. Dispatches: Robert Wynyard/Sir Henry Labouchere, no. 67, 5 June 1855, ANZ, Wellington, ACHK 16585, G 30/25.
25. Ibid.
26. Dispatches: Sir Henry Labouchere, no. 27, 27 November 1855, ANZ, Wellington, ACHK 8604 G1/41, printed in *LT*, 14 June 1856.
27. Ibid.
28. Ibid.
29. Dispatches: Thomas Gore Brown/Sir Henry Labouchere, no. 53, 29 May 1856, ANZ, Wellington, ADCZ 18844, GORE BROWNE2/1/1.
30. Ibid.
31. *AJHR*, 1858, Session 1, A–02, 1; Dispatch: H. Labouchere/Governor Gore Browne, no. 90, 10 December 1856.
32. *AJHR*, 1874, Session 1, A–01, 11; Dispatches: Sir James Fergusson/The Earl of Kimberley, no. 51, 30 June 1873.

33. *AJHR*, 1874, Session 1, A–02, 12; Dispatches: The Earl of Kimberley/Sir James Fergusson, General, 23 September 1873.

34. *OW*, 25 September 1852.

35. *OW*, 2 October 1852.

36. *OW*, 20 May 1854; *OW*, 25 August 1855. Macandrew resigned in anger in June 1857 over the decision of the board and the provincial council to develop Maclaggan Street rather than Stafford Street as the main south road; *OW*, 26 April 1856; *OW*, 27 September 1856.

37. Constitution Act, 1852, clause 18. The Dunedin Town Board had been elected in August 1855 to maintain urban infrastructure.

38. William Cargill had 17 children, 10 of whom survived him, and the six who accompanied him to Otago established a powerful network of allied families.

39. McLintock, *The History of Otago*, 235.

40. John Godley (ed.), *Letters from Early New Zealand by Charlotte Godley 1850–1853*, Christchurch: Whitcombe & Tombs, 1951, 18.

41. *OW*, 24 September 1853. Macandrew in turn nominated Cutten for a Town of Dunedin seat.

42. Erik Olssen has lodged a paper with the Hocken Collections that contains a detailed analysis of all of Macandrew's election results: MS 2146/97. Olssen's data has been used throughout this book.

43. *OW*, 1 and 7 October 1853. John Cargill, 1818–1889, b. Scotland, landed New Zealand 1848, 6th child and 3rd surviving son of William Cargill; married 1) Sarah, daughter of John Jones of Waikouaiti, 2) Kate, daughter of Dr Featherston, superintendent of Wellington Province; served in Royal Navy; coffee planter in Ceylon; Dunedin merchant, pastoralist (Tokomairiro, Taieri Plains and Teviot Station). Member OPC 1855–59, 1863–67; MHR 1853–58, 1866–70; colonel in command of Otago Volunteers and Militia. Left NZ 1884, retired to England then British Columbia, where he died.

44. *OW*, 7 January 1854. The members were James Adam, William Cutten and Alexander Rennie representing the Town of Dunedin district; Archibald Anderson, John Gillies, John Hyde Harris, Edward McGlashan, James Macandrew and William Hunter Reynolds (absent this day) represented the Dunedin Country district. Harris was the only 'Little Enemy' representative, but he had lapsed when he married one of Captain Cargill's daughters.

45. Ibid.

46. T.M. Hocken, *Contributions to the Early History of New Zealand (Settlement of Otago)*, London: Sampson, Low, Marston and Co, 1898, 155.

47. V&P, OPC, Session I, 10 January 1854, Summary of Proceedings on Bills, vi.

48. John Gillies, 1802–1871, b. Scotland, landed New Zealand 1852. Dunedin lawyer, partner of John Hyde Harris. Member OPC 1853–55, Speaker OPC 1854–55.
John Hyde Harris, 1825–1886, b. England, landed New Zealand 1850. Son-in-law of William Cargill, Dunedin lawyer, initially a member of 'The Little Enemy'. Member OPC 1853–58; OEC 1858–59; superintendent of Otago 1863–65; MLC 1858–64, 1867–68; solicitor-general (Stafford ministry) 1867–68. As an example of the interwoven Cargill descendents, one of Harris' sons married a cousin, a daughter of John Cargill.
Edward McGlashan, 1817–1889, b. Scotland, landed New Zealand 1850. Younger brother of John McGlashan, partner Young & McGlashan, Dunedin merchants; member OPC 1853–55, 1871–76; MHR 1860–62, 1871–75.

49. *OW*, 6 August 1853, 'Report of a meeting held in Dunedin in support of reducing land prices in Otago.'

50. V&P, OPC, Session I, 12 January 1854, 6.

51. V&P, OPC, 14 March 1854, 22: Message Respecting the Intestate Estate Funds. Cargill was unaware or unsupportive of the role of a loyal opposition.
52. V&P, OPC, 25 April 1854, Appendix, 29–34: Superintendent's Speech of Prorogation. Cargill was reported as saying: 'Your Council has shown a tendency, not unnatural perhaps, in the novelty of our circumstances, to exceed its proper bounds, and to trench upon the functions of the Executive.' Gillies was so offended by the speech that he resigned his seat immediately (V&P, OPC, Session I, 25 April 1854, 17).
53. Scholefield, *Parliamentary Record*, 31–41.
54. Raewyn Dalziel, 'The politics of settlement', in W.H. Oliver & B.R. Williams (eds), *The Oxford History of New Zealand*, Oxford: Clarendon Press, 1981, 97.
55. Malcolm Moncrief-Spittle, ed., *The Lost Journal of Edward Jerningham Wakefield: Being an account of his exploits and adventures in New Zealand in the years 1850–1858, including: His various visitations, conversations & observations &c. &c. To which is added an introduction.* Dunedin: Kilmog Press, 2008, 1.
56. W.D. McIntyre, ed., *The Journal of Henry Sewell 1853–7* (2 vols.), Christchurch: Whitcoulls, 1980, vol. II, 16 July 1854, 57.
57. McLintock, *The History of Otago*, 361. McLintock claims that the fighting was actually over Cargill's trust in Macandrew to the exclusion of Cutten, his own son-in-law. The split was healed in 1860 when Macandrew appointed Cutten to his first provincial Executive Council, although Cutten was always wary of Macandrew's behaviour.
58. Letter: William Cutten/Christiana Cutten, undated but likely to be June 1854, in Stuart Greif and Hardwicke Knight, *Cutten: Letters revealing the life and times of William Henry Cutten the forgotten pioneer*, Dunedin: Stuart Greif and Hardwicke Knight, 1979, 55.
59. *NZPD*, 24 May 1854, 2.
60. *NZPD*, 26 May 1854, 4.
61. Letter: James Macandrew/Eliza Macandrew, 25/27 May 1854, KWMSS.
62. *SC*, 30 May 1854.
63. Scholefield, *Parliamentary Record*, 27.
64. Parliament did not sit in 1855 while consultation with the British government was under way. On 7 May 1856 the first executive to be fully responsible to parliament was chosen. It was led by Henry Sewell, making him New Zealand's first prime minister. His ministry survived for 13 days and was succeeded by William Fox, who also ruled for 13 days. Stability came finally on 2 June 1856 with the election of Edward Stafford, an Anglo-Irish gentleman settler who was the first superintendent of Nelson from 1853 to 1856, a member of the House from 1855 (to 1878) and a skilful manager of parliamentary procedure. He remained at the helm until 12 July 1861.
65. FitzGerald's ministry survived for 50 days and was followed by one led by Thomas Forsaith which lasted just three days. Peter Stuart, *Edward Gibbon Wakefield in New Zealand: His political career 1853–54*, Wellington: Price Milburn for Victoria University of Wellington, 1971, chapters 8–11 provides a detailed account of Wakefield's political manoeuvrings; Philip Temple, *A Sort of Conscience: The Wakefields*, Auckland: Auckland University Press, 2003, 503–16.
66. *NZ*, 19 August 1854: Macandrew's letter to the editor.
67. *SC*, 18 August 1854.
68. *Votes and Proceedings of the House of Representatives*, 1854, Sessions I–II, 'Select Committees Appointed During (Sessions 1 & II) of 1854'.
69. *NZPD*, 2 June 1854, 32.

70. *NZPD*, 15 August 1854, 332.
71. *NZPD*, 11 July 1854, 190.
72. The 'clean shirt ministry' was so-called because Forsaith insisted on returning home to change his clothes before accepting his nomination as a member of the Executive Council. Members were Thomas Forsaith, William Travers, Edward Jerningham Wakefield (EGW's son) and Macandrew, who joined the officials on the administrator's Executive Council.
73. Jeanine Graham, *Frederick Weld*, Auckland: Auckland University Press, 1983, 63.
74. Letter: Macandrew/Thomas Reynolds, 16 June 1854, KWMSS. Thomas and family arrived in Dunedin on 28 March 1857 on the ship *John Masterman* and took up land in Southland. *ODT*, 27 August 1868 reported the arrival of a number of merino rams from Lisbon: 'We believe this is the first importation of Spanish merino sheep direct from Spain into any of the Australasian Colonies. Mr. Thomas Reynolds, their owner, has accompanied them in all their wanderings through Spain and Portugal to our shores, and has spared neither expense nor trouble to effect his object of introducing pure Spanish merino blood into New Zealand.'
75. Ibid.
76. McLintock, *The History of Otago*, 361. Harris, another Cargill son-in-law, added fuel to the flames when '[w]ith prophetic insight he held that the administration of public affairs should not be entrusted to a man whose whole public career had been marked by extreme rashness, inconsideration for others and a determination to achieve his own ends. No one panted for power more than Macandrew and no one was more unwilling to part with it'; V&P, OPC, Session II, 1854–55. Macandrew and Reynolds voted together in 13 of the 15 recorded divisions and opposed each other only once. Gillies and Harris never voted with Macandrew.
77. V&P, OPC, Session II, 6 August 1855, 69: Superintendent's Message No. 18. Cargill said he had asked for the dissolution on 4 May 1855.
78. V&P, OPC, Session II, 26 October 1855, Appendix, 74: 'NOTE. The Journals of Council from 17th September, to 20th October, 1855, inclusive, are deleted in terms of resolution of 17th March, 1856, in consequence of the Council having been dissolved by His Excellency the Governor immediately previous to the first mentioned day.'
79. V&P, OPC, Session IV, 12 March 1856, 13.
80. Ibid., 12: Reply to the Opening Address of His Honor the Superintendent; 14 March 1856, 18: 'Resolved that the Provincial Solicitor be requested to prepare and introduce an Ordinance, for the purpose of providing a remedy against any misconduct of individuals not members of this Council.'
81. V&P, OPC, Session V, 2 December 1856, 12: Superintendent's Address.
82. V&P, OPC, Session VII, 3 November 1858, 1: Superintendent's Address. These years had the shortest sittings in the council's existence. The council held three sessions in 1856 of 1, 9 and 7 days. In its life of 34 sessions, the council's longest was 65 sitting days, its shortest was 1 sitting day and the median length was 19 sitting days.
83. Waste Lands Act 1854; Provincial Waste Lands Act 1854.
84. V&P, OPC, Session II, 10 November 1854, 7.
85. Ibid.
86. V&P, OPC, Session II, 14 November 1854, 9. Gillies: 'before taking into consideration the Appropriation Bill intended to be introduced into the House on Tuesday next, it is necessary that the Executive give satisfactory explanations as to the line of policy they intend to adopt: – On what subjects they intend to introduce Bills this Session.'
87. OW, 25 November 1854. Macandrew resigned on 23 November 1854. On 14 November Cutten had described Macandrew's approach to politics: 'When Mr Gillies had accused the Executive of having no policy, Mr Macandrew had cheered. He delighted in having no policy, and he admitted the fact.' Reynolds resigned on 17 November.

88. *OW*, 2 December 1854.
89. V&P, OPC, Session II, 12 December 1854, 27: Superintendent's Message No. 6.
90. *OW*, 29 September 1855: Summary of Land Regulations of the Province of Otago.
91. McLintock, *The History of Otago*, 395.
92. *OW*, 29 September 1855.
93. V&P, OPC, Session II, 7 May 1855, 52. Macandrew proposed, 'That in the present circumstances of the Province, with abundance of real property, but a scarcity of circulating medium, it is inexpedient and impolitic that the money deposited for lands, under the temporary Regulations for the immediate occupation thereof now in force, should be locked up in the Provincial chest for an indefinite period; and that it would greatly conduce to encourage and aid the efforts of the industrious settlers … were the money so deposited lent out to the individual by whom it has been so deposited.'
94. *OW*, 19 May 1855.
95. *OW*, 20 April 1861: 'For sale, By order of the Mortgagee, The Valuable Estate of Carisbrook … extending to 240 acres, or thereby.' *OW*, 10 November 1860: the estate may have extended beyond the Glen as Macandrew had auctioned 80 quarter-acre sections the previous year. The sections were in the 'Newly Surveyed Township of Richmond Hill, being part of the Carisbrook Estate, situated at the top of Mclaggan-street, within twenty minutes' walk of the Custom House'.
96. *OW*, 23 July 1853: 'Electoral Roll for the Dunedin Country District for the Year 1853–4' listed Macandrew as a 'Leaseholder and Freeholder' of 'Carisbrook, near Dunedin'; *ODT*, 9 October 1976, Douglas Skene. The geographical origin of Carisbrook may be corroborated by Osborne Terrace, the name of a street adjoining Glen Road. The Presbyterian Church Trustees owned flat land at the foot of the Glen that later become the site of Carisbrook sports ground, named after the estate.
97. Charles Waddy, 2016, 'A Casa Reynolds: The personal, commercial and political adventures of one generation of a British family in Great Britain, Spain, Portugal and New Zealand', unpublished history of the Reynolds family, 91. Rachel Pinkerton married William Reynolds in 1856 and her trustees purchased land there as part of her marriage settlement.
98. Olive Trotter, *Pioneers Behind Bars: Dunedin Prison and its earliest inmates, 1850–1870*, Dunedin: Olive Trotter, 2002, 36. Colin did not become a farmer; James was the only member of the family who did; According to Waddy, 117, Macandrew bought land in Upper Harbour East on 17 June 1858 but sold it in 1860 to Walker & Healey, who sold it to the Reynolds family for Eliza's trust fund.

Chapter 5

1. *OW*, 22 December 1855. Macandrew was the highest polling of five candidates on election day, 1 December 1855, with 28 votes.
2. Macandrew was elected to the Dunedin Town Board in August 1855 and to the Waste Lands Board in September 1856. Membership of both boards allowed him to manipulate events in a way that supported his business interests, but he was later exposed.
3. V&P, OPC, Session V, 2 December 1856, 2.
4. *AJHR*, 1858, B–5: Correspondence Relative to the New Zealand Loan of £500,000.
5. Governor Thomas Gore Browne assented to the ordinance on 27 January 1857.
6. Schedule and Synopsis of the Ordinances passed by the Provincial Council of Otago during Sessions I to XXVII inclusive, Dunedin, 1853–1871.
7. *LT*, 24 June 1857.

8. A.H. McLintock, *The History of Otago: The origins and growth of a Wakefield class settlement*, Dunedin: Otago Centennial Historical Publications, 1949; reprint, Christchurch: Capper Press, 1975, 374.
9. *OW*, 1 October 1853.
10. V&P, OPC, Session I, 8 March 1854, 13.
11. Ibid. The committee of Gillies, Harris, Reynolds, Macandrew and Anderson, usually opponents, were in agreement.
12. V&P, OPC, Session II, Appendix, 89: Report of Committee on Education, Adopted 18 December 1854.
13. Schedule and Synopsis of the Ordinances passed by Provincial Council of Otago during Sessions I, 1853–54, to XXVII, 1870, inclusive, 13.
14. V&P, OPC, Session IV, 5 and 14 March 1856, 3, 20. Macandrew, Reynolds, John McGlashan and Peter Proudfoot made up the commission.
15. V&P, OPC, Session V, 10 December 1856, 26; Session VI, 9 November 1857, 31; Session VII, 12 November 1858, 19; Session VIII, 25 October 1859, 3: Superintendent's Address.
16. McLintock, *The History of Otago*, 386.
17. Ibid., 509.
18. Ibid., 511. Learmonth Dalrymple, 1827–1901, b. Scotland, landed New Zealand 1852. She successfully lobbied for women's admission to the University of Otago which was approved in 1871, a first in Australasia. She was also active in the Kindergarten movement.
19. *ODT*, 17 December 1896.
20. Ibid.
21. Eileen Wallis, *A Most Rare Vision*, Dunedin: Otago Girls' High School Board of Trustees, 1995, 26.
22. *OW*, 26 December 1857.
23. *OW*, 5 November 1853.
24. *OW*, 8 July 1854.
25. *OW*, 31 December 1859.
26. 'Minute Book of the Trustees', Trust Fund for Religious and Educational Uses, Dunedin, 1848–67, held at the office of the Otago Foundation Trust Board, Dunedin: 31 December 1857.
27. *New Zealand Spectator and Cook's Strait Guardian*, 10 February 1855.
28. *New Zealand Spectator and Cook's Strait Guardian*, 30 August 1856.
29. *OW*, 20 September 1856.
30. McLintock, *The History of Otago*, 365.
31. *OW*, 20 September 1856; Gavin McLean, *Otago Harbour: Currents of controversy*, Dunedin: Otago Harbour Board, 1985, 17, confirms Macandrew was the owner of the sailing vessels *Gil Blas*, *Star* and *Endeavour*. *ODT*, 3 April 1899.
32. V&P, OPC, Session V, 9 December 1856, 23; *OW*, 20 December 1856.
33. *LT*, 17 January 1857.
34. *OW*, 24 January 1857.
35. V&P, OPC, Session VII, 11 November 1858, Appendix, 41: Report, Select Committee on Immigration Correspondence.
36. Ibid., 40–41.
37. *OC*, 24 February 1860.
38. *OW*, 29 December 1860. In protesting his innocence of embezzlement in a letter 'To the People of Otago', Macandrew said, 'I can safely say, that of the £40,000 to £50,000 of public

money which has been paid to me on account of steam and immigration, I never received a sixpence before it was fairly earned.' Reynolds left the firm in September 1858.

39. V&P, OPC, Session XI, 18 December 1860, Appendix, iv–xxv: Report, Select Committee on the State of the Public Accounts, Public funds, &c.

40. *New Zealander*, 30 April 1856.

41. *Votes and Proceedings of the House of Representatives*, 1856, D–2: Report of the Select Committee on the Bank of Issue.

42. *NZPD*, 2 May 1856, 39.

43. *NZPD*, 16 May 1856, 84; *Votes and Proceedings of the House of Representatives*, 1856, D–5: Report of the Select Committee on the Bank Charters and Private Paper Money Bills. Macandrew had submitted a bill to amend two ordinances enacted by the Legislative Council of New Zealand (before 1852), but this emerged from the parliamentary process as two bills, and so amended that he disowned them and pressed instead for a new bill.

44. *Votes and Proceedings of the House of Representatives*, 1856, D–14: Report of the Select Committee on Inter-Provincial Communication.

45. Sir Edward Stafford, 1819–1901, b. Scotland, landed New Zealand 1843. Landowner, superintendent Nelson PC 1853–56; MHR 1855–78; premier 1856–61, 1865–69, 1872; KCMG 1879; GCMG 1887.

46. *NZPD*, 19 June 1856, 180–83; AJHR 1858, B–05, 3–7: Memorandum: C.W. Richmond/ Thomas Gore Browne explains the ministry's reasons for the loan. The debts were to the New Zealand Company and the Union Bank of Australia.

47. *Votes and Proceedings of the House of Representatives*, no. 52, 3 July 1856.

48. Waste Lands Act 1856; Waste Lands Act 1858.

49. *OW*, 14 November 1857.

50. *OW*, 21 November 1857.

51. Ibid.

52. V&P, OPC, Session VI, 3 November 1857, 11. Cargill exceeded his legal authority by appointing his son-in-law Cutten, without the support of his executive, to be Proudfoot's successor as chief commissioner of the Waste Lands Board, which Macandrew chaired. Cargill's second offence resulted in a reprimand approved by all the councillors except his son, John Cargill, which stated, 'That this Council strongly disapproves of His Honor the Superintendent delivering an Address to the Council without the concurrence of his Executive.'

53. V&P, OPC, Session VI, 16 November 1857, Appendix, 52–80: Report, Select Committee on the State of the Land Office.

54. *OW*, 20 March 1858.

55. T.M. Hocken, *Contributions to the Early History of New Zealand (Settlement of Otago)*, London: Sampson, Low, Marston and Co, 1898, 182.

56. V&P, OPC, Session VII, 9 November 1858, 12.

57. *OW*, 20 November 1858; V&P, OPC, Session VII, 1858, xiv: Table IV, Summary of Proceedings on Bills.

58. V&P, OPC, Session VII, November 1858, 12. Macandrew's opposition to the payment of members evaporated once he was in power, perhaps because he needed all the friends he could get; V&P, OPC, Session IX, 26 April 1860, 36: Message 14 included his request for payment of country members, and council voted to pay '10s per day and 1s per mile each way, for members residing beyond four miles from Town, from commencement of business'.

59. V&P, OPC, Session VII, 11 November 1858, 18; OW, 20 November 1858.

60. Hocken, *Contributions*, 329.
61. *GRA*, 8 December 1866; OW, 28 July 1877; OW, 25 November 1882; AWJ, 26 January 1883: the watch was described as 'one of Bennett's gold self-winding hunters, bearing the recipient's monogram on the outer case; whilst on the inner is the following inscription:– "Presented to James Macandrew, Esq., M.H.R. for the Port Chalmers electoral district, as a slight recognition of his eminent political services, by his constituents and a few other friends". The chain is of massive gold, whilst as an appendage it has a large amethyst set as a seal.'
62. *OW*, 7 May 1853; OW, 15 April 1854 to 30 August 1856.
63. James Adam, *Twenty Five Years of Emigrant Life in the South of New Zealand*, Edinburgh: Bell and Bradfute, 1876, 63. 'Previous to that time trade had been under the dominion of an old Sydney merchant, whose great object was to make money, which he did rapidly. Our young friend [Macandrew] commenced business on an apparently opposite principle, viz., to create a trade … He encouraged the farmers to cultivate more largely. He advanced money on their grain and wool, and in a short time made his influence felt far and near.'
64. *OW*, 31 October to 12 December 1857.
65. Summons: James Macandrew/Octavious Harwood, District Court of Dunedin, undated, MS–0438/156, HC.
66. McLean, *Otago Harbour*, 38: 'Wool comprised the bulk of that season's [1856] £22,908 worth of exports.'
67. *OW*, 29 May 1858.
68. Ibid; Alex Bathgate, *Picturesque Dunedin*, Dunedin: Mills, Dick and Co, 1890.
69. Bathgate, *Picturesque Dunedin*.
70. McLintock, *The History of Otago*, 422.
71. *OW*, 26 June 1858.
72. *OC*, 3 September 1858.
73. McLintock, *The History of Otago*, 420.
74. *LT*, 8 December 1858; McLean, *Otago Harbour*, 39.
75. *OW*, 8 January 1859.
76. *OW*, 30 April 1859.
77. V&P, OPC, Session VII, 3 November 1858, 2: Superintendent's Address.
78. Ibid.
79. The Waste Lands Act 1858, passed 19 August 1858.
80. V&P, OPC, Session VII, 15 November 1858, 39: Appendix, Report of the Select Committee on the New Provinces Act, 1858.
81. V&P, OPC, Session VII, 3 November 1858, 1: Superintendent's Address.
82. V&P, OPC, Session VII, 7 November 1858, 5: Reply to the Opening Address of His Honor the Superintendent.
83. V&P, OPC, Session VIII, 26 October 1859, Appendix, i: Proposed Additions to and Amendments of the Land Regulations of the Province of Otago, New Zealand.
84. *OW*, 19 November 1859, 'Reports of Sheep Inspectors, Northern District'; OW, 15 December 1860; ST, 16 July 1901, Obituary for Mrs John MacGibbon senr: 'Mr MacGibbon, in partnership with Mr James Macandrew (Superintendent of Otago) had taken up the Otapiri run.' This was Run 146.
85. *OW*, 4 September 1858; OW, 1 January 1859.

Chapter 6

1,   T.M. Hocken, *Contributions to the Early History of New Zealand (Settlement of Otago)*, London: Sampson, Low, Marston and Co, 1898, 189; V&P, OPC, Session VIII, 25 October 1859: Superintendent's Address, 3; OW, 29 October 1859.
2.   A.H. McLintock, *The History of Otago: The origins and growth of a Wakefield class settlement*, Dunedin: Otago Centennial Historical Publications, 1949; reprint, Christchurch: Capper Press, 1975, 415.
3.   *LT*, 30 July 1859.
4.   *OW*, 20 August 1859.
5.   *OW*, 23 July 1859.
6.   McLintock, *The History of Otago*, 417.
7.   *OW*, 7 January 1860.
8.   Guy Scholefield, *A Dictionary of New Zealand Biography* (2 vols.), Wellington: Department of Internal Affairs, 1940, vol. I, 99. Some early superintendents who had successful business careers were William Brown (Auckland, Mar–Sep 1855); John Logan Campbell (Auckland, Oct 1855–Sep 1856); Charles Brown (Taranaki, Jul 1853–Dec 1856); Isaac Featherston (Wellington, Jul 1853–Apr 1858 and Jun 1858–Mar 1871); Edward Stafford (Nelson, Aug 1853–Sep 1856); and James FitzGerald (Canterbury, Jul 1853–Sep 1857). Serving in the General Assembly may have improved Macandrew's electability as superintendent; 22 of New Zealand's 44 superintendents sat in parliament before taking on the role, while 38 of the 44 were members of both a council and parliament.
9.   Hocken, *Contributions*, 196.
10. WI, 16 March 1860.
11. *OW*, 14 April 1860.
12. V&P, OPC, Session IX, 11 April 1860: Superintendent's Address, 2.
13. *OW*, 14 April 1860.
14. *LT*, 1 February 1860. Thomas Dick, 1823–1900, b. Scotland, landed Dunedin 1857; merchant and auctioneer; member OPC 1859–65; OEC 1859–60, 1862–64; Otago superintendent 1865–67; MHR 1860–63, 1866–67, 1879–84.
15. *OW*, 28 April 1860.
16. James Alexander Robertson Menzies, 1821–1888, b. Scotland, landed New Zealand 1853. Doctor of medicine; Mataura runholder; MLC 1858–88; member Southland PC 1861, 1864–67, 1869–70; Southland superintendent 1861–64; member OPC 1871–76.
17. *OW*, 7 April 1860.
18. *OW*, 28 April 1860. The vote was close run because there was 'some hesitation as to the right of some present, who were geographically excluded, and the temporary absence of a few who were indulging in the fragrant weed, beneath the shelter of the house'.
19. For a full description of this period in Southland's history see André Brett, 'Wooden rails and gold: Southland and the demise of the provinces', in Lloyd Carpenter and Lyndon Fraser, *Rushing for Gold*, Dunedin, Otago University Press, 2016, 253–67.
20. Scholefield, *Parliamentary Record*, 224.
21. *ST*, 18 October 1870.
22. Charles Waddy, 'A Casa Reynolds: The personal, commercial and political adventures of one generation of a British family in Great Britain, Spain, Portugal and New Zealand', unpublished history of the Reynolds family, 115.
23. Nathaniel Chalmers, 1830–1910, b. Scotland, landed New Zealand 1849. Explorer, landowner, sheep farmer, timber miller; member Southland PC 1861–64; Southland EC 1861–64;

treasurer & deputy superintendent Southland PC 1863–64. As deputy superintendent he turned the first sod of Southland's ill-fated wooden railway in 1863, having approved the use of the soft timber that led to its failure. Emigrated to Fiji 1868; cotton and sugar planter, magistrate, member Fiji LC 1879–83.

24. Waddy, 'A Casa Reynolds', 116–17.
25. Olive Trotter, *Pioneers Behind Bars: Dunedin Prison and its earliest inmates, 1850–1870*, Dunedin: Olive Trotter, 2002, 39. Macandrew was gazetted superintendent on 3 January 1860.
26. V&P, OPC, Session XI, 18 December 1860: Appendix, Report of Select Committee on the State of the Public Accounts, Public Funds, &c, v. He borrowed £486 in February and £600 in March.
27. *OW*, 15 September 1860.
28. McLintock, *The History of Otago*, 410. On 12 October 1860 T.B. Gillies introduced a bill to suspend the New Provinces Act. It was lost by one vote on its second reading.
29. V&P, OPC, Session XI, 12 December 1860: Superintendent's Address, 1.
30. Cargill had suggested the reclamation project earlier. See V&P, OPC, Session VIII, 25 October 1859: Superintendent's Opening Address, 2.
31. *TimH*, 1 June 1867. On his re-election as superintendent, one of Macandrew's first actions was to seek advice from Governor Gore Brown, now governor of Tasmania, on the best way to introduce salmon to Otago; 'Introduction of Salmon and Trout. £1,000' was an item in the Appropriation Ordinance 1867; *ODT*, 17 November 1871, Macandrew reported that the General Assembly had included £500 for the importation of salmon ova to New Zealand; *OW*, 25 October 1875, Macandrew is reported as saying, 'I have taken an interest in this salmon business for years. I have now got matters fairly into training, for a supply of ova to Otago.'
32. 'Boosterism was infectious, and you had to catch it to keep up with the competition. "He who confined his transactions, in those times, to his actual capital could stand no chance with his neighbours who availed themselves of loans."' R.E. Wright, 'Bank ownership and lending patterns in New York and Pennsylvania, 1781–1831', *Business History Review*, 73 (1999), cited in James Belich, *Replenishing the Earth: The settler revolution and the rise of the Anglo World 1783–1939*, Oxford: Oxford University Press, 2009, 203.
33. V&P, OPC, Session XI, 19 December 1860: Reply to the Opening Address of His Honor the Superintendent, 14.

Chapter 7

1. Letter written by Eliza Macandrew. *OC*, 26 August 1859.
2. The store and auction departments were sold to James Paterson and Co. *OW*, 24 September 1859.
3. *OW*, 5 May 1860. He was still trading under the name of James Macandrew & Co., despite having sold his firm to James Paterson in September the previous year.
4. *OW*, 27 July 1861: '16th August 1860 … I also made over to them three properties in the town, and gave them a second charge on a property on the side of the Harbour … This left me no real property unencumbered'; OW, 26 November 1860: Horse-shoe Bush Run advertised for sale; OW, 9 March 1861: Hokanui Run reported sold; OW, 10 November 1860: some land at Carisbrook sold as '80 Quarter-Acre Sections … in the newly surveyed Township of Richmond Hill, being part of the Carisbrook Estate'; *AJHR*, 1867, D–1, Papers Relative to the Case of Mr. Macandrew, 19. He repaid £970.

5. *OW*, 20 April 1861.
6. *OW*, 2 February 1861.
7. V&P, OPC, Session XI, 12 December 1860, 8.
8. Ibid., 9, Appendix 1: Reports of Auditors of Public Accounts, i.
9. Ibid., iv.
10. Letter: James Macandrew/T.B. Gillies, chairman of the select committee, 15 December 1860, F&J, vol. 02, no. 05, HC.
11. *OW*, 29 December 1860.
12. V&P, OPC, Session XI, 18 December 1860: Appendix, Report of Select Committee on the State of the Public Accounts, Public Funds, &c, iv–xxv.
13. V&P, OPC, Session XI, 19 December 1860, 12.
14. Ibid.
15. Ibid., 15.
16. Ibid., Superintendent's Message No. 2.
17. Ibid.
18. Ibid., 17.
19. *OW*, 29 December 1860.
20. Sir John Larkins Cheese Richardson, 1810–1878, b. India, landed New Zealand 1856. Farmed South Otago: member OPC 1860–61, 1863–67, 1873; superintendent Otago 1861–63, acting 1865; MHR 1862, 1863–67; MLC 1867–78; minister of customs, postmaster-general (Weld ministry) 1864–65; member EC (Stafford ministry) 1866–68: speaker LC 1868–78; chancellor University of Otago 1869–71; Kt., 1875.
21. V&P, OPC, 4 January 1861, 38: Superintendent's message No. 17.
22. Robert Gilkison, *Early Days in Dunedin*, Auckland: Whitcombe and Tombs, 1938, 2.
23. V&P, OPC, Session VI, 5 November 1857, 21.
24. Henry Monson, Journal, 28 January 1861, 316, MS–0088, HC.
25. Ibid., 317.
26. Ibid., 31 January 1861, 319.
27. Ibid.
28. Letter: Macandrew, Superintendent/Robert Chapman, factor of the Church Trustees, 18 February 1861, Presbyterian Church Archives, Knox College, Dunedin. The letter is regarding land for a church at Kaitangata, and is signed by Macandrew as superintendent.
29. Monson, Journal, 21 March 1861, 116.
30. 'To the People of Otago', *OW*, 15 April 1861; *OW*, 25 May 1861.
31. *Otago Provincial Gazette*, 7 June 1861, 199.
32. A 'warrant for payment' was similar to a modern-day cheque.
33. V&P, OPC, Session XII, 1861, xix: Appendix: letter: Richardson, Superintendent/John McGlashan, 26 June 1861. The council softened the blow when they agreed to McGlashan's dismissal on 4 July by including in their motion the words: 'This Council concurs in His Honor's opinion that the charges made against Mr. McGlashan of having used the Public Funds for his own private purposes have not been substantiated; that under the circumstances, the Council considers Mr. McGlashan's dismissal to be no bar to his holding any other Government appointment for which the Government may consider him fitted'.
34. *AJHR*, 1867, D–1, Papers Relative to the Case of Mr. Macandrew, 37. Enclosure in Letter No. 11.
35. Ibid., 38: Letter No. 14.
36. *OW*, 27 July 1861.
37. Ibid.

38. Dunedin Supreme Court Archives: Petition for discharge, cited in Charles Waddy, 2016, 'A Casa Reynolds: The personal, commercial and political adventures of one generation of a British family in Great Britain, Spain, Portugal and New Zealand', unpublished history of the Reynolds family, 121.
39. *OW*, 21 September 1861.
40. The 'Index to Unassisted Passengers' held by the Public Record Office, Victoria, Australia, lists a Mr Jas Macandrew aged 39, landed from the barque *Oscar* in October 1861, making his year of birth 1822. Another anomaly with his age!
41. Olive Trotter, *Pioneers Behind Bars: Dunedin Prison and its earliest inmates, 1850–1870*, Dunedin: Olive Trotter, 2002, 48: 'It has often been supposed that Macandrew was sequestered there (Carisbrook) almost under house arrest, but it cannot have been a very strict arrangement'; OW, 18 September 1875: 'Four years' probation was the time imposed upon the young merchant.' It is uncertain when his debts were paid or by whom.
42. Trotter, *Pioneers Behind Bars*, 36: 'He had a prosperous business as a general merchant and importer, and was also a stock agent. All this brought him a profit it was said of £20,000 a year. He had invested in land all over Otago – at Portobello and Waikari and South Otago, even as far off as Invercargill.' This would be more than $2,250,000 in today's currency. All calculations made on the Reserve Bank of New Zealand website: www.rbnz.govt.nz/monetary-policy/inflation-calculator
43. Jim McAloon, *No Idle Rich: The wealthy in Canterbury & Otago 1840–1914*, Dunedin: University of Otago Press, 2002, 33. Jones's estate was valued at £60,000 (2016 = $7,132,244).
    • William Barnard Rhodes, 1807–1878, b. England. 'By 1853 he was already being referred to as "the millionaire of Wellington". At his death he was described as "one of the richest men in the country"', 'Rhodes v. Rhodes', in F.M. Ollivier, H.D. Bell and W. Fitzgerald (eds), *Ollivier, Bell, & Fitzgerald's Reports of Cases*, Wellington: Lyon and Blair, 1878–89–80, 1880, 17. Rhode's estate was valued at £272,796.0.5 (2016 = $40,408,012). Brad Patterson, 'Rhodes, William Barnard', from the Dictionary of New Zealand Biography: www.TeAra.govt.nz/en/biographies/1r7/1
    • Edward Reece, 1834–1887, b. England, ironmonger, Christchurch. Reece's estate was valued at £81,798 (2016 = $15,064,743). McAloon, *No Idle Rich*, 57.
    • Nathaniel Levin, 1819–1903, b. England, merchant and trader. 'At the time of his death, even though much of his colonial property had been passed on to Willie and his family, Levin still had assets in New Zealand worth £104,818.' (2016 = $17,803,482). Roberta Nicholls, 'Levin, Nathaniel William', from the Dictionary of New Zealand Biography: www.TeAra.govt.nz/en/biographies/1l7/1
    • John Logan Campbell, 1817–1912, b. Scotland. Brown & Campbell was a merchant firm established in Auckland in 1840. *The Colonist* (Nelson), 27 June 1913, reports Campbell's estate was valued at £227,966 (2016 = $35,625,000).
    • Donald Reid, 1833–1919, b. Scotland. Reid's estate was valued at £170,000 (2016 = $16,741,896). McAloon, *No Idle Rich*, 57.
44. *ODT*, 4 March 1887.
45. A. Menzies, Journal, 7 December 1855, Toitū Otago Settlers Museum.

Chapter 8

1. He was rescued from a capsized boat on Otago Harbour and taken to the Provincial Hotel, where he 'for some hours lay in a very precarious state'. *OC*, 26 November 1861.
2. *The Southern Provinces Almanac, Directory & Year Book for 1864*, Christchurch, 1863, 53.

3. Ibid., 54.
4. Hunter's date and place of birth are recorded in the Macandrew family Bible. Thanks to Charles Waddy for details about the purchase of Colinswood.
5. Last will and testament of Eliza Hunter Macandrew, signed 11 December 1874: ANZ, Dunedin, DAAC D239 23 435.
6. Sir Julius Vogel, 1835–1899, b. London, landed Dunedin 1861 from the Victorian goldfields, wrote for Macandrew's weekly newspaper the *Otago Colonist*, established the *Otago Daily Times* in 1861; member OPC 1863–69, OEC 1866–69; MHR 1863–76, 1884–89; colonial treasurer 1869–72, 1872–73, 1884–87; premier 1873–75, 76; postmaster-general 1875–76; agent-general, London, 1876–80; CMG 1871; KCMG 1874.
7. *ODT*, 28 May 1863.
8. Speech: Julius Vogel at Complimentary Banquet, Odd Fellows Hall, Wellington, 17 February 1876. Vogel Papers, ATL, MSY–1337.
9. Raewyn Dalziel, *Julius Vogel: Business politician*, Auckland: Auckland University Press, 1986, 44.
10. *ODT*, 12 May 1862. The meeting was held on 10 May.
11. *OW*, 6 April 1899. The assembly seat was won by Eliza's brother William Reynolds.
12. *OW*, 1 June 1863.
13. *Press*, quoted in *ST*, 19 June 1863.
14. *The Colonist* (Nelson), 6 November 1863.
15. *OW*, 23 December 1882.
16. *NE*, 12 May 1869.
17. Dalziel, *Julius Vogel*, 35.
18. *ODT*, 16 January 1865.
19. *ODT*, 21 January 1865.
20. *ODT*, 25 January 1865.
21. A.H. McLintock, *The History of Otago*, Dunedin: Centennial Historical Publications, 1949; Christchurch: Capper Press, 1975, 561.
22. William P. Morrell, *The Provincial System in New Zealand: 1852–76*, 2nd edn, Christchurch: Whitcombe & Tombs, 1964, 157; 168.
23. *BH*, 8 February 1866.
24. *OW*, 10 October 1863.
25. *Press*, 2 May 1865, 'Manifesto of the Southern Separation League'.
26. *NOT*, 9 March 1865.
27. V&P, OPC, Session XX, 5 and 10 May 1865, 50; 57.
28. Ibid., 12 May 1865, 65. Donald Reid, 1833–1919, b. Scotland, landed Dunedin 1849. Farmed Salisbury on Taieri Plain 1857–1912, became extremely wealthy transporting freight to goldfields; member OPC 1863–76, OEC 1868 (2 days), 1869–72, 1874–76; MHR 1866–69, 1871–78; minister of public works 1872; minister of Crown lands and immigration 1877.
29. *NOT*, 27 April 1865.
30. *BH*, 20 April 1865.
31. *NOT*, 27 April 1865.
32. *EP*, 19 June 1865.
33. Alan McRobie, *New Zealand Electoral Atlas*, Wellington: Department of Internal Affairs, 1989, 36. The seat of Bruce was established in 1860 but in 1866 was divided into two seats, Bruce and Clutha; *OW*, 19 April 1862. Colinswood was in the Bruce electorate at this time.
34. *ODT*, 20 July 1865.
35. *BH*, 20 July 1865.

36. *ODT*, 1 August 1865; Erik Olssen, election analysis, MS 2146/97, HC.
37. *NOT*, 27 July 1865.
38. *AJHR*, 1864, D-02, 'Papers Relative to the Removal of the Seat of Government to Cook's Strait'. This details the appointment of three Australian commissioners and their recommendation that Wellington become the capital. It was moved in an attempt to appease the Middle Island separationists who wanted a more accessible site for parliament. For a detailed exposition see A. Brett, *Acknowledge No Frontier: The creation and demise of New Zealand's provinces, 1853–76*, Dunedin: Otago University Press, 2016, 156; Guy Scholefield, *New Zealand Parliamentary Record*, Wellington: Government Printer, 1950, 68; 121: 'The Assembly sat from 26 July–30 October 1865 and was dissolved on 27 January 1866.'
39. *BH*, 10 August 1865.
40. *EP*, 10 August 1865.
41. *TimH*, 2 September 1865.
42. *The Colonist* (Nelson), 10 November 1865.
43. *WI*, 29 August 1872.
44. *DSC*, 11 September 1865.
45. *NZPD*, 2 August 1865, 236.
46. Ibid., 7 September 1865, 432.
47. Ibid., 9 September 1865, 438. The motion was presented by the Auckland member Thomas Russell.
48. Ibid., 483.
49. Ibid., 12 September 1865, 494.
50. Ibid., 525; Dalziel, *Julius Vogel*, 66.
51. Premier Whitaker resigned in 1864 over the British government's insistence that New Zealand pay for the Imperial troops used to mount major campaigns in the land wars. Frederick Weld succeeded to the premiership on the understanding that his government would take full responsibility for Māori affairs.
52. *NZPD*, 1864–66, 6 September 1865, 421–23.
53. Dalziel, *Julius Vogel*, 65. The Stamp Duties Act was gazetted on 17 August 1866 to become law on 1 January 1867.
54. V&P, OPC, Session XXI, 15 November 1865, 1.
55. V&P, OPC, Session XXI, 27 November 1865, 1–2: Reports of Select Committees, Relations Between General and Provincial Governments. Members were George Brodie, Arthur Burns, Frederick Moss, William Reynolds, Macandrew and Vogel.
56. *ODT*, 8 November 1865, contains Macandrew's address.
57. V&P, OPC, Session XXI, 8 December 1865, 45.
58. *NE*, 2 December 1865.
59. *TarH*, 9 December 1865.
60. *Press*, 10 March 1866.
61. *BH*, 15 March 1866.
62. *WI*, 11 August 1866. Macandrew 'objected to a standing army existing in this Colony, for it would be composed principally of mercenaries, and might, some day, in the hands of a faction, become the means of taking away the liberties of the people'.
63. *BH*, 23 August, 1866.
64. *NE*, 1 September 1866.
65. *WI*, 1 September 1866.
66. *WI*, 29 September 1866.
67. *DSC*, 4 October 1866.
68. *NE*, 1 September 1866.

69. Ibid.
70. *NE*, 12 June 1866.
71. *NZPD*, 24 July 1866, 801.
72. Ibid., 808.
73. *NZPD*, 26 July 1866, 824.
74. Ibid., 821.
75. Ibid., 31 July 1866, 845. Four of the six superintendents in the House (Donald McLean, Isaac Featherston, William Eyes and William Moorhouse) voted against; superintendents Whitaker and Dick were in favour.
76. Edmund Bohan, *Edward Stafford: New Zealand's first statesman*, Christchurch: Hazard Press, 1994, 227. Colonial unity is sardonically defined as 'that deplorable notion that there was a wider community of national interest beyond mere local self-interest'.
77. *ODT*, 5 September 1866.
78. *ODT*, 19 October 1866. The Otago Association's aim was 'obtaining the largest possible amount of self-government'.
79. *NZPD*, 24 August 1866, 895.
80. *ODT*, 23 July 1866.
81. *NZPD*, 19 July 1866, 788.
82. *NZPD*, 24 July 1866, 796.
83. *NE*, 26 July 1866: 'The conclusion would seem to be that the General Government must recall the letters of delegation. The mover (Macandrew), and Mr. Dick, the Superintendent of Otago, declared that they would prefer this to the present arrangement.'
84. *ODT*, 12 September 1866.
85. *WCT*, 22 October 1866.
86. McLintock, *The History of Otago*, 478. The visitor was novelist Anthony Trollope, writing in 1872.
87. V&P, OPC, Session XXII, 21 November 1866, 11.
88. *NOT*, 27 November 1866.
89. *ODT*, 30 November 1866.
90. Ibid.
91. *NEM*, 5 January 1867.
92. *GRA*, 8 January 1867. The families came together in 1889 when Macandrew's fifth child, Herbert, married Richardson's granddaughter Lissie Rich. Richardson did not witness this union of the two families, having died in 1878.
93. *BH*, 27 December 1866; V&P, OPC, Session XXII, 20 December 1866, 44.

Chapter 9

1. *BH*, 17 January 1867.
2. Letter: Joseph Mackay/James Macandrew, 13 August 1866, KWMSS.
3. Ibid.
4. *BH*, 31 January 1867.
5. The Harbour Endowment Ordinance 1861; the Otago Harbour Improvement Ordinance 1862; the Port of Otago Marine Board Ordinance 1863.
6. A.H. McLintock, *The History of Otago: The origins and growth of a Wakefield class settlement*, Dunedin: Otago Centennial Historical Publications, 1949; reprint, Christchurch: Capper Press, 1975, 497.
7. Raewyn Dalziel, *Julius Vogel: Business politician*, Auckland: Auckland University Press, 1986, 71.

8. 'The Report of the Commissioner Appointed to Examine the Public Accounts of the Province of Otago', originally published in *Otago Provincial Gazette*, 7 June 1861, 199 and reprinted in *ODT* on 1, 2, 5, 6, 7 & 8 February 1867.
9. *ODT*, 1 February 1867.
10. *ODT*, 4 February 1867.
11. Ibid.
12. *BH*, 7 February 1867.
13. *ODT*, 14 February 1867.
14. *ODT*, 19 February 1867.
15. *OW*, 2 February 1867.
16. *BH*, 7 February 1867.
17. *BH*, 14 February 1867.
18. Ibid.
19. *BH*, 21 February 1867.
20. *ODT*, 20 February 1867.
21. Ibid.
22. Alan McRobie, *New Zealand Electoral Atlas*, Wellington: Department of Internal Affairs, 1989, 36.
23. Otago Provincial Council: Miners' Provincial Representation Ordinance 1862; Otago Representation Ordinance 1862.
24. *Dunstan Times*, 15 February 1867.
25. *Dunstan Times*, 28 February 1867; Erik Olssen, election analysis, MS 2146/97, HC. Macandrew won with 2260 votes, Thomas Dick received 1392 and the third contender, J.G.S. Grant, received two.
26. *NOT*, 26 February 1867.
27. *TimH*, 27 February 1867.
28. *WI*, 28 February 1867.
29. *GRA*, 2 March 1867.
30. *DSC*, 14 March 1867.
31. *TarH*, 16 March 1867.
32. *The Leeds Mercury*, 1 July 1867.
33. *NE*, 26 July 1866; *AJHR*, 1867, D–1, 'Papers Relative to the Case of Mr. Macandrew', no. 15, 38. This appendix is a full and valuable record of Macandrew's behaviour when he was superintendent in 1860, and was resurrected on his return to that position in 1867. The papers contain Otago Provincial Council's 1860 select committee report and evidence; Knight's 1861 report and evidence; subsequent letters regarding his report; and further correspondence concerning the delegated powers, between the premier's office and Macandrew, written between February and June 1867. Stafford's instructions to Knight are in no. 17, 8 March 1867, 39; Knight's report on his 1867 review is in no. 19, Enclosure 2, 18 March 1867, 41.
34. Ann Tyndale-Biscoe, 'The struggle for responsible government in the Province of Otago 1854–76', MA thesis, University of New Zealand, 1954, examines the evolution of the authority of Otago Provincial Council's Executive Council. Chapter X, 108–18, analyses the events and outcomes of the delegated powers episode.
35. *AJHR*, 1867, D–1, 'Papers Relative to the Case of Mr. Macandrew', no. 19, 42: Sub-Enclosure 2 to Enclosure 2, letter Macandrew/Dr. Knight, 15 March 1867.
36. Ibid., Enclosure 2, 18 March 1867, 42.
37. Ibid., no. 20, 16 April 1867, 43.

38. *GRA*, 30 April 1867; *AJHR*, 1867, D–1, 'Papers Relative to the Case of Mr. Macandrew', no. 24, 44: Telegram Macandrew/Governor Grey, 27 April 1867, suggesting an uprising in Otago was possible.

39. *NE*, 14 May 1867: Port Chalmers residents had resolved to form 'the Port Chalmers Vigilance Association for the preservation of their political liberties'.

40. *ODT*, 23 April 1867.

41. Ibid.

42. *AJHR*, 1867, D–1, 'Papers Relative to the Case of Mr. Macandrew', no. 28, 45: Enclosure, letter Macandrew/Major-General Chute, 1817–86, G.O.C. Imperial Forces, 24 April 1867.

43. *ODT*, 10 June 1867, 15 June 1867; Letter: J.C. Richmond/Edward Stafford, 4 May 1867: Stafford Papers, ANZ, MS Papers 2045–2050.

44. Letter: J.C. Richmond/C.W. Richmond, 3 May 1867, in Guy Scholefield (ed.), *The Richmond–Atkinson Papers*, Vol. II, Wellington: R.E. Owen, Government Printer, 1960, 243.

45. Ibid.

46. *OW*, 18 May 1867.

47. Ibid.

48. *ODT*, 19 February 1867.

49. *ODT*, 16 March 1867; Dispatch: Governor George Grey/Edward Cardwell, secretary of state for the colonies, 30 May 1867: ANZ, Wellington, ACHK 16580, G 25 10/77.

50. Letter: J.C. Richmond/Edward Stafford, 16 May 1867: Stafford Papers, ANZ, Wellington, MS Papers 2045–2050.

51. Vincent Pyke was the chief commissioner and secretary of the Otago goldfields 1862–67. This was an Otago provincial appointment, rather like the modern-day CEO of a local body, and he was responsible for administrating the goldfields (not the electorates). The position was abolished by Premier Stafford when the government took back control of the goldfields in 1867.

52. Letter: J.C. Richmond/Edward Stafford, 28 May 1867: Stafford Papers, ANZ, Wellington, MS Papers 2045–2050.

53. Letter: J.C. Richmond/C.W. Richmond, 13 June 1867, in Scholefield, *The Richmond–Atkinson Papers*, vol. II, 249.

54. Ibid.

55. *OW*, 15 June 1867.

56. V&P, OPC, Session XXIII, 1 May 1867, 4: Superintendent's Address.

57. V&P, OPC, Session XXIII, 28 May 1867, 9: Reports of Select Committees, XVI – Separation Petition. 7325 people signed this petition; William P. Morrell, *The Provincial System in New Zealand: 1852–76*, 2nd edn, Christchurch: Whitcombe & Tombs, 1964, 182, fn. 1. The secretary of state refused to advise the Queen to comply with the petition.

58. McLintock, *The History of Otago*, 572, fn. 8.

59 *NZPD*, vol. 1, 16 July 1867, 69.

60. *NZPD*, vol. 1, 17 July 1867, 112.

61. *BH*, 31 July 1867.

62. Clause 2 of both Acts.

63. Letter: Joseph Rhodes/Donald McLean, 31 August 1867: McLean Papers, ATL, MS 0032-0527.

64. *WH*, 14 April 1868.

65. *NZPD*, vol. 1, 17 July 1867, 91.

66. *NZPD*, vol. 1, part I, 15 August 1867, 481–84. Macandrew also attempted to reduce central government's expenditure by opposing the formation of an armed constabulary force. He

demanded that 'the Middle Island should take the stand, and protest against being compelled not only to support its own police but to support the police of the Northern Island also'. The Armed Constabulary Bill's second reading was passed by 40 votes to 5 (Macandrew, Vogel, Reynolds, Burns, Graham – all southerners – were opposed); *NZPD*, vol. 1, part I, 26 September 1867, 1126: Macandrew also moved to abolish the subsidy on interprovincial mail services, but even Vogel opposed him on this issue.

67. *NZPD*, vol. 1, part II, 5 September 1867, 787–88.
68. *EP*, 6 September 1867.
69. *NE*, 5 October 1867, 6.
70. *AJHR*, 1868, A–3, 'Report of the Pokaikai Commission'.
71. Major (Sir) Harry Atkinson, 1831–1892, b. England, landed New Zealand 1853. Farmed in Taranaki from 1853; member Taranaki PC 1857–65, 1873–74; Taranaki EC 1868, 1874; deputy superintendent 1861–62; MHR 1861–69, 1872–91; MLC 1891–92; minister of colonial defence (Weld ministry) 1864–65; minister of Crown lands and immigration (Vogel ministry) 1874–77; colonial treasurer, minister of Crown lands and immigration (Pollen ministry) 1875–76; minister of Crown lands, immigration and customs (Vogel ministry) 1876; colonial treasurer, minister of customs and stamp duties (Hall ministry) 1879–82; colonial treasurer, minister of customs, stamp duties and marine (Whitaker ministry) 1882–83, 1887–91; premier 1876–77, 1883–84, 1887–91; KCMG 1888.
72. *NZPD*, vol. 1, 31 August 1867, 515 on. The bill was enacted as the Public Offenders Disqualification Act 1867.
73. *HBH*, 3 September 1867.
74. Ibid.
75. *WI*, 2 November 1867.
76. *WCT*, 5 November 1867.
77. *ST*, 18 December 1867.

Chapter 10

1. V&P, OPC, Session XXV, 22 April 1869, 1–3: Superintendent's Address.
2. 'The estimates' – a parliamentary term for committing money for projects, usually at budget time.
3. V&P, OPC, Session XI, 12 December 1860, 8: Superintendent's Address. Simon Nathan, *James Hector*, Wellington: Geoscience Society of New Zealand, 2015, 44, 116; see also *AJHR*, 1870, F–6, Interim Report of the Committee on the Public Accounts. Macandrew was not party to Hector's appointment but they encountered each other again in 1870. Hector had not delivered the final report of his three-year Otago Geological Survey when he moved to central government employment in 1865, and Macandrew wanted the costs of the survey refunded to Otago. He was unsuccessful.
4. V&P, OPC, Session XVIII, 7 April 1864, 4: Superintendent's Address.
5. V&P, OPC, Session XXIV, 9 April 1868, 5.
6. V&P, OPC, Session XXIV, 8 June 1868, 20: Reports of Select Committees, VIII. West Coast.
7. The section on railways is shaped by discussions with Dr André Brett of the University of Wollongong, and by his article, 'Dreaming on a railway track: Public works and the demise of New Zealand's provinces', *Journal of Transport History*, 36, no. 1, 2015, 77–96; and his book, *Acknowledge No Frontier: The creation and demise of New Zealand's provinces, 1853–76*, Dunedin: Otago University Press, 2016.

8. *AJHR*, 1880, E–3: Report of the Railways Commission.
9. *OW*, 7 January 1860.
10. V&P, OPC, Session IX, 11 April 1860: Superintendent's Address.
11. V&P, OPC, Session XVII, 1863, 7–12: Report of Select Committee on Roads and their Deviation.
12. The Otago Southern Trunk Railway Act 1866, clauses IX and X.
13. V&P, OPC, Session XXIII, 1 May 1867, 2: Superintendent's Address.
14. V&P, OPC, Session XXVI (Special), 8 December 1869, 1: Superintendent's Address.
15. *ODT*, 1 January 1873. Letter: George Bowen/Eliza Macandrew, 10 January 1873, KWMSS. The governor enjoyed his stay in Dunedin and gave Eliza a pair of slippers when he departed.
16. V&P, OPC, Session XXXI, 6 May 1873, 2: Superintendent's Address; *AJHR*, 1873, Session 1, E–07a, Dunedin and Port Chalmers Railway, (Correspondence Relative to the Purchase of), 5, letter 17: 'The Hon Mr Richardson [Minister of Public Works]/His Honor the Superintendent of Otago, 15 April 1873'. The central government bought the railway from David Proudfoot's Dunedin and Port Chalmers Railway Company (Limited) and leased it back to the province.
17. By 1876, despite a shrinking economy and an uncooperative council, Macandrew had propelled a large number of building projects to completion. A.H. McLintock, *The Port of Otago*, Dunedin: Whitcombe & Tombs, 1951, 64.
18. *ODT*, 16 March 1872.
19. V&P, OPC, Session XXV, 22 April 1869, 2: Superintendent's Address.
20. *NOT*, 8 May 1875.
21. *ODT*, 7 January 1874.
22. McLintock, *Port of Otago*, 107, claims Macandrew 'made good use of his position as chairman to safeguard the interests of Port Chalmers', and this division continued until his death.
23. *ODT*, 10 June 1878.
24. *Otago Journal*, no. 1, January 1848, quoted in G.E. Thompson, *A History of the University of Otago (1869–1919)*, Dunedin: J. Wilkie & Co., 1919, 9–10.
25. Dunedin Church Lands Ordinance 1861, Sect 4; Thompson, A History of the University of Otago, 11.
26. The Presbyterian Church of Otago Lands Act 1866, Clauses VII & IX.
27. *NZPD*, vol. 1, 24 July 1867, 154; 30 July 1867, 214.
28. *AJHR*, 1867, F–01, Report of the Select Committee on the Establishment of University Scholarships; Together with the Proceedings of the Committee, and the Evidence.
29. *ODT*, 20 August 1867.
30. V&P, OPC, Session XXIV, 8 April 1868, 2: Superintendent's Address.
31. Ibid., 9–20: Report: Select Committee on College.
32. Letter: Macandrew, Superintendent/Rattray & Co., 27 June 1868, McLean Papers, ATL, MS 0032–0400. (Rattray & Co. were attorneys for Donald McLean, superintendent of Hawke's Bay Province, MHR for Napier, and a partner in Hawkesburn Station near Clyde in Central Otago.)
33. University of Otago Ordinance 1869, Clause XIV.
34. University of Otago Endowment Ordinance 1870. Thompson, *A History of the University of Otago*, 143. The endowment comprised the Burwood and Mararoa runs in Southland of 70,000 acres (28,328ha) and Barewood Run near Middlemarch of 30,000 acres (12,140ha).
35. W.P. Morrell, *The University of Otago: A centennial history*, Dunedin: University of Otago Press, 1969, 37–42. Eighty-one students enrolled for the first year. The council resolved on 8

April 1871 'that women be admitted to all classes, and allowed to compete for all certificates, equivalent to degrees, conferred by the University of Otago'. The council awarded only one degree, however (to a man), before surrendering their degree-granting power to the University of New Zealand. The first woman to receive a degree from a New Zealand university was Kate Edger, who gained a BA in 1877 following study at Auckland University College.

36. Thompson, *A History of the University of Otago*, 143. The endowment was Benmore Run in the Waitaki Valley.
37. Ibid. These were Forest Hill Estate near Winton, and Lamb Hill Estate near Dunedin.
38. *ODT*, 11 November 1869.
39. *ODT*, 9 February 1881.
40. Hugh Parton, *The University of New Zealand*, Auckland: Auckland University Press, 1979, 16.
41. Thompson, *A History of the University of Otago*, 30.
42. *WI*, 4 November 1871.
43. Parton, *The University of New Zealand*, 17.
44. V&P, OPC, Session XXX, 30 April 1872, 3: Superintendent's Address.
45. V&P, OPC, Session XXXIII, 29 April 1874, 2: Superintendent's Address.
46. The New Zealand University Act 1874.
47. *ODT*, 10 June 1878. Report of a meeting of the Otago University Council, 6 June 1878.
48. *ODT*, 25 February 1887; 11 June 1887.
49. Thompson, *A History of the University of Otago*, illustration facing 64. University of Otago Calendar 1947, 45.
50. *ODT*, 26 November 1885. The portrait hangs in the university's Clocktower Building.
51. *ODT*, 13 February 1869.
52. Ibid.
53. *ODT*, 21 February 1870.
54. The school was later renamed the Dunedin School of Art and Design and, in 1921, amalgamated with King Edward Technical College. It became a department of Otago Polytechnic in 1966, and now offers degrees in fine arts.
55. J.D.S. McKenzie, 'Local authority and educational development: A study of the OEB from 1877–1899', PhD thesis, University of Otago, 1973, 1.
56. V&P, OPC, Session XXXI, 6 May 1873, 3: Superintendent's Address.
57. V&P, OPC, Session XXXII, 3 July 1873: Report of the Commission 'To inquire into, and report upon, the present condition of the Boys' High School, Dunedin, and to make such general suggestions as to the Advancement of the Higher Education of the Province as may commend themselves to their consideration'. Recommendation 52, p. xiv.
58. V&P, OPC, Session XXXII, 29 July 1873, 104. Sir Robert Stout, 1844–1930, b. Shetlands, landed Dunedin 1864. Schoolteacher, lawyer; member OPC 1872–76, OEC 1874–76; MHR 1875–79, 1884–87, 1893–98; MLC 1926–30; attorney-general and minister of lands and immigration (Grey ministry) 1878–79; premier 1884, 1884–87; KCMG 1886, chief justice 1899–1926; privy councillor 1921.
59. Carol Morton Johnston and Harry Morton, *Dunedin Teachers' College: The first hundred years*, Dunedin: Dunedin Teachers College Publications Committee, 1976, 10.
60. V&P, OPC, Session XXIII, 1 May 1867, 3: Superintendent's Address.
61. Ibid. Assent given 5 June 1867.
62. Alex Bathgate, *Picturesque Dunedin: or Dunedin and its neighbourhood in 1890*, Dunedin: Mills, Dick & Co., 1890, 201. The Act was enacted on 10 October 1867.
63. V&P, OPC, Session XXIV, 8 April 1868, 2: Superintendent's Address. The Industrial School became the responsibility of the Education Department in 1880 and closed in 1927, when

it metamorphosed into the Dunedin Boys' Receiving Home, Lookout Point, which in turn closed in 1991. Erin Williams: www.nzta.govt.nz/assets/projects/caversham-highway/docs/caversham-industrial-school-archaelogical-assessment.pdf

64. V&P, OPC, Session XXXIII, 29 April 1874, 3: Superintendent's Address.
65. NZPD, vol. 28, 27 August 1878, 508.
66. *Transactions and Proceedings of the New Zealand Institute, 1869*, vol. II, Wellington, 1870, 438; *AJHR*, 1870, D–25: Second Annual Report of the Governors of the New Zealand Institute.
67. Francis Reid, 'The province of science: James Hector and the New Zealand Institute, 1867–1903', PhD thesis, University of Cambridge, 2007, quoted in Nathan, *James Hector*, 91.
68. *ES*, 18 October 1917.
69. *ODT*, 2 June 1868.
70. *ES*, 5 December 1868.

Chapter 11

1, *WI*, 22 August 1867.
2. A Miss Macandrew departed for the south on 10 November 1871 (*EP*, 10 November 1871); 'Arrived … Hon Mr Macandrew, Master Macandrew' on 14 July 1872 (*WI*, 15 July 1872); Mrs and Miss Macandrew returned from the north on 28 April 1874 (*OW*, 2 May 1874); Master Macandrew arrived from the south on 18 September 1876 (*ODT*, 25 September 1876).
3. *ODT*, 28 April 1869.
4. *ODT*, 30 April 1869.
5. *NZPD*, vol. 1, 8 August 1867, 391.
6. William Morrell, *The Provincial System in New Zealand: 1852–76*, 2nd edn, Christchurch: Whitcombe & Tombs, 1964, 192–93.
7. *NE*, 20 August 1867.
8. Morrell, *The Provincial System*, 193–96. The bills became the County of Westland Act 1867 and the Timaru and Gladstone Board of Works Act 1867; *TimH*, 5 February 1868. Timaru and Gladstone settlers petitioned the Assembly five times in 1866–67. Westland requested separation from Canterbury Province on the grounds of 'diversity of interests, distance from the seat of Provincial Government, and difficulty of communication, insufficient representation, injudicious legislation, parsimonious expenditure, and excessive cost of administration'.
9. V&P, OPC, Session XXIV, 8 April 1868, 3: Superintendent's Address.
10. Ibid.
11. *BH*, 10 June 1868.
12. A.H. McLintock, *The History of Otago: The origins and growth of a Wakefield class settlement*, Dunedin: Otago Centennial Historical Publications, 1949; reprint, Christchurch: Capper Press, 1975, 489.
13. *EP*, 20 June 1868.
14. V&P, OPC, Session XXIV, April 1868, Appendix, 3: Statement of Expenditure. Macandrew's salary increased from £900 to £1200 and the salaries of the provincial treasurer and the secretary of land and works from £600 to £800. The council sat for 26 days in 1867, an increase on the lifetime median session length (19 sitting days), but in 1868 it sat for 45 days, the second longest session in its history. Many subsequent sessions were also much longer than the median.
15. V&P, OPC, Session XXIV, 11 June 1868, 133: Superintendent's Address.

Slippery Jim or Patriotic Statesman?

16. McLintock, *The History of Otago*, 578. Vogel was dismissed as editor of the *ODT* in April 1868 and established a new Dunedin newspaper, the *New Zealand Sun*, on 16 November 1868. It promoted provincial separation and federal government, but folded after three months.

17. Sir William Fox, 1812–1893, b. England, landed New Zealand 1842. Lawyer, landowner. Resident agent NZ Company Nelson 1843–48; principal agent NZ Company, Wellington, 1848–50; member Wellington PC 1854–62, Wellington EC 1854–58, 1861; MHR 1855–65, 1868–81; colonial secretary with Native affairs (Whitaker ministry) 1863–64; premier 1856, 1861–62, 1869–72, 1873; attorney-general 1856; attorney-general and first minister 1861; colonial secretary 1861–62, 1869, 1873; KCMG 1879.

18. *NZPD*, vol. 2, 30 July 1868, 185–206.

19. Ibid., 197.

20. *NZPD*, vol. 2, 7 August 1868, 362–65.

21. Ibid.

22. *NZPD*, vol. 2, 12 August 1868, 449.

23. Vogel's motion became the basis for the Immigration Act 1868.

24. *NZPD*, vol. 3, 16 September 1868, 300.

25. *NZPD*, vol. 4, 16 October 1868, 358–59.

26. *TT*, 10 October 1868.

27. V&P, OPC, Session XXV, 22 April 1869, 1: Superintendent's Address. The Consolidated Loan Act 1867 had removed the provinces' power to raise loans; the Public Debts Act 1867 made provision to convert existing provincial debentures into colonial stock.

28. McLintock, *The History of Otago*, 578.

29. V&P, OPC, Session XXV, 22 April 1869, 4: Superintendent's Message No. 1.

30. *ODT*, 26 April 1869.

31. *BH*, 15 September 1869.

32. V&P, OPC, Session XXV, 3 June 1869, 84: Superintendent's Address.

33. V&P, OPC, Session XXVI, 23 December 1869, 32–33: Superintendent's Address.

34. *The Colonist* (Nelson), 25 June 1869.

35. Danny Keenan, 'New Zealand wars – New Zealand wars overview', Te Ara – the Encyclopedia of New Zealand: www.TeAra.govt.nz/en/new-zealand-wars/

36. Ibid.

37. Letter: Thomas Hirst/Thomas Hirst (son), 30 July 1869, Hirst Family Letters, MS-0994-1006, vol. 6, 54, ATL, MS-0999.

38. *NZPD*, vols. 5, 9, 14 & 15, 16 July 1869, 423, 476–93, 511–27, 530–54; vol. 6, 20 July 1869, 10.

39. *WI*, 15 July 1869.

40. *ODT*, 28 July 1869.

41. *NZPD*, vol. 6, 20 July 1869, 10.

42. *NZPD*, vol. 6, 22 July 1869, 73. The Otago Settlements Act 1869 became law on 6 August 1869.

43. *NZPD*, vol. 6, 17 August 1869, 500–05; 18 August 1869, 534–47.

44. Ibid., 502.

45. *NZPD*, vol. 6, 18 August 1869, 540.

46. *OW*, 11 September 1869. Idaburn Run was known locally as 'the ministerial run'. Sir Francis Dillon Bell, 1821–1898. A relative of Edward Gibbon Wakefield, employed by NZ Company, London, 1839, then NZ 1843–51; commissioner of Crown lands Wellington 1851–55; pastoralist; member Wellington PC 1853–56; Wellington EC 1854; member OPC 1865–67, 1869–70, 1871–73; MHR 1855–56, 1859–75; member of EC (FitzGerald ministry) 1854; colonial treasurer (Sewell ministry) 1856; colonial treasurer, minister of Native affairs and customs (Domett ministry) 1862–63; member EC (Fox ministry) 1869–71; Speaker HR 1871–75; MLC 1854–56, 1877–80; agent-general 1880–91; KB 1873; KCMG 1881; CB 1886.

47. *NZPD*, vol. 6, 31 August 1867, 853.
48. V&P, OPC, Session XXVII, 18 May 1870, 42.
49. V&P, OPC, Session XXVIII, 21 November 1870, 12.
50. V&P, OPC, Session XXVIII, 24 November 1870, 24.
51. V&P, OPC, Session XXVIII, 25 November 1870, 26: Superintendent's Message No. 3.
52. V&P, OPC, Session XXVIII, 5 December 1870, 48.

Chapter 12

1. *OW*, 7 January 1860; V&P, OPC, Session XXIV, 8 April 1868, 2: Superintendent's Address.
2. V&P, OPC, Session XXVII, 26 April 1870, 2: Superintendent's Address.
3, Jonathan West, *The Face of Nature: An environmental history of the Otago Peninsula*, Dunedin: Otago University Press, 2018, 76.
4. *ODT*, 23 February 1864, reported 18,805 miners working in Otago. V&P, OPC, Session XXI, 15 November 1865, Departmental Reports XIII, Gold Fields Department, 39A; this reported 6000 miners.
5. *OW*, 14 October 1865. The experience of Chinese miners in Otago is discussed at length by James Ng in *Windows on a Chinese Past*, vol. 1, chapters 2B, 2D, 2E.
6. Manying Ip, 'Chinese – The first immigrants', Te Ara – the Encyclopedia of New Zealand: www.TeAra.govt.nz/en/chinese/page-2
7. *ODT*, 23 February 1864.
8. Ibid. The reporter completed his item in the argot of the day: 'The introduction of the Celestials to our gold fields, especially to those within the district of the Dunstan, would be productive of an immense amount of good, not only to the favoured locality in which the sons of the moon might take up their mundane abode, but to the province at large.'
9. *AJHR*, 1871, Session 1, H–05: Interim Report of the Chinese Immigration Committee, 23.
10. *ODT*, 3 February 1868. It was also printed in other Otago newspapers that month.
11. *OW*, 20 August 1870.
12. K.C. McDonald, *City of Dunedin: A century of civic enterprise*, Dunedin: Dunedin City Corporation, 1965, 34.
13. V&P, OPC, Session XXIX, 5 June 1871, Appendix: Report, Otago Mining Commission, 6, 11.
14. *AJHR*, 1871, Session 1, H–05b: Final Report of the Chinese Immigration Committee, presented 27 October 1871.
15. Ibid., 8.
16. *AJHR*, 1867, Session 1, G–01. no. 6: Petition of John Topi Patuki, presented 22 August 1867, 6.
17. V&P, OPC, Session XX, April 1865: Reports of Select Committees, III, Message no. 4, 11.
18. *AJHR*, Session I, 1858, E–04, Reports of Commissioners of Native Reserves, 13–16.
19. Teone Topi Patuki (?1810–1900). Warrior, paramount Ngāi Tahu chief 1844, Wesleyan teacher and expert whaler. Alexander Mackay, *A Compendium of Official Documents Relative to Native Affairs in the South Island, Vol. 1*, Wellington: Government Printer, 1873; vol. 1, no. 72, 'Petition of John Topi Patuki to Her Majesty the Queen, 17 August 1867': http://nzetc. victoria.ac.nz/tm/scholarly/tei-Mac01Comp-t1-g1-t6-g1-t5-g1-t1.html#n205
20. *AJHR*, 1867, Session 1, G–01, no. 6, Petition of John Topi Patuki, presented 22 August 1867.
21. Ibid.
22. Ibid.
23. William Mantell, 1820–95, landed New Zealand June 1840; employed by New Zealand Company, 1851–56; commissioner of Crown lands in Otago, MHR 1861–66; minister Native affairs 1861; postmaster-general, minister of Crown lands 1862–63; Native secretary, minister of Native affairs 1864-65; MLC 1966-95; a founder of the New Zealand Institute.

24. McDonald, *City of Dunedin*, 24.
25. Dunedin Public Lands Ordinance 1854, Clause 1.
26. McDonald, *City of Dunedin*, 25; V&P, OPC, 1854, 47–50: Appendix, Correspondence Respecting the Moray Place Reserve. In April 1852 Mantell, no friend of the Presbyterians and acting on direction from Resident Magistrate Chetham Strode with the backing of the colonial secretary, and thus the seemingly unwitting governor, reserved the centre of the Octagon for an Anglican church, without consultation or publicity. When building materials arrived for the church there was a protest. Newly elected Superintendent Cargill commented, 'Any such occupation of the Octagon would be similar to erecting buildings in the gardens of Moray Place, Edinburgh, or of St. James's Square, London, and would be so regarded by the proprietors of Dunedin.' Johnny Jones donated money to buy land on the corner of the Octagon and Stuart Street, where St Paul's Church was consecrated in 1863 (Norman Ledgerwood, *The Heart of a City: The story of Dunedin's Octagon*, Dunedin: Norman Ledgerwood, 2008, 50–58).
27. Ibid.
28. Waitangi Tribunal, *The Ngai Tahu Sea Fisheries Report 1991*: www.justice.govt.nz/tribunals/waitangi-tribunal/Reports/wai0027 per cent201991 per cent20Report/doc_008, 7.3.18.
29. *NZPD*, 1864–66, 1 August 1865, 214.
30. *AJHR*, 1865, F–2, Report of the Select Committee on the Otago Reserves, 3.
31. Ibid., 2.
32. *ODT*, 15 October 1870.
33. *AJHR*, 1876, H–27, Rent of the Princes Street Reserve, (Correspondence Respecting), 1. Letter: George Grey/Duke of Buckingham, 8 October 1867. Grey explained that he signed the January 1866 Crown grant giving over the reserves to the province in ignorance, and blamed his executive council which 'inadvertently advised me to sign'. He later suggested that the Crown Lands Office had accidentally included it in a collection of special grants for reserves for schools for him to sign. Ironically, it was Stafford who advised him to sign it when Grey questioned the process. By the time the mistake was discovered the document had already been dispatched to Dunedin.
34. Waitangi Tribunal, *The Ngai Tahu Sea Fisheries Report 1991*.
35. *NZPD*, 1864–66, 28 September 1866, 1015. The bill was titled 'An Act to declare the Superintendent of the Province of Otago to be entitled to certain Rents received on account of a Reserve situated in Princes Street, in the City of Dunedin'; its short title was 'The Princes Street (Dunedin) Reserve Act 1866'. It was presented again the following year but lapsed in the Legislative Council on 12 September 1867.
36. Hori Kerei Taiaroa ?–1905, younger son of Te Matenga Taiaroa; MHR (Southern Māori) 1871–78, 1881–85; MLC 1879–80, 1885–1905. Taiaroa was a vigorous advocate for the return of land to Ngāi Tahu. He believed signing Kemp's deed (1848, between Ngāi Tahu and Henry Kemp for the purchase of 5,500,000ha, which included most of Canterbury, Westland and parts of Otago) and the Murihiku deed (1853, between Ngāi Tahu and Mantell for the purchase of 2,833,00ha in the Southland region) was a mistake. He contended the sales were carried out under threat of force (Guy Scholefield, *A Dictionary of New Zealand Biography* (2 vols.), Wellington: Department of Internal Affairs, 1940, vol 1., 357).
37. Alexander Mackay, *A Compendium of Official Documents*, vol. 1, no. 57: 'The Hon. the Colonial Secretary to His Honor the Superintendent, Otago', 16 October 1866.
38. Ibid.
39. Alexander Mackay, *A Compendium of Official Documents*, vol. 1, no. 58: 'His Honor the Superintendent, Otago, to the Hon. the Colonial Secretary', 30 October 1866; Dunedin

Reserves Management Ordinance 1866. V&P, OPC, Session XXIII, April 1867, 1: Council Paper (no. 1), Ordinances Disallowed.

40. *AJHR*, 1877, I–3B, Native Affairs Committee: Report on the Petition of Hori Kerei Tairoa, Together with the Minutes of Evidence Thereupon, 6.

41. Mackay, *A Compendium of Official Documents*, vol. 1, no. 59: 'The Hon. J. Hyde Harris, and other Residents in the Province of Otago, to the Hon. the Colonial Secretary', 12 July 1867.

42. Ibid., no. 60: 'The Hon. the Colonial Secretary to Mr. J. Hyde Harris, and other Residents in the Province of Otago', 23 July 1867.

43. Ibid., no. 61: 'The Hon. the Colonial Secretary to His Honor the Superintendent, Otago' [Macandrew], 24 July 1867.

44. Ibid., no. 62: 'His Honor the Superintendent, Otago, to the Hon. the Colonial Secretary', 25 July 1867.

45. Ibid., no. 87: 'His Honor the Superintendent, Otago, to the Hon. J. C. Richmond', 12 September 1867.

46. *AJHR*, 1868, Session 1, F–04, Proceedings of the Select Committee on the Dunedin Disputed Reserves.

47. Mackay, *A Compendium of Official Documents*, vol. 1, no. 83: 'His Honor the Superintendent, Otago, to the Hon. J. C. Richmond', 27 August 1867.

48. Ben Schrader, *The Big Smoke: New Zealand cities 1840–1920*, Wellington: Bridget Williams Books, 2016, 197. See also West, *The Face of Nature*, 180–81.

49. Mackay, *A Compendium of Official Documents*, vol. 1, no. 82, Enclosure 3: 'Order in Council', 26 October 1867.

50. *ODT*, 15 October 1870, William H. Reynolds, Letter to the Editor.

51. Supreme Court of New Zealand, *Regina v. Macandrew* (1869), 1 CA 172; *ES*, 27 September 1869.

52. *ODT*, 11 November 1869.

53. *AJHR*, 1877, I–3B, Native Affairs Committee: Report on the Petition of Hori Kerei Tairoa, Together with the Minutes of Evidence Thereupon, 15, Appendix 1: 'Memorandum between Mr. Vogel and Mr. Izard [C.B. Izard, solicitor acting for John Topi Patuki]. In consideration of the Superintendent making the said payments of £4650 and £500, all proceedings on behalf of the Natives to be stopped, and the present action to be discontinued; each side to pay its own costs; Mr. Izard to telegraph England to stop the [Privy Council] appeal on payment of the above amounts.' A Dunedin Reserves Management Ordinance was rejected in 1869 and 1871, and assented to in 1873.

54. *AJHR*, 1876, H–27, Rent of the Princes Street Reserve, (Correspondence Respecting), 4, Letter no. 12, 'Memorandum by Mr. H.T. Clarke', 16 October 1875. This contains an excerpt from a letter from Macandrew to the colonial secretary, 20 November 1872.

55. *ES*, 23 January 1874.

56. *AJHR*, 1876, H–27, Rent of the Princes Street Reserve, (Correspondence Respecting), 3, Letter no. 8, 'Hori Kerei Tairoa to the Hon. Sir D. McLean', 6 March 1874.

57. *Waka Maori*, 25 August 1874.

58. *AJHR*, 1877, I–3B, Native Affairs Committee. Report on the Petition of Hori Kerei Tairoa, Together with the Minutes of Evidence Thereupon, 3.

59. Ibid.

60. *NZPD*, vol. 27, 6 December 1877, 761. The committee of the whole House in a British parliament for the purpose of considering and voting the ordinary state expenditure of the year.

61. Ibid.

62. Ibid.

63. *ES*, 6 May 1880.

64. Waitangi Tribunal, *The Ngai Tahu Sea Fisheries Report 1991*, 7.5.6.

65. Ibid.

66. Harry Evison, *Ngāi Tahu Land Rights and the Crown Pastoral Lease Lands in the South Island of New Zealand*, 3rd edn, Christchurch: Ngāi Tahu Māori Trust Board, 1986, 52.

67. Harry Evison, *Te Wai Pounamu/The Greenstone Island: A history of the Southern Māori during the European colonisation of New Zealand*, Christchurch: Aoraki Press in association with Ngāi Tahu Trust Board, 1993, 426.

68. *NZH*, 25 September 1869.

69. James Belich, *'I Shall Not Die': Titokowaru's war, New Zealand, 1868–9*, Wellington: Allen & Unwin in association with Port Nicholson Press, 1989, 278.

70. *ODT*, 26 October 1869.

71. Ibid.

72. *ODT*, 23 March 2011.

73. *ES*, 20 March 1872.

74. Ibid. Taurua's name was mispelled as 'Taurau'.

75. *ODT*, 10 February 1874.

Chapter 13

1. *NZPD*, vol. 6, 20 July 1869, 10.

2. Guy Scholefield, *A Dictionary of New Zealand Biography*, (2 vols.), Wellington: Department of Internal Affairs, 1940. See the entries for these men for details of their activities.

3. His salary peaked at £1200 in 1867 and was reduced to £800 in 1872.

4. *AJHR*, 1870, B–2, 12: Financial Statement by the Hon. The Colonial Treasurer.

5. *NZPD*, vol. 7, 28 June 1870, 98–115; Raewyn Dalziel, *Julius Vogel: Business politician*, Auckland: Auckland University Press, 1986, 107. New Zealand's debt at that time was already £8 million.

6. *NZPD*, vol. 7, 28 June 1870, 115.

7. *NZPD*, vol. 7, 12 July 1870, 349.

8. Ibid., 343.

9. *NZPD*, vol. 8, 21 July 1870, 31.

10. NZPD, vol. 7, 6 July 1870, 215.

11. *NZPD*, vol. 12, 7 August 1872, 337. This is Reynolds' report of a comment made by Vogel in the 1870 debate.

12. *NZPD*, vol. 7, 28 June 1870, 104.

13. The Immigration and Public Works Act 1870, the Immigration and Public Works Loan Act 1870, the Payments to Provinces Act 1870, and the Defence and other Purposes Loan Act 1870.

14. *NZPD*, vol. 7, 28 June 1870, 100, Financial Statement. First reading of bill, 20 July 1870, 546.

15. *NZPD*, vol. 7, 20 July 1870, 546; for the bill's progress through the House and the Legislative Council see vol. 8, 3 August 1870, 271 and 10 August 1870, 431; vol. 9, 24 August 1870, 252.

16. *NZPD*, vol. 9, 29 August 1870, 381.

17. *ODT*, 9 December 1870.

18. Ibid.

19. *ODT*, 18 January 1871.

20. Ibid.

21. *NZPD*, vol. 8, 22 July 1870, 60.
22. *ODT*, 8 February 1871.
23. *ST*, 27 September 1870.
24. *TT*, 13 October 1870; 20 October 1870.
25. *OW*, 29 October 1870.
26. *ST*, 18 November 1870.
27. *BH*, 13 July 1870.
28. *ODT*, 26 December 1870.
29. *NOT*, 13 January 1871.
30. *OW*, 14 January 1871.
31. Letter: C.A. de Lautour/G.H. Scholefield, 10 March 1928, ATL, MS-Papers-0212-C/02A.
32. *ODT*, 9 December 1870.
33. *ODT*, 1 March 1871. Erik Olssen, election analysis, MS 2146/97, HC. Macandrew 3365 votes, Reid 3015.
34. *EP*, quoted in *ODT*, 28 February 1871.
35. *ODT*, 11 February 1871; 16 February 1871.
36. *WI*, 4 February 1871.
37. *ODT*, 11 April 1871.
38. *NOT*, 9 May 1871.
39. V&P, OPC, Session XXIX, 11 July 1871, 88.
40. Alfred Leslie Murray, 'The general election of 1871 and its importance in the history of New Zealand', MA thesis, University of New Zealand, 1956, 85–105.
41. *NZPD*, vol. 11, 19 October 1871, 439.
42. *NZPD*, vol. 11, 30 October 1871, 643.
43. *NZPD*, vol. 11, 13 October 1871, 337.
44. *ODT*, 19 March 1872.
45. *ODT*, 20 January 1875.
46. *NZPD*, vol. 10, 14 September 1871, 421–25.
47. *Auckland Morning News*, quoted in *ODT*, 18 September 1871.
48. *EP*, 24 August 1871.
49. Letters: Stevens/Stafford, 27 and 31 August 1871, Stafford Papers, ATL, MS–2050.
50. *NZPD*, vol. 10, 14 September 1871, 427.
51. *NZPD*, vol. 11, 12 October 1871, 280.
52. Dalziel, *Julius Vogel*, 125.
53. *NZPD*, vol. 11, 25 October 1871, 525.
54. Dalziel, *Julius Vogel*, 125.
55. *NZPD*, vol. 11, 10 November 1871, 980.
56. *EP*, 28 October 1871.
57. *WI*, 15 December 1871.
58. Austin Gee, 'Moving house: A peripatetic parliament', *Otago Settlers News*, Spring 2017, issue 134, 1–3, Dunedin: Otago Settlers Association.
59. *LT*, 14 August 1872.
60. *NZPD*, vol. 12, 24 July 1872, 68–70.
61. Ibid.
62. *NZPD*, vol. 12, 7 August 1872, 326–28.
63. Ibid., 330.
64. Ibid., 334.

65. *NZPD*, vol. 13, 5 September 1872, 155.
66. *NZPD*, vol. 12, 27 August 1872, 673.
67. *NZPD*, vol. 13, 5 September 1872, 156.
68. George Marsden Waterhouse, 1824–1906. Member South Australia LC 1851–54, 1857, 1860–63; chief secretary South Australia 1861–63; Wairarapa pastoralist, MLC 1870–90; member without portfolio (Fox ministry) 1871; premier 1872–73; Speaker LC 1887. Waterhouse, Whitaker and Pollen were the only premiers who sat in the Legislative Council.
69. *ODT*, 31 August 1874.
70. Letter: Henry Sewell/Stafford, 31 October 1872, Stafford Papers, ATL, MS–2050.
71. *WI*, 16 May 1872.
72. Dalziel, *Julius Vogel*, 155.
73. William P. Morrell, *The Provincial System in New Zealand: 1852–76*, 2nd edn, Christchurch: Whitcombe & Tombs, 1964, 243. The legislation was the Superintendents of Marlborough Election Act 1872, the Superintendent of Taranaki Empowering Act 1873, the Superintendents of Hawke's Bay Election Act 1873 (although this Act was never applied) and the Province of Westland Act 1873.
74. *TT*, 5 September 1872, records his first departure from Wellington on the *Luna*; *NOT*, 27 September 1872 records his second departure on the *Nebraska*; *ODT*, 15 November 1872 records Reid's dismissal on 25 September 1872.
75. V&P, OPC, Session XXXI, 8 May 1873, 10.
76. V&P, OPC, Session XXXI, 19 May 1873, 14.
77. *ODT*, 1 July 1873.
78. V&P, OPC, Session XXXII, 30 July 1873, 113: Superintendent's Message.
79. Ibid.
80. *NZPD*, vol. 16, 4 August 1874, 401.
81. Ibid., 415–26.
82. Ibid., 417.
83. *NZPD*, vol. 16, 13 August 1874, 581.
84. *ODT*, 8 August 1874.
85. *NZPD*, vol. 16, 24 August 1874, 888–90.
86. *ODT*, 8 August 1874.
87. *NZPD*, vol. 16, 18 August 1874, 699.
88. *ODT*, 29 August 1874.

Chapter 14

1, V&P, OPC, Session XXXIV, 3 May 1875: Superintendent's Address, 5, 6; 5 May 1875: Reply, 10; 15 June 1875, 111.
2. *ST*, 19 May 1875.
3. *ODT*, 16 July 1875.
4. *BH*, 7 May 1875.
5. *NZPD*, vol. 17, 20 July 1875, Governor's Speech, 2.
6. Jonathon Lucas Hunt, 'The election of 1875–6 and the abolition of the provinces', MA thesis, University of Auckland, 1961, 323.
7. *NOT*, 31 August 1875.
8. *NZPD*, vol. 17, 27 August 1875, 705.
9. *NZPD*, vol. 17, 24 August 1875, 522–27.
10. Ibid.

11. Ibid.
12. William P. Morrell, *The Provincial System in New Zealand: 1852–76*, 2nd edn, Christchurch: Whitcombe & Tombs, 1964, 257; NZPD, vol. 18, 1 September 1875, 166: second reading, 37 in favour, 15 opposed.
13. An Act to Provide for the Abolition of Provinces, 1875, Section 28.
14. *NZPD*, vol. 18, 22 September 1875, 529; 23 September 1875, 560.
15. *NZPD*, vol. 19, 29 September 1875, 74.
16. *OW*, 9 October 1875.
17. *ODT*, 23 October 1875.
18. *Mount Ida Chronicle*, 30 October 1875.
19. *Mount Ida Chronicle*, 28 October 1875.
20. Ibid.
21. James Macandrew, 'Address to the People of Otago', Dunedin: Mills, Dick and Co, 1875.
22. *BH*, 19 November 1875.
23. Letter: Edward McGlashan/Sir Donald McLean, 16 November 1875, McLean Papers, ATL, MS 0032-0416.
24. *CL*, 1 September 1876. The editorial summarises the issues.
25. Letter: Jane Maria Atkinson/C.W. Richmond, 10 February 1876, in Guy Scholefield, ed., *The Richmond–Atkinson Papers* (2 vols.), Wellington: R.E. Owen, Government Printer, 1960, 413.
26. *AJHR*, 1876, A–4, Abolition of the Provinces: The Commissioners' Visits (Papers Relating to). Letter: Macandrew/Vogel, 6 April 1876, 3. This correspondence was distributed in a private pamphlet in 1877, printed by Mills, Dick & Co., Dunedin.
27. Ibid., 8. Letter: Macandrew/Vogel, 22 April 1876.
28. Ibid., 12. Letter: Vogel/Macandrew, 3 May 1876.
29. A.H. McLintock, *The History of Otago: The origins and growth of a Wakefield class settlement*, Dunedin: Otago Centennial Historical Publications, 1949; reprint, Christchurch: Capper Press, 1975, 210, 608.
30. Province of Otago, Departmental Reports and Other Papers, 10 June 1876, 1–5, uncatalogued, HC.
31. Letter: Daniel Pollen/Julius Vogel, 19 October 1876, Vogel Papers, ATL, MS–papers–2072–Folder 25. Vogel's letter of appointment as agent-general indicates that the colonial government had a target at this time of 5000 immigrants per annum, which Otago alone had more than surpassed.
32. Province of Otago, Departmental Reports and Other Papers, 10 June 1876, 1–5.
33. *NZPD*, vol. 21, 3 August 1876, 55.
34. *NZPD*, vol. 21, 16 August 1876, 377–79.
35. The Counties Act 1876, No. 47.
36. *NZPD*, vol. 21, 22 August 1876, 509–11.
37. Ibid.
38. *WCT*, 15 August 1876.
39. *NZPD*, vol. 22, 19 September 1876, 373–406.
40. *NZPD*, vol. 22, 26 October 1876, 634–47.
41. *BH*, 29 September 1876.
42. *OW*, 7 October 1876, printed Macandrew's telegram, Atkinson's memorandum and Macandrew's reply.
43. *GRA*, 14 October 1876.
44. Ibid.
45. *Marlborough Express*, 11 October 1876.

46. *Star*, 20 October 1876.
47. *CL*, 3 November 1876.
48. Speech: Julius Vogel, Banquet at Wanganui, 16 March 1876, Vogel Papers, ATL, MSY-1337. There were of course other reasons: Morrell in *The Provincial System* (270–85) suggests overextended borrowing; transfer of functions to the centre; decentralisation of other functions to local bodies; provincial extravagance; diversity of legislation and lack of uniformity; land issues; discontent of outliers; growth of national consciousness; and growing apathy with politics. Brett in *Acknowledge No Frontier* considers Vogel's public works policy was the primary event that led to change because it 'deprived the provinces of their two main functions, public works and immigration, and imposed a national form on infrastructural planning' (246).
49. Speech: Julius Vogel, Banquet at Wanganui, 16 March 1876, Vogel Papers, ATL, MSY-1337.
50. Letter: William Rolleston/Hugh Carleton, 10 December 1870, Rolleston Papers, ATL, MS-77-248-01/4.
51. Letter: Robert Gillies/William Cutten, 25 October 1875, in Stuart W. Greif and Hardwicke Knight, *Cutten: Letters revealing the life and times of William Henry Cutten the forgotten pioneer*, Dunedin: Stuart Greif and Hardwicke Knight, 1979, 73.

Chapter 15

1. Letter: Stevens/Stafford, 2 August 1871, Stafford Papers, ATL, MS-2050.
2. Guy Scholefield, *New Zealand Parliamentary Record*, Wellington: Government Printer, 1950, 37. Macandrew held the Crown lands and immigration portfolios from 15 October 1877 to 25 July 1878, and public works from 28 March 1878 to 8 October 1879.
3. *NZPD*, vol. 32, 3 October 1879, 162; WH, 11 October 1879, 'Report of Liberal Party Caucus' held on 10 October 1879.
4. *BoPT*, 28 May 1887.
5. For more information on the Government Building see Heritage New Zealand: www.heritage.org.nz/the-list/details/37
6. *NZPD*, vol. 24. 20 July 1877, 5.
7. Raewyn Blackstock, 'The office of agent-general for New Zealand in the United Kingdom, 1870–1905', PhD thesis, Victoria University of Wellington, 1970, 358. Between 1871 and 1878 a total of 84,125 assisted migrants landed in New Zealand, peaking in 1875 with 31,785. Atkinson reduced the flow to 7413 in 1877. Grey trimmed it further, and Hall's ministry in 1880 reduced it to near zero.
8. Judith Bassett, *Sir Harry Atkinson: 1831–1892*, Auckland: Auckland University Press, 1975, 46.
9. *ST*, 1 September 1876.
10. Paul Goldsmith, *We Won, You Lost, Eat That! A political history of tax in New Zealand since 1840*, Auckland: David Ling, 2008, 54.
11. John Stuart Mills' text *Principles of Political Economy* was published in 1848 and was probably the most widely read economics text for the rest of the century.
12. Goldsmith, *We Won, You Lost, Eat That!*, 55.
13. Letter: C.A. de Lautour/G.H. Scholefield, 10 March 1928, ATL MS-Papers-0212-C/02A. 'Each year in Wellington these two men chose to seek an unpretentious hotel in Molesworth Street: they two, the only members as a rule in that house. It was rarely, but what, after each recess they returned to the House together. Men, these two, very different in natures, but at one in this: they shared a passionate devotion to New Zealand and her people. Grey, who made it his

business to know all that was to be known about those he had to work with, must have been satisfied with Macandrew's past history before allowing him to become his friend.'

14. Raewyn Dalziel, *Julius Vogel: Business politician*, Auckland: Auckland University Press, 1986, 223; Wilson, *The Grey Government*, 4: 'To the ardent provincialists, the most important goal to be attained was the placing in power of a government sympathetic to their provincial interests, irrespective of whether the principles of that Government were conservative or radical.' William Montgomery, 1821–1914, b. London, landed New Zealand 1860. Christchurch merchant, runholder. Member Canterbury PC 1866–70, 1873–76; Canterbury EC 1866–69, 1874–75; MHR 1874–87; colonial secretary (Stout ministry) 1884; member EC (Seddon ministry) 1893–95; MLC 1892–1907.

15. Bassett, *Sir Harry Atkinson*, 55; *NZPD*, vol. 24, 31 July 1877, 127. Atkinson continued: 'Time is needed for the completion and development of our public works: quiet is needed for the consolidation of the social results without which a scheme of immigration and railways in any new country would be a failure.' Some things do not change: in January 1988 Prime Minister David Lange called for a pause for 'a cup of tea'.

16. *NZPD*, 17 August 1877, vol. 24, 499.

17. Ibid., 507.

18. David Hamer, 'The Agricultural Company and New Zealand politics, 1877–1886', *Historical Studies: Australia and New Zealand*, 10, no. 38, 1962, 141–64.
John Ballance, 1839–1893, b. Ireland, landed New Zealand 1865. Merchant Wanganui; owner and editor *Wanganui Herald*; MHR 1875–81, 1884–93; colonial treasurer and minister of customs, education and stamp duties (Grey ministry) 1878–79; minister of Native affairs and defence (Stout ministry) 1884; minister of Native affairs, defence, lands and immigration (Stout ministry) 1884–87; premier 1891–93; Native minister 1891; commissioner of stamp duties 1891–92; colonial treasurer, commissioner of trade and customs 1891–93.

19. *NZPD*, vol. 26, 8 October 1877, 284.

20. Wilson, *The Grey Government*, 12.

21. J. Rutherford, *Sir George Grey: A study in colonial government*, 2nd edn, London: Cassell, 1961, 598. *The Colonist* (Nelson), 3 February 1860, used the term 'Liberal Party' to describe a party in Nelson Provincial Council, and it was used widely of Grey's faction, even though it was not a party in the modern sense of the word. Morrell says, 'It is not altogether surprising that the first political development after abolition was the emergence of a Liberal party in the General Assembly': Morrell, *New Zealand*, London: Ernest Benn, 1935, 59.

22. *TA*, 18 October 1877.

23. Wilson, *The Grey Government*, 3–4, 60–63.

24. W.D. Stewart, *William Rolleston*, Christchurch: Whitcombe & Tombs, 1940, 126–27.

25. William Gisborne, *New Zealand Rulers and Statesmen 1840 to 1885*, London: Sampson Low, Marston, Searle & Rivington, 1886, 266.

26. *AES*, 16 October 1877, 'Ministerial statement by Sir George Grey'.

27. *Press*, 16 October 1877.

28. *AES*, 16 October 1877, 'Ministerial statement by Sir George Grey'.

29. *GRA*, 15 October 1877: '[Grey] will carry into the Cabinet – in fact he cannot help it – all the positiveness and self-obstinacy which made it almost impossible for him to maintain amicable relations with any Ministry during the time he was Governor.'

30. *ODT*, 27 October 1877.

31. *New Zealand Tablet*, 26 July 1878.

32. *Marlborough Express*, 17 October 1877.

33. *BH*, 30 October 1877.

34. Letter: James Farmer (London)/James Hector (Wellington), 14 November 1877, Sir James Hector Letters, MS–0443–3/16, HC.
James Farmer, 1823–1895, estate manager for John Logan Campbell. Member Auckland PC 1861–63, 1867–69, 1871–72; MHR 1859–60, 1867–70; MLC 1871–74. Farmer retired to London where he monitored New Zealand affairs; he acted as agent for and corresponded with James Hector until 1891. He consistently criticised Grey and is a useful counterpoint to some of the effusive newspaper reports of the period.
35. Alfred Saunders, *History of New Zealand, Vol. II*, Christchurch: Smith, Anthony, Sellars & Co., 1899, 383.
36. Dispatches: Lord Normanby/Henry Herbert, 4th Earl of Carnarvon, 23 August 1876 and 16 October 1877, Carnarvon Papers, 30/6/39, Public Record Office, London; in Dalziel, *Julius Vogel*, 223.
37. *GRA*, 5 December 1877.
38. *ST*, 26 November 1877. Parliament eventually approved a loan bill of just £2,500,000; *EP*, 20 November 1877.
39. *EP*, 7 December 1877: "'Saved by the casting vote of the Speaker.' Surely that is not a dignified or creditable position for a Ministry to occupy. Moreover, had Messrs. Travers, Gisborne, and Johnston been present, and voted in accordance with their previously expressed opinions, the motion of "no confidence" would have been carried and the Ministry defeated.'
40. Erik Olssen, *A History of Otago*, Dunedin: John McIndoe, 1984, 48.
41. William Gisborne, *New Zealand Rulers and Statesmen*, 270.
42. An Act to Regulate the Sale or other Disposal of the Lands of the Crown in New Zealand 1877, no. 29. A.H. McLintock, *The History of Otago: The origins and growth of a Wakefield class settlement*, Dunedin: Otago Centennial Historical Publications, 1949; reprint, Christchurch: Capper Press, 1975, 630–33. For a detailed description of this Act see W.R. Jourdain, *Land Legislation and Settlement in New Zealand*, Wellington: Government Printer, 1925, 26.
43. Ibid.
44. *CL*, 22 February 1878. They left Wellington on 18 February.
45. *EP*, 22 February 1878.
46. *WCT*, 25 February 1878.
47. *GRA*, 23 February 1878.
48. *WCT*, 25 February 1878.
49. *WCT*, 28 February 1878.
50. *New Zealand Tablet*, 26 July 1878.
51. *WT*, 27 June 1878; *Star*, 3 July 1878.
52. *GRA*, 4 July 1878. Telegram: James Macandrew/Chairman, Greymouth County Council.
53. *The Belfast News-Letter*, 17 March 1879.
54. *ST*, 13 June 1879.
55. *HBH*, 11 September 1879; Denis Hogan and Bryce Williamson, eds., *New Zealand is Different: Chemical milestones in New Zealand history*, Christchurch: New Zealand Institute of Chemistry, 1999, 260.
56. *HBH*, 22 July 1878.
57. *OW*, 10 August 1878.

Chapter 16

1. *AJHR*, 1878, E–1, Public Works Statement, ix.
2. Erik Olssen, *A History of Otago*, Dunedin: John McIndoe, 1984, 48.
3. *AJHR*, 1877, I–5, Report of the Select Committee to Inquire into the Present System of Railways Management.
4. *NZPD*, vol. 28, 27 August 1878, 500–09.
5. *AJHR*, 1878, E–1, Public Works Statement, by the Minister for Public Works, The Hon. James Macandrew, Tuesday, 27th August, 1878, iv–vi.
6. *AJHR*, 1877, E–1, Public Works Statement, by the Minister for Public Works, The Hon. John Davies Ormond, Friday, 10th August, 1877.
7. *AJHR*, 1878, E–1, Public Works Statement, ix.
8. *EP*, 28 August 1878.
9. Reprinted in the *HBH*, 6 September 1878.
10. Ibid.
11. *New Zealand Tablet*, 30 August 1878.
12. *OW*, 14 September 1878.
13. Letter: Thomas Hirst/Grace Hirst (daughter), 14 September 1878, Hirst Family Letters, ATL, MS-0994-1006, vol. 13, MS-1006, 50.
14. Railways Construction Act 1878.
15. *NZPD*, vol. 29, 22 October 1878, 1009: Arthur Seymour, member for Wairau.
16. Ibid., 1015: Richmond Hursthouse, member for Motueka.
17. *NZPD*, vol. 29, 24 October 1878, 1071: Alfred Saunders, member for Cheviot.
18. Ibid., 1058: Harry Atkinson, member for Egmont.
19. *AJHR*, 1878, E–1, Public Works Statement, vi.
20. *NZPD*, vol. 29, 24 October 1878, 1089.
21. Ibid.
22. District Railways Act 1877 Amendment Act 1878 and Public Works Act 1876 Amendment Act 1878.
23. Alfred Cox, *Recollections*, Christchurch: Whitcombe & Tombs, 1884, 133.
24. Alfred Saunders, *History of New Zealand. Vol. II*, Christchurch: Smith, Anthony, Sellars & Co., 1899, 456.
25. Dick Scott, *Ask That Mountain: The story of Parihaka*, Auckland: Reed/Southern Cross, 1975, 28.
26. *AJHR*, 1880, G–2, Reports of the Royal Commission on 'The Confiscated Lands Inquiry and Maori Prisoners' Trials Act, 1879', xxv.
27. Larnach had resigned as colonial treasurer. The Taranaki Land Board was responsible for the sale of Crown lands, including confiscated land. Ballance composed an advertisement to be run in New Zealand and Australian newspapers: 'New Zealand Waimate Plains. Notice is hereby given that about 16,000 acres of the well-known Waimate Plains, on the West Coast of the North Island of New Zealand, will be disposed of by public auction, at Carlyle (Patea) on Tuesday, the 6th May next. The whole of the land proposed to be sold has been surveyed and sub-divided into allotments and will be disposed of partly upon deferred payments and partly upon immediate payment under the provisions of the "Land Act, 1877". Full particulars and details of the sections and allotments will be published shortly. –C.D. Whitcombe, commissioner of Crown lands office, New Plymouth, 25th March, 1879.' It was printed in the *Patea Mail*, 29 March; the *Taranaki Herald*, 2 April; *The Age* and *The Argus* (Melbourne), 27 March; *The Mercury* (Hobart), 27 March; *The Queenslander*, 29 March; the *Brisbane Courier*,

31 March; the *Adelaide Observer* and the *South Australian Chronicle & Weekly Mail*, 5 April. On 4 April the advertisements were suspended, and on 24 April the Taranaki Land Board was told to place an advertisement that was printed in the *Taranaki Herald*, 25 April 1878, and many other New Zealand and Australian newspapers: 'Referring to advertisement dated 25th March last, the SALE of the WAIMATE PLAINS is POSTPONED until further notice.' No further action was taken with the sale.

28. Timothy McIvor, *The Rainmaker: A biography of John Ballance journalist and politician 1839–1893*, Auckland: Heinemann Reid, 1989, 81.

29. Tūkāroto Matutaera Pōtatau Te Wherowhero Tāwhiao 1825?–1894 (Ngāti Mahuta, Tainui), son of Pōtatau Te Wherowhero, the first Māori king, who he succeeded in 1860. Tāwhiao's 34-year reign was dominated by land issues following the 1863 invasion of the Waikato and the confiscation of Māori lands by British settlers. He placed the King Country off-limits to Europeans until a peace agreement was made in 1881. He visited England in 1884 to petition Queen Victoria for a separate Māori parliament and the return of confiscated lands, but was refused an audience and his petition was denied. In the 1880s he established his own parliament, Te Kauhanganui at Maungakawa near Cambridge, but its authority was not recognised by other iwi.

30. *AJHR*, 1878, E–1, Public Works Statement, v.

31. J. Rutherford, *Sir George Grey: A study in colonial government*, 2nd edn, London: Cassell, 1961, 612.

32. Ibid., 74.

33. *NZPD*, vol. 29, 6 August 1878, 81 onwards. The Beer Tax Bill and the Company Income Tax Bill were withdrawn by Grey on 4 October 1878.

34. McIvor, *The Rainmaker*, 80.

35. *NZPD*, vol. 29, 10 October 1878, 590: William Russell (Captain, later Sir), member for Napier.

36. NZPD, vol. 30, 31 October 1878, 1263; McIvor, *The Rainmaker*, 79.

37. A full account of the events surrounding the Agricultural Company is in David Hamer, 'The Agricultural Company and New Zealand politics, 1877–1886', *Historical Studies: Australia and New Zealand*, 10, no. 38, 1962, 141–64.

38. *ODT*, 28 January 1879.

39. *NZPD*, vol. 27, 26 November 1877, 467 & 472; Raewyn Dalziel, *Julius Vogel: Business politician*, Auckland: Auckland University Press, 1986, 224, claims that Vogel's quarrels with Macandrew 'had always been political rather than personal and after Vogel left New Zealand they carried on a desultory but amicable correspondence'. Some of these letters are in Vogel Papers, ATL, MSY-1335.

40. *AJHR*, 1880, B–4A, Five Million Loan. Papers Relating to its Negotiation, Etc., 32, Enclosure no. 93, telegram dated 7 November 1879.

41. *AJHR*, 1881, A–05, Sir Julius Vogel: Papers Relating to his Resignation of the Agent-Generalship: also, as to his Position and Claims Respecting the £5,000,000 Loan, and Inscription of Stock (in Continuation of Correspondence Printed in B–4 and B–4a, 1880), 1.

42. Hamer, *The Agricultural Company*, 147. William Rees, member for Auckland City East and Patrick Dignan, member for Auckland City West.

43. *NZPD*, vol. 49, 14 October 1884, 426–33.

44. Ibid., 444. Macandrew voted in the next division of the House that day. See also David Hamer, 'The law and the prophet: A political biography of Sir Robert Stout (1844–1930)', MA thesis, University of Auckland, 1960, 119.

45. Edmund Bohan, *To Be a Hero: Sir George Grey 1812–1898*, Auckland: HarperCollins (New Zealand), 1998, 267.

46. Ibid., 269.
47. *ST*, 15 July 1879.
48. *WC*, 30 July 1879: 'Thames Railway Map. The Hon James Macandrew, the Minister of Public Works, stands convicted of having tampered with a public document after it had been laid upon the table of the House.' Edward Richardson, 1831–1915, b. England, civil and mechanical engineer, appointed 1861 to construct the Lyttelton rail tunnel. Member Canterbury PC 1870–76; MHR 1871–90; minister of public works (Waterhouse Ministry) 1872–73; minister of public works (Fox ministry) 1873; minister of public works (Vogel ministry) 1873–75; minister of public works (Pollen ministry) 1875; minister of public works (Vogel ministry) 1876; minister of public works (Atkinson ministry) 1876; minister of public works (Atkinson ministry reconstituted) 1876–77; minister of public works (Stout–Vogel ministry) 1884–87; MLC 1892–99.
49. *AJHR*, 1879, I–2, Report of the Railway Map Inquiry Committee, 23 July 1879.
50. *NZPD*, vol. 31, 24 July 1879, 210; *NZPD*, vol. 31, 7 August 1879, 454.
51. *AJHR*, 1879, I–2A, Report of the Railway Map Inquiry Committee (Revived).
52. *AJHR*, 1880, E–3, vii, Report of the Railways Commission.
53. *AJHR*, 1879, Session I, E–1, iii, Public Works Statement.
54. Judith Bassett, *Sir Harry Atkinson: 1831–1892*, Auckland: Auckland University Press, 1975, 72.
55. *NZPD*, vol. 31, 29 July 1879, 304.
56. *AJHR*, 1879, Session 1, A–01, Dissolution of Parliament (Memorandum by His Excellency the Governor); A–02, Election of a New Parliament (Memoranda Respecting the Issue of Writs for The); Dispatch, Confidential: Sir Hercules Robinson/Sir Michael Hicks Beach, 9 August 1879, Wellington, ACGO 8333 IA1/427/[79] 1879/3408; Gavin McLean, *The Governors: New Zealand's governors and governors-general*, Dunedin: University of Otago Press, 2006, 92.
57. *OW*, 6 September 1879.
58. *ODT*, 4 September 1879.
59. Utilitarians believe that the purpose of morality is to make life better by increasing the good things in the world (such as pleasure and happiness) and decreasing the bad things (such as pain and unhappiness).
60. Ibid.
61. *ODT*, 4 September 1879.
62. *OW*, 6 September 1879.
63. Letter: James Macandrew/Mabel (Mavie) Macandrew, 18 August 1879, KWMSS: Colin, his oldest son, was now 30; Alice was 15, Mabel was 13 and Arthur, the youngest, was 10.
64. *AJHR*, 1879, Session II, H–18, The General Election, 1879. Return Showing the Adult Male Population of Each Electoral District, the Number of Electors on the Rolls, the Total Number who Voted in Each Contest, and the Number of Votes for the Successful and Unsuccessful Candidates Respectively, 3. Eighty per cent of the eligible voters of Port Chalmers voted in this election; the New Zealand figure for voter turnout in contested seats was 66.5 per cent.

Chapter 17

1. *NZPD*, vol. 32, 3 October 1879, 162.
2. Keith Sinclair, 'The significance of the "Scarecrow Ministry", 1887–1891', in Robert Chapman and Keith Sinclair, eds., *Studies of a Small Democracy: Essays in honour of Willis Airey*, Auckland: Blackwood and Janet Paul, 1963, 107.
3. *ODT*, 13 September 1879.

4. *Press*, 2 June 1880: 'Sir George Grey, acting apparently in distinct independence of Mr. Macandrew's party, has given a week's notice of his intention to move for the repeal of the property tax.'
5. *WCT*, 7 May 1880.
6. These became the Triennial Parliaments Act 1879 and the Qualification of Electors Act 1879. Women almost attained the vote when an amendment moved by Ballance to replace 'man' with 'person' was lost by just 34 to 29 votes (NZPD, vol. 33, 7 November 1879, 173).
7. Jean Garner, *By His Own Merits: Sir John Hall – pioneer, pastoralist and premier*, Hororata: Dryden Press, 1995, 165.
8. J. Rutherford, *Sir George Grey: A study in colonial government*, 2nd edn, London: Cassell, 1961, 626.
9. *WC*, 16 October 1879: 'The Liberal Association have decided to support the Liberal Party under the leadership of Mr. Macandrew'; *WH*, 1 November 1879: 'All this time the actual position of parties was this – Ministerialists 41, Opposition 45; and could a division have been forced this would have been the report of the tellers.'
10. *GRA*, 13 October 1879. The Otago Daily Times and Witness Board minutes indicate that family support was not forthcoming. The board, chaired by his brother-in-law William Reynolds, instructed the editor not to support Macandrew's run for the premiership. This animosity appears to have survived from Vogel's days as editor and the *ODT*'s opposition to Macandrew's election campaign for the superintendency in 1867. Otago Daily Times and Witness Board Minutes, 17 October 1879, AG4, HC, cited in Fergus Sinclair, 'High Street quaking: A history of Dunedin's "inner circle"', PhD thesis, University of Otago, 1996, 116.
11. William Colbeck, member for Marsden; William Hurst, member for Auckland City West; William Swanson, member for Newton; Reader Wood, member for Waitemata.
12. *WT*, 28 October 1879.
13. *WH*, 5 November 1879.
14. For example, *EP*, 28 August 1878.
15. *EP*, 15 October 1879. It continued, 'They have spent all their ordinary revenue, all their first surplus and £3,500,000 of borrowed money, and yet are nearly a million short.'
16. Letter: James Farmer/JamesHector, 1 January 1880, Sir James Hector Letters, MS–0443–3/19, HC.
17. *AJHR*, 1879, Session II, B–02: Speech of the Colonial Treasurer on the Financial Position of the Colony, 14 October 1879, 1 & 7.
18. Ibid.
19. *AJHR*, 1879, Session II, B–02A: Financial Statement in Committee of Ways and Means, 17th November 1879, by the Colonial Treasurer, 5.
20. Harry Atkinson, 'Notes upon the Taxation and Indebtedness of New Zealand', 12 December 1879, Vogel Papers, ATL, MSY–1335.
21. Letter: John Hall/Julius Vogel, 1 January 1880, Hall Papers, ATL, MSX–0908, 82.
22. *AJHR*, 1880, E–3, Report of the Railways Commission; H–2, Report of the Royal Commission on the Civil Service of New Zealand.
23. *AJHR*, 1880, H–2, 8.
24. Ibid., 7.
25. *AJHR*, 1880, H–2E, Correspondence Relative to a Supply of Galvanised Iron; and H–2D, Telegram from Locomotive Engineer, Christchurch, Relative to Defective Railway Wagons.
26. *AJHR*, 1880, E–3, Report of the Railways Commission, iv.
27. Gary Hawke, *The Making of New Zealand: An economic history* (Cambridge: Cambridge University Press, 1985), 81: 'Claims that railways were built in the wrong places are unsubstantiated but difficult to refute. That they were spread amongst the provinces for

political reasons does not imply that they varied much from optimal locations … A map of the railway system at the end of the 1870s suggests progress towards the eventual national system, not a set of rewards for political allegiance.'
28. Alfred Saunders, *History of New Zealand. Vol. II* (Christchurch: Smith, Anthony, Sellars & Co., 1899), 452. Saunders was a severe critic and chaired the Royal Commission on the Civil Service of New Zealand in 1880. From 1878 to 1881 he was the member for Cheviot, which benefitted from Macandrew's railway building programme.

Chapter 18

1. *TimH*, 26 June 1882: 'On the motion of Mr. Macandrew, seconded by Mr. Stewart, Mr. Montgomery was appointed leader'; *WC*, 16 March 1881: 'Mr Macandrew [elected 1853, 24 years non-continuous service] is the "father of the House", having been elected previously to any other member, but is closely followed by Sir W. Fox [elected 1855, 23 years non-continuous service] and Sir G.M. O'Rorke [elected 1861].'
2. *WCT*, 4 July 1882.
3. *OW*, 29 May 1880.
4. *NZPD*, vol. 34, 17 December 1879, 1041.
5. *Press*, 25 May 1880.
6. *EP*, 13 March 1882.
7. *OW*, 31 May 1884.
8. *NZPD*, vol. 35, 24 June 1880, 489.
9. Ibid., 490.
10. *AES*, 25 June 1880.
11. *CL*, 27 May 1881.
12. *TA*, 10 May 1882.
13. These were: the familiar customs duties, courts of law, currency, weights and measures, mail, bankruptcy proceedings, navigational aids, shipping dues, native affairs, marriage, criminal law and inheritance laws.
14. *CL*, 28 October 1881.
15. *BH*, 4 November 1881.
16. *ODT*, 30 May 1885.
17. *NZPD*, vol. 53, 8 September 1885, 569–73; *The New Zealand Tablet*, 11 September 1885.
18. *ODT*, 27 May 1884.
19. *NZPD*, vol. 50, 8 November 1884, 516. For the British amendments to the draft bill before it was enacted, see *AJHR*, 1885, Session 1, A–02, Despatches from the Secretary of State to the Governor of New Zealand, 23, Letter 31: Earl of Derby/Governor Jervois, 11 December 1884.
20. *NZPD*, vol. 53, 7 September 1885, 531.
21. Ibid.
22. Miles Fairburn, 'New Zealand and Australian Federation, 1883–1901', *New Zealand Journal of History*, 4, no. 2, 1970, 138–59.
23. *NZPD*, vol. 55, 6 July 1886, 276.
24. Ged Martin, *Australia, New Zealand, and Federation, 1883–1901*, London: Menzies Centre for Australian Studies, 2001, 88: 'Canberra Avenue was projected as Wellington Avenue. As late as the planning of their federal capital in 1913, Australians assumed that New Zealand would one day become the seventh state of their Commonwealth.'
25. The Land Act 1877 Amendment Act, 1884, clause 42. Macandrew maintained his ties with Scotland throughout his life and consistently encouraged migration from there to New Zealand, e.g. *ODT*, 24 September 1884: 'Mr Macandrew has a plan by which he proposes not

only to relieve New Zealand of unemployed, but also to alleviate the distress of the Highland crofters, of whose hardships so much has recently been said in the Home newspapers.'

26. The Land Act 1885, clause 165.

27. *NEM*, 12 February 1885; TT, 22 September 1886.

28. George Vesey Stewart, 1832–1920, Irish estate agent, sponsor of a special settlement for Ulstermen in New Zealand. Selected land at Katikati in 1874, and more near Te Puke in 1878. Reputedly sponsored over 4000 migrants; sponsored construction of the Tauranga–Rotorua railway, which was abandoned after Mt Tawarewa eruption of 1887; emigration agent, London, 1883–87; owner *Bay of Plenty Times* 1879; first Tauranga mayor 1882, and member of many local bodies.

29. *The Times* of London, 9 September 1886.

30. *AES*, 9 April 1885.

31. *ODT*, 22 March 1883.

32. Letter: James Macandrew/Mabel Macandrew, 11 July 1881, KWMSS.

33. Raewyn Dalziel, *Julius Vogel: Business politician*, Auckland: Auckland University Press, 1986, 245.

34. *OW*, 23 December 1882.

35. *TimH*, 14 August 1884. A megatherium is a genus of elephant-sized ground sloths endemic to South America.

36. *NZH*, quoted in *ODT*, 16 August 1884.

37. Letter: James Macandrew/Mabel Macandrew, 23 August 1884, KWMSS.

38. Letter: Robert Stout/Julius Vogel, 15 December 1884, quoted in Raewyn Blackstock, 'The office of Agent-General for New Zealand in the United Kingdom, 1870–1905', PhD thesis, Victoria University of Wellington, 1970, 361.

39. V&P, OPC, Session II, 7 May 1855, 52.

40. *WH*, 29 July 1884.

41. *NZPD*, vol. 50, 28 October 1884, 147.

42. *AJHR*, 1885, I–6, Report of the Advances on Land Committee, 1.

43. *NZPD*, vol. 55, 8 July 1886, 404–29.

44. Ibid.

45. Ibid.

46. Ibid.

47. *The Colonist* (Nelson), 13 September 1886.

48. Michael Bassett, *Sir Joseph Ward: A political biography*, Auckland: Auckland University Press, 1993, 53.

49. *ODT*, 27 May 1884.

50. NZPD, vol. 56, 18 August 1886, 865–66.

51. Land Act 1877 Amendment Act 1879, no. 21; Timothy McIvor, *The Rainmaker: A biography of John Ballance journalist and politician 1839–1893*, Auckland: Heinemann Reid, 1989, 98.

52. *NZPD*, vol. 56, 18 August 1886, 865–66. The Usher of the Black Rod is an officer of parliament who is responsible for keeping order in the Legislative Council. The role was retained after abolition of the council, as a messenger between the governor-general and the House. The Black Rod is his staff of office, hence his shortened title.

53. Letter: James Macandrew/Mabel Macandrew, 23 August 1884, KWMSS.

54. Letter: James Macandrew/Hunter Macandrew, 22 August 1885, KWMSS.

55. *ODT*, 30 May 1885.

56. *ODT*, 29 June 1886.

57. The Otago Harbour Bridge Act 1886. First reading 11 June 1886, third reading 22 July 1886.

58. McLintock (*The Port of Otago*, 155–57) and McLean (*Otago Harbour*, 95–97) give details of the saga of the proposed harbour bridge. The latter includes a plan of the bridge.
59. *ODT*, 8 July 1886.
60. *ODT*, 26 November 1885. The painting was destroyed by fire on 11 December 1907. *ES*, 10 May 1888.
61. *EP*, 17 May 1884.
62. 'Sketch of the Life of James Macandrew', *Otago, Southland and South Canterbury Provincial Almanac & Directory (1875–1909)*, Dunedin: Mills, Dick & Co., 1886, 2.
63. *The Colonist* (Nelson), 13 September 1886.

Chapter 19

1. John Wilson, 'The voyage out: Journeys to New Zealand', Te Ara – the Encyclopedia of New Zealand: www.TeAra.govt.nz/en/the-voyage-out/page-1
2. *AJHR*, 1856, Report of the Select Committee on Inter-Provincial Communication.
3. *AJHR*, 1869, Session 1, F–05, Report of the Select Committee on Postal Communication.
4. *NZPD*, vol. 6, 24 August 1869, 684–87. He recommended that the government should pay no more than £20,000 annually, for three years.
5. *TarH*, 15 January 1870.
6. Raewyn Dalziel, *Julius Vogel: Business politician*, Auckland: Auckland University Press, 1986, 141.
7. *NZPD*, vol. 19, 4 October 1875, 165.
8. See Appendix 1.
9. *NZPD*, vol. 19, 8 October 1875, 326.
10. V&P, OPC, Session XXVII, 26 April 1870, 2: Superintendent's Address.
11. *AJHR*, 1878, Session 1, D–01, Emigration to New Zealand. (Letters to the Agent-General), 5. Letter No. 11, James Macandrew/Julius Vogel, 16 April 1878.
12. Ibid.
13. *ES*, 28 April 1881.
14. *Star*, 27 July 1878.
15. *NZPD*, vol. 30, 30 October 1878, 1243–46.
16. *ST*, 30 November 1878.
17. *NZPD*, vol. 39, 3 August 1881, 215–17.
18. *AJHR*, 1881, Session 1, I–09, Direct Steam Service Committee (Report of, Together with Minutes of Evidence), 1.
19. *NZPD*, vol. 40, 13 September 1881, 559.
20. *NZPD*, vol. 43, 28 August 1882, 603–33.
21. Ibid., 626. Richard John Seddon, 1845–1906, b. Lancashire, landed New Zealand 1869. Merchant, miners' advocate; member Westland PC 1874–76; MHR 1879–1906; minister of public works, mines, defence, marine (Ballance ministry) 1891–93; premier 1893–1900; prime minister 1900–06; minister of mines, Native minister 1893; public works, defence 1893–96; Native minister 1893–99; postmaster-general, electric telegraph commissioner 1896–99; commissioner of trade and customs 1896–1900; colonial treasurer, minister of labour 1896–1906; minister of defence 1900–06; minister of education, immigration 1903–06; privy councillor 1897.
22. *WH*, 14 June 1883.
23. *NZPD*, vol. 45, 7 August 1883, 365–91. For the communications with the shipping companies, see *AJHR*, 1883, Session 1, F–04, Conveyance of Immigrants and Cargo by Direct Steam Line to the Colony (Further Correspondence Relative to).

24. *AJHR*, 1883, Session 1, I–10, Joint Committee on Direct Steam Service (Report of the), Together with Minutes of Proceedings, 1.
25. *NZPD*, vol. 50, 5 November 1884, 408–13.

Chapter 20

1. *OW*, 4 March 1887. The Macandrew family Bible records his age at death as 68.
2. Telegrams: Julius Vogel/Colin Macandrew, 28 February 1887; William Reynolds/Colin Macandrew, two dated 25 February 1887. Held by Ruth Anderson, Dunedin.
3. Reynolds was ignored but was proved correct. Colin Macandrew was given permission in 1889 to move the remains of James and Eliza to Macandrew Bay cemetery, where several of their children and other members of the extended family are now buried with them. ANZ, Wellington, ACGO 8333 IA1/576/[18] 1889/3436.
4. *OW*, 4 March 1887.
5. *BH*, 1 March 1887.
6. *Mataura Ensign*, 1 March 1887.
7. *OW*, 4 March 1887.
8. *ODT*, 25 February 1887.
9. Letter: W.H. Mansford, Registrar, University of Otago/Colin Macandrew, 18 April 1887, held by Ruth Anderson.
10. *The New Zealand Tablet*, 4 March 1887.
11. *EP*, 26 March 1887.
12. *TT*, 19 March 1887.
13. *NEM*, 29 March 1887.
14. *AWJ*, 5 April 1887.
15. *The Times* of London, 15 April 1887.
16. *TT*, 2 March 1887.
17. *OW*, 4 March 1887; *WC*, 4 March 1887.
18. *BH*, 8 March 1887.
19. *BH*, 18 March 1887.
20. *ODT*, 16 March 1887.
21. *OW*, 11 March 1887.
22. *ES*, 9 April 1887.
23. *EP*, 9 April 1887.
24. *ME*, 12 April 1887.
25. *ME*, 21 June 1887.
26. *ES*, 10 August 1887.
27. *Press*, 25 June, 6 July 1891. Premier Ballance sent a telegram to say he regretted he could not be present.
28. *ODT*, 11 July 1891.
29. *ES*, 24 October 1891.
30. *CL*, 17 July 1891.
31. Appendix 2: Last will and testament, James Macandrew, died 24 February 1887. Probate James Macandrew dated 7 June 1887, ANZ, Dunedin, DAAC D239 9074 251 A917.
32. Jane Smallfield, personal communication, 1 June 2016.
33. *NZPD*, vol. 66, 14 September 1889, 553–54.
34. Ibid
35. Ibid., 589–90.
36. Ibid.

37. *AJHR*, 1890, B–1, Public Accounts of the Government of New Zealand, for Financial Year Commencing 1st April, 1889 and ending 31st March, 1890, 41.
38. Brian and Diane Miller, *Macandrew Bay*, Dunedin: Lifelogs Ltd, 2009, 33.
39. J.A. Menzies, Journal, 7 December 1855, Toitū Otago Settlers Museum.
40. *ST*, 3 March 1887.
41. *OW*, 4 March 1887. Rev Dr Donald McNaughton Stuart, 1819–1894, b. Scotland, landed Dunedin 1860. Established Knox Church, second Presbyterian church in Otago; member of Senate, University of New Zealand 1873–81; chancellor University of Otago 1879–94.
42. *The NZ Presbyterian*, 1 April 1887, 190–91. Greig was the minister of Macandrew's Otago Peninsula parish 1868–1904.
43. Letter: Thomas Hirst/Grace Hirst (wife), 2 January 1862, Hirst Family Letters, ATL, MS-0994-1006, vol. 3, MS-0996, 179.
44. Michael Bassett, *The State in New Zealand: 1840–1984*, Auckland: Auckland University Press, 1998, 10.
45. *ODT*, 30 May 1885.
46. W.P. Morrell, *The Provincial System in New Zealand: 1852–76*, Christchurch, Whitcombe & Tombs, 1964 (2nd edn), 270–85, 'The Causes of Abolition.'
47. *AJHR*, 1876, A–4, Abolition of the Provinces: The Commissioners' Visits (Papers Relating To).
48. *NZPD*, 26 July 1866, 824.
49. Ron Palenski, *The Making of New Zealanders*, Auckland: Auckland University Press, 2012, 18.
50. Jeanine Graham, 'Settler society', in Geoffrey Rice, ed., *Oxford History of New Zealand*, 2nd edn, Auckland: Oxford University Press, 1992, 132.
51. James Belich, *Paradise Reforged: A history of the New Zealanders from the 1880s to the year 2000*, Auckland: Allen Lane, 2001, 221.
52. *ODT*, 30 May 1885.
53. *EP*, 27 November 1879.
54. *WT*, 21 June 1883; *NZPD*, vol. 51, 24 June 1885, 128–35; 25 June 1885, 165–66, 179–90.
55. John E. Martin, *Parliament's Library 150 years*, Wellington: Steele Roberts, 2008, 13.
56. New Zealand Parliament, Library Lending Register, Wellington. Parliamentary Librarian, *Classified Catalogue of the Library of the General Assembly of New Zealand*, Wellington, Government Printer, 1885. In July 1879 Macandrew borrowed *Far from the Madding Crowd* (Thomas Hardy, 1874), and in November, *Race for Wealth* and *Austin Friars* (by the popular Mrs J.H. Riddell, 1866, 1870) and *Sir Gibbie* (by popular novelist George MacDonald, 1879). His non-fiction diet included the latest publications, especially on politics and biography: in August, *Diderot and the Encyclopædists* (John Morley, 1878); in September, *War in Bulgaria: A narrative of personal experiences* (LtGen Valentine Baker, 1879); in October, when he was plain Mr Macandrew again, *English Party and Party Leaders, from Walpole to Peel* (W.H. Davenport Adams, 1878), and in August 1881, the *Life of Lord Clyde* (LtGen Shadwell, 1881).
57. Martin, *Parliament's Library 150 years*, 58, 54.
58. *NZPD*, vol. 12, 8 August 1872, 368.
59. Sir John McKenzie, 1838–1901, b. Scotland, landed New Zealand 1860. Farmed North Otago; member OPC 1871–76; MHR 1881–1900; MLC 1901; minister of lands and immigration, agriculture (Ballance ministry) 1891–93; minister immigration 1893–96; minister lands, agriculture, commissioner of forests (Seddon ministry) 1893–1900; KCMG 1901.
60. *ODT*, 30 August 1882.

61. Tom Brooking, *Lands for the People? The Highland Clearances and the colonisation of New Zealand: A biography of John McKenzie*, Dunedin: University of Otago Press, 1996, 60.

62. *NZPD*, vol. 54, 17 June 1886, 558.

63. Ibid.

64. Tom Brooking, *Richard Seddon: King of God's own*, Auckland: Penguin Books, 2015, 48. Macandrew's bankruptcy was not an unusual event in those times. Richard Seddon was another politician who got off to a shaky start – he filed for bankruptcy in 1878. Imprisonment of debtors ended in 1874.

65. The following ministers were knighted: Wilson in 1872, Bell in 1873, Richardson, Vogel and McLean in 1874, Fitzherbert in 1877, Stafford and Fox in 1879, O'Rorke in 1880, Hall and Whitmore in 1882, Whitaker in 1884, Stout in 1886 and Atkinson in 1888.

66. Guy Scholefield, *New Zealand Parliamentary Record*, Wellington: Government Printer, 1950, 169.

67. *ODT*, 18 April 1916: Macandrew Street, which separates First Church and the Garrison Hall, was renamed Burlington Street to avoid the duplication of street names following the amalgamation of the boroughs of Andersons Bay, Maori Hill and Mornington with the City of Dunedin in 1915.

68. *OW*, 10 August 1878.

Appendices

1. Obituary, Mr Colin Macandrew, *ODT*, 19 March 1928.
2. Obituary, Nurse Marion Macandrew: *Kai Taki*, vol. XV, issue 1, January 1926.
3. Memorandum: James Macandrew/Herbert Macandrew, 12 February 1880, in Denis Le Cren, *The Rich and Macandrew Families*, Nelson: Denis Le Cren, 1993, 87. Always the concerned parent, Macandrew gave Herbert very specific and clear guidance when he left to train as a doctor in Scotland.
4. *ODT*, 26 January 1917.
5. Letter: James Macandrew/Hunter Macandrew, 22 August 1885, KWMSS. Macandrew was prepared to use his influence in Wellington with the Railways Department when Hunter wanted a transfer.
6. *Dominion*, 2 March 1915.
7. *Dominion*, 17 May 1917; EP, 14 June 1917.
8. *EP*, 22 January 1917.

Bibliography

PRIMARY SOURCES

Manuscripts

Alexander Turnbull Library, Wellington
Atkinson, Harry, MS–Papers 91
Ballance, John, MS–Papers 25
Hall, John, MS–Group 0033
Hirst Family Letters, MS–0994-1006
McLean, Donald, MS–Group–1551
Rolleston, William, MS–77–248
Stafford, Edward, MS–Papers 2045 to 2050
Stout, Robert, MS–Papers–0040
Vogel, Julius, MS–Papers–2072

Archives New Zealand, Wellington
Governors' Papers

Archives New Zealand, Dunedin
Macandrew, James/Superintendent correspondence: 'Making Stafford Street
    passable for winter. He is starting a brick and tile works near the Town Belt', 16 March
    1859, AAAC 707 D500 130/c 118
Last Will and Testament of Eliza Hunter Macandrew: signed 11 December
    1874, DAAC D239 23 435
Last Will and Testament of James Macandrew: died 24 February 1887, DAAC
    D239 9074 251 A917

Hocken Collections, Dunedin
Cargill, William, correspondence: 'Papers relating to the establishment of Otago', MS-0075
    and MS-0076
Cargill, William, letter book, MS-0095
Cargill, William, correspondence re applications for depasturage licences, MS-0211/3
Cargill, William, 'Receipts for payment in Otago settlement', MS-1751 00
Depasturage Licences Applications, Otago, MS-0209/006
Dispatches from the New Zealand Company and correspondence with New Zealand agents,
    MS-0079 to MS-0083
Elder, James Brown, 'Notes for Early History Society of Otago', MS-0043
Hector, James/Farmer, James, correspondence, MS-0443-3/15 to MS-0443-3/28
Hocken, Thomas, correspondence, MS-0451/003 in Collected Papers of Thomas Hocken,
    ARC-0180
------ *Flotsam and Jetsam*, vols. 1–20, SER-07789, in Collected Papers of Thomas Hocken,
    ARC-0180

Macandrew, James, correspondence with relatives, MS–00111/2

Macandrew & Co./Octavius Harwood, correspondence and summons over unpaid bills, MS–0438/127 and MS–0438/128

Macandrew, James, Arithmetic Exercise book, Misc–MS–0619

McGlashan, John, correspondence, MS–0463/2 to MS–0463/36

Minute Book 1851, Otago Settlers' Association, MS–0032

Monson, Henry, Journal, MS–0088

New Zealand Agricultural Company agreement, 14 November 1878, MS–0585

Olssen, Erik, analysis of Macandrew's election results, MS–2146/97

Papers of the Otago Lay Association, MS–0077 and MS–0078

Reid, Donald, letters, Misc–MS–0178

Terms of Purchase of Land in the Settlement of Otago, June 1847, MSS–Pam–124/2

Toitū Otago Settlers Museum

Macandrew, James: 'Address to the People of Otago', pamphlet, 1875

Macandrew Family Bible

Menzies, J.A., Dr, Journal

Minute Book of the James Macandrew Testimonial Committee 1878

Richardson, J.C.L., papers

National Library of Scotland

Oliver & Boyd, Booksellers of Edinburgh, and Robert Garden, then Garden & Macandrew of London, correspondence 1841–1850, National Library of Scotland MSS, Acc 5000/vols. 201, 203, 204, 205, 206, 207.

Other

Annual Report of the First Church of Otago for the year ending 31 December 1852, Presbyterian Church Archives, Knox College, Dunedin

Macandrew Family papers in possession of Ruth Anderson, Dunedin, New Zealand

Macandrew Family papers in possession of Marsha Donaldson, Waikanae, New Zealand

Macandrew Family papers in possession of Kate Wilson, Middlemarch, New Zealand

Martin, Ged, "Edward Gibbon Wakefield: Abductor and Mystagogue", Paper presented at 'Edward Gibbon Wakefield and New Zealand 1830–1865: A reconsideration conference': Wellington: National Library, 1996

New Zealand Parliament Library Lending Register, Wellington: unpublished manuscript.

Rates book of the Dunedin Town Board (established 1857), vol. 4/1: Dunedin City Council

The Minute Book of the Trustees, Dunedin, 1848 to 1867, Trust Fund for Religious and Educational Uses: Otago Foundation Trust Board, Dunedin

Waddy, Charles, 'A Casa Reynolds: The personal, commercial and political adventures of one generation of a British family in Great Britain, Spain, Portugal and New Zealand': unpublished history of the Reynolds family, Seddon, New Zealand, 2016

Newspapers

Aberdeen Journal

Aberdeen Weekly Journal

Ashburton Guardian

Auckland Herald
Auckland Morning News
Bay of Plenty Times
Bruce Herald
Clutha Leader
Colonial Journal
Colonist
Daily Free Press
Daily News London
Daily Southern Cross
Dunedin Leader
Dunstan Times
Evening Post, Wellington
Evening Star, Dunedin
Glasgow Herald
Grey River Argus
Hawke's Bay Herald
Lake Whakatip Mail
Leeds Mercury
Lyttelton Times
Marlborough Express
Mataura Ensign
Mount Ida Chronicle
Nelson Examiner and New Zealand Chronicle (later *Nelson Examiner*)
Nelson Evening Mail
New Zealand Journal
New Zealand Herald
New Zealand Spectator and Cook's Strait Guardian
New Zealand Tablet
New Zealander
North Otago Times
Oamaru Mail
Otago Daily Times
Otago Colonist
Otago Journal
Otago Witness
Press
Southern Cross
Southland Times
Star, Christchurch
Taranaki Herald
Thames Advertiser
The Times
Tuapeka Times
Timaru Herald

Waikato Times
Wanganui Chronicle
Wanganui Herald
Wellington Independent
West Coast Times

Official printed sources

Votes and Proceedings of Otago Provincial Council, 1853–76
Otago Provincial Government Gazette, 1853–76
New Zealand Parliamentary Debates, 1854–88
Votes and Proceedings of the House of Representatives, 1854–56
Appendices to the Journals of the House of Representatives, 1858–88

SECONDARY SOURCES

Books

Adam, James, *Twenty Five Years of Emigrant Life in the South of New Zealand*, Edinburgh: Bell and Bradfute, 1876

Anderson, Robert David, *Education and the Scottish People 1750–1918*, Oxford: Clarendon Press, 1995.

Arnold, Rollo, *The Farthest Promised Land: English villagers, New Zealand immigrants of the 1870*, Wellington: Price Milburn, 1981

------*New Zealand's burning: The settler's world in the mid 1880s*, Wellington: Victoria University Press, 1994

Atkinson, Alan, *The Europeans in Australia*, vol. 2, Melbourne: Oxford University Press, 2004.

Barr, James, *The Old Identities*, Dunedin: Mills, Dick & Co., 1879

Bassett, Judith, *Sir Harry Atkinson: 1831–1892*, Auckland: Auckland University Press, 1975

Bassett, Michael, *Sir Joseph Ward: A political biography*, Auckland: Auckland University Press, 1993

------*The State in New Zealand: 1840–1984*, Auckland: Auckland University Press, 1998.

Bathgate, Alexander, *Colonial Experiences or Sketches of People and Places in the Province of Otago, New Zealand*, Glasgow: James Maclehose, 1874

------*Picturesque Dunedin*, Dunedin: Mills, Dick and Co, 1890

Belich, James, *'I Shall Not Die': Titokowaru's War, New Zealand, 1868–9*, Wellington: Allen & Unwin in association with the Port Nicholson Press, 1989

------*Making Peoples: A history of the New Zealanders from Polynesian settlement to the end of the nineteenth century*, Auckland: Penguin, 1996

------*The New Zealand Wars and the Victorian Interpretation of Racial Conflict*, Auckland: Penguin Books, 1988

------*Paradise Reforged: A history of the New Zealanders from the 1880s to the year 2000*, Auckland: Allen Lane, 2001

------*Replenishing the Earth: The Settler Revolution and the Rise of the Anglo World 1783–1939*, Oxford: Oxford University Press, 2009

Beaglehole, J.C., *New Zealand: A short history*, London: George Allen & Unwin, 1936

Binney, Judith, ed., *The Shaping of History: Essays from the New Zealand Journal of History*, Wellington: Bridget Williams Books, 2001

Boast, Richard, *Buying the Land, Selling the Land: Governments and Maori land in the North Island 1865–1921*, Wellington: Victoria University Press, 2008

Bohan, Edmund, *Edward Stafford: New Zealand's first statesman*, Christchurch: Hazard Press, 1994

------*To Be a Hero: Sir George Grey 1812–1898*, Auckland: HarperCollins, 1998

------*'Blest Madman' FitzGerald of Canterbury*, Christchurch: Canterbury University Press, 1998

Bracken, Thomas, *Musings in Maoriland*, Dunedin: Arthur T. Keirle, 1890

Brett, André, *Acknowledge No Frontier: The creation and demise of New Zealand's provinces, 1853–76*, Dunedin: Otago University Press, 2016

Brock, Jeanette M., *The Mobile Scot: A study of emigration and migration 1861–1911*, Edinburgh: John Donald, 1999.

Brooking, Tom, *'And Captain of their Souls'*, Dunedin: Heritage Books, 1984

------*Lands for the People? The Highland Clearances and the colonisation of New Zealand: A biography of John McKenzie*, Dunedin: University of Otago Press, 1996

------*Richard Seddon: King of God's Own*, Auckland: Penguin Books, 2014

Brooking, Tom and Coleman, Jennie, (eds), *The Heather and the Fern: Scottish migration & New Zealand settlement*, Dunedin: University of Otago Press, 2003

Buchanan, Neil Harkness and Buchanan, Andrew Hamilton, (eds), *Andrew Buchanan Diaries 1865, 1873*, Christchurch: N.H. Buchanan and A.H. Buchanan, 1997

Bueltmann, Tanja, *Scottish Ethnicity and the Making of New Zealand Society 1850–1930*, Edinburgh: Scottish Historical Review Monographs Series No. 19, Edinburgh University Press, 2011

Burdon, Randal, *The Life and Times of Sir Julius Vogel*, Christchurch: Caxton Press, 1948.

Bush, Graham, *Local Government & Politics in New Zealand*, 2nd edn., Auckland: Auckland University Press, 1995

Butterworth, Susan and Butterworth, Graham, *Chips off the Auld Rock: Shetlanders in New Zealand*, Wellington: Shetland Society of Wellington, 1997

Cage, R.A., ed., *The Scots Abroad: Labour, capital, enterprise, 1750–1914*, London: Croom Helm, 1985

Cameron, George G., *The Scots Kirk in London*, Oxford: Becket Publications, 1979

Carpenter, Lloyd and Fraser, Lyndon, *Rushing for Gold*, Dunedin: Otago University Press, 2016

Carrington, C.E., *John Robert Godley of Canterbury*, Christchurch: Whitcombe & Tombs, 1950

Chapman, Robert and Sinclair, Keith, (eds), *Studies of a Small Democracy: Essays in Honour of Willis Airey*, Auckland: Blackwood and Janet Paul, 1963

Cowan, A.H., *Sir Donald McLean*, Dunedin: A.H. & A.W. Reed, 1940

Cox, Alfred, *Recollections*, Christchurch: Whitcombe & Tombs, 1884

Curthoys, Ann, Genovese, Ann and Reilly, Alex, *Rights and Redemption: History, law and indigenous people*, Sydney: University of New South Wales Press, 2008

Cyclopedia of New Zealand, Christchurch: The Cyclopedia Company, 1905

Dalziel, Raewyn, *Julius Vogel: Business politician*, Auckland: Auckland University Press, 1986

Davidoff, Leonore and Hall, Catherine, *Family Fortunes: Men and women of the English middle class, 1780–1850*, London: Hutchinson, 1987

Davidson, William Soltau, *William Soltau Davidson 1846–1924: A sketch of his life covering a period of fifty-two years, 1864–1916, in the employment of the New Zealand and Australian Land Company Limited*, Edinburgh: Printed for private circulation by Oliver & Boyd, 1930

Devine, Tom, *The Great Highland Famine: Hunger, emigration and the Scottish Highlands in the nineteenth century*, Edinburgh: John Donald, 1988

——————*Scottish Emigration and Scottish Society: Proceedings of the Scottish Historical Studies Seminar, University of Strathclyde, 1990–91*, Edinburgh: John Donald, 1992

——————*The Scottish Nation: A modern history*, London: Penguin, 1999

——————*Scotland's Empire: The origins of the global diaspora*, London: Penguin, 2004

——————*To the Ends of the Earth: Scotland's global diaspora, 1750–2010*, London: Penguin, 2012

Devine, Tom, ed., *Conflict and Stability in Scottish Society 1700–1850: Proceedings of the Scottish Historical Studies Seminar, University of Strathclyde 1988–89*, Edinburgh: John Donald, 1990

Devine, Tom and Mitchison, Rosalind, eds, *People and Society in Scotland: Volume 1, 1760–1830*, Edinburgh: John Donald in association with the Economic and Social History Society of Scotland, 1988

Donnachie, Ian and Whatley, Christopher, eds, *The Manufacture of Scottish History*, Edinburgh: Polygon, 1992

Dumett, R.E., *Gentlemanly Capitalism and British Imperialism: The new debate on empire*, New York: Longman, 1999

Dunmore, John, *Wild Cards: Eccentric characters from New Zealand's past*, Auckland: New Holland Publishers, 2006

Dunn, W.H. & Richardson, I.L.M., *Sir Robert Stout: A biography*, Wellington: A.H. & A.W. Reed, 1961

Elliot, John, *History in the Making*, New Haven: Yale University Press, 2012

English, Henry, ed., *The Mining Almanack for 1849*, London: The Mining Journal Office, 1849

——————*The Mining Manual and Almanack for 1851*, London: The Mining Journal Office, 1850

Evans, Julie, *Edward Eyre: Race and colonial governance*, Dunedin: University of Otago Press, 2005

Evison, Harry, *Ngāi Tahu Land Rights and the Crown Pastoral Lease Lands in the South Island of New Zealand*, 3rd edn., Christchurch: Ngāi Tahu Māori Trust Board, 1986

——————*Te Wai Pounamu/The Greenstone Island: A history of the Southern Māori during the European colonisation of New Zealand*, Christchurch: Aoraki Press in association with Ngāi Tahu Trust Board, 1993

Fargher, Ray, *The Best Man Who Ever Served the Crown? A life of Donald McLean*, Wellington: Victoria University Press, 2007

Fitzpatrick, Brian, *The British Empire in Australia: An economic history 1834–1939*, Melbourne: Melbourne University Press, 1941

Fox, William, *The Six Colonies of New Zealand*, London: John W. Parker and Son, 1851

Fulton, Christina, *Lella: A Poem*, Dunedin: Evening Star, 1868

Gardner, W.J., *Colonial Cap and Gown: Studies in mid-Victorian universities of Australasia*, Christchurch: University of Canterbury, 1979

Garner, Jean, *By His Own merits: Sir John Hall – Pioneer, pastoralist and premier*, Hororata, New Zealand: Dryden Press, 1995

Gilkison, Robert, *Early Days in Dunedin*, Auckland: Whitcombe and Tombs, 1938

Gisborne, William, *New Zealand Rulers and Statesmen 1840 to 1885*, London: Sampson Low, Marston, Searle & Rivington, 1886

Godley, John R., ed., *Letters from Early New Zealand by Charlotte Godley 1850–1853*, Christchurch: Whitcombe & Tombs, 1951

Goldsmith, Paul, *We Won, You Lost, Eat That! A political history of tax in New Zealand since 1840*, Auckland: David Ling, 2008

Graham, Jeanine, *Frederick Weld*, Auckland: Auckland University Press, 1983

––––––'Settler society', in Geoffrey Rice, ed., *Oxford History of New Zealand*, 2nd edn., Auckland: Oxford University Press, 1992

Greif, Stuart W. and Knight, Hardwicke, *Cutten: Letters revealing the life and times of William Henry Cutten the forgotten pioneer*, Dunedin: Stuart Greif and Hardwicke Knight, 1979

Hall-Jones, F.G., *Historical Southland*, Invercargill: Southland Historical Committee, 1945

Hall-Jones, John, *Goldfields of the South*, Invercargill: Craig Printing Co, 1982

––––––*Martins Bay*, Invercargill: Craig Printing Co, 1987

Hamer, David, *The New Zealand Liberals: The years of power, 1891–1912*, Auckland: Auckland University Press, 1988

Hamilton, Nigel, *Biography: A brief history*, Cambridge, Mass: Harvard University Press, 2007

Harper, Marjory, *Emigration from North East Scotland, Vol. 1: 'Willing Exiles'*, Aberdeen: Aberdeen University Press, 1988

––––––*Emigration from North East Scotland, Vol. 2: 'Beyond the Broad Atlantic'*, Aberdeen: Aberdeen University Press, 1988

––––––*Adventurers and Exiles: The great Scottish exodus*, London: Profile, 2003

Harper, Marjory, ed., *Emigrant Homecomings: The return movement of emigrants, 1600–2000*, Manchester: Manchester University Press, 2005

Harper, Marjory and Vance, Michael E., eds, *Myth, Migration and the Making of Memory: Scotia and Nova Scotia c. 1700–1900*, Published for the Gorsebrook Research Institute for Atlantic Canada Studies by Fernbrook Publishing, Halifax, and John Donald, Edinburgh, 1999

Hawke, Gary, *The Making of New Zealand: An economic history*, Cambridge: Cambridge University Press, 1985

Hay, J.N., *Epidemics and pandemics: Their impacts on human history*, Santa Barbara, Ca: ABC–CLIO, 2005

Herman, Arthur, *How the Scots Invented the Modern World*, New York: Crown Publishers, 2001

Hight, James and Straubel, C.R., eds, *A History of Canterbury* (3 vols.), Christchurch: Whitcombe & Tombs, 1957–1971

Hirst, John, *The Australians: Insiders & outsiders on the national character since 1770*, Melbourne: Black, 2007

Hocken, T.M., *Contributions to the Early History of New Zealand (Settlement of Otago)*, London: Sampson, Low, Marston and Co, 1898

Hogan, Denis and Williamson, Bryce, eds, *New Zealand is Different: Chemical milestones in New Zealand history*, Christchurch: New Zealand Institute of Chemistry, 1999

Horsman, Alan, ed., *The Diary of Alfred Domett, 1872–85*, London: Oxford University Press, 1953

Houston, R.A. and Knox, W.W.J., eds, *The New Penguin History of Scotland: From the earliest days to the present day*, London: Allen Lane/Penguin in association with the National Museums of Scotland, 2001

Hursthouse, Charles, *New Zealand: The 'Britain of the South'*, 2nd edn. London: Edward Stanford, 1861

Johnston, Carol Morton and Morton, Harry, *Dunedin Teachers' College: The first hundred years*, Dunedin: Dunedin Teachers College Publications Committee, 1976

Jourdain, W.R., *Land Legislation and Settlement in New Zealand*, Wellington: Government Printer, 1925

Kennedy, Junior, David, *Kennedy's Colonial Travel: A narrative of a four years' tour through Australia, New Zealand, Canada, &c*, London: Edinburgh Publishing Company, 1876

King, Michael, *The Penguin History of New Zealand*, Auckland: Penguin, 2003

Le Cren, Denis J., *The Rich and Macandrew Families 1280–1993*, Nelson: Denis Le Cren, 1993

Ledgerwood, Norman, *The Heart of a City: The story of Dunedin's Octagon*, Dunedin: Norman Ledgerwood, 2008

Locke, Elsie, *The Gaoler*, Palmerston North: Dunmore Press, 1978

Macandrew, James, *Address to the People of Otago*, Dunedin: Mills, Dick and Co, 1875

Macdonald, Phillida, *Eliza's Journal*, Christchurch: P. Macdonald, 2000

Mackay, Alexander, *A Compendium of Official Documents Relative to Native Affairs in the South Island, Vol. 1*, Wellington: Government Printer, 1873

MacKenzie, John M., ed., *The Victorian Vision: Inventing New Britain*, London: V. & A. Publications, 2004

MacLaren, Alan A., *Religion and Social Class: The Disruption years in Aberdeen*, London & Boston: Routledge & Kegan Paul, 1974

Macmillan, David S., *Scotland and Australia, 1788–1850: Emigration, commerce and investment*, Oxford: Clarendon, 1967

McAloon, Jim, *Nelson: A regional history*, Whatamango Bay, New Zealand: Cape Catley Ltd, 1997

------*No Idle Rich: The wealthy in Canterbury & Otago 1840–1914*, Dunedin: University of Otago Press, 2002

McCalla, Doug, *Planting the Province: The economic history of Upper Canada*, Toronto: University of Toronto Press, 1993

McDonald, K.C., *City of Dunedin: A century of civic enterprise*, Dunedin: Dunedin City Corporation, 1965

McEldowney, Dennis, ed., *Presbyterians in Aotearoa 1840–1990*, Wellington: Presbyterian Church of New Zealand, 1990

McIntosh, A.D., *Marlborough: A provincial history*, Blenheim: Marlborough Provincial Historical Committee, 1940

McIntyre, W.D., ed., *The Journal of Henry Sewell 1853–7* (2 vols.), Christchurch: Whitcoulls, 1980

McIvor, Timothy, *The Rainmaker A biography of John Ballance journalist and politician 1839–1893*, Auckland: Heinemann Reid, 1989

McLean, Gavin, *Otago Harbour: Currents of controversy*, Dunedin: Otago Harbour Board, 1985

------*The Southern Octopus: The rise of a shipping empire*, Wellington: New Zealand Ship & Marine Society, 1990

------*The Governors: New Zealand's Governors and Governors-General*, Dunedin: Otago University Press, 2006

McLintock, A.H., *The Port of Otago*, Dunedin: Whitcombe & Tombs, 1951

------*Crown Colony Government in New Zealand*, Wellington: Government Printer, 1958

------*The History of Otago: The origins and growth of a Wakefield class settlement*, Dunedin: Otago Centennial Historical Publications, 1949; reprint, Christchurch: Capper Press, 1975

McLintock, A.H. and Wood, G.A., *The Upper House in Colonial New Zealand*, Wellington: Government Printer, 1987

McKean, John, *The Church in a Special Colony: A history of the Presbyterian Synod of Otago & Southland 1866–1991*, Dunedin: Synod of Otago and Southland, Presbyterian Church of Aotearoa New Zealand, 1994

McRobie, Alan, *New Zealand Electoral Atlas*, Wellington: Department of Internal Affairs, 1989

Mander-Jones, Phyllis, *Manuscripts in the British Isles Relating to Australia, New Zealand, and the Pacific*, Canberra: Australian National University Press, 1972

Martin, Ged., *Australia, New Zealand, and Federation, 1883–1901*, London: Menzies Centre for Australian Studies, 2001

Martin, John E., *The House: New Zealand's House of Representatives 1854–2004*, Palmerston North: Dunmore Press, 2004

------*Parliament's Library 150 years*, Wellington: Steele Roberts, 2008

Merrington, E.N., *A Great Coloniser: Rev Dr Thomas Burns*, Dunedin: Otago Daily Times and Witness Newspapers, 1929

Miller, Brian and Miller, Diane, *Macandrew Bay*, Dunedin: Lifelogs Ltd, 2009

Milne, J., *The Romance of a Pro-Consul: Being the Personal Life of the Right Hon. Sir George Grey, KCB*, London: Chatto & Windus, 1899

Moncrieff-Spittle, Malcolm, ed., *The Lost Journal of Edward Jerningham Wakefield: Being an account of his exploits and adventures in New Zealand in the years 1850–1858, including: His various visitations, conversations & observations &c. &c. To which is added an introduction.* Dunedin: Kilmog Press, 2008

Morrell, William P., *British Colonial Policy in the Age of Peel and Russell*, Oxford: Clarendon Press, 1930

------*New Zealand*, London: Ernest Benn, 1935

------*The Provincial System in New Zealand: 1852–76*, 2nd edn., Christchurch: Whitcombe & Tombs, 1964

------*The University of Otago: A centennial history*, Dunedin: University of Otago Press, 1969

Morrell, William, and Hall, D.O.W., *A History of New Zealand Life*, Christchurch: Whitcombe and Tombs, 1957

Morris, R.J., *Class, Sect and Party: The making of the British middle class, Leeds, 1820–1850*, Manchester: Manchester University Press, 1990

------*Men, Women and Property in England, 1780–1870: A social and economic history of family strategies amongst the Leeds middle classes*, Cambridge: Cambridge University Press, 2005

Nathan, Simon, *James Hector*, Wellington: Geoscience Society of New Zealand, 2015

Ng, James, *Windows on a Chinese Past: How the Cantonese goldseekers and their heirs settled in New Zealand* (4 vols.), Dunedin: Otago Heritage Books, 1993

Nolan, Melanie, *Kin: A collective biography of a New Zealand working-class family*, Christchurch: Canterbury University Press, 2005

Oliver, W.H. & Williams, B.R., eds, *The Oxford History of New Zealand*, Oxford: Clarendon Press, 1981

Olssen, E., *A History of Otago*, Dunedin: John McIndoe, 1984

Otago Provincial Government, *The Province of Otago in New Zealand: Its progress, present condition, resources, and prospects*, Dunedin: Otago Provincial Government, 1868

Palenski, Ron, *The Making of New Zealanders*, Auckland: Auckland University Press, 2012

M. Brook Taylor, ed., *Canadian History, A Reader's Guide, Vol. 1: Beginnings to Confederation*, Toronto: University of Toronto Press, 1994

Parliamentary Librarian, *Classified Catalogue of the Library of the General Assembly of New Zealand*, Wellington: Government Printer, 1885

Parton, Hugh, *The University of New Zealand*, Auckland: Auckland University Press, 1979

Patterson, Brad, Brooking, Tom and McAloon, Jim, *Unpacking the Kists: The Scots in New Zealand*, Dunedin: Otago University Press, 2013

Pearce, G.L., *The Scots of New Zealand*, Auckland: Collins, 1976

Phillips, Jock & Hearn, Terry, *Settlers: New Zealand immigrants from England, Ireland & Scotland 1800–1945*, Auckland: Auckland University Press, 2008

Polaschek, R.J., ed., *Local Government in New Zealand*, Wellington and London: New Zealand Institute of Public Administration and Oxford University Press, 1956

Reed, A.H., *The Story of Early Dunedin*, Wellington: A.H. & A.W. Reed, 1956

Registrar-General of New Zealand, *Statistics of New Zealand for 1853, 1854, 1855, and 1856*, Auckland: 1858

------*Statistics of New Zealand for 1887*, Auckland: 1888

Richards, Eric, *Britannia's Children*, London: Hambledon and London, 2004

Robinson, Neil, *To the ends of the earth: Norman McLeod and the Highlanders' migration to Nova Scotia and New Zealand*, Auckland: HarperCollins, 1997

Roxburgh, Irvine, *Jacksons Bay: A centennial history*, Wellington: A.H. & A.W. Reed, 1976.

Rutherford, J., *Sir George Grey: A study in colonial government*, 2nd edn., London: Cassell, 1961.

Salmon, J.H.M., *A History of Goldmining in New Zealand*, Wellington: R.E. Owen, Government Printer, 1963

Saunders, Alfred, *History of New Zealand. Vol. II*, Christchurch: Smith, Anthony, Sellars and Co, 1899

Scholefield, Guy, *A Dictionary of New Zealand Biography* (2 vols.), Wellington: Department of Internal Affairs, 1940

------*Notable New Zealand Statesmen: Twelve prime ministers*, Christchurch: Whitcombe and Tombs, 1946

------*New Zealand Parliamentary Record*, Wellington: Government Printer, 1950

------, (ed.), *The Richmond-Atkinson Papers* (2 vols.), Wellington: R.E. Owen, Government Printer, 1960

Schrader, Ben, *The Big Smoke: New Zealand cities 1840–1920*, Wellington: Bridget Williams Books, 2016

Scott, Dick, *Ask That Mountain: The story of Parihaka*, Auckland: Reed/Southern Cross, 1975

Siegfried, Andre, trans. E.V. Burns, *Democracy in New Zealand*, London: G. Bell and Sons, 1914

Simpson, Tony, *The Immigrants: The great migration from Britain to New Zealand, 1830–1890*, Auckland: Godwit Press, 1997

Sinclair, Keith, *A History of New Zealand*, London: Penguin, 1959

Slocombe, Stanley, ed., *The Riversdalians: Centennial story of Riversdale and district 1873–1973*, Riversdale: Riversdale and Districts Centennial Committee, 1973

Smith, Janet Adam, *John Buchan, a Biography*, London: Rupert Hart-Davies, 1965

Smout, T.C., *A Century of the Scottish People 1830–1950*, London: Collins, 1986

Snedden, Fleur, *King of the Castle: A biography of William Larnach*, Auckland: David Bateman, 1997

Stewart, William Downie, ed. *The Journal of George Hepburn*, Dunedin: Coulls Somerville Wilkie and A.H. Reed, 1934

——————*The Right Honourable Sir Francis H.D. Bell: His life and times*, Wellington: Butterworth & Co., 1937.

——————*William Rolleston*, Christchurch: Whitcombe & Tombs, 1940.

Stone, R.C.J., *Young Logan Campbell*, Auckland: Auckland University Press, 1982

——————*The Father and his Gift: John Logan Campbell's later years*, Auckland: Auckland University Press, 1987

Stuart, Peter, *Edward Gibbon Wakefield in New Zealand: His political career 1853–54*, Wellington: Price Milburn for Victoria University of Wellington, 1971

Sullivan, Jim, *Reading Matters: A history of the Dunedin Athenaeum and Mechanics' Institute*, Dunedin: Dunedin Athenaeum and Mechanics' Institute, 2013

Temple, Philip, *A Sort of Conscience: The Wakefields*, Auckland: Auckland University Press, 2003

The Southern Provinces Almanac, Directory & Year Book for 1864, Christchurch: 1863

Thompson, G.E., *A History of the University of Otago (1869–1919)*, Dunedin: J. Wilkie & Co., Ltd., 1919

Trotter, Olive, *Pioneers Behind Bars: Dunedin Prison and its earliest inmates, 1850–1870*, Dunedin: Olive Trotter, 2002

——————*Dunedin's Spiteful Socrates, J.G.S. Grant*, Dunedin: Olive Trotter, 2005

——————*John Larkins Cheese Richardson: 'The gentlest, bravest and most just of men'*, Dunedin: Otago University Press, 2010

Turnbull, Michael, *The New Zealand Bubble: The Wakefield theory in practice*, Wellington: Price, Milburn, 1959

University of Otago Calendar, Dunedin: University of Otago, 1947

Wade, Richard, *The Urban Frontier: Pioneer life in early Pittsburgh, Cincinnati, Lexington, Louisville, and St Louis*, Chicago: University of Chicago Press, 1976

Wakefield, Edward Jerningham, *Adventure in New Zealand*, ed. Joan Stevens, abridged edn., Christchurch: Whitcombe and Tombs, 1955

——————*The London Journal of Edward Jerningham Wakefield*, ed. Joan Stevens, Alexander Turnbull Library Monograph No 4. Wellington: Alexander Turnbull Library & Victoria University of Wellington, 1972

Wallis, Eileen, *A Most Rare Vision: Otago Girls' High School – The first 125 years*, Dunedin: Otago Girls' High School Board of Trustees, 1995

Watt, W.J., *Dunedin's Historical Background: An historical geography of Dunedin covering the period 1840–1900*, Dunedin: Dunedin City Council, 1972

West, Jonathan, *The Face of Nature: An environmental history of the Otago Peninsula*, Dunedin: Otago University Press, 2018

Westgarth, William, *The Colony of Victoria*, London: Sampson Low, Son and Marston, 1864

Wilkinson, J.D., *Early New Zealand Steamers. Vol. I*, Wellington: Maritime Historical Productions, 1866

Wilson, Ben, *Heyday: Britain and the birth of the modern world*, London: Weidenfeld & Nicolson, 2016

Wilson, John, *Reminiscences of the Early Settlement of Dunedin and South Otago*, Dunedin: J Wilkie and Co, 1912

Wilson, T.G., *The Grey Government 1877–9*, Auckland: Auckland University College, History Series No. 5, Bulletin No. 45, 1954

------*The Rise of the New Zealand Liberal Party 1880–90*, Auckland: Auckland University College, History Series No. 6, Bulletin No. 48, 1956

Wolmar, Christian, *Fire & Steam: A new history of the railways in Britain*, London: Atlantic Books, 2007

Wright-St Clair, Rex E., *Thoroughly a Man of the World: A biography of Sir David Monro, M. D.*, Christchurch: Whitcombe & Tombs, 1971

Electronic sources

A Compendium of Official Documents Relative to Native Affairs in the South Island, compiled by Alexander Mackay; Nelson, New Zealand, The Govt. of N.Z., 1871–1872, two volumes: http://nzetc.victoria.ac.nz/tm/scholarly/tei-Mac01Comp-t1-g1-t6-g1-t5-g1-t1.html#n205

AtoJsOnline, National Library of New Zealand: https://atojs.natlib.govt.nz/cgi-bin/atojs?a=p&p=home&e=-------10--1------0--7

Baptismal Register, Old Machar Church, Aberdeen, 18/05/1819 MCANDREW, JAMES [O. P. R. Births 168/B00 0050 0610 OLD MACHAR]: www.scotlandspeople.gov.uk/

Encyclopaedia Britannica, 9th edn, (1875) and 10th edn. (1902), Encyclopaedia Britannica Co, London: www.1902encyclopedia.com/A/ABE/aberdeen.html

Hall, D., 1966, 'Macandrew, James', Te Ara – the Encyclopaedia of New Zealand: www.TeAra.govt.nz/1966/M/MacandrewJames/en

Heritage New Zealand: www.heritage.org.nz/the-list/details/37

Inflation calculator, UK: www.moneysorter.Co,uk/calculator_inflation2.html#calculator

Inflation calculator, NZ: http://www.rbnz.govt.nz/monetary-policy/inflation-calculator

London Census 1841 0bbba32d01db8027d3a224b2464d608e.pdf Folio Reference, HO107/1052/4/~F39: www.ukcensusonline.com/search/index.php?fn=james&sn=macandrew&phonetic_mode=1&event=1841

New Zealand Legal Information Institute, Otago Provincial Ordinances and New Zealand Acts: www.nzlii.org/databases.html#nz_cases

Nicholls, Roberta, 1990, 'Levin, Nathaniel 1818–1887', from the Dictionary of New Zealand Biography: www.TeAra.govt.nz/en/biographies/1l7/1

Papers Past: http://paperspast.natlib.govt.nz/cgi-bin/paperspast

Olssen, Erik, 'Macandrew, James 1819?–1887', from the Dictionary of New Zealand Biography: http://www.teara.govt.nz/en/biographies/1m1/macandrew-james

Patterson, Brad, 'William Barnard Rhodes, 1807–78', from the Dictionary of New Zealand Biography: http://www.TeAra.govt.nz/en/biographies/1r7/1

Statistics New Zealand, Long Term Data Series: www.stats.govt.nz/browse_for_stats/economic_indicators/NationalAccounts/long-term-data-series.aspx

The Grand Lodge of Scotland: www.grandlodgescotland.com/masonic-subjects/lodge-histories/174-lodge-celtic-no477

Waitangi Tribunal, 'The Ngāi Tahu Sea Fisheries Report 1991': http://www.justice.govt.nz/tribunals/waitangi-tribunal/Reports/wai0027 per cent201991 per cent20Report/doc_008

Wikipedia, 'George Street, Dunedin': http://en.wikipedia.org/wiki/George_Street,_Dunedin

Wilson, John, *The Gazetteer of Scotland*, published 1882, 3rd printing, 2002: https://archive.org/stream/gazetteerofscotl00wilsuoft/gazetteerofscotl00wilsuoft_djvu.txt

Williams, Erin, 'Caversham Industrial School: 181 Mornington Road, Dunedin', Site Record No. 144/526. Archaeological Assessment, Dunedin, Guy Williams and Associates, 2011: www.nzta.govt.nz/assets/projects/caversham-highway/docs/caversham-industrial-school-archaelogical-assessment.pdf

Articles and book chapters

Attard, Bernard, 'From free-trade imperialism to structural power: New Zealand and the capital market, 1856–68', *Journal of Imperial and Commonwealth History*, 35, no. 4, 2007, 505–27.

Banner, Lois W., 'Biography as history', *American History Review*, 114, no. 3, 2009, 579–86.

Barber, L.H., 'James Gibbs' heresy trial, 1890', *New Zealand Journal of History*, 12, no. 2, 1978, 146–57.

Bowie, Patricia, 'The shifting gold rush scenario: California to Australia to New Zealand', *Californians*, 6, no. 1, 1988, 12–30.

Brett, André, 'Dreaming on a railway track: Public works and the demise of New Zealand's provinces', *Journal of Transport History*, 36, no. 1, 2015, 77–96.

––––––'Wooden rails and gold: Southland and the demise of the provinces', in Lloyd Carpinter and Lyndon Fraser, *Rushing for Gold*, Dunedin: Otago University Press, 2016, 253–67.

Brooking, Tom, '"Busting up" the greatest estate of all', *New Zealand Journal of History*, 26, no. 1, 1992, 78–98.

––––––'Silences of grass: Retrieving the role of pasture plants in the development of New Zealand and the British Empire', *Journal of Imperial and Commonwealth History*, 35, no. 3, 2007, 417–35.

Brown, Judith, '"Life histories" and the history of modern South Asia', *American History Review*, 114, no. 3, 2009, 587–95.

Brown, Kate, 'Gridded lives: Why Kazakhstan and Montana are nearly the same place', *American Historical Review*, 106, no. 1, 2001, 17–48.

Bruckner, Phillip, 'Presidential Address: Whatever happened to the British Empire?' *Journal of the Canadian Historical Association*, 4, no. 1, 1993, 3–32.

Bulletin, Friends of the Hocken Collections, 'New Zealand's Nine Provinces (1853–76)', No. 31, Dunedin, 2000.

------'Importers, merchants & warehousemen', no. 52, Dunedin, 2006.

------'Shipping', no. 57, Dunedin, 2008.

------'The Squatters Club', no. 58, Dunedin, 2008.

Cannadine, D., 'The Empire strikes back', *Past & Present*, 147, 1995, 180–94.

Cookson, John, 'How British? Local government in New Zealand to c. 1930', *New Zealand Journal of History*, 41, NçO. 2, 2007, 143–60.

Crawford, Scott A.G.M. 'Recreation in pioneering New Zealand: Some early newspaper sources in Otago province, 1848–1861', *Victorian Periodicals Review*, 23, no. 3, 1990, 97–103.

Dalziel, Raewyn, 'The "continuous ministry" revisited', *New Zealand Journal of History*, 21, no. 1, 1987, 46–61.

------'Book review: *The New Zealand Liberals. The years of power, 1891–1912*', *New Zealand Journal of History*, 23, no. 2, 1989, 193–95.

Dunbabbin, J.P.D., '"The revolt of the field": The Agricultural Labourers' Movement in the 1870s', *Past & Present*, 26(1), 1963, 68–97.

Fairburn, Miles, 'New Zealand and Australian Federation, 1883–1901', *New Zealand Journal of History*, 4, no. 2, 1970, 138–59.

Gee, Austin, ed. 'Moving house: A peripatetic parliament', *Otago Settlers News*, 134, Spring 2017, 1–3.

Gibbons, Peter, 'Cultural colonization and national identity', *New Zealand Journal of History*, 36, no. 1, 2002, 4–15.

Hall, Jacquelyn Dowd, '"You must remember this": Autobiography as social critique', *Journal of American History*, 85, no. 2, 1998, 439–65.

Hamer, David, 'The agricultural company and New Zealand politics, 1877–1886', *Historical Studies: Australia and New Zealand*, 10, no. 38, 1962, 141–64.

Harper, Marjory, 'A century of Scottish emigration to New Zealand', *Immigrants & Minorities*, 29(2), 2011, 221–22.

Herron, David Gordon, 'The circumstances and effects of Sir George Grey's delay in summoning the first New Zealand General Assembly', *Historical Studies Australia and New Zealand* 8(32), 1959, 364–82.

------'The franchise and New Zealand politics, 1853–8', *Political Science*, 12(28), 1960, 28–44.

Hopkins, A.G., 'Back to the future: From national history to imperial history', *Past & Present*, 164(1), 1999, 198–243.

------'Gentlemanly capitalism in New Zealand', *Australian Economic History Review*, 43, no. 3, 2003, 287–97.

Hunt, Chris, 'Banking crises in New Zealand: An historical perspective', *Bulletin, Reserve Bank of New Zealand*, 72, no. 4, 2009.

Kearsley, G.W., Hearn, T.J. and Brooking, T.W.H., 'Land settlement and voting patterns in the Otago Provincial Council, 1863–1872', *New Zealand Journal of History*, 18, no. 1, 1984, 19–33.

McAloon, Jim, 'The colonial wealthy in Canterbury and Otago: No idle rich', *New Zealand Journal of History*, 30, no. 1, 1996, 43–60.

------'New Zealand and the economics of empire', *History Now*, no. 7, 2001, 12–16.

------'Gentlemanly capitalism and settler capitalists: Imperialism Dependent development and colonial wealth in the South Island of New Zealand', *Australian Economic History Review*, 42, no. 2, 2002, 204–23.

------'Class in colonial New Zealand', *New Zealand Journal of History*, 38, no. 1, 2004, 3–21.

Mackenzie, John M., 'On Scotland and the Empire', *International History Review*, 15, no. 4, 1993, 714–39.

MacKenzie, John & Patterson, Brad, 'The New Zealand Scots in international perspective: An introduction', *Immigrants & Minorities*, 29(2), 2011, 153.

Morris, R.J., 'Samuel Smiles and the genesis of self-help: The retreat to a petit bourgeois utopia', *Historical Journal*, 24, no. 1, 1981, 89–109.

Nasaw, David, 'Introduction. Historians and biography', *American Historical Review*, 114, no. 3, 2009.

Nenadic, Stana, 'The rise of the urban middle classes', in Devine, Tom and Mitchison, Rosalind, eds, *People and Society in Scotland Volume I: 1760–1830*, Edinburgh: John Donald Publishers in association with The Economic and Social History Society of Scotland, 1988, 109–26.

------'Political reform and the "ordering" of middle-class protest'. in Devine, Tom, ed., *Conflict and Stability in Scottish Society 1700–1850: Proceedings of the Scottish Historical Studies Seminar, University of Strathclyde 1988–89*, Edinburgh: John Donald Publishers, 1990, 65–82.

------'The Victorian middle classes', in Fraser, W. Hamish and Maver, Irene, eds, *Glasgow, People and Society in Scotland, Volume II: 1830 to 1912*, Manchester and New York: Manchester University Press, 1996, 265–69.

Olssen, Erik, 'Where to from here? Reflections on the twentieth-century historiography of nineteenth-century New Zealand', *New Zealand Journal of History*, 26, no. 1, 1992, 54–77.

------'Mr. Wakefield and New Zealand as an experiment in post-enlightenment experimental practice', *New Zealand Journal of History*, 31, no. 2, 1997, 197–218.

Otago, Southland and South Canterbury Provincial Almanac & Directory (1875–1909), 'Sketch of the life of James Macandrew', Dunedin: Mills, Dick & Co., 1886.

Pickens, K.A., 'The writing of New Zealand history: A Kuhnian perspective', *Historical Studies*, 17, 1977, 384–98.

Pickles, Kate, 'Empire settlement and single British women as New Zealand domestic servants during the 1920s', *New Zealand Journal of History*, 35, no. 1, 2001, 22–44.

Rosanwoski, G.J., 'The West Coast railways and New Zealand politics, 1878–1888', *New Zealand Journal of History*, 4, no. 1, 1970, 34–53.

Ross, Angus, 'The New Zealand Constitution Act of 1852: Its authorship', *Historical and Political Studies*, 1(1), 1969, 61–67.

Rubinstein, William D., 'No idle rich: The wealthy in Canterbury and Otago, 1840–1914', *The English Historical Review*, 118, no. 479, 2003, 14–17.

Solomon Roberts, 'Obituary of George Crane', *Journal of the Franklin Institute*, 41, no. 3, 1846, 214.

Stone, R.C.J., 'The Maori lands question and the fall of the Grey government, 1879', *New Zealand Journal of History*, 1, 1967, 51–74.

Wakefield, Edward Jerningham, 'What will they do in the General Assembly?' *Times*, Christchurch, 1863.

Wright, R.E., 'Bank ownership and lending patterns in New York and Pennsylvania, 1781–1831', *Business History Review*, 73, 1999.

Theses

Blackstock, Raewyn, 'The office of Agent-General for New Zealand in the United Kingdom, 1870–1905', PhD thesis, Victoria University of Wellington, 1970.

Bunce, Roderick, 'The trust funds for religious and educational uses at Otago, 1842 to 1866', MA thesis, University of Otago, 1982.

Bunce, Roderick, 'James Macandrew of Otago: Slippery Jim or a leader staunch and true?', PhD thesis, Victoria University of Wellington, 2013.

Cook, A.H., 'The slowly dying cause: A study of Otago Provincialism after the abolition of the provinces 1975–1884', MA thesis, University of Otago, 1969.

Ellis, M.A., 'James Macandrew and his times', MA thesis, University of Otago, 1926.
Hamer, David, 'The law and the prophet: A political biography of Sir Robert Stout (1844–1930)', MA thesis, University of Auckland, 1960.

Herron, David Gordon, 'The structure and course of New Zealand politics, 1853–1858', PhD thesis, University of Otago, 1959.

Hunt, Jonathon Lucas, 'The election of 1875–6 and the abolition of the provinces', MA thesis, University of Auckland, 1961.

Lenihan, Rebecca, 'From Alba to Aotearoa: Profiling New Zealand's Scots migrants, 1840–1920', PhD thesis, Victoria University of Wellington, 2010.

Leslie, Alfred Murray, 'The general election of 1871 and its importance in the history of New Zealand', MA thesis, University of New Zealand, 1956.

McIvor, Timothy, 'On Ballance: A biography of John Ballance, journalist and politician, 1839–1893', PhD thesis, Victoria University of Wellington, 1984.

Mullins, R.M., 'The division of power between the general and provincial governments 1853–67', MA thesis, Victoria University of Wellington, 1953.

Sinclair, Fergus, 'High Street quaking: A history of Dunedin's "Inner circle"', PhD thesis, University of Otago, 1996.

Tyndale-Biscoe, Ann, 'The struggle for responsible government in the province of Otago 1854–76', MA thesis, University of Otago, 1954.

Index